KIWI Pathfinder
New Zealand
Travellers Road Atlas

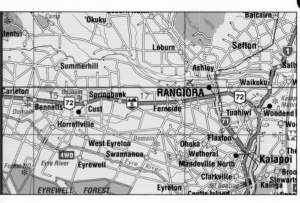

Congratulations. You have chosen to purchase New Zealands newest and most comprehensive Road Atlas, designed and published by New Zealands leading map company. The dedicated team of cartographers at Kiwimaps Ltd take pride in presenting this publication to you. Considerable time and effort has been put into the production of this product. We would also like to thank the various information centres, local councils and Transit New Zealand for the invaluable information received.

How to use this directory: As you look at the contents below you will see that this directory is divided into colour sections. Select the section you require and look for the corresponding border colour. For more information on how to use this street directory turn to pages 4-5. For ease of use, the index is located in the rear section of this book.

Contents	Page 1
Map Coverage & Page Locations	Pages 2-3
Instructions, Reference & Map Scales	Page 4-5
Travel Times & Distances	Page 6-7
North Island Touring	Maps 1-28
South Island Touring	Maps 29-62
Northland and Auckland	Maps 63-66
Waikato and Bay of Plenty	Maps 67-70
Hawkes Bay, Manawatu & Wellington	Maps 71-74
Nelson and Marlborough	Maps 75-76
Christchurch, Otago and Southland	Maps 77-80
North Island Town Centres	Maps 81-93
South Island Town Centres	Maps 94-101
Index Introduction and Instructions	Index 1
Index	Index 1- Index 36

KIWIMAPS LTD

Head Office: P.O. Box 2472, Christchurch.
Phone: (03) 366 3809.
Fax: (03) 379 1763.
Auckland Area Office: P.O. Box 101878, NSMC, Auckland.
Phone: (09) 444 0427.
Fax: (09) 444 1381.

ISBN 1-877201-65-0 4th
ISBN 3rd Edition 1-877201-

D1283363

KIWI Maps Quality you can trust

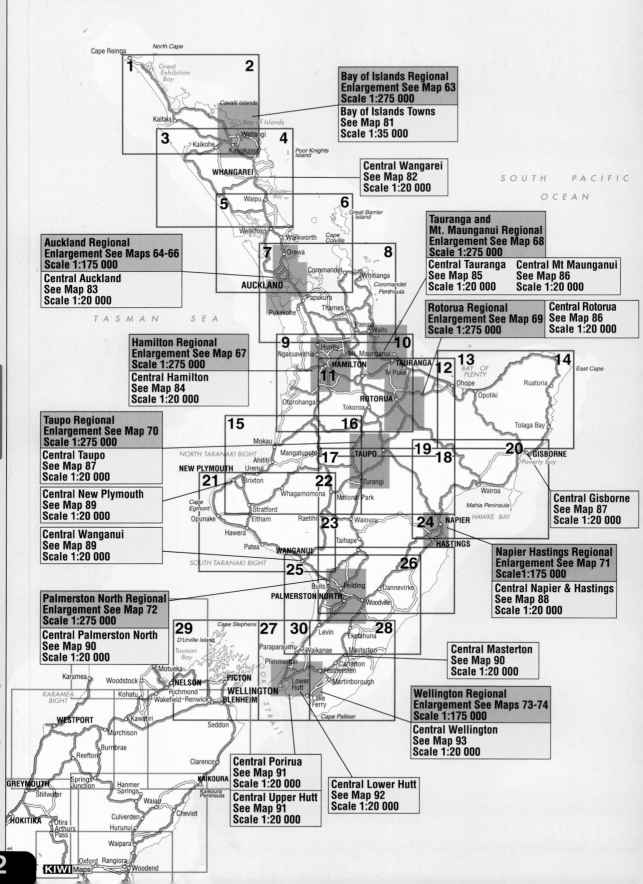

North Island

Bay of Islands Regional
Enlargement See Map 63
Scale 1:275 000
Bay of Islands Towns
See Map 81
Scale 1:35 000

Central Wangarei
See Map 82
Scale 1:20 000

Tauranga and
Mt. Maunganui Regional
Enlargement See Map 68
Scale 1:275 000
Central Tauranga
See Map 85
Scale 1:20 000
Central Mt Maunganui
See Map 86
Scale 1:20 000

Rotorua Regional
Enlargement See Map 69
Scale 1:275 000
Central Rotorua
See Map 86
Scale 1:20 000

Auckland Regional
Enlargement See Maps 64-66
Scale 1:175 000
Central Auckland
See Map 83
Scale 1:20 000

Hamilton Regional
Enlargement See Map 67
Scale 1:275 000
Central Hamilton
See Map 84
Scale 1:20 000

Taupo Regional
Enlargement See Map 70
Scale 1:275 000
Central Taupo
See Map 87
Scale 1:20 000
Central New Plymouth
See Map 89
Scale 1:20 000
Central Wanganui
See Map 89
Scale 1:20 000

Central Gisborne
See Map 87
Scale 1:20 000

Napier Hastings Regional
Enlargement See Map 71
Scale1:175 000
Central Napier & Hastings
See Map 88
Scale 1:20 000

Palmerston North Regional
Enlargement See Map 72
Scale 1:275 000
Central Palmerston North
See Map 90
Scale 1:20 000

Central Masterton
See Map 90
Scale 1:20 000

Wellington Regional
Enlargement See Maps 73-74
Scale 1:175 000
Central Wellington
See Map 93
Scale 1:20 000

Central Porirua
See Map 91
Scale 1:20 000
Central Upper Hutt
See Map 91
Scale 1:20 000

Central Lower Hutt
See Map 92
Scale 1:20 000

SOUTH PACIFIC
OCEAN

TASMAN SEA

KIWI Maps

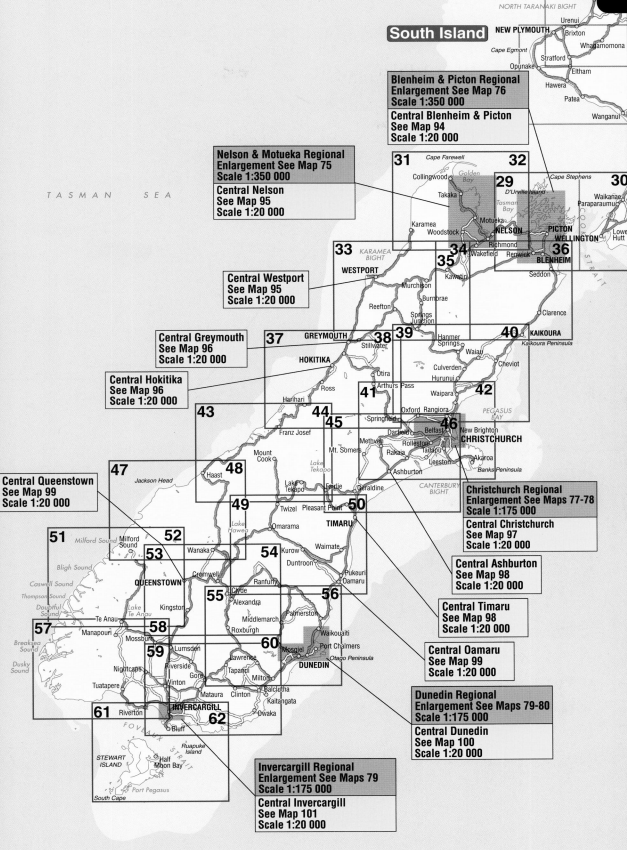

South Island

Blenheim & Picton Regional Enlargement See Map 76
Scale 1:350 000

Central Blenheim & Picton See Map 94
Scale 1:20 000

Nelson & Motueka Regional Enlargement See Map 75
Scale 1:350 000

Central Nelson See Map 95
Scale 1:20 000

Central Westport See Map 95
Scale 1:20 000

Central Greymouth See Map 96
Scale 1:20 000

Central Hokitika See Map 96
Scale 1:20 000

Central Queenstown See Map 99
Scale 1:20 000

Christchurch Regional Enlargement See Maps 77-78
Scale 1:175 000

Central Christchurch See Map 97
Scale 1:20 000

Central Ashburton See Map 98
Scale 1:20 000

Central Timaru See Map 98
Scale 1:20 000

Central Oamaru See Map 99
Scale 1:20 000

Dunedin Regional Enlargement See Maps 79-80
Scale 1:175 000

Central Dunedin See Map 100
Scale 1:20 000

Invercargill Regional Enlargement See Maps 79
Scale 1:175 000

Central Invercargill See Map 101
Scale 1:20 000

Map Coverage & Page Locations

South Island

KIWI Maps

PAGE 3

Reference to New Zealand Touring Maps 1 to 81

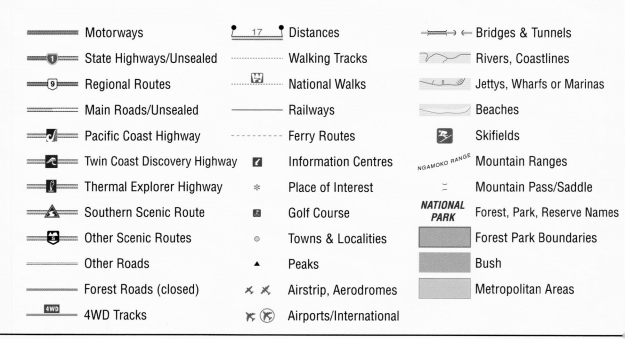

Motorways		Distances	17	Bridges & Tunnels	
State Highways/Unsealed		Walking Tracks		Rivers, Coastlines	
Regional Routes		National Walks		Jettys, Wharfs or Marinas	
Main Roads/Unsealed		Railways		Beaches	
Pacific Coast Highway		Ferry Routes		Skifields	
Twin Coast Discovery Highway		Information Centres		Mountain Ranges	NGAMOKO RANGE
Thermal Explorer Highway		Place of Interest		Mountain Pass/Saddle	
Southern Scenic Route		Golf Course		Forest, Park, Reserve Names	NATIONAL PARK
Other Scenic Routes		Towns & Localities		Forest Park Boundaries	
Other Roads		Peaks		Bush	
Forest Roads (closed)		Airstrip, Aerodromes		Metropolitan Areas	
4WD Tracks		Airports/International			

Reference to New Zealand City & Town Maps 82-101

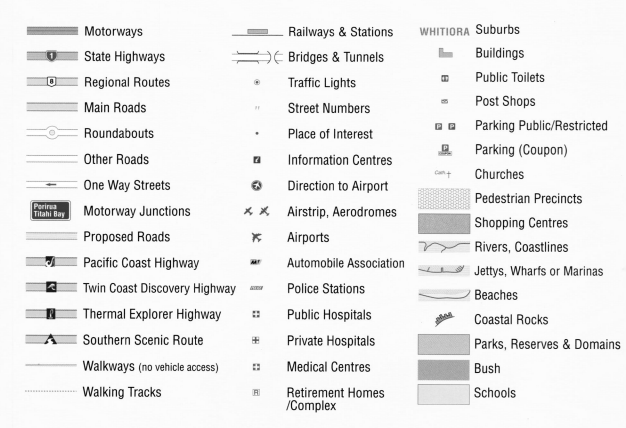

Motorways	Railways & Stations	Suburbs	WHITIORA
State Highways	Bridges & Tunnels	Buildings	
Regional Routes	Traffic Lights	Public Toilets	
Main Roads	Street Numbers	Post Shops	
Roundabouts	Place of Interest	Parking Public/Restricted	
Other Roads	Information Centres	Parking (Coupon)	
One Way Streets	Direction to Airport	Churches	
Motorway Junctions (Porirua Titahi Bay)	Airstrip, Aerodromes	Pedestrian Precincts	
Proposed Roads	Airports	Shopping Centres	
Pacific Coast Highway	Automobile Association	Rivers, Coastlines	
Twin Coast Discovery Highway	Police Stations	Jettys, Wharfs or Marinas	
Thermal Explorer Highway	Public Hospitals	Beaches	
Southern Scenic Route	Private Hospitals	Coastal Rocks	
Walkways (no vehicle access)	Medical Centres	Parks, Reserves & Domains	
Walking Tracks	Retirement Homes /Complex	Bush	
		Schools	

 All maps are north facing

Map Scales

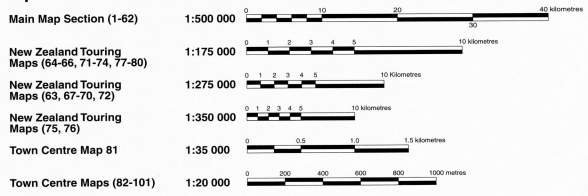

Main Map Section (1-62)	1:500 000	0 10 20 30 40 kilometres
New Zealand Touring Maps (64-66, 71-74, 77-80)	1:175 000	0 1 2 3 4 5 10 kilometres
New Zealand Touring Maps (63, 67-70, 72)	1:275 000	0 1 2 3 4 5 10 Kilometres
New Zealand Touring Maps (75, 76)	1:350 000	0 1 2 3 4 5 10 kilometres
Town Centre Map 81	1:35 000	0 0.5 1.0 1.5 kilometres
Town Centre Maps (82-101)	1:20 000	0 200 400 600 800 1000 metres

How To Find A Town or Location:

LOCATION NAME   MAP NO. REFERENCE

Example: **TE KAO** ....**1 B2 SE**

NW	NE
SW	SE

Locate **TE KAO** in the index. Note the reference and turn to the map number (**1**) - the bold number following the suburb name. The location will appear on this map in the square found by intersecting the letter **B** and the number **2** - these are in the map border. To help you find the location quickly, each square can be further subdivided into four parts: NorthWest, NorthEast, SouthWest & SouthEast. **TE KAO** will be found in the **S**outh**E**ast part.

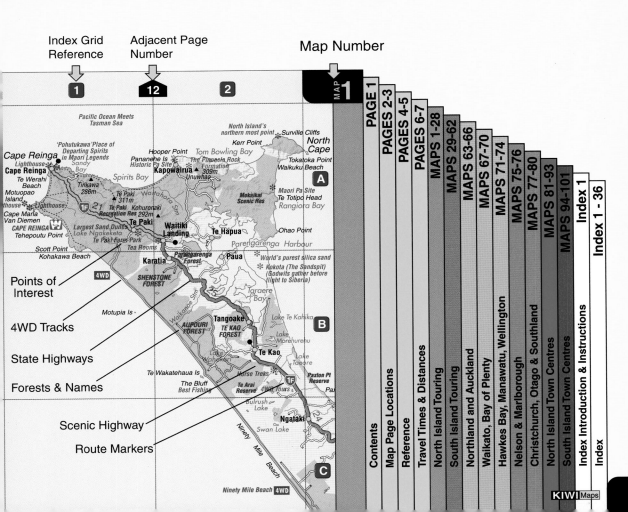

Index Grid Reference

Adjacent Page Number

Map Number

Points of Interest

4WD Tracks

State Highways

Forests & Names

Scenic Highway

Route Markers

PAGE 1 — Contents
PAGES 2-3 — Map Page Locations
PAGES 4-5 — Reference
PAGES 6-7 — Travel Times & Distances
MAPS 1-28 — North Island Touring
MAPS 29-62 — South Island Touring
MAPS 63-66 — Northland and Auckland
MAPS 67-70 — Waikato, Bay of Plenty
MAPS 71-74 — Hawkes Bay, Manawatu, Wellington
MAPS 75-76 — Nelson & Marlborough
MAPS 77-80 — Christchurch, Otago & Southland
MAPS 81-93 — North Island Town Centres
MAPS 94-101 — South Island Town Centres
Index 1 — Index Introduction & Instructions
Index 1 - 36 — Index

Instructions

Instructions, Reference & Scales

KIWI Maps

North Island

Travel Times & Distances

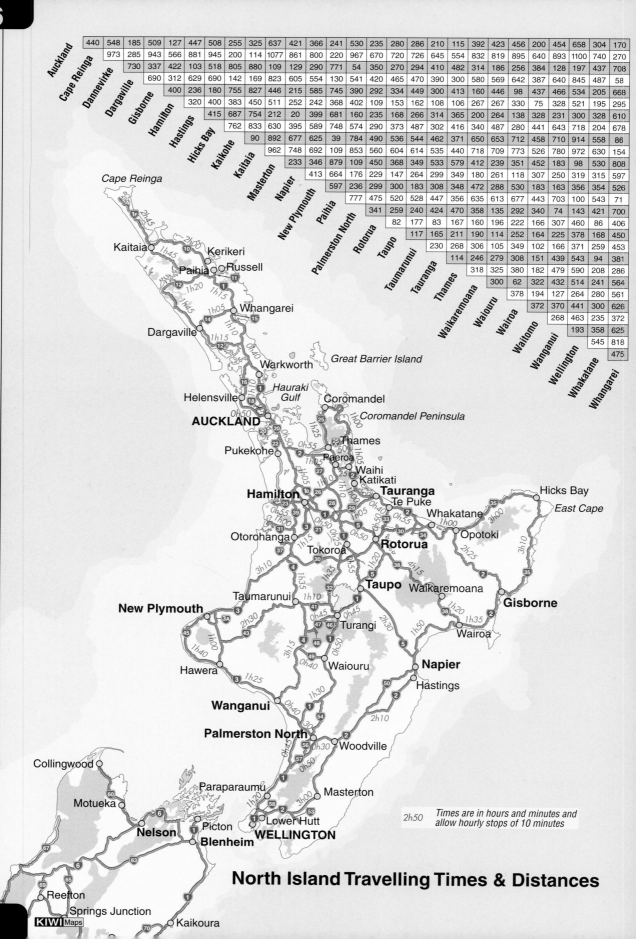

	Cape Reinga	Dannevirke	Dargaville	Gisborne	Hamilton	Hastings	Hicks Bay	Kaikohe	Kaitaia	Masterton	Napier	New Plymouth	Paihia	Palmerston North	Rotorua	Taupo	Taumarunui	Tauranga	Thames	Waikaremoana	Waiouru	Wairoa	Waitomo	Wanganui	Wellington	Whakatane	Whangarei
Auckland	440	548	185	509	127	447	508	255	325	637	421	366	241	530	235	280	286	210	115	392	423	456	200	454	658	304	170
Cape Reinga		973	285	943	566	881	945	200	114	1077	861	800	220	967	670	720	726	645	554	832	819	895	640	893	1100	740	270
Dannevirke			730	337	422	103	518	805	880	109	129	290	771	54	350	270	294	410	482	314	186	256	384	128	197	437	708
Dargaville				690	312	629	690	142	169	823	605	554	130	541	420	465	470	390	300	580	569	642	387	640	845	487	58
Gisborne					400	236	180	755	827	446	215	585	745	390	292	334	449	300	413	160	446	98	437	466	534	205	668
Hamilton						320	400	383	450	511	252	242	368	402	109	153	162	108	106	267	267	330	75	328	521	195	295
Hastings							415	687	754	212	20	399	681	160	235	168	266	314	365	200	264	138	328	231	300	328	610
Hicks Bay								762	833	630	395	589	748	574	290	373	487	302	416	340	487	280	441	643	718	204	678
Kaikohe									90	892	677	625	39	784	490	536	544	462	371	650	653	712	458	710	914	558	86
Kaitaia										962	748	692	109	853	560	604	614	535	440	718	709	773	526	780	972	630	154
Masterton											233	346	879	109	450	368	349	533	579	412	239	351	452	183	98	530	808
Napier												413	664	176	229	147	264	299	349	180	261	118	307	250	319	315	597
New Plymouth													597	236	299	300	183	308	348	472	288	530	183	163	356	354	526
Paihia														777	475	520	528	447	356	635	613	677	443	703	100	543	71
Palmerston North															341	259	240	424	470	358	135	292	340	74	143	421	700
Rotorua																82	177	83	167	160	196	222	166	307	460	86	406
Taupo																	117	165	211	190	114	252	164	225	378	168	450
Taumarunui																		230	268	306	105	349	102	166	371	259	453
Tauranga																			114	246	279	308	151	439	543	94	381
Thames																				318	325	380	182	479	590	208	286
Waikaremoana																					300	62	322	432	514	241	564
Waiouru																						378	194	127	264	280	561
Wairoa																							372	370	441	300	626
Waitomo																								268	463	235	372
Wanganui																									193	358	625
Wellington																										545	818
Whakatane																											475

2h50 — Times are in hours and minutes and allow hourly stops of 10 minutes

North Island Travelling Times & Distances

KIWI Maps

	Westport	Wanaka	Timaru	Te Anau	St. Arnaud	Reefton	Queenstown	Picton	Oamaru	Nelson	Mt. Cook	Milford Sound	Kaikoura	Invercargill	Hokitika	Hanmer Springs	Haast	Greymouth	Gore	Franz Joseph	Dunedin	Collingwood	Christchurch	Bluff	Blenheim	Ashburton	Arthur's Pass
Alexandra	644	87	312	249	794	617	92	800	227	870	241	370	657	204	520	590	235	661	139	375	190	964	455	232	786	383	559
Arthur's Pass	200	528	250	800	320	162	645	458	334	382	408	922	337	694	104	264	381	100	647	248	477	476	150	723	424	180	
Ashburton	420	348	76	564	515	339	401	423	160	503	246	685	275	492	300	221	490	345	427	476	275	596	86	522	393		
Blenheim	264	745	471	960	100	250	794	29	555	117	639	1081	132	887	370	260	643	330	821	486	670	251	308	922			
Bluff	884	320	441	185	1020	886	218	952	362	1043	472	308	792	27	729	744	463	799	96	600	245	1120	605				
Christchurch	334	428	162	650	352	253	487	336	247	418	330	770	187	578	260	135	535	255	513	395	360	509					
Collingwood	314	842	671	1115	211	316	960	245	756	136	840	1240	380	1088	418	392	720	384	1022	580	870						
Dunedin	695	276	199	289	710	608	280	698	114	786	331	410	545	217	570	495	424	551	150	562							
Franz Joseph	280	285	492	560	400	260	404	531	506	470	500	678	550	575	140	395	140	181	510								
Gore	810	224	352	138	902	752	167	849	266	937	380	260	700	65	648	648	369	705									
Greymouth	102	469	352	732	222	80	583	360	450	290	510	860	338	769	41	214	317										
Haast	438	146	426	418	563	395	262	671	384	609	360	539	710	433	281	532											
Hanmer Springs	218	560	300	785	238	140	620	300	380	306	466	908	133	714	256												
Hokitika	145	426	361	690	260	120	513	400	456	337	530	810	428	690													
Invercargill	869	285	417	158	932	818	190	915	330	1016	445	280	767														
Kaikoura	340	612	351	839	230	324	676	160	436	249	518	960															
Milford Sound	958	394	610	121	1089	930	291	1121	524	1145	550																
Mt. Cook	664	214	210	434	682	576	271	667	215	747																	
Nelson	230	587	587	1025	119	217	693	114	671																		
Oamaru	580	234	85	408	600	500	319	583																			
Picton	292	774	499	988	128	281	822																				
Queenstown	659	117	336	168	839	633																					
Reefton	83	545	410	807	152																						
St. Arnaud	158	769	514	1005																							
Te Anau	828	273	486																								
Timaru	497	278																									
Wanaka	588																										

Collingwood
Motueka
WELLINGTON
Picton
Nelson
Blenheim
Westport
Reefton
Punakaiki
Springs Junction
Greymouth
Lewis Pass
Hanmer Springs
Kaikoura
Hokitika
Arthur's Pass
Waipara
Franz Josef
CHRISTCHURCH
Banks Peninsula
Akaroa
Mount Cook
Haast
Ashburton
Haast Pass
Twizel
Fairlie
Rangitata
Timaru
Omarama
Milford Sound
Wanaka
Queenstown
Cromwell
Alexandra
Oamaru
Te Anau
Manapouri
DUNEDIN
Gore
Milton
Invercargill
Halfmoon Bay
(Oban)
Stewart Island

2h50 *Times are in hours and minutes and allow hourly stops of 10 minutes*

South Island Travelling Times & Distances

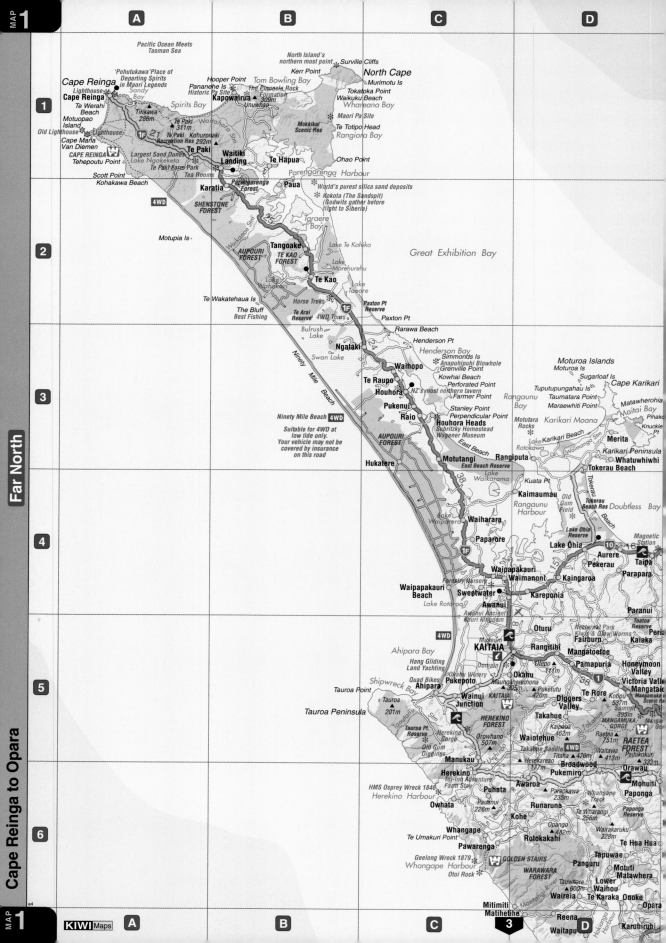

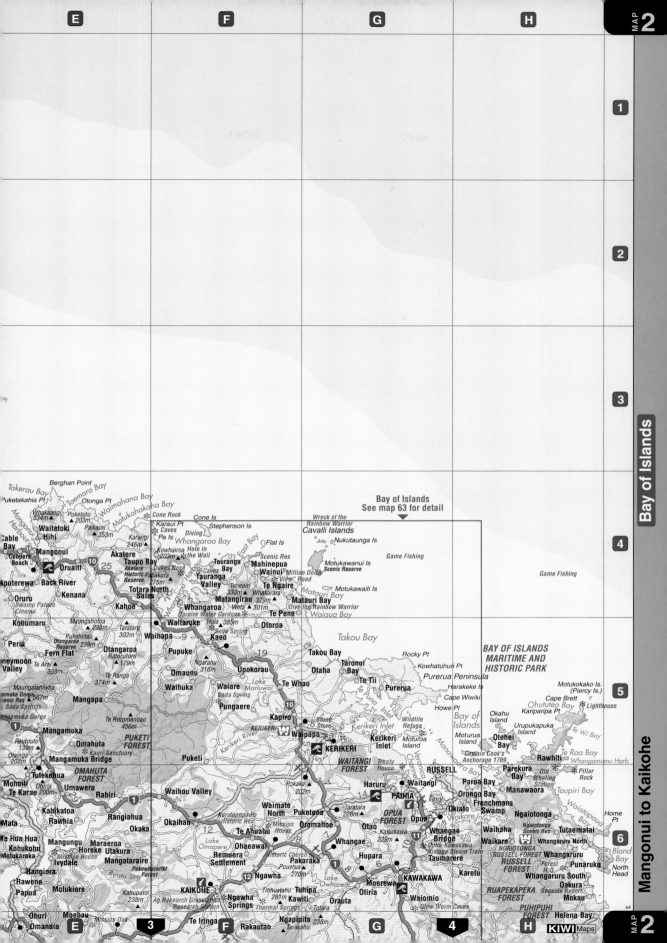

MAP 2

MAP 2

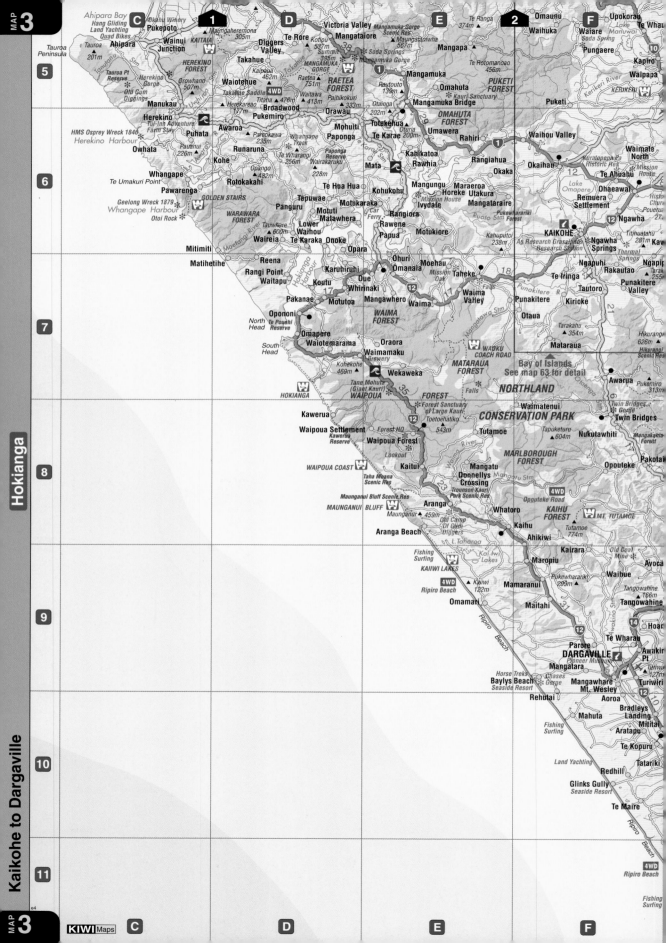

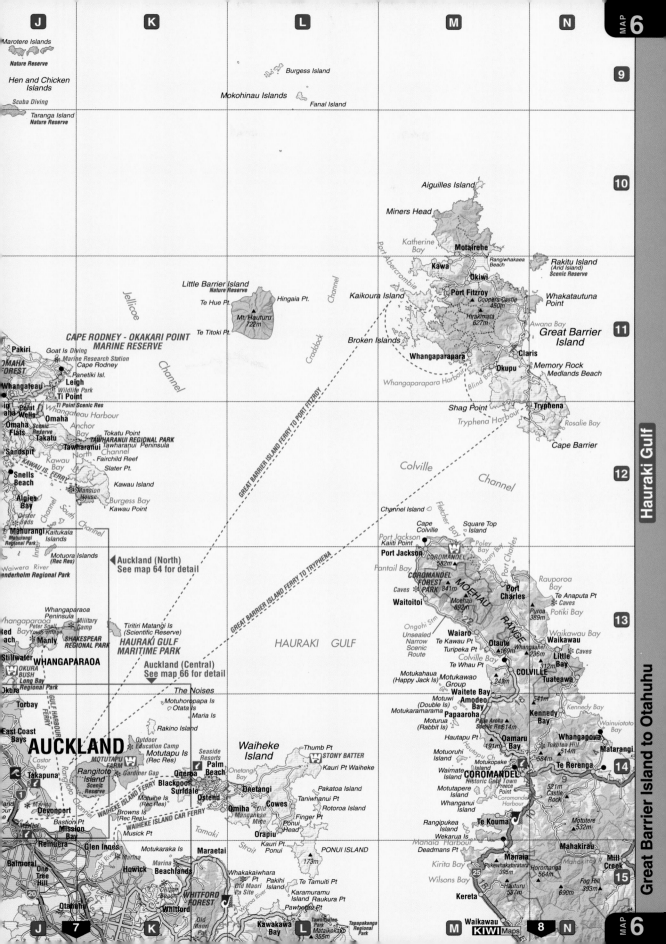

MAP 6

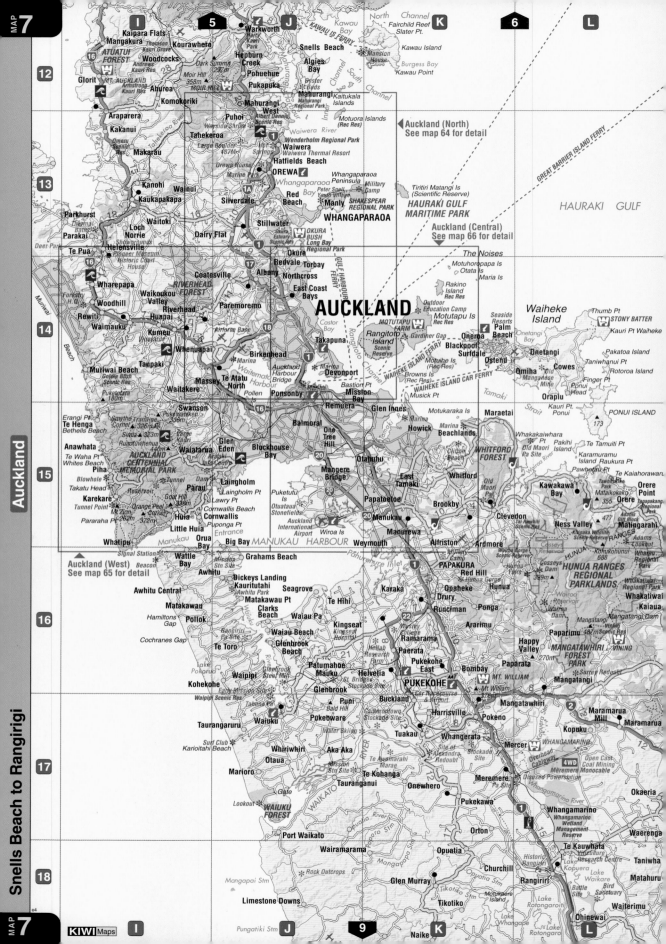

MAP 7
5
6

Auckland

Snells Beach to Rangiriri

AUCKLAND

HAURAKI GULF

HAURAKI GULF MARITIME PARK

Waiheke Island

Auckland (North)
See map 64 for detail

Auckland (Central)
See map 66 for detail

Auckland (West)
See map 65 for detail

MANUKAU HARBOUR

WHITFORD FOREST

HUNUA RANGES REGIONAL PARKLANDS

MANGATAWHIRI FOREST PARK

PONUI ISLAND

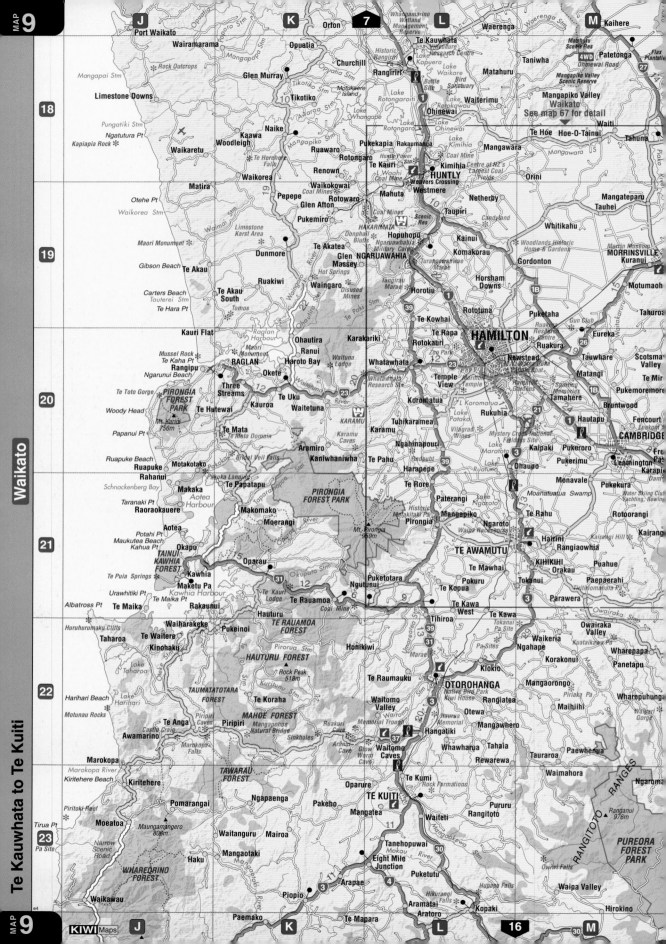

MAP 10

Bay of Plenty

Waihi to Mangakino

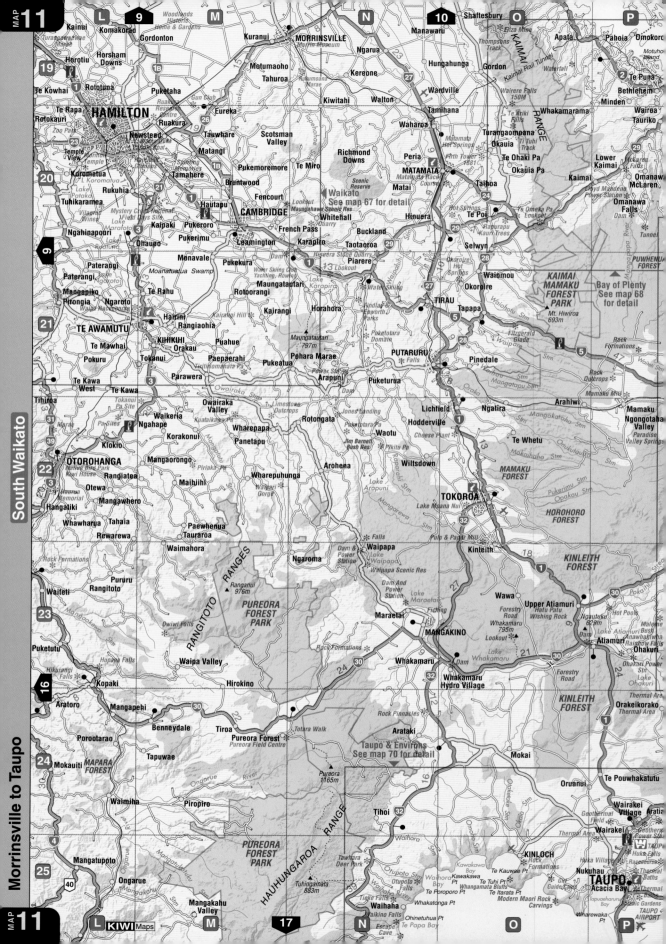

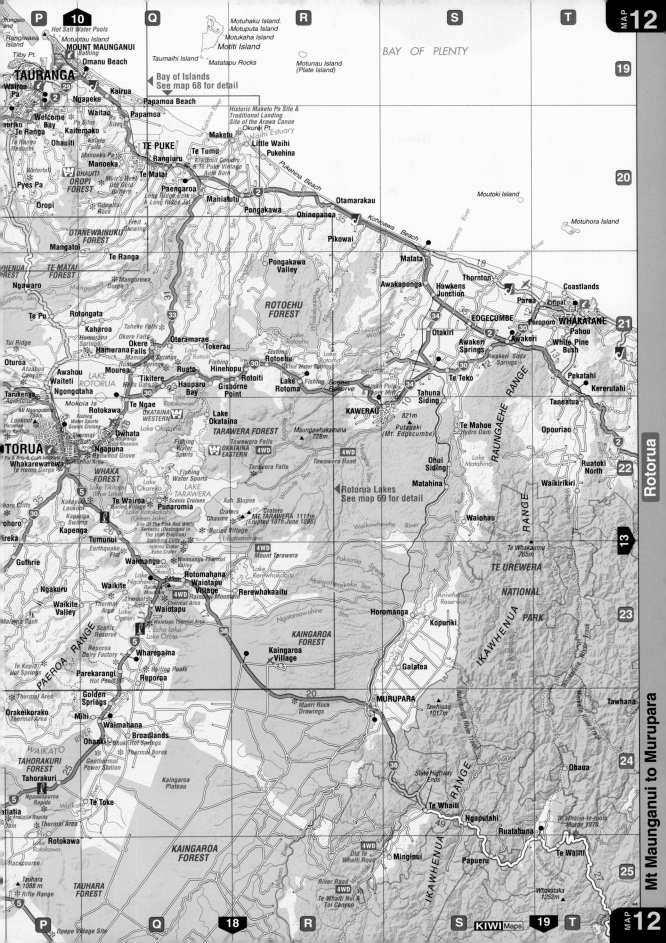

Otarawhata Is
Cape Runaway
First Landing of the Tainui &
Arawa Canoes from Hawaiki
Kopongatahi Pt
Tahurua Pt
Lottin Pt
Midway Pt

Whangaparaoa
Whangaparaoa
Bay
Old Post Office (1870's)
Waihau Bay
Taratuia Pt
Potaka
Matakaoa Pt
Hicks Bay
Hicks Bay Tuwhakairiora Marae
Haupara Pt

Orete Pt
Otamaroa
44
Te Waha o Rerekohu
Largest Pohutukawa

Oruaiti Beach
Tokata
Awatere River
Raukokore
Historic Church Papatea Bay
Pukeamaru
992m
Te Araroa
Horoera
Horoera Pt

Waikawa
Pt
Papatea
PUKEAMARU
SCENIC
RES
East Cape

Te Kopua
Kereua River
Whanarua Bay
Kariangi
Pre European Lookout
(Excavated Whare Site)
Tapatu
East Cape
East Island

4WD
19
Whakaangiangi
Awatere
Lighthouse
Most Easterly
in the World

Maungaroa Marae
Whale Boat
Kereu River
RUATORIA
FOREST
Maraehara
20

Raukumara
1414m
Rangitukia
Waiapu River

Rangipoua
1041m
Waiomatatini
Wairoa
Tikitiki
Ngata Homestead
Porourangi Marae

Potts Peak
1426m
Whakawhitira
Kakariki
Te Upokoohinepaki Pt

RAUKUMARA
CONSERVATION
AREA
Takamore
Reporua

Hikurangi
1754m
Rotokautuku
Papawera
RUATORIA
Manghahea Marae
Mahora
Koutuamoa Pt

Whakapourangi
Hiruharama
Pohatukura
Tuparoa

RAUKUMARA
RANGE
Aorangi
Kaimoho Pt

Kopuaroa
26
Wharepanga
Waikahawai Pt

RANGE
Ohineakai
Waipiro Bay

Takapau
35
Waipiro Bay

Ihungia
Te Puia Springs
Hot Pools
Koutunui Head
Moutahiauru Is
Motuaiuri Is

Huiarua
Hautanoa
Waima
Te Puka
Koutunui Pt
Te Ariuru
Tokomaru Bay

Mangatarata
Tuatini
Tokomaru Bay
Ongaruru

TOKOMARU
FOREST
Hikuwai
Mawhai Pt

MANGATU
FOREST
Waiau
ANAURA BAY
Tutamoe
998m
Arero
The Three
Bridges
Anaura Bay
Anaura Bay
Motuoroi Island

Arowhana
1440m
Puakato
675m
36
Mangatuna
Marau Pt
Tokatea Rocks
Kaiaua Pt

Tauwhareparae
Huanui
Paerau Pt
Karaka Bay

Arakihi
639m
The Five Bridges
Wharekaka
23

Whatatutu
Takapau
Tolaga Bay
Tolaga Bay
Mitre Rocks
Pourewa Island

Kanakanaia
Bird Sanctuary
Hauiti
COOKS COVE

Puha
2
Paremata
23
Te Karaka
Waihau Beach
Waihau Bay
24

Waimata
35
47

Waipaoa
Kaitaratahi
Pakarae
Waiharehare Bay
Gable End Foreland
Gable Islet
Te Ikaarongamai Bay

Ngatapa
Pukeakura
497m
Pakarae

W X 20 Y Z KIWI Maps A
MAP 14
Lake
Repongaere
Waituhi
Whangara
Whangara Is
e4

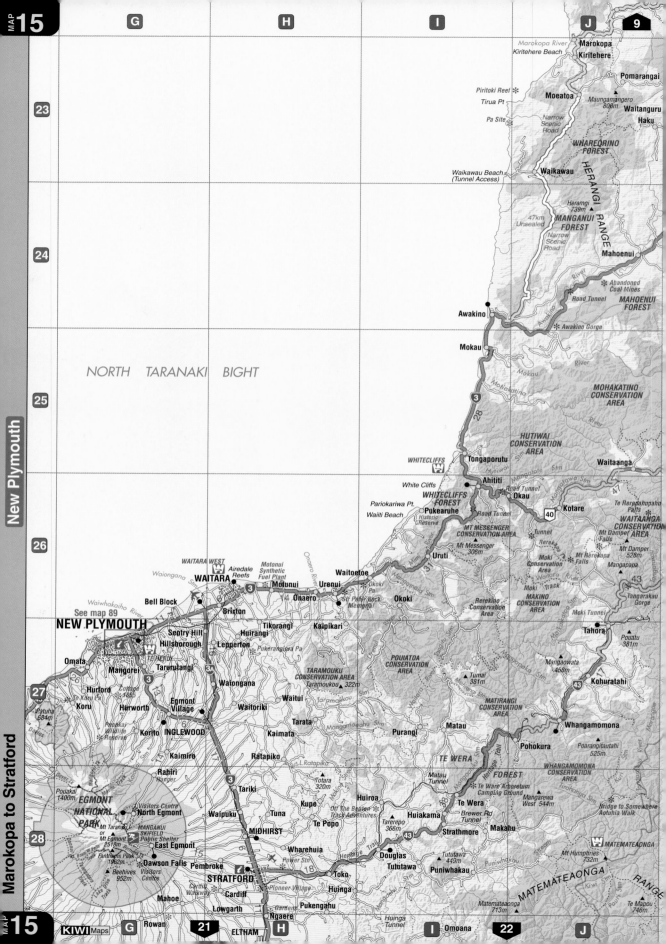

MAP
15
G   H   I   J   9

Marokopa River
Kiritehere Beach
Marokopa
Kiritehere

Pomarangai

Piritoki Reef
Tirua Pt
Pa Site

Moeatoa
Maungamangero
806m
Waitanguru
Haku

Narrow
Scenic
Road

WHAREORINO
FOREST

HERANGI RANGE

Waikawau Beach
(Tunnel Access)

Waikawau

Herangi
739m

MANGANUI
FOREST

Mahoenui

47km
Unsealed

Narrow
Scenic
Road

Awakino

Abandoned
Coal Mines

Road Tunnel

MAHOENUI
FOREST

Awakino Gorge

NORTH TARANAKI BIGHT

Mokau

3

28

Mokau River

MOHAKATINO
CONSERVATION
AREA

Mohakatino

HUTIWAI
CONSERVATION
AREA

WHITECLIFFS

Tongaporutu

Waitaanga

White Cliffs

Ahititi

Road Tunnel

47

Te Rerepahupahu
Falls

WHITECLIFFS
FOREST

Okau

Kotare

40

WAITAANGA
CONSERVATION
AREA

Pariokariwa Pt.

Pukearuhe

Road Tunnel

Mt Dampet
Falls

Mt Damper
528m

Waiiti Beach

Historic
Reserve

MT MESSENGER
CONSERVATION
AREA

Tunnel

Mt Rerekapa
Falls

Mangapapa

Mt Messenger
306m

Moki
Conservation
Area

43

See map 89

WAITARA WEST

Airedale
Reefs

Motunui
Synthetic
Fuel Plant

Waiongana Stm

Onaero River

Waitoetoe

Uruti

31

Moki Track

Rerekino
Conservation
Area

MAKINO
CONSERVATION
AREA

Moki Tunnel

Tangarakau
Gorge

WAITARA

Motunui

Urenui

Okoki
Pa

Tahora

Pouatu
381m

Waiwhakaiho River

Bell Block

Brixton

Onaero

St Peter Jock
Memorial

Okoki

Mangaowata
458m

43

Kohuratahi

NEW PLYMOUTH

Sentry Hill

Tikorangi

Kaipikari

Hillsborough

Huirangi

Lepperton

Pukerangiora Pa

TARAMOUKU
CONSERVATION
AREA

POUIATOA
CONSERVATION
AREA

Tumai
381m

MATIRANGI
CONSERVATION
AREA

Whangamomona

Omata

Mangorei

Tarurutangi

3A

Waiongana

Taramoukou 322m

Pohokura

Poarangitautahi
525m

Hurford

Koru

Hurworth

Egmont
Village

Waitoriki

Waitui

Tarata

Matau

TE WERA
FOREST

WHANGAMOMONA
CONSERVATION
AREA

Patuha
684m

Cottage
1855

3

Korito

INGLEWOOD

Kaimata

Purangi

Matau
Tunnel

Te Ware Arboretum
Camping Ground

Mangarewa
West 544m

Bridge to Somewhere
Aotuhia Walk

Rewa
Wildlife
Reserve

Kaimiro

Ratapiko

L.Ratapiko

Te Wera

Brewer Rd
Tunnel

Rahiri
Ranger

Totara
320m

Huiroa

Makahu

Mt Humphries
732m

EGMONT
NATIONAL
PARK

Pouakai
1400m

Visitors Centre
North Egmont

Tariki

Kupe

Off the Beaten
Track Adventures

Huiakama

MATEMATEAONGA

Waipuku

Tuna

Te Popo

Tarerepo
366m

43

Strathmore

Mt Taranaki
or Mt Egmont
2518m

MANGANUI
SKIFIELD
Public Shelter

Fanthams Peak
1962m

East Egmont

Wharehuia

MIDHIRST

Power Stn

Douglas

Tututawa
449m

Matemateaonga
713m

Te Mapou
746m

MATEMATEAONGA
RANGE

Beehives
952m

Dawson Falls
Visitors Centre

Pembroke

Toko

Tututawa

Puniwhakau

18

Mahoe

Pioneer Village

STRATFORD

Cardiff

Huinga

Gardens
Walkway

Pukengahu

Huinga
Tunnel

Lowgarth

Ngaere

MAP 16

King Country

Te Kuiti to Mt Ruapehu

Grid references (top): K 9 L M 11 N
Grid references (right): 32, 23, 11, 32, 24, 16, 32, 25, 32, 26, 17, 27, 1, 46, 28
Grid references (bottom): K 22 L M 17 N

Waitomo Caves · Paewhenua · Tauraroa · Ngaroma · Waipapa · Falls · Dam & Power Station · Dam and Power Station

Rewarewa · Waimahora · Maraetai

Te Kumi · Rock Formations · Mangakino

TE KUITI · Waiteti · Pururu · Rangitoto · Ranganui 976m · Rock Formations · Whakamaru · Whakamaru Hydro Village · Dam

Ngapaenga · Pakeho · Mangatea · Rangitoto

Waitanguru · Mairoa · Tanehopuwai · Eight Mile Junction · Puketutu · Owiwi Falls · Waipa Valley · Hirokino · Rock Pinnacles · Arataki

Arapae · Mokau River · Hupapa Falls

Piopio · Aramatai · Kopaki · Mangapehi · Benneydale · Tiroa · Totara Walk · Pureora Forest · Pureora Field Centre

Paemako · Te Mapara · Aratoro · Tihoi

Ngatamahine · Omaru Falls · Porootarao · Tapuwae · Pureora 1165m

Aria · Mokauiti Stm · Wairere Falls · Mokauiti · Mapiu · Mapara Forest · Waimiha · Piropiro

Totoroa Gorge · Mangaokewa Stm · Tangitu · Ongarue River · Pureora Forest Park

WAITEWHENA FOREST · Karaka Forest · Mangakahu Valley · Tawhiara Deer Park · Otupoto Falls · Tieke Falls · Waihaha · Waikino Falls · Te Papa Bay · Escape Cave · Te Tiroa Pt · Te Tawai Pt · Cherry Bay

PANIRAU FOREST · Abandoned Coal Mine · Mangatupoto · Ongarue · HAUHUNGAROA RANGE · Tuhingamata 883m · Whanganui

Otangiwai · Maniatangaroa Falls

Matiere · Tuhua · Te Koura · Taringamotu Valley · Meringa · Hauhungaroa 1078m · Te Aputa · Whareroa Stm

Nihoniho · Nihoniho Conservation Area · Okahukura · Manuariki Marae · Ngakonui · Oruaiwi · PUREORA FOREST PARK · Waituhi Saddle Lookout Scenic Res · Te Raina · Lake Kuratau

Ohura · Te Arohakere 565m · Waipa Pa · Taringamotu · Tuhua Domain · Lairdvale · Echolands · Ngapuke · Kuratau Junction · Kuratau · Whareroa

Mangaparo · Tatu 600m · Otunui · TAUMARUNUI · Taumaruiti · Manunui · Moerangi · Hirata · Pukawa

Tatu · Blue Coal Mine Tatu · Motutara Conservation Area · Pungapunga · Whangaporoto · PUKEPOTO FOREST · Historic Mission House · Omori

Tokirima · Aukopae · Heritage Trail · Tunakotekote · Kakahi Glow Worms · Waihi Village (Private) · Stump Bay

Opatu · Te Maire · Hikumutu · Piriaka · Lookout · Taupo & Environs See map 70 for detail · Thermal Area & Hot Pools · Tokaanu · Thermal Area · Historic Church · Tail Fishing Race

Kirikau · Scenic Reserve · Bush Walk · Owhango

TANGARAKAU CONSERVATION AREA · Scenic Reserve · Kawautahi · Oio · TONGARIRO FOREST CONSERVATION AREA · Outdoor Pursuit Centre · Tongariro · Papakai · Motuopuhi Island · TONGARIRO NATIONAL PARK · 1325m Pihanga

Tawhata · Hukapapa · Te Porere Redoubt · LAKE ROTOAIRA · Camp · Rangipo

Retaruke · Mansons Siding · Kaitieke · Railway Spiral (200M Rise) · Matariki Falls · Car Park · The Tongariro Crossing Mt Tongariro 1967m · Soda Springs · Blue Lake · Explosion Craters · WARNING ROAD MAY BE CLOSED IN WINTER

Upper Retaruke · Raurimu · Scenic Reserves · Tawhai Falls · Emerald Lakes · Mt Ngauruhoe 2291m Active Volcano

WHANGANUI NATIONAL PARK · Bridge to Nowhere · National Park · Waikune · Whakapapa · Silica Rapids · Whakapapa Visitors Centre · Tama Lakes

TAHEKE CONSERVATION AREA · Whitianki 635m · Conservation Area · Erua · ERUA CONSERVATION AREA · Makatote Viaduct · Hauhungatahi Wilderness Area · Iwikau Village · WHAKAPAPA SKIFIELD · TONGARIRO NATIONAL PARK (World Heritage Site) · TUKINO SKIFIELD

Ruatiti · Final Railway Spike (1908) · Crater Lake · Mt Ruapehu 2797m Active Volcano · TUROA SKIFIELD · 4WD · Tukino Skifield

Paripokai 475m · MURUMURU CONSERVATION AREA · Pokaka · Mountain Views · RANGIPO DESERT · Desert Road Summit 1074m

Ramanui · Horopito

MATEMATEAONGA · Orautoha · Tohunga Junction · RANGATAUA CONSERVATION AREA

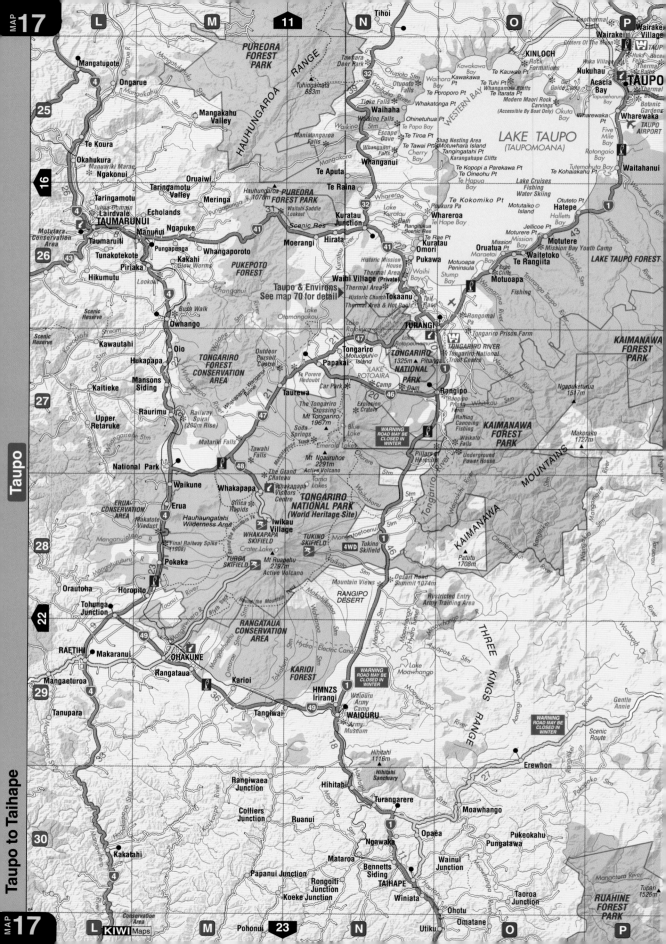

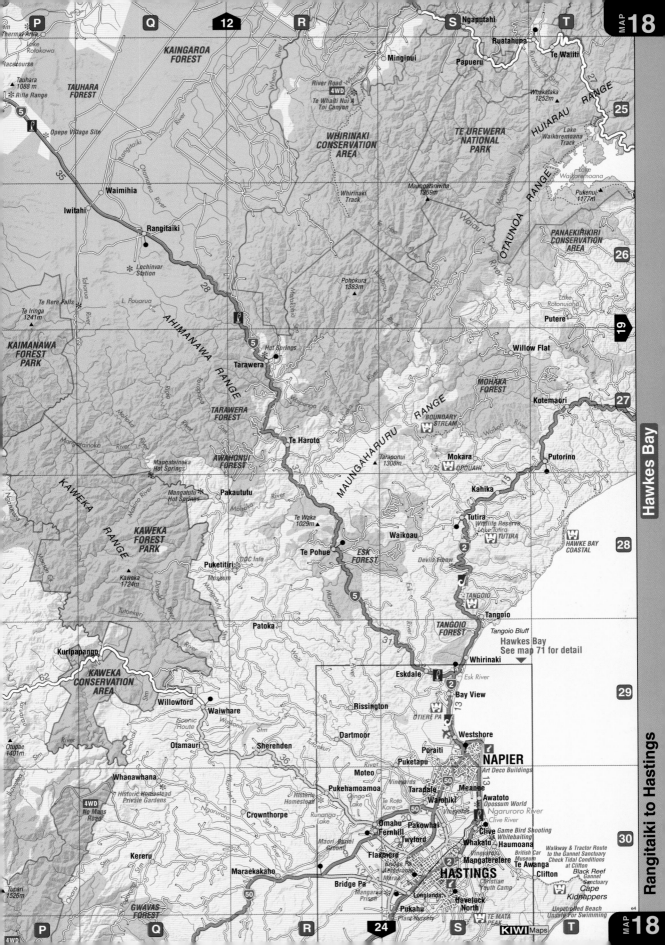

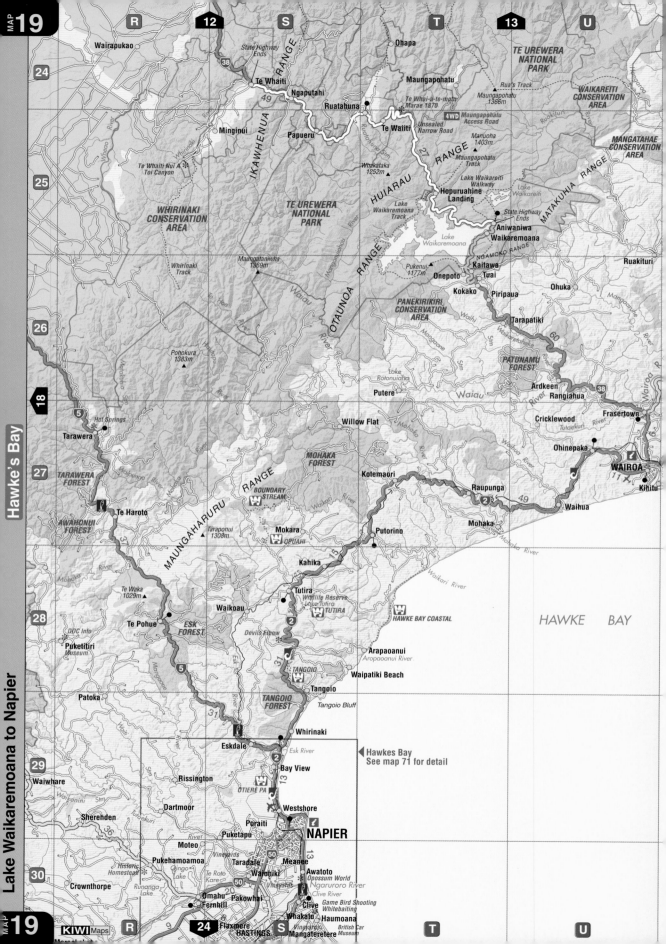

MAP 19

R | 12 | S | T | 13 | U

24
25
26
18
27
28
29
30

Wairapukao

State Highway Ends
38

Te Whaiti
Ngaputahi
49
Ruatahuna

Ohapa

Maungapohatu

TE UREWERA NATIONAL PARK

Rua's Track

WAIKAREITI CONSERVATION AREA

Minginui
Papueru

Te Waiiti

Te Whaiti Nui A Toi Canyon

IKAWHENUA RANGE

Whakataka 1252m

Te Whai-a-te-motu Marae 1870

Maungapohatu 1366m

4WD Maungapohatu Access Road

27

Unsealed Narrow Road

RANGE

Manuoha 1403m

Maungapohatu Track

MATAKUHIA RANGE

MANGATAHAE CONSERVATION AREA

WHIRINAKI CONSERVATION AREA

TE UREWERA NATIONAL PARK

Whirinaki Track

Maungataniwha 1369m

HUIARAU RANGE

Lake Waikaremoana Track

Hopuruahine Landing

Lake Waikareiti Walkway

Lake Waikareiti

State Highway Ends

Aniwaniwa
Waikaremoana

NGAMOKO RANGE

Ruakituri

Te Hoe

Waiau River

OTAUNOA RANGE

Lake Waikaremoana

Pukenui 1177m

Onepoto
Tuai
Kaitawa

Kokako
Piripaua

Ohuka

Pohokura 1383m

Metahua Stm

PANEKIRIKIRI CONSERVATION AREA

Waihi

Tarapatiki
60

PATUNAMU FOREST

18

5 Hot Springs
Tarawera

Waiotapu River

Lake Rotonuiaha

Putere

Waiau River

Mangaone

Waikaretaheke River

Ardkeen
Rangiahua
38

Wairoa R

Willow Flat

Mohaka River

Cricklewood
Tutaekuri River

Frasertown

Ohinepaka

WAIROA
11

27

TARAWERA FOREST

MAUNGAHARURU RANGE

MOHAKA FOREST

Kotemaori

Raupunga
2

Mohaka

49

Waihua

Kihitu

AWAHOHU FOREST

Te Haroto

BOUNDARY STREAM

Taraponui 1308m

OPUAHI

Mokara

Putorino

Mohaka River

31

Te Waka 1029m

Te Pohue

ESK FOREST

Waikoau

15

Kahika

28

DOC Info
Puketitiri
Museum

Tutira
Wildlife Reserve
Lake Tutira
TUTIRA

Waikari River

HAWKE BAY COASTAL

HAWKE BAY

5

Devils Elbow

2

Arapaoanui
Aropaoanui River

Patoka

TANGOIO FOREST

31

TANGOIO

Waipatiki Beach

Tangoio

Tangoio Bluff

Mangaone River

Whirinaki

Eskdale
2
Esk River

Hawkes Bay
See map 71 for detail

Waiwhare

29

Rissington

Bay View
13

OTIERE PA

Waiwhare

Dartmoor

Sherenden

36

Westshore

Poraiti

NAPIER

Moteo
Pukehamoamoa
Puketapu

Taradale
50
Waiohiki

Meanee

Awatoto
Opossum World

Game Bird Shooting
Whitebaiting

Crownthorpe

Omahu
Fernhill

Pakowhai

20

Clive
Whakatu

Historic Homestead

Te Roto Kare

Vineyards

Ngaruroro River
Clive River

British Car Museum

MAP 19

KIWI Maps

R | 9 | 24 | S | T | U

Flaxmere
HASTINGS
Mangateretere
Haumoana

MAP 20

Te Wera
V
13
W
Te Karaka
X
14
Y

Wharekopae
Rere
Wharekopae River
East Woodhill Arboretum
Waipaoa
Kaitaratahi
Waimata
Pakarae
Gable End Foreland
24
Waihau Bay
Waiharehare Bay

Ngatapa
Rongopai Marae 1888
Lake Waituhi
Repongaere
Ormond
Waihirere
Pukeakura 497m
Pakarae River
Te Ikaarongamai Bay

Tahunga
Pehiri
Hangaroa
Gentle Annie (Gisborne District)
Waerengaahika
Patutahi
Hexton
Makauri
Makaraka
See map 87
Whangara
Whangara Is
Waiomoko River
Pouawa
Pariokonohi Pt
TE TAPUWAE O RONGOKAKO MARITIME RESERVE
25

Waerengaokuri
Matawhero
Manutuke
GISBORNE
Makorori
Tatapouri
Turihaua Pt
35
Tatapouri Pt
Makorori Pt

Doneraille Park
Tiniroto
Waikura River
Whakapunake 962m
Te Arai River
Waingake
Waipaoa River
Poverty Bay
Tuamotu Is
Okitu
Wainui
Tuaheni Pt
Tuaheni Pt

Te Reinga
Muriwai
Young Nicks Head
Maraetaha River
26

Marumaru
Tukemokihi
Maraetaha
Bartletts
WHARERATA
FOREST

Tuhara
Whakaki
Morere
Hot Springs
Mahanga
Kopuawhara
27

Kihitu
Whakaki Lagoon
Nuhaka
Opoutama
Oraka Beach
Mahia
Auroa Pt

Waikokopu
Mahia Beach
Whakatakahe Head
Table Cape

Te Heruotaraia Pt
MAHIA PENINSULA SCENIC RESERVE
Te Kapu 366m
28

Long Pt
Mahia Peninsula
Tawapata

Hekerangi Pt

HAWKE BAY
Ahuriri Point
29

Portland Island

30

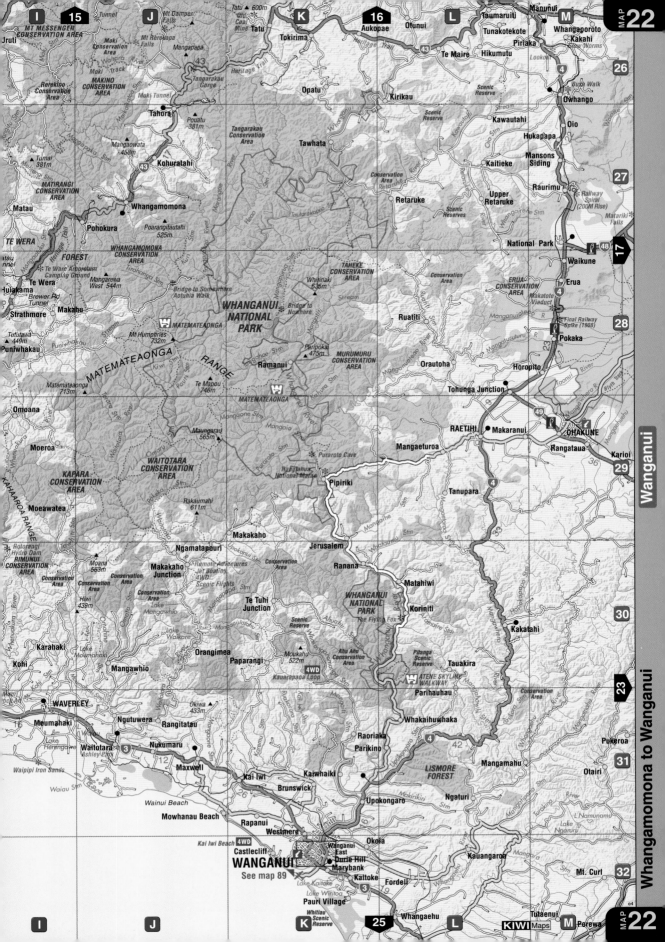

MAP 22
MAP 22

MAP 24

MAP 26

MAP 28

MAP
29

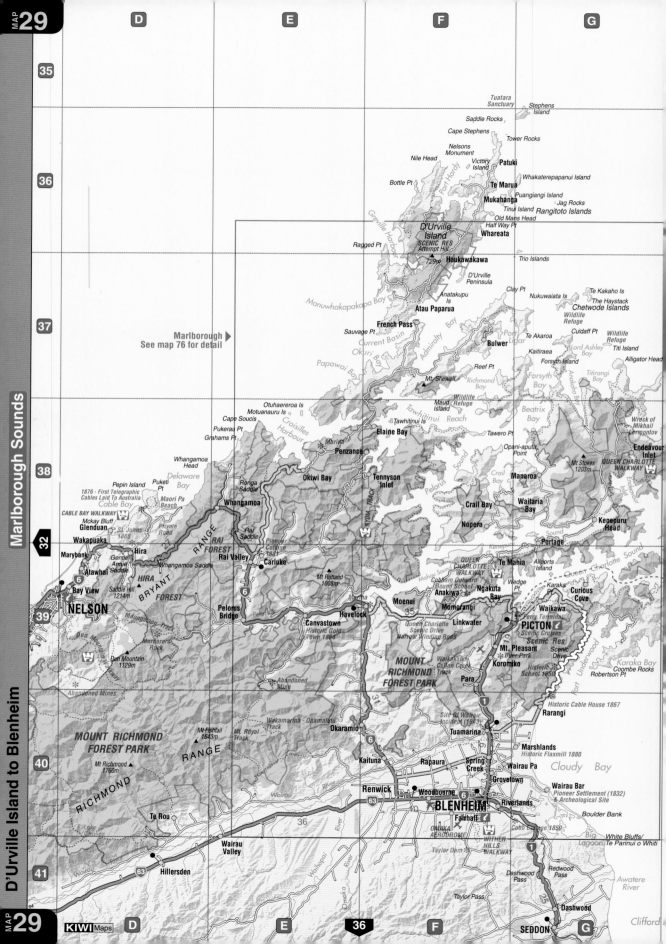

Tuatara
Sanctuary
Stephens
Island
Saddle Rocks
Cape Stephens
Tower Rocks
Nelsons
Monument
Nile Head
Victory
Island
Patuki
Bottle Pt
Te Marua
Whakaterepapanui Island
Mukahanga
Puangiangi Island
Jag Rocks
Tinui Island
Rangitoto Islands
Old Mans Head
Half Way Pt
D'Urville
Island
Whareata
SCENIC RES
Attempt Hill
Ragged Pt
729m
Haukawakawa
Trio Islands
D'Urville
Peninsula
Clay Pt
Nukuwaiata Is
Te Kakaho Is
The Haystack
Anatakupu
Is
Chetwode Islands
Atau Paparua
Wildlife
Refuge
Manuwhakapakapa Bay
French Pass
Te Akaroa
Culdaff Pt
Wildlife
Refuge
Sauvage Pt
Bulwer
Kaitiraea
Titi Island
Current Basin
Port
Ligar
Lord Ashley
Bay
Alligator Head
Okuri Bay
Reef Pt
Forsyth Island
Papawai Bay
Admiralty
Mt Shewell
Richmond
Bay
Forsyth
Bay
Titirangi
Bay
Maud
Island
Wildlife
Refuge
Beatrix
Bay
Tawhitinui Reach
Otuhaereroa Is
Tawhitinui Is
Motuanauru Is
Wreck of
Mikhail
Lermontov
Cape Soucis
Tawero Pt
Marina
Elaine Bay
Opani-aputa
Point
Endeavour
Inlet
Pukerau Pt
Grahams Pt
Penzance
Mt Stokes
1203m
QUEEN CHARLOTTE
WALKWAY
Whangamoa
Head
Pelorus
Okiwi Bay
Tennyson
Inlet
Crail
Bay
Manaroa
Delaware
Bay
Ronga
Saddle
Sound
1876 - First Telegraphic
Cables Laid To Australia
Pepin Island
Puketi
Pt
Whangamoa
Crail Bay
Waitaria
Bay
Kenepuru
Head
Cable Bay
Maori Pa
Beach
Rai
Saddle
Nopera
CABLE BAY WALKWAY
Mckay Bluff
St Johns
1868
Private
Road
Pioneer
Cottage
1861
Portage
Glenduan
RAI
FOREST
Wakapuaka
RANGE
Kenepuru
Marybank
Hira
Rai Valley
Carluke
QUEEN
CHARLOTTE
WALKWAY
Te Mahia
Allports
Island
Gentle
Annie
Saddle
HIRA
Whangamoa Saddle
Mt Rutland
1008m
Cobham Outward
Bound School
Te Mahia
Queen Charlotte Sound
Bay View
BRYANT
Saddle Hill
1214m
Moenui
Karaka
Bay
Curious
Cove
NELSON
FOREST
Pelorus
Bridge
Anakiwa
Ngakuta
Bay
Wedge
Pt
Waikawa
Canvastown
Havelock
35
Momorangi
Ferry Terminal
Dun Mountain
Historic Gold
Town 1864
Linkwater
PICTON
Murderers
Rock
Queen Charlotte
Scenic Drive
Narrow Winding Road
SCENIC RES
Scenic
Drive
Dun Mountain
1129m
27
Mt Pleasant
Deer Park
Karaka Bay
Coombe Rocks
Abandoned
Mine
Koromiko
Historic
School 1859
Robertson Pt
Abandoned Mines
MOUNT
RICHMOND
FOREST PARK
Waikakaho
Cullen Creek
Track
Para
Wakamarina - Onamalutu
Track
Historic Cable House 1867
Mt Fishtail
1643m
Mt Royal
Track
Okaramio
Site of Wairau
Incident (1843)
Rarangi
MOUNT RICHMOND
FOREST PARK
Tuamarina
Marshlands
Historic Flaxmill 1880
Mt Richmond
1760m
Kaituna
Rapaura
Spring
Creek
Wairau Pa
Cloudy Bay
RICHMOND
RANGE
Renwick
Woodbourne
Grovetown
Wairau Bar
Pioneer Settlement (1832)
& Archeological Site
Te Rou
63
BLENHEIM
Riverlands
Boulder Bank
Fairhall
Cobb Cottage 1859
Wairau
Valley
OMAKA
AERODROME
WITHER
HILLS
WALKWAY
Big
Lagoon
White Bluffs
Te Parinui o Whiti
Hillersden
Taylor Dam
Awatere
River
Dashwood
Pass
Redwood
Pass
Taylor Pass
25
Dashwood
SEDDON
Clifford

Marlborough
See map 76 for detail

MAP
29
KIWI Maps   D   E   36   F   G

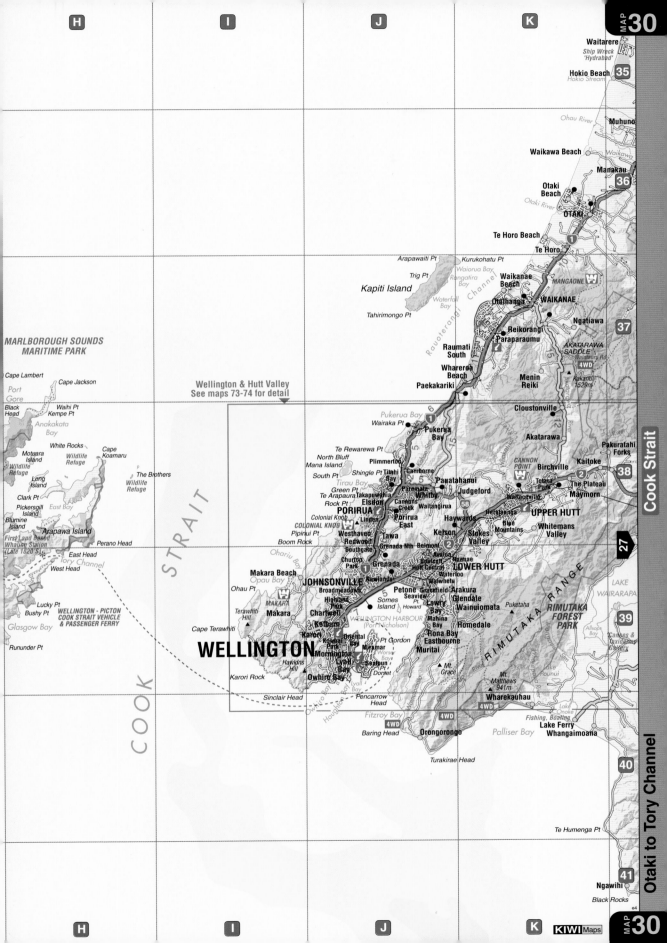

Waitarere
Ship Wreck 'Hydrabad'

Hokio Beach
Hokio Stream

Muhunoa

Ohau River

Waikawa Beach
Waikawa

Manakau

Otaki Beach

Otaki River

OTAKI

Te Horo Beach

Te Horo

Arapawaiti Pt

Kurukohatu Pt

Waiorua Bay

Trig Pt

Rangatira Bay

Waikanae Beach

Kapiti Island

Waikanae

MANGAONE

Otaihanga

Tahirimongo Pt

Waterfall Bay

Reikorangi

Ngatiawa

Raumati South

Paraparaumu

AKATARAWA SADDLE
Waitaanui Rd

Whareroa Beach

4WD

MARLBOROUGH SOUNDS MARITIME PARK

Paekakariki

Menin Reiki

Kakanui 1529m

Cloustonville

Cape Lambert

Cape Jackson

Waihi Pt
Kempe Pt

Black Head

Anakakata Bay

Pukerua Bay

Akatarawa

White Rocks

Wildlife Refuge

Cape Koamaru

Pukerua Bay

Wairaka Pt

Pakuratahi Forks

Motuara Island

Wildlife Refuge

Long Island

The Brothers
Wildlife Refuge

Te Rewarewa Pt

North Bluff

Mana Island

Plimmerton

Camborne

Kaitoke

Birchville

CANNON POINT

Totara Park

The Plateau
Maymorn

Clark Pt

South Pt

Shingle Pt

Tilahi Bay

Pauatahanui

Pickersgill Island

Green Pt
Te Arapaura

Takapuwahia

Paremata

Judgeford

58

Whiteemans

Blumine Island

First Land Based Whaling Station (Late 1820's)

Rock Pt

Elsdon

PORIRUA

Cannons Creek

Waitangirua

UPPER HUTT

Arapawa Island

Perano Head

Colonial Knob

COLONIAL KNOB

Porirua East

Haywards

Heretaunga

Blue Mountains

Whitemans Valley

East Head
West Head

Pipinui Pt

Linden

Tawa

Grenada Nth

Kelson

Stokes Valley

Tory Channel

Boom Rock

Westhaven

Redwood

Southgate

Belmont

2

Lucky Pt
Bushy Pt

WELLINGTON - PICTON COOK STRAIT VEHICLE & PASSENGER FERRY

Churton Park

Grenada

Aotea

Naenae

LOWER HUTT

RIMUTAKA FOREST PARK

LAKE WAIRARAPA

Glasgow Bay

Ohariu Bay

Newlands

Hutt Central

Waterloo
Waiwhetu

Runander Pt

MAKARA BEACH
Opau Pt

JOHNSONVILLE

Broadmeadows

Petone

Gracefield
Seaview

Arakura

Glendale

Puketaha

Allsops Bay

Canoes & Taxidexine Gallery

Ohau Pt

Highland Park

Somes Island

Lowry Bay

Wainuiomata

Terawhiti Hill

Makara

Chartwell

Howard

Mahina Bay

Homedale

Mt Matthews 941m

Kelburn

Karori

Kowhai Park

Oriental Bay

Pt Gordon

Rona Bay

Eastbourne

Muritai

RIMUTAKA RANGE

Lake Pounui

Cape Terawhiti

Mornington

Miramar

Mt Grace

Karori Rock

WELLINGTON

Lyall Bay

Seatoun

Pt Dorset

Worser Bay

Lake Onoke

Hawkins Hill

Owhiro Bay

Lyall Bay

Fishing, Boating

Lake Ferry

Whangaimoana

COOK STRAIT

Sinclair Head

Pencarrow Head

Fitzroy Bay

4WD

4WD

Wharekauhau

Houghton Bay

4WD

Baring Head

Orongorongo

Palliser Bay

Turakirae Head

Te Humenga Pt

Ngawihi

Black Rocks

e4

KIWI Maps

MAP 30

Wellington & Hutt Valley
See maps 73-74 for detail

Pukerua Bay

WELLINGTON HARBOUR
(Port Nicholson)

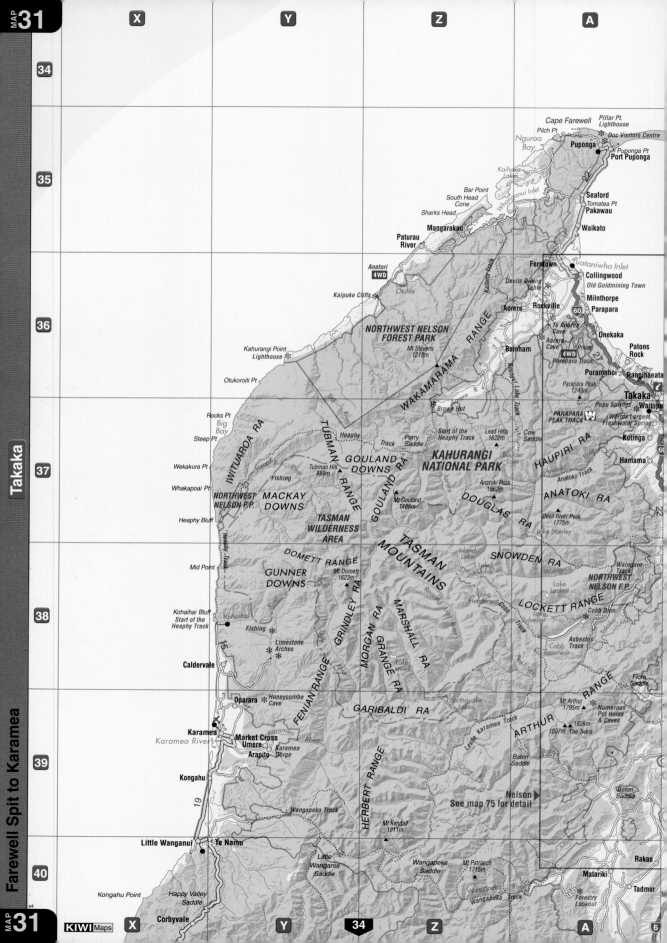

MAP
31

34
35
36
37
38
39
40

Cape Farewell
Pillar Pt.
Lighthouse
Pilch Pt
Doc Visitors Centre
Nguroa Bay
Puponga
Puponga Pt
Port Puponga

Kaihoka Lakes
Bar Point
South Head Cone
Seaford
Tomatea Pt
Pakawau
Sharks Head
Mangarakau
Whanganui Inlet
Waikato

Paturau River
Ruataniwha Inlet
Ferntown
Collingwood
Old Goldmining Town
Anatori
4WD
Devils Dining Table
Milnthorpe
Parapara
Lake Otuhie
Kaipuke Cliffs
Aorere
Rockville
60

NORTHWEST NELSON FOREST PARK
Te Anaroa Cave
Onekaka
Mt Stevens 1213m
Bainham
Aorere Cave
4WD
Private
Patons Rock

Kahurangi Point Lighthouse
Parapara Track
Puramahoi
Rangihaeata

Otukoroiti Pt
Brown Hut
PARAPARA PEAK TRACK
Parapara Peak 1249m
Pupu Springs
Takaka
7
Waitapu

Rocks Pt
Big Bay
Heaphy
Perry Saddle
Start of the Heaphy Track
Lead Hills 1622m
Cow Saddle
(Worlds Largest Freshwater Spring)
Kotinga

Steep Pt
Track
Boulder Lake
Hamama

Wekakura Pt
Fishing
GOULAND DOWNS
KAHURANGI NATIONAL PARK
Anatoki Track

Whakapoai Pt
Tubman Hill 889m
Anatoki Peak 1662m
ANATOKI RA

Heaphy Bluff
NORTHWEST NELSON F.P.
MACKAY DOWNS
TASMAN WILDERNESS AREA
Mt Gouland 1468m
DOUGLAS RA
Devil River Peak 1775m
Lake Stanley

Mid Point
DOMETT RANGE
GUNNER DOWNS
Mt Domett 1623m
TASMAN MOUNTAINS
Island Lake
SNOWDEN RA
Lake Cobb
Waingaro
Waingaro Track
NORTHWEST NELSON F.P.

Kohaihai Bluff
Start of the Heaphy Track
Lake Ellen
Lake Lockett
Cobb Dam

Kohaihai
Fishing
Lake Sylvester
LOCKETT RANGE

Caldervale
Limestone Arches
Cobb Reservoir
Asbestos Track

Oparara
Honeycombe Cave
GRINDLEY RA
MORGAN RA
MARSHALL RA
GRANGE RA
Lake Lewell
Earthquake Lakes
Flora Saddle

Karamea
Karamea River
Market Cross
Umere
Arapito
Karamea Gorge
FENIAN RANGE
GARIBALDI RA
Leslie Karamea Track
Mt Arthur 1795m
Numerous Pot Holes & Caves
1826m
1807m The Twins
ARTHUR RANGE

Kongahu
HERBERT RANGE
Baton Saddle

Wangapeka Track
Nelson
See map 75 for detail
Baton Saddle

Little Wanganui
Te Namu
Mt Kendall 1811m

Little Wanganui Saddle
Wangapeka Saddle
Mt Patriarch 1715m
Rakau

Kongahu Point
Happy Valley Saddle
Wangapeka Track
Wangapeka Track
Matariki
Tadmor

Forestry Lookout

Corbyvale

Tasman Bay

Takaka to Rai Valley

Farewell Spit

Bird Sanctuary

FAREWELL SPIT
NATURE RESERVE
(LIMITED ACCESS)

Lighthouse

Golden Bay

Separation Pt

Taupo Pt
Tata Is
Wainui
Inlet
Anapai
Bay

Tata Beach
Tarakehe
Totaranui

akaka

Awaroa
Bay

Waitapu
Pohara
Clifton

Birds Clearing

Motupipi
4WD

East Takaka

Manson
Cave

Totaranui Track

Awaroa Head

Moa Park

ABEL
TASMAN
NATIONAL PARK

Marine Reserve

Tonga Island
Tonga Roadstead
Foul Pt
South Head

Harwood
Hole

Mt Evans
1156m

North Head
Torrent Bay
Pitt Head
Astrolabe Plaque

Numerous
Sinkholes

Horse Treks

Adele Island
Fisherman Island

Uruwhenua

Caves

Marahau

Sandy Bay
Sea Kayaking/Water Taxi
Toko Ngawa Pt

Upper
Takaka

Split Apple Rock

Lookout
Eureka Bend

Kaiteriteri
Launch Cruises

Historic Plaque

Riwaka

Fisrt Settlers
Landing

Brooklyn

Motueka

White Water
Rafting

Tasman Bay

Port Motueka

Lower
Moutere

Marini
Jackett Island

Pangatotara

Kina
Tame Eels

Braeburn

Tasman

Ngatimoti

Moutere Bluff

Ruby Bay

Pokororo
Orinoco

Harakeke

Old
Highway
61

Woodstock

Mahana

Mapua
Bronte

Rabbit Island

Thorpe

Bells Is
Beats Is

Upper
Moutere

Neudorf
Saddle

Dovedale

Redwood
Valley

Saxton
Is

Stanley
Brook

28

St Paul's 1657

Brightwater

Lord Rutherford
Birthplace

Tapawera

GOLDEN DOWNS
FOREST

Wakefield

Spring
Grove

Rakau

26

St John's 1646

Mararewa

Wai-iti
Foxhill

Motupiko

Belgrove

Kohatu

WAIMEA
FOREST

WAIMEA
FOREST

Marlborough ▶
See map 76 for detail

◀ Nelson, Motueka & Environs
See map 75 for detail

NELSON

See map 95

STOKE

RICHMOND

Hope

Maungatapu Track

Dun Mountain Track

Murderers'
Rock

Dun Mountain
1129m

Abandoned Mines

Mt Fishtail
1643m

MOUNT RICHMOND
FOREST PARK

Mt Royal
Track

Wakamarina - Onamalutu
Track

Okaramio

Kaituna

Pepin Island
Puketi
Pt

1876 - First Telegraphic
Cables Laid To Australia

Cable Bay

Maori Pa
Beach

Private
Road

CABLE BAY
WALKWAY

Mckay Bluff

Glenduan

St Johns
1886

Wakapuaka

Marybank

Hira

Gentle Annie
Saddle

Atawhai

Whangamoa Saddle

Bay View

Saddle Hill
1214m

HIRA
FOREST

Whangamoa
Head

Delaware
Bay

Whangamoa

Ronga
Saddle

Rai
Saddle

RAI
FOREST

Rai Valley

Carluke

Mt Rutland
1008m

Pelorus
Bridge

Canvastown
Historic Gold
Town 1864

27

Moenui

Abandoned
Mine

Greville Harbour

Ragged Pt

Manuwhakapakapa Bay

Sauvage Pt

Current Basin
Okuri Bay

Papawai Bay

Otuhaereroa Is
Motuanauru Is

Cape Soucis

Pukerau Pt

Grahams Pt

Croisilles
Harbour

Elaine Bay

Marina

Okiwi Bay

Tennyson
Inlet

BRYANT
RANGE

Pioneer
Cottage
1862

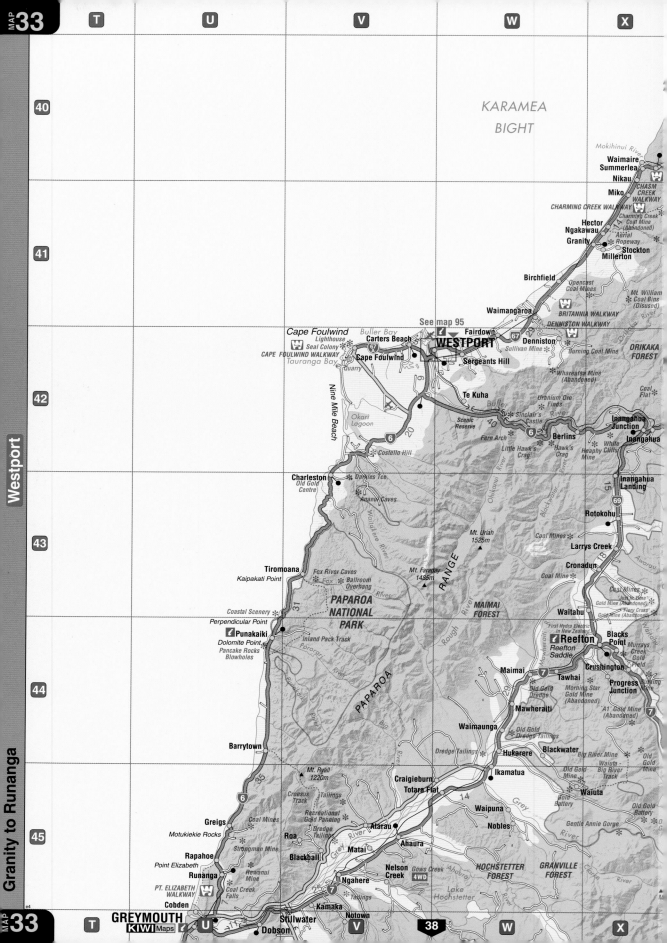

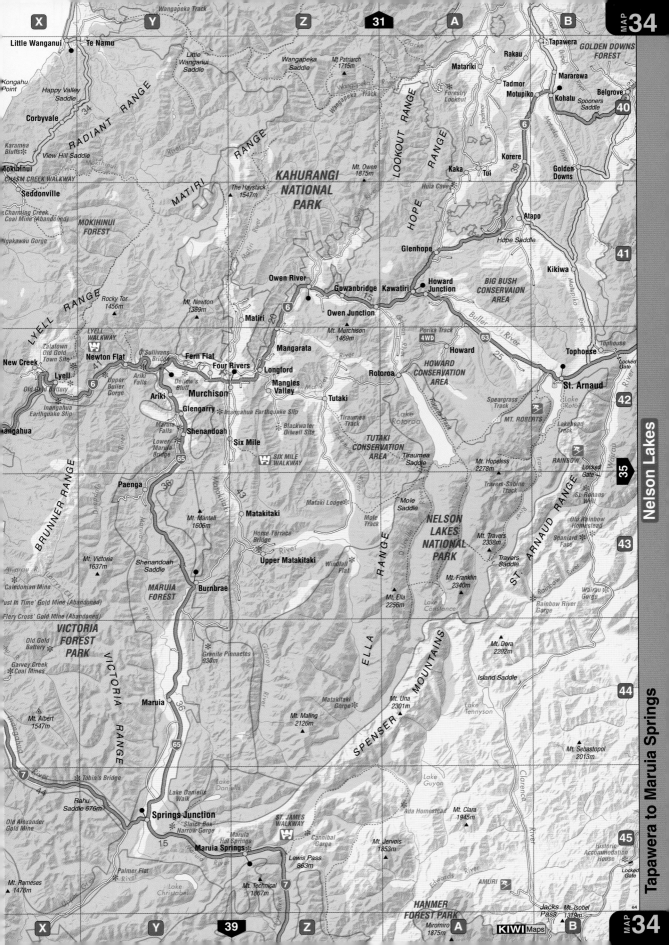

Nelson Lakes

Tapawera to Maruia Springs

Little Wanganui · Te Namu
Wangapeka Track
Little Wanganui Saddle
Wangapeka Saddle
Mt Patriarch 1715m
Tapawera
GOLDEN DOWNS FOREST
Rakau
Matariki
Mararewa
Kongahu Point
Happy Valley Saddle
Tadmor
Motupiko
Belgrove
Kohatu
Spooners Saddle
40
Corbyvale
RADIANT RANGE
34
Forestry Lookout
6
Karamea Bluffs
View Hill Saddle
39
Kaka
Tui
Korere
Golden Downs
Mokihinui
KAHURANGI NATIONAL PARK
Mt. Owen 1875m
Huia Cave
Atapo
41
CHASM CREEK WALKWAY
Seddonville
MATIRI RANGE
RANGE
The Haystack 1547m
LOOKOUT RANGE
HOPE RANGE
Glenhope
Hope Saddle
Kikiwa
Charming Creek Coal Mine (Abandoned)
MOKIHINUI FOREST
Ngakawau Gorge
LYELL RANGE
Mt Newton 1389m
Owen River
Gowanbridge
Kawatiri
Howard Junction
BIG BUSH CONSERVAION AREA
Rocky Tor 1456m
Matiri
Owen Junction
Mt Murchison 1469m
Porika Track 4WD
Howard
63
Tophouse
New Creek
Zalatown Old Gold Town Site
LYELL WALKWAY
O'Sullivans Bridge
Fern Flat
Mangarata
Mt. Murchison 1469m
HOWARD CONSERVATION AREA
Tophouse
Locked Gate
Lyell
Newton Flat
Four Rivers
Longford
Rotoroa
Speargrass Track
St. Arnaud
42
6
Upper Buller Gorge
Ariki Falls
Dellow's Bluff
Mangles Valley
Mangles River
Tutaki
Lake Rotoroa
MT. ROBERTS
Lake Rotoiti
Lakehead Track
Ariki
Murchison
Glengarry
Inangahua Earthquake Slip
Tiraumea Track
RAINBOW
Inangahua
Maruia Falls
Shenandoah
Six Mile
Blackwater Oilwell Site
TUTAKI CONSERVATION AREA
Tiraumea Saddle
Mt Hopeless 2278m
Locked Gate
35
Lower Maruia Bridge
65
SIX MILE WALKWAY
Travers-Sabine Track
St Ronans Well
BRUNNER RANGE
Paenga
36
43
Mataki Lodge
Mole Saddle
NELSON LAKES NATIONAL PARK
Mt Travers 2338m
Old Rainbow Homestead
Spaniard Face
43
Mt. Victoria 1637m
Mt. Mantell 1606m
Matakitaki
Mole Track
Travers Saddle
Awarua R.
Caledonian Mine
Shenandoah Saddle
Horse Terrace Bridge
Upper Matakitaki
Windfall Flat
Mt. Franklin 2340m
Rainbow River Gorge
Wairau Gorge
'Just In Time' Gold Mine (Abandoned)
'Fiery Cross' Gold Mine (Abandoned)
MARUIA FOREST
Burnbrae
Mt. Ella 2256m
Lake Constance
ST. ARNAUD RANGE
VICTORIA FOREST PARK
Old Gold Battery
Granite Pinnacles 930m
ELLA RANGE
Mt. Dora 2202m
44
Garvey Creek Coal Mines
Maruia
36
Matakitaki Gorge
Mt. Una 2301m
Island Saddle
Mt Sebastopol 2013m
Mt. Albert 1547m
SPENSER MOUNTAINS
Lake Tennyson
7
65
Mt. Maling 2126m
44
Tobin's Bridge
Lake Daniells Walk
Lake Daniells
Glenroy River
Lake Guyon
Rahu Saddle 676m
Springs Junction
15
'Sluice Box' Narrow Gorge
ST. JAMES WALKWAY
Ada Homestead
Mt Clara 1945m
Historic Accommodation House
45
Old Alexander Gold Mine
Maruia Springs
Maruia Hot Springs
Cannibal Gorge
Mt Jervois 1853m
Locked Gate
Palmer Flat
Lewis Pass 863m
7
Mt. Rameses 1478m
Mt. Technical 1867m
Lake Christabel
AMURI
HANMER FOREST PARK
Miromiro 1875m
Jacks Pass
Mt. Isobel 1319m

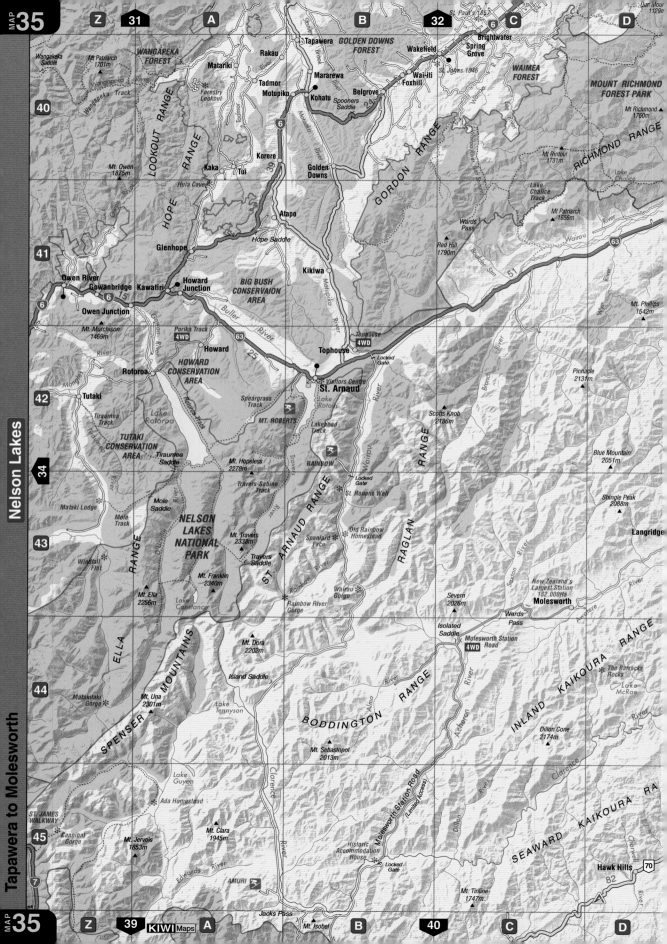

MAP
37

P   Q   R   S   T

West Coast

Hokitika to Franz Josef

45

46

TASMAN SEA

47

HOKITIKA
See map 96
Takutai

Mananui   MAHINAP
                 WALKW
Lake Mahinapua
Ruatapu

30

6

48
Historic
Gold Town   Hokitika R.
Ross

Historical
Monument
*   Mt. Greenland
Ferguson   905m   TOTARA
Bush   FOREST

Kakapotahi   Fergusons   Totara
                                       Saddle
Pukekura
                   Waitaha
        IANTHE
        FOREST   MIKONUI
49   *Lake.   FOREST
Wanganui Bluff   Ianthe/
        Matahi
        Wanganui   River
        WANGANUI   WAITAHA
        FOREST   FOREST
Saltwater Lagoon   SMYTH
Abut Head
White Heron *   Herepo   RANGE
Sanctuary   Waitaha
                                   River
        Lake.   Harihari
        Rotokino   Mt. Whitcombe
Okarito Lagoon   POERUA   2644m
        OKARITO   Rotokino   FOREST   WILBERG
50   FOREST   RANGE
Okarito   Te Taho
Three Mile Lagoon   Lake   6   30
& Walk   Wahapo
Blanchards Bluff Alps
                  Panoramic   Whataroa   Mt. Adams
Five Mile Beach   View   2223m
        The Forks
        Lake
        Mapourika   WAITANGI   SOUTHERN
        WAIANGI   FOREST
                                            ALPS
        Weheka   Gunn Peak
        River   1753m   Ka Tiritiri o te Moana
51
        Old
        Terminal
        Moraine
        Tatare   Scenic Flights
Omoeroa
Saddle   Visitors   Franz Josef
MAP   Centre   Douglas Track
37   P KIWI Maps   Q   Lookout Point   R   S   T
              44

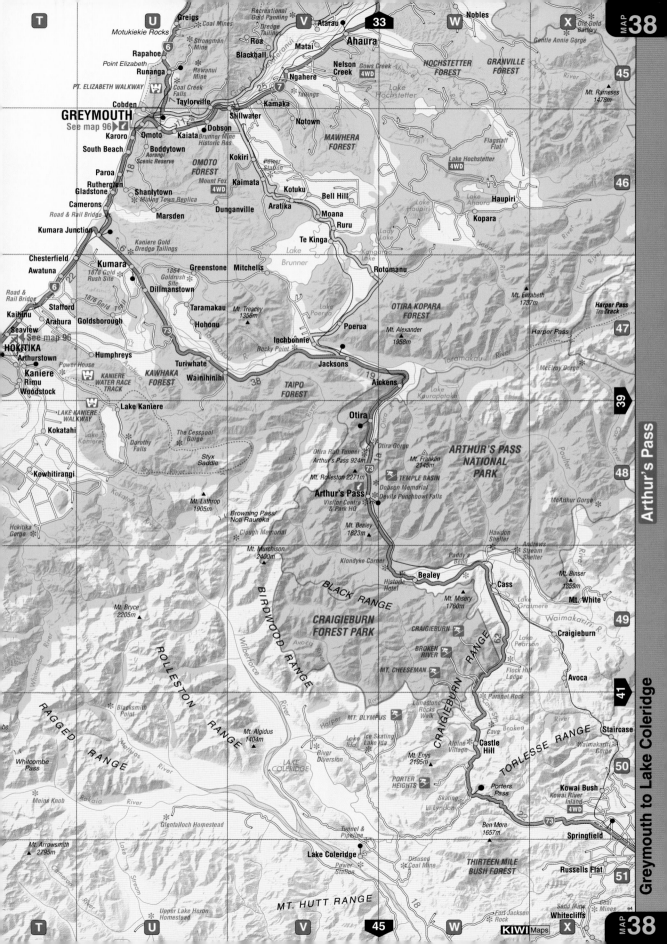

MAP 40

B · 35 · C · D · 36 · E

Mt. Sebastopol 2013m
Historic Accommodation House
Locked Gate
Mt. Tinline 1747m
MT. LYFORD
Jacks Pass
Mt. Isobel 1319m
Jollies Pass 4WD
Jollies Pass
mer ngs
HANMER FOREST
Walking Tracks
7A
Hanmer River 4WD
Hanmer River
Mt Lyford Village
Whales Back Saddle
Limestone Sinkholes (Tomos)
70
30
Waiau
Jet Boating
70 11
Leslie Hills Homestead
7
Rotherham
Mouse Point
Culverden Homestead
Red Post Corner
Culverden
3
AMURI
PLAIN
LOWRY PEAKS RANGE
Mt. Parnassus 697m
Waiau River

Molesworth Station Road (Limited Access)
Dillon River
Charwell River
Kahutara River
Swyncombe
Lynton Downs
Hawk Hills
70
82
Limestone Rock Formations
Conway River
Kowhai River
Kekerengu River
Mt. Fyffe 1602m
Mount Fyffe 4WD
Locked Gate
Mt. Fyffe
Mt. Furneaux
Kowhai
Maori Leap Caves
5
KAIKOURA
Nga Niho Pa
Whale & Dolphin Watching
45
Parititahi Tunnel
Raramai Tunnel
Peketa
South Bay
Seal Colony
KAIKOURA PENINSULA WALKWAY
Goose Bay
Rock Art
Oaro
1
46
Hundalee
Claverley
Ferniehurst
Conway Flat
17
Hawkswood
Mt. Wilson 644m
Parnassus
Spotswood
47
Phoebe
16
Caverhill
Leamington
Waiau River
Random Spur Road 4WD
Mina
Cheviot
1
Shag Rock
Beckenham Hills
Domett
Gore Bay
Cathedral Cliffs
Port Robinson
Ethelton
36
Lighthouse
PORT ROBINSON TRACK
Greta
Hurunui Mouth
Blythe Valley
Hurunui River
48
Scargill
Napenape Coastal Reserve
Waikari River
4WD
Limestone Road
Spye
22
Greta Valley
18
Omihi
1
Motunau Beach
Motunau Island
49
Omihi Forest
Cliffs 90m High
4WD Kowai River - Coast

PEGASUS BAY

50

B · C · D · E

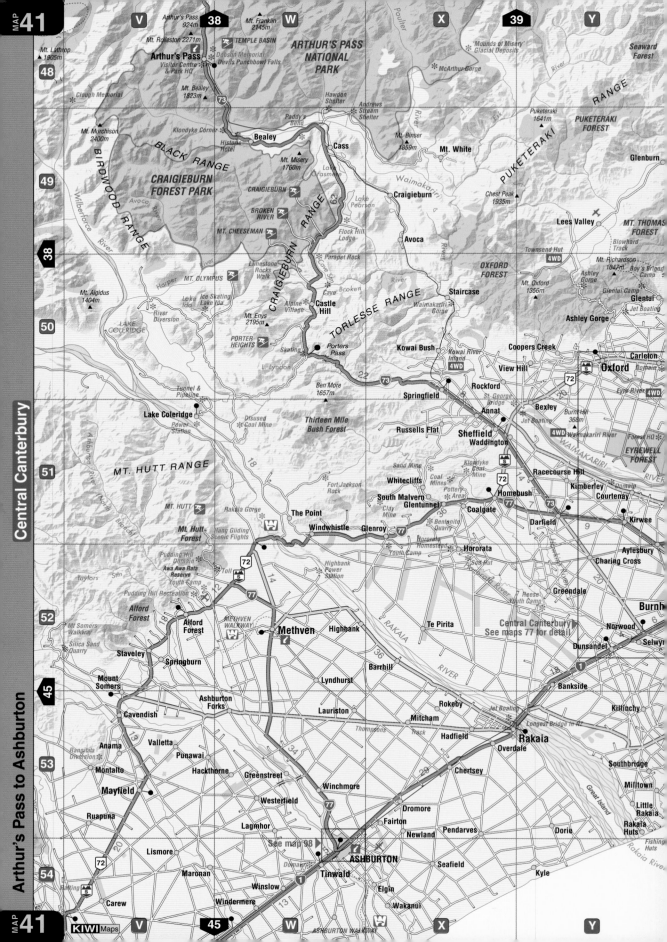

MAP
41

V 38 W X 39 Y

48

49

38

50

51

52

45

53

54

Mt. Lathrop ▲1905m

Arthur's Pass 924m

Mt. Rolleston 2271m

TEMPLE BASIN

Mt. Franklin 2145m

ARTHUR'S PASS NATIONAL PARK

'Mounds of Misery' Glacial Deposits

Seaward Forest

Arthur's Pass Visitor Centre & Park HQ

Dobson Memorial
Devils Punchbowl Falls

McArthur Gorge

Clough Memorial

Mt. Bealey 1823m

73

Hawdon Shelter

Andrews Stream Shelter

Puketeraki 1641m

PUKETERAKI FOREST

Mt. Murchison 2400m

Historic Hotel

Klondyke Corner

Bealey

Paddy's Bend

Cass

Mt. Binser 1859m

Mt. White

Glenburn

BLACK RANGE

BIRDWOOD RANGE

Mt. Misery 1760m

Lake Grasmere

Waimakariri

Chest Peak 1935m

PUKETERAKI RANGE

CRAIGIEBURN FOREST PARK

CRAIGIEBURN

Lake Pearson

Craigieburn

Lees Valley

MT. THOMAS FOREST

Avoca

BROKEN RIVER

Flock Hill Lodge

Avoca

River

Mt. Richardson 1047m

Boy's Brigad Camp

MT. CHEESEMAN

Parapet Rock

Cave Stm

OXFORD FOREST

Mt. Oxford 1356m

Ashley Gorge

Glentui Camp

Mt. Algidus 1404m

Harper

MT. OLYMPUS

Limestone Rocks Walk

Lake Ida

Ice Skating Lake Ida

Cave

Broken

River

Staircase

Waimakariri Gorge

Glentui

Jet Boating

Wilberforce River

LAKE COLERIDGE

River Diversion

Alpine Village

Castle Hill

TORLESSE RANGE

Ashley Gorge

Mt. Enys 2195m

CRAIGIEBURN RANGE

Kowai Bush

Kowai River Inland 4WD

Coopers Creek

Carleton

PORTER HEIGHTS

Skating

Porters Pass

Oxford

72

L. Lyndon

22

73

View Hill

Rockford

St. George Bridge

Springfield

Annat

Bexley

Burnt Hill 368m

Eyre River 4WD

Tunnel & Pipeline

Ben More 1657m

Jet Boating

4WD

Waimakariri River

Lake Coleridge Power Station

Disused Coal Mine

Thirteen Mile Bush Forest

Russells Flat

Sheffield

Waddington

Racecourse Hill

Kimberley

Courtenay

Forest HQ

EYREWELL FOREST

RIVER

MT. HUTT RANGE

Fort Jackson Rock

18

Whitecliffs

Sand Mine

Klondyke Coal Mine

72

Homebush

73

Kirwee

Ashburton River North Branch

Rakaia Gorge

MT. HUTT

South Malvern

Glentunnel

Coal Mines

Pottery Area

77

Coalgate

Darfield

9

Aylesbury

Charing Cross

Mt. Hutt Forest

The Point

Windwhistle

Glenroy

77

Clay Mine

36

Bentonite Quarry

Hororata Homestead

Se Hut

Hororata

Reese Youth Camp

Greendale

20

Burnh

Mt. Hutt Domain

Hang Gliding Scenic Flights

Pudding Hill Domain

Awa Awa Rata Reserve Youth Camp

72

Toll

Highbank Power Station

Nororata Youth Camp

Central Canterbury See maps 77 for detail

Norwood

Taylors Stm

12

14

77

RAKAIA

Dunsandel

Selwyr

Pudding Hill Recreation

Alford Forest

METHVEN WALKWAY

Methven

Highbank

Te Pirita

RIVER

18

Norwood

6

Mt Somers Walkway

Silica Sand Quarry

Staveley

Springburn

Barrhill

Bankside

Kilfinchy

Mount Somers

Lyndhurst

Rokeby

Jet Boating

Longest Bridge in N7

13

Cavendish

Ashburton Forks

Lauriston

Mitcham

Hadfield

Rakaia

Southbridge

Anama

Rangitata Diversion

Valletta

Punawai

Hackthorne

Greenstreet

Winchmore

77

Overdale

Chertsey

Montalto

34

Milltown

Mayfield

Westerfield

Dromore

Fairton

Pendarves

Dorie

Little Rakaia

Ruapuna

Lagmhor

See map 98

Newland

Seafield

Rakaia Huts

Lismore

20

72

Maronan

Winslow

1

ASHBURTON

Tinwald

Kyle

Fishing Huts

Great Island

Rakaia River

Carew

Windermere

Elgin

Wakanui

13

Domain

ASHBURTON WALKWAY

MAP
41

KIWI Maps

V 45 W X Y

BANKS PENINSULA

PEGASUS BAY

◄ Christchurch & Central Canterbury
See maps 77-78 for detail

CHRISTCHURCH

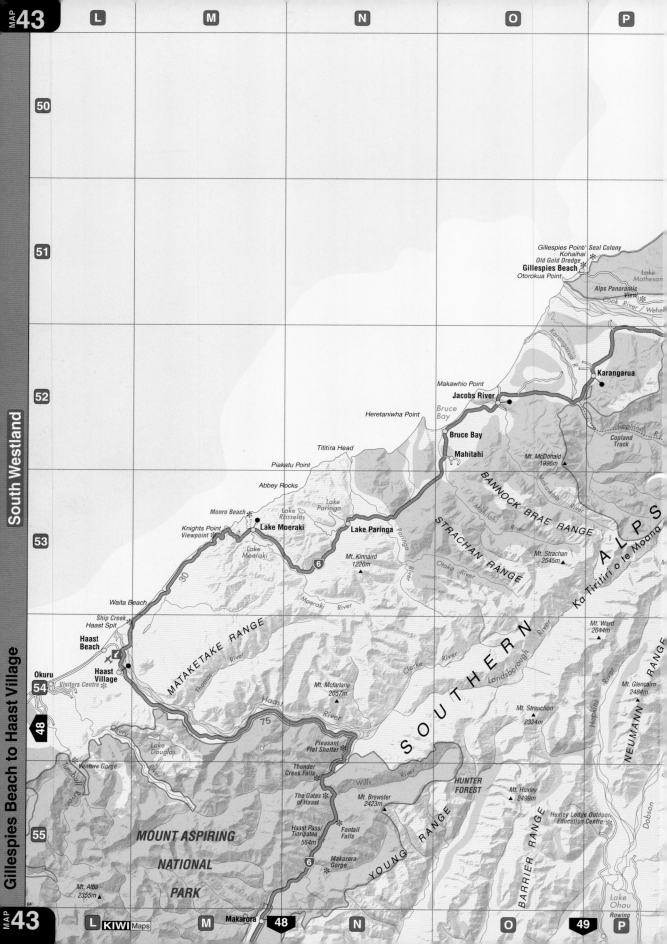

MAP
43

L   M   N   O   P

50

51

52

53

54

55

Gillespies Point/ Seal Colony
Kohaihai
Old Gold Dredge
Gillespies Beach
Otorokua Point

Lake Matheson

Alps Panoramic View

Cook River / Wehel

Karangarua R.

Karangarua

Makawhio Point

Jacobs River

Heretaniwha Point

Bruce Bay

Bruce Bay

Mahitahi

Mt. McDonald 1996m

Copland Track

Copland R.

Tititira Head

BANNOCK BRAE RANGE

Piakatu Point

Abbey Rocks

Lake Rasselas

Lake Paringa

Mt. Strachan 2545m

STRACHAN RANGE

Monro Beach

Lake Moeraki

Knights Point Viewpoint

Lake Paringa

Mt. Kinnaird 1226m

Lake Moeraki

Paringa River

Otoka River

KA Tiritiri o te Moana

ALPS

Waita Beach

30

Moeraki River

SOUTHERN

Mt. Ward 2644m

Ship Creek Haast Spit

Haast Beach

MATAKETAKE RANGE

Thomas River

Clarke River

Landsborough River

Hopkins River

NEUMANN RANGE

Mt. Glencairn 2484m

Okuru

Haast Village

Visitors Centre

48

Lake Douglas

Mt. Mcfarlane 2057m

Haast River

75

Mt. Strauchon 2324m

Okuru River

Pleasant Flat Shelter

Turnbull River

Venture Gorge

Thunder Creek Falls

Wills River

HUNTER FOREST

Mt. Huxley 2499m

YOUNG RANGE

BARRIER RANGE

Dobson

The Gates of Haast

Mt. Brewster 2423m

Huxley Lodge Outdoor Education Centre

MOUNT ASPIRING

Haast Pass/ Tioripatea 564m

Fantail Falls

6

Makarora Gorge

NATIONAL

PARK

Mt. Alba 2355m

Lake Ohau

Rowing

MAP 44

P Q Abut Head R Herepo 37 S T

White Heron Sanctuary
Okarito Rotokino FOREST
Lake Rotokino
Waitangitaona River
Harihari
Whataroa River
SMYTH RANGE
Mt. Whitcombe 2644m
50

POERUA FOREST
Te Taho
6
Okarito Lagoon
Lake Wahapo
WILBERG RANGE
Ramsay Glacier
Okarito
Three Mile Lagoon & Walk
Blanchards Bluff
Alps Panoramic View
The Forks
Whataroa
Mt. Adams 2223m
Lyell Glacier
Five Mile Beach
Lake Mapourika
WAITANGI FOREST
33
Clyde River
A L P S
51

Old Terminal Moraine
Tatare
Gunn Peak 1753m
Perth River
CLOUDY PEAK RANGE
Lawrence River
Erewhon
Waiho River
Omoeroa River
25
Franz Josef / Waiau
Douglas Track Lookout Point
Ka Tiritiri o te Moana
Tatare Sun
Totara Sun
Havelock River
Erewhon Park
52

Visitors Centre
Omoeroa Saddle
Cook Saddle
Franz Josef Glacier / Ka Roimata o Hine Hukatere
Geike Snowfield
Elie de Beaumont 3117m
Godley Gl
Mt. D'Archiac 2865m
MOUNT COOK NATIONAL PARK
Mt. Sibbald 2804m
SIBBALD RANGE
Macauley River
The Thumbs 2545m
Dr Sinclair's Grave
Mesopotamia
Mt. Sinclair 2065m
Historic Stone Hut 1860's
Site of Samuel Butler's "V" Hut
45

Mirror Lake
Scenic Flights
Fox Glacier
Glow Worm Dell
Chalet Lookout
Fox Glacier / Te Meaka o Tuawe
Visitors Centre
S O U T H E R N
Tasman Glacier
Mt. Tasman 3498m
Malte Brun 3155m
Murchison River
Murchison Glacier
LIEBIG RANGE
HALL RANGE
Godley River
Island
53

WESTLAND NATIONAL PARK
Aoraki/Mt. Cook 3754m
Mt. Radove 2431m
Lilybank Station
THUMB RANGE
Mt. Musgrave 2246m
Fox Peak 2332m
BEN MCLEOD RANGE
Meikleburn Saddle
Clayton
Hot Springs
Copland Pass
Tasman Glacier
Blue Lakes & Walk
Glacier Snout & Lake
[Rental Cars Prohibited]
GAMACK RA
Cass River
Fork Stream
TWO
FOX PEAK
Mt. Sefton 3157m
Hooker Glacier
Hooker Glacier Lake & Walk
Kea Point
The Hermitage
Aoraki Mount Cook
Mt. Blackburn 2416m
Jollie River
Domain Tarras
Sherwood Downs
54

Karangarua Saddle
Mt. Sebastopol 1468m
MT COOK AIRPORT & SCENIC FLIGHTS
Mt. Stevenson 2366m
South Opuha River
North Opuha River
Lake Opuha (hydro lake)
Ashwick Flat
Mt. Hopkins 2682m
Tasman River
LAKE TEKAPO
Lake Alexandrina
Mt. Dobson
Opuha Dam
Trentham
RANGE
Glentanner Park Scenic Flights
Ice Skating
Scenic Flights
Mt. John Observatory
Church of the Good Shepherd
Mt. Edwards 1916m
Kimbell
Allandale
79
Cattle Valley

Dun Fiunary 2499m
55
Tekapo Military Camp
Lake Tekapo
Power Station
Eversley
Fairlie
8
25
Dobson River
BEN OHAU
80
LAKE PUKAKI
Scenic Route
Salmon Farm
Power Station
Peter's Lookout
Tekapo Hydro
Mary Burn
47
Tekapo River
Canal
Sawdon River
18
Dog Kennel Corner Plaque
Burkes Pass
Burkes Pass
Sims
Winscombe
16
Opihi Gorge
55

Pukaki Hydro Electricity Canal
Mt. Cook Lookout
8
Grays River
Mackenzie Pass
Sinkholes
Limestone Valley
Cricklewood
8
Camp Valley
Sinkholes
Chamberlain

P 49 Q R S KIWI Maps 50 T

MAP 44

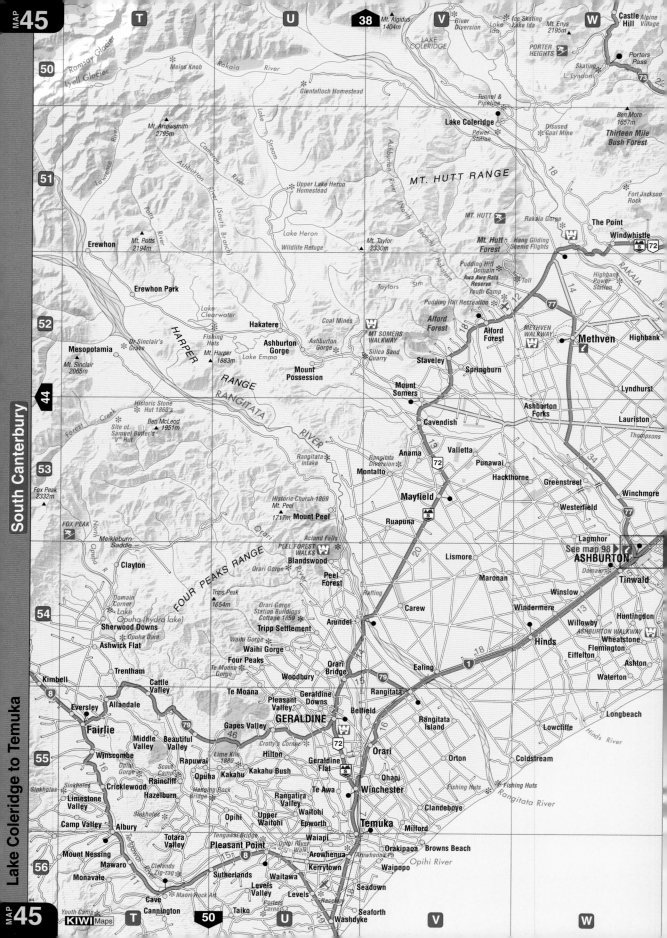

MAP
47

G   H   I   J   K

Milford Sound

Jacksons Bay to Milford Sound

53

54

55

56

57

58

59

Jackson Head
Smoothwater Point   Jackson
                            Jackson
                            /Oka

Seal Rocks   Neils Beach

Cascade Point

Cascade River
Iota Bluff   Lake Ellery

Barn Islands

CASCADE
FOREST   Monkey Puzzle
                    Gorge

Sandrock Bluff

Browne Island   Collyer
                                                     1647m

Bonar Knob   Dagon
Cutter Rocks   1693m

Gorge Islands   Gorge   River

Longridge Point   M A L C O L M   ARAWHATA
                                                        FOREST
                          R A N G E   O
Mt. Beck   Cascade Gorge   L
1091m   I
Awarua Point   V
                                                I
             Waluna   N
             Lagoon   E

Big Bay   R
                     Pyke-Big Bay   A
                     Route   Toreador Peak N
Long Reef   1942m   G
Hollyford River   E

Martins Bay   Lake
                       Wilmot

             Mt. Pyke
             1217m   S
Site of   K   Climax Peak   Mt. Edward
Early Settlement   I   2432m   2586m
                        P
             Hollyford P
             Track   E
                        R
Musket Bay   S

Lake McKerrow
Whakatipu Waitai

Yates Point   Lake
                               Alabaster
Brig Rock   D   Wawahi
                   A   Waka   F O R B E S   M T S
Milford Sound   R
/Piopiotahi   R   Rees - Dart
                   A   Poseidon Peak   Track
Stripe Point   N   2222m   Lochnagar
St. Anne Point   Mt. Pembroke   Mt. Earnslaw/
                 ▲ 2000m   Lake   Pikirakatahi
                   M Mt. Tutoko Unknown   ▲ 2816m
                   O 2749m   Centaur Peak
                   U   Lake   2518m
Mitre Peak ▲   N   Nerine
1692m   T
       Scenic   A   Hollyford   Chinaman's Bluff
Lake   Cruises   I   Track
Ronald   N   Somnus
                   S   2281m
                                Humboldt Falls Lake
       Milford Sound   Sylvan   Paradise
Milford   'Invincible'
Track Scenic   Disused Gold Mine
Lake   Flights
Moreton Lake   Lake
       Ada   The Chasm   Harris   Diamond
Lake   Lake
Marian Gunns Camp   Routeburn
        & Museum   Track
Mt. Elliot   Hollyford
▲ 2003m Homer Tunnel Lake
                       Mariar

MAP
47

G KIWI Maps   H   52   I   J   53   K

64

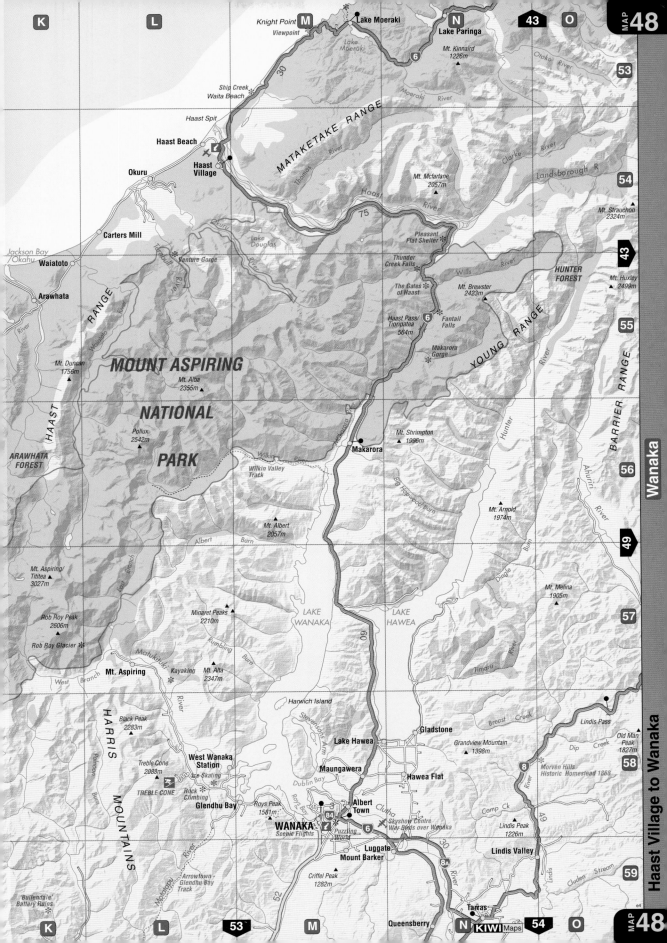

Knight Point
Viewpoint
Lake Moeraki
Lake Paringa

53

Mt. Kinnaird
1226m

6

Otoko River

Ship Creek
Waita Beach

MATAKETAKE RANGE

30

Lake
Moeraki

Thomas River

Moeraki River

Clarke River

Landsborough R

Haast Spit

54

Haast Beach

Haast River

Mt. Mcfarlane
2057m

Mt. Strauchon
2324m

Okuru

Haast
Village

Carters Mill

75

Pleasant
Flat Shelter

Wills River

43

Jackson Bay
/Okahu

Lake
Douglas

Thunder
Creek Falls

HUNTER
FOREST

Mt. Huxley
2499m

Waiatoto

Venture Gorge

The Gates
of Haast

Mt. Brewster
2423m

Arawhata

Turnbull River

Okuru River

Haast Pass/
Tioripatea
564m

6

Fantail
Falls

YOUNG RANGE

55

Makarora
Gorge

Mt. Duncan
1756m

MOUNT ASPIRING

Mt. Alba
2355m

Woodolo River

Hunter River

BARRIER RANGE

ARAWHATA
FOREST

NATIONAL

Pollux
2542m

Mt. Shrimpton
1996m

Makarora

Ahuriri River

PARK

HAAST RANGE

Wilkin River

Wilkin Valley
Track

Big Hopwood Burn

56

Mt. Albert
2057m

Mt. Arnold
1974m

East Branch

Albert Burn

49

Mt. Aspiring/
Tititea
3027m

Mt. Melina
1905m

Rob Roy Peak
2606m

Minaret Peaks
2210m

LAKE
WANAKA

LAKE
HAWEA

Diagle Burn

57

Rob Roy Glacier

Rumbling Burn

Matukituki River

Mt. Aspiring

Kayaking

Mt. Alta
2347m

Timaru River

West Branch

HARRIS

Black Peak
2283m

Harwich Island

Lindis Pass

Gladstone

Breast Creek

Lindis Pass

MOUNTAINS

Treble Cone
2088m

Ice-Skating

West Wanaka
Station

Stevensons Arm

Lake Hawea

Grandview Mountain
1398m

Old Man
Peak
1827m

58

Dublin Bay

Maungawera

Hawea Flat

8

Morven Hills
Historic Homestead 1868

TREBLE CONE

Rock
Climbing

Glendhu Bay

Roys Peak
1581m

Roys Bay

Albert
Town

Clutha River

Camp Ck

Lindis Peak
1226m

49

WANAKA
Scenic Flights

84

Puzzling
World

6

Skyshow Centre
War Birds over Wanaka

Lindis Valley

Palmora Burn

Luggate
Mount Barker

8A

30 River

'Bullendale'
Battery Ruins

Arrowtown -
Glendhu Bay
Track

Criffel Peak
1282m

52

Motatapu River

59

Tarras

Lindis

Cluden Stream

Wanaka

Haast Village to Wanaka

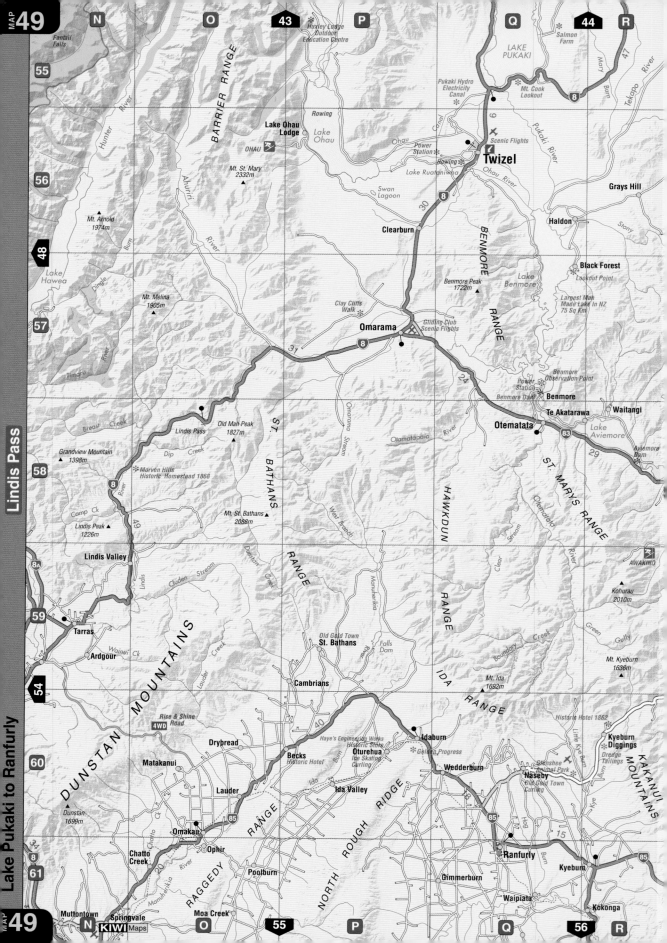

MAP
49

N   O   **43**   P   Q   **44**   R

Fantail
Falls

55

BARRIER RANGE

Huxley Lodge
Outdoor
Education Centre

LAKE
PUKAKI

Salmon
Farm

Hunter River

56

Rowing

Lake Ohau
Lodge

Lake
Ohau

OHAU

Pukaki Hydro
Electricity
Canal

Mt. Cook
Lookout

Scenic Flights

Twizel

Mt. St. Mary
2332m

Swan
Lagoon

Power
Station

Rowing

Lake Ruataniwha

Ohau River

Grays Hill

Mt. Arnold
1974m

30

8

Clearburn

Haldon

48

Lake
Hawea

Ahuriri River

Dingle Burn

Mt. Melina
1905m

Clay Cliffs
Walk

Benmore Peak
1722m

BENMORE RANGE

Lake
Benmore

Black Forest
Lookout Point

Largest Man
Made Lake in NZ
75 Sq Km

57

Timaru River

31

Omarama

8

Gliding Club
Scenic Flights

24

Benmore
Observation Point

Power
Station

Benmore

Waitangi

Benmore Dam

Breast Creek

Lindis Pass

Old Man Peak
1827m

ST.

Omarama Stream

Olamatapaio River

Otematata

Te Akatarawa

83

Lake
Aviemore

Grandview Mountain
1398m

Dip Creek

Morven Hills
Historic Homestead 1868

BATHANS

West Branch

29

Aviemore
Dam

ST. MARYS RANGE

Otematata River

58

Camp Ck

8

49

River

Mt. St. Bathans
2088m

RANGE

Dunstan Creek

Manuherikia

HAWKDUN

RANGE

Clear Stream

AWAKINO

Kohurau
2010m

59

Lindis Peak
1226m

Lindis Valley

Lindis

Cluden Stream

Lauder Creek

Old Gold Town
St. Bathans

Falls
Dam

Manuherikia

IDA

RANGE

Boundary Creek

Green Gully

Mt. Kyeburn
1636m

8A

Tarras

Wainui Ck

DUNSTAN

Cambrians

Bree

Mt. Ida
1692m

Little Kyeburn

Ardgour

MOUNTAINS

54

Historic Hotel 1862

Kyeburn
Diggings
Dredge
Tailings

KAKANUI

60

Rise & Shine
Road

4WD

Drybread

Haye's Engineering Works
Historic Store

Gellas Progress

Idaburn

Stenshee
Animal Park

MOUNTAINS

Matakanui

Becks
Historic Hotel

40

Lauder Burn

Oturehua
Ice Skating
Curling

Wedderburn

Naseby
Old Gold Town
Curling

Dunstan
1699m

Lauder

Ida Burn

Ida Valley

85

Hog Burn

Kye Burn

Omakau

85

RANGE

NORTH

RIDGE

15

8

Chatto
Creek

Ophir

ROUGH

Ranfurly

Kyeburn

85

61

20

Manuherikia River

RAGGEDY

Chatto Ck

Poolburn

Gimmerburn

Waipiata

Kokonga

MAP
49

Muttontown
N
Springvale
KIWI Maps
O   **55**   P
Moa Creek
Q   **56**   R

MAP
51

D   E   F   G

57

58   St. Anne Po

Seabreeze Point
Poison Bay   Lake
Ronald

Bell Point

Sutherland Sound

59   Tommy Point   Mt. Longsight
1472m
Bligh Sound
Flat Point

Bounty
Haven   Lake
Grave

George Sound   Bare Cone
985m   Dark River

FRANKLIN MTS

Round Head
Looking Glass Bay   George River

60   Lake
Alice
Two Thumb Bay   Mt. McDougall
2036m
Mt. Tanilba   Lake   George Sound
Caswell Sound   1242m   Katherine   Track
Lake
Nugget Point   Thomson   STUART
Islet Point   Stillwater   River   L. Wade   MTS
Charles Sound   Fleetwood Peak   Mt. Donald   Lake   Lake
Hawes Head   1298m   1585m   Wapiti   Hankinson
Lake
Marchant   Howitt Peaks
1646m
61   Nancy Sound   Emelius Arm   Lake   Lake   Mt. Pisgah
Anxiety Point   Gold Arm   Mackinnon   McIvor   1556m

Thompson Sound   Command Peak   Myrtle   South West Arm   Middle Fi
Colonial Head   1256m   Tarn   Lake
Bloxham   Mt. Irene
1879m

Foot Arm   MURCHISON

L. Duncan

L. Dora   MTS

South West Point   Thompson   Hidden   L. Te Au
Secretary Island   Sound   Lake   L.Hilda   Mt. Lyall
62   Nee Island   1905m
Doubtful Sound   Bradshaw   L.Hall
Shelter Island   The Gut   Gear   Camelot   River   KEPLER
Febrero Point   Bauza Is.   Arm   L. Minerva   South Fiord
Scenic Cruises   Lake
Malaspina Reach   Herries   Mt. Luxmore
1472m
Mt. Forbes   First Arm   Mt. Soaker   MTS   Jacksons Peaks
1305m   1593m   1699m   Kepler
63   Track
Dagg Sound   Ardo   Burn   Cathedral Peaks
Towing Head   Crooked Arm   Lake   1699m
Brown   Burn
Scenic Cruises   Mt. Gorge   West Arm
Deep Cove   1598m
Norwest
Tailrace   Lake
Tunnel

MAP
51
KIWI Maps   D   E   57   F   G
e4

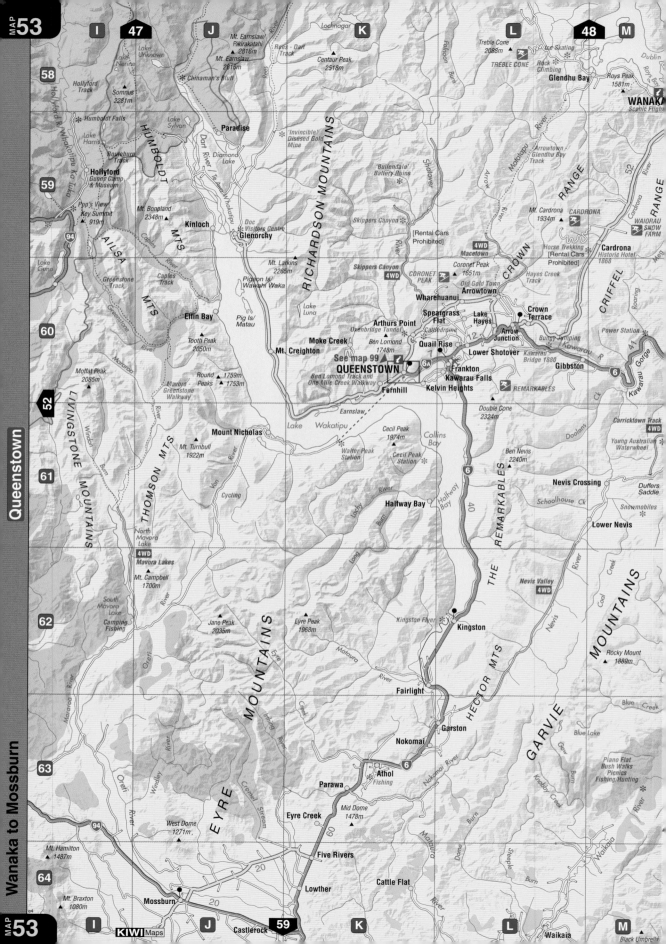

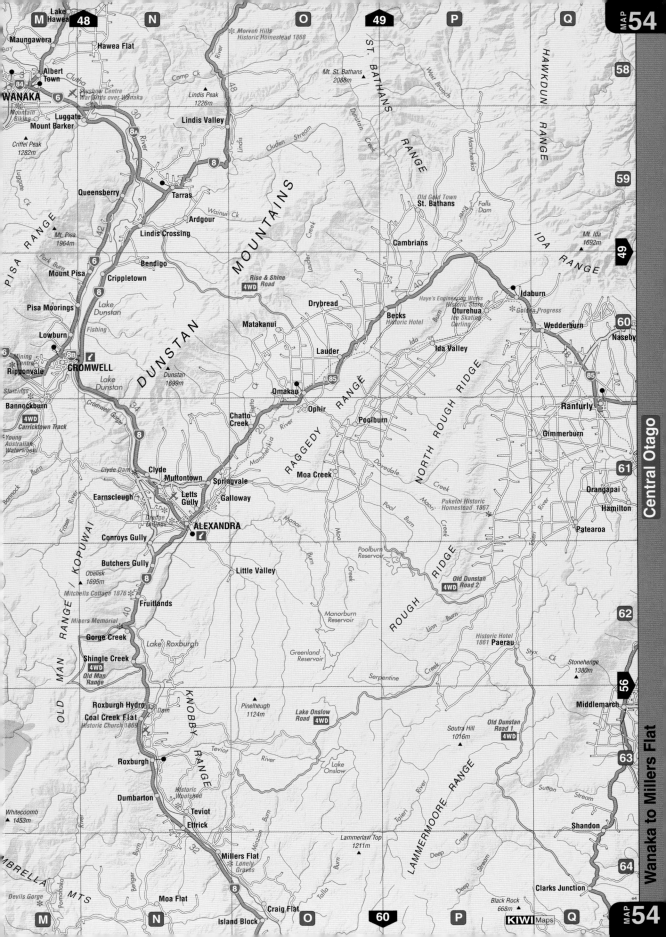

MAP 54

M 48 N O 49 P Q

Lake Hawea
Maungawera
Hawea Flat
Morven Hills Historic Homestead 1868
HAWKDUN RANGE
Albert Town
WANAKA
Warbirds over Wanaka
Flyshow Centre
Mount Biking
Mount Barker
Luggate
Criffel Peak 1282m
Queensberry
Mt. St. Bathans 2088m
ST. BATHANS RANGE
Lindis Peak 1226m
Lindis Valley
Tarras
Ardgour
Camp Ck
West Branch
Clutha River
PISA RANGE
Mt. Pisa 1964m
Lindis Crossing
Wainui Ck
Lindis
Cluden Stream
Dunstan Creek
Manuherikia River
Old Gold Town
St. Bathans
Falls Dam
IDA RANGE
Mt. Ida 1692m
Bendigo
Crippletown
Mount Pisa
Park Burn
Pisa Moorings
Lake Dunstan
Fishing
Rise & Shine Road
4WD
Lauder Creek
Cambrians
Golden Progress
Idaburn
Lowburn
Drybread
Matakanui
Becks Historic Hotel
Haye's Engineering Works Historic Store
Oturehua
Ice Skating Curling
Wedderburn
Naseby
Ripponvale
CROMWELL
8B
Mining Centre
Lauder
Ida
Ida Valley
85
Bannockburn
4WD
Carricktown Track
Young Australian Waterwheel
Lake Dunstan
Dunstan 1699m
Cromwell Gorge
DUNSTAN MOUNTAINS
Chatto Creek
Omakau
Ophir
Poolburn
NORTH ROUGH RIDGE
Ranfurly
Gimmerburn
RAGGEDY RANGE
Moa Creek
Dovedale Creek
Orangapai
Hamilton
Clyde Dam
Clyde
Muttontown
Springvale
Galloway
Puketoi Historic Homestead 1867
Earnscleugh
Letts Gully
Manor Burn
Patearoa
Dredge Tailings
ALEXANDRA
Moa Creek
Pool Burn
OLD MAN RANGE / KOPUWAI
Conroys Gully
Poolburn Reservoir
Moon Creek
Butchers Gully
Little Valley
ROUGH RIDGE
Obelisk 1695m
Old Dunstan Road 2
4WD
Mitchells Cottage 1876
Fruitlands
Manorburn Reservoir
Linn Burn
Historic Hotel 1861 Paerau
Miners Memorial
Gorge Creek
Stonehenge 1380m
Shingle Creek
4WD
Old Man Range
Lake Roxburgh
Greenland Reservoir
Serpentine Creek
Middlemarch
Soutra Hill 1016m
Old Dunstan Road 1
4WD
KNOBBY RANGE
Roxburgh Hydro
Coal Creek Flat
Historic Church 1869
Teviot River
Lake Onslow Road
4WD
Pinelheugh 1124m
Lake Onslow
Roxburgh
Whitecoomb 1453m
Sutton Stream
Dumbarton
Historic Woolshed
Teviot
Ettrick
LAMMERMOORE RANGE
Shandon
UMBRELLA MTS
Devils Gorge
Pomahaka River
Benger Burn
Millers Flat
Lonely Graves
Lammerlaw Top 1211m
Moa Flat
Clarks Junction
Black Rock 668m
Pomahaka River
Tollo Burn
Minzion Burn
Deep Creek
Island Block
Craig Flat
8

M N O 60 P Q

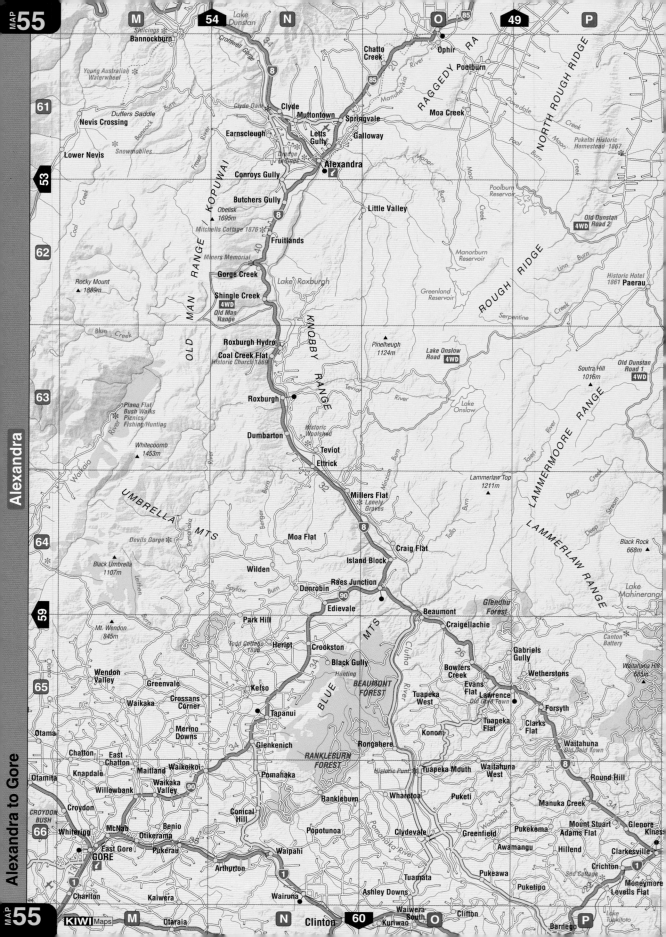

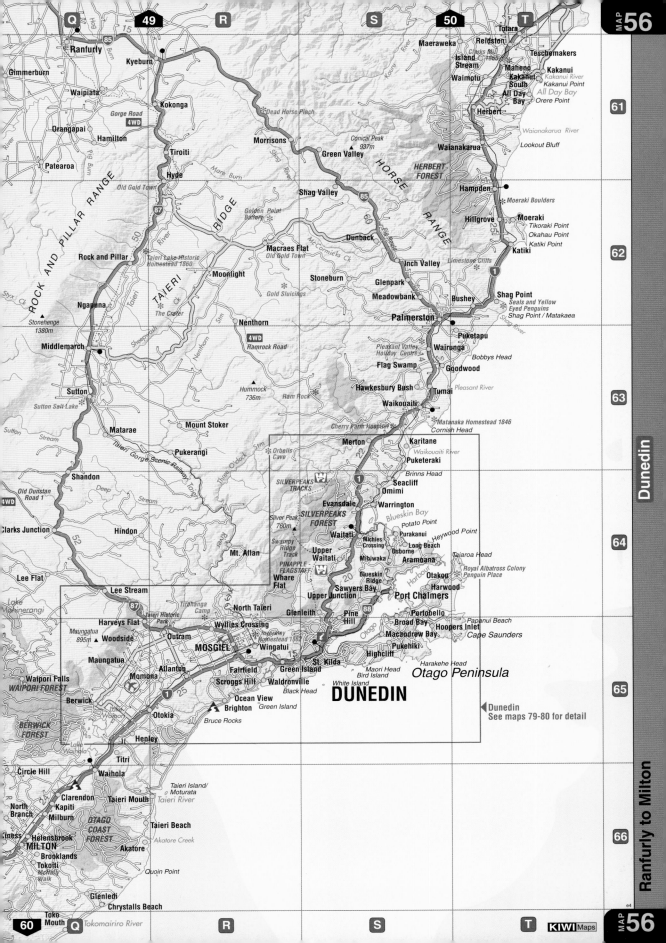

MAP 56

61

62

63

64

65

66

Dunedin

Ranfurly to Milton

Q   49   R   S   50   T

Ranfurly · Kyeburn

Gimmerburn

Waipiata

Orangapai · Kokonga

Hamilton

Patearoa · Tiroiti

Hyde

Gorge Road 4WD

Old Gold Town

Dead Horse Pinch

Morrisons

Conical Peak 937m

Green Valley

Waianakarua River

Maeraweka

Reidston

Totara

Island Stream · Teschemakers

Maheno · Kakanui

Waimotu · Kakanui South · Kakanui Point

All Day Bay · Orere Point

Herbert

HERBERT FOREST

Waianakarua · Lookout Bluff

Hampden · Moeraki Boulders

Shag Valley

Golden Point Battery

Macraes Flat
Old Gold Town

Moonlight

Dunback

McCormicks Ck

Inch Valley

Stoneburn

Glenpark

Meadowbank

Bushey

Hillgrove · Moeraki

Tikoraki Point · Okahau Point · Katiki Point

Katiki

Limestone Cliffs

Shag Point
Seals and Yellow Eyed Penguins
Shag Point / Matakaea

Palmerston

Puketapu

Wairunga

Bobbys Head

Goodwood

Pleasant River

Pleasant Valley Holiday Centre

Flag Swamp

Hawkesbury Bush

Tumai

Waikouaiti

Matanaka Homestead 1846
Cornish Head

Cherry Farm Hospital

ROCK AND PILLAR RANGE

Rock and Pillar

Ngapuna

Stonehenge 1380m

Middlemarch

Sutton

Sutton Salt Lake

Matarae

Shandon

TAIERI RIDGE

Old Gold Town

Moonlight

The Crater

Nenthorn

4WD
Ramrock Road

Hummock 736m

Ram Rock

Gold Sluicings

Mount Stoker

Pukerangi

Hindon

Taieri Gorge Scenic Railway

Deep Stream

Three O'clock Stm

Orbells Cave

SILVERPEAKS TRACKS

Silver Peak 760m

SILVERPEAKS FOREST

Swampy Ridge Track

PINAPPLE FLAGSTAFF

Whare Flat

Merton

Karitane

Waikouaiti River

Puketeraki

Brinns Head

Seacliff

Omimi

Warrington

Evansdale

Blueskin Bay

Waitati

Potato Point

Purakanui

Michies Crossing

Long Beach

Mihiwaka · Osborne

Aramoana

Taiaroa Head

Royal Albatross Colony
Penguin Place

Upper Waitati

Blueskin Ridge Track

Sawyers Bay

Otakou

Harwood

Port Chalmers

Upper Junction

Glenleith

Pine Hill

Portobello

Broad Bay · Hoopers Inlet

Papanui Beach

Macandrew Bay · Cape Saunders

Pukehiki

Highcliff

Harakehe Head

Maori Head
Bird Island

Otago Peninsula

St Kilda

Otago Peninsula

Clarks Junction

Lee Flat

4WD

Old Dunstan Road 1

52

Lee Stream

87

Taieri Historic Park

Tirohanga Camp

North Taieri

Harveys Flat

Wyllies Crossing

Invermay Homestead 1862

Wingatui

Maungatua 895m · Woodside

MOSGIEL

Maungatua

Allanton

Fairfield

Momona

Scroggs Hill

Waldronville

Green Island

White Island

Black Head

Berwick

WAIPORI FOREST

Waipori Falls

Otokia

Ocean View

Brighton · Green Island

Bruce Rocks

DUNEDIN

◀ Dunedin
See maps 79-80 for detail

BERWICK FOREST

Lake Mahinerangi

Lake Waihola

Henley

Titri

Circle Hill

Waihola

Clarendon

Kapiti · Milburn

North Branch

iness

Helensbrook

MILTON

Brooklands

Tokoiti · McNally Walk

Glenledi

Chrystalls Beach

Toko Mouth

Taieri Island/ Moturata
Taieri River

OTAGO COAST FOREST

Taieri Beach

Akatore Creek

Akatore

Quoin Point

MAP
57

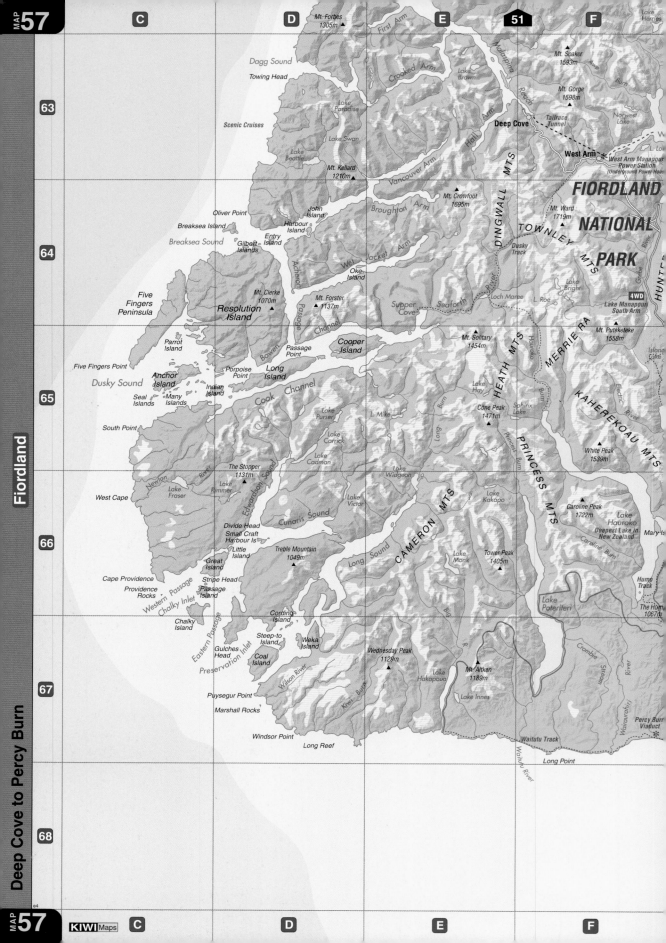

63

64

65

66

67

68

Mt. Forbes
1305m ▲

First Arm

Dagg Sound

Towing Head

Crooked Arm

Lake
Brown

Mt. Spaker
1593m ▲

Mt. Gorge
1598m ▲

Lake
Herries

Norwest
Lake

Deep Cove

Tailrace
Tunnel

Scenic Cruises

Lake
Paradise

Lake Swan

West Arm ☆

West Arm Manapouri
Power Station
(Underground Power House)

L. Lor

Lake
Beattie

Mt. Kellard
1210m ▲

Vancouver Arm

Hall Arm

FIORDLAND

Oliver Point

John
Island

Mt. Crowfoot
1695m ▲

Mt. Ward
1719m ▲

NATIONAL

Breaksea Island

Harbour
Island

Broughton Arm

DINGWALL MTS

TOWNLEY MTS

PARK

Breaksea Sound

Gilbert
Islands

Entry
Island

Acheron

Wet

Jocket Arm

Dusky
Track

Lake
Bright

HUNTE

Five
Fingers
Peninsula

Mt. Clerke
1070m ▲

**Resolution
Island**

Oke
Island

Passage

Mt. Forster
1137m ▲

Supper
Cove

Seaforth

Loch Maree

L. Roe

4WD

Lake Manapouri
South Arm

Parrot
Island

Bowen

Passage
Point

**Cooper
Island**

Channel

Mt. Solitary
1454m ▲

HEATH MTS

Hauroko

MERRIE RA

Mt. Puteketeke
1558m ▲

Island
Lake

Five Fingers Point

**Anchor
Island**

Porpoise
Point

**Long
Island**

L. Mike

Lake Hay

KAHEREKOAU MTS

Electric River

Dusky Sound

Seal
Islands

Many
Islands

Indian
Island

Cook Channel

Lake
Purser

Long Burn

Cone Peak
1471m ▲

Sphinx
Lake

Princess Burn

White Peak
1539m ▲

South Point

Lake
Carrick

Lake
Cadman

Lake
Widgeon

PRINCESS MTS

The Stopper
1131m ▲

Newton
River

Lake
Rimmer

Edwardson Sound

Lake
Victor

CAMERON MTS

Lake
Kakapo

Caroline Peak
1722m ▲

Lake
Hauroko
Deepest Lake in
New Zealand

Mary Is

West Cape

Lake
Fraser

Cunaris Sound

Lake
Monk

Caroline Burn

Divide Head

Small Craft
Harbour Is

Treble Mountain
1049m ▲

Long Sound

Tower Peak
1405m ▲

Hump
Track

Cape Providence

Great
Island

Little
Island

The Hum
1067m

Lake
Poteriferi

Providence
Rocks

Stripe Head

Passage
Island

Western Passage

Crombie Stream

River

Chalky Island

Chalky Inlet

Cording
Island

Big

Steep-to
Island

Weka
Island

Eastern Passage

Gulches
Head

Coal
Island

Wilson River

Wednesday Peak
1129m ▲

Lake
Hakapoua

Mt. Aitken
1189m ▲

Preservation Inlet

Kiwi Burn

Lake
Innes

Waititu Track

Wairaurahiri
River

Percy Burn
Viaduct

Puysegur Point

Marshall Rocks

Windsor Point

Long Reef

Waihiru River

Long Point

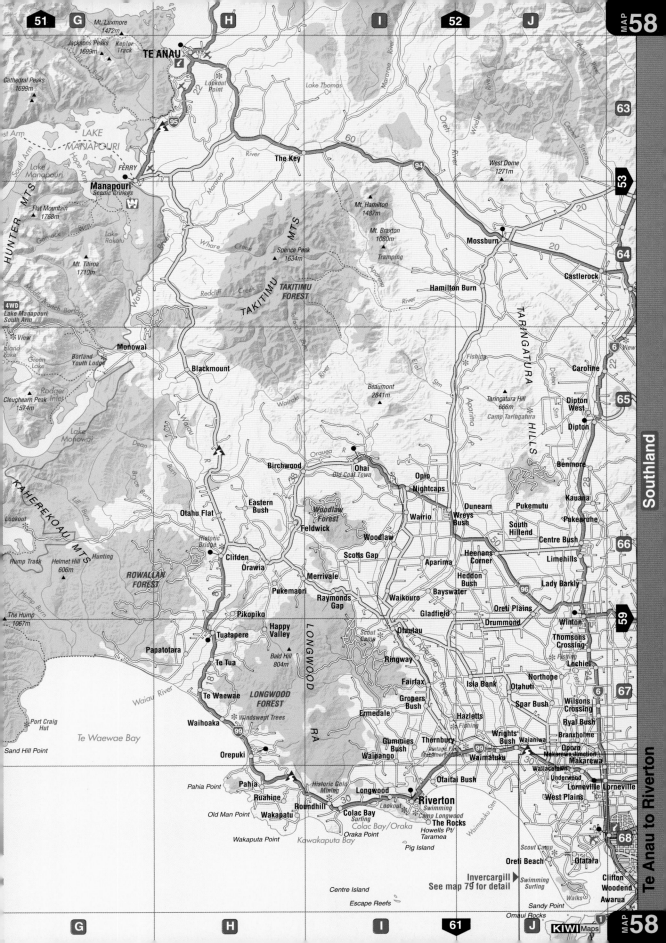

MAP 60

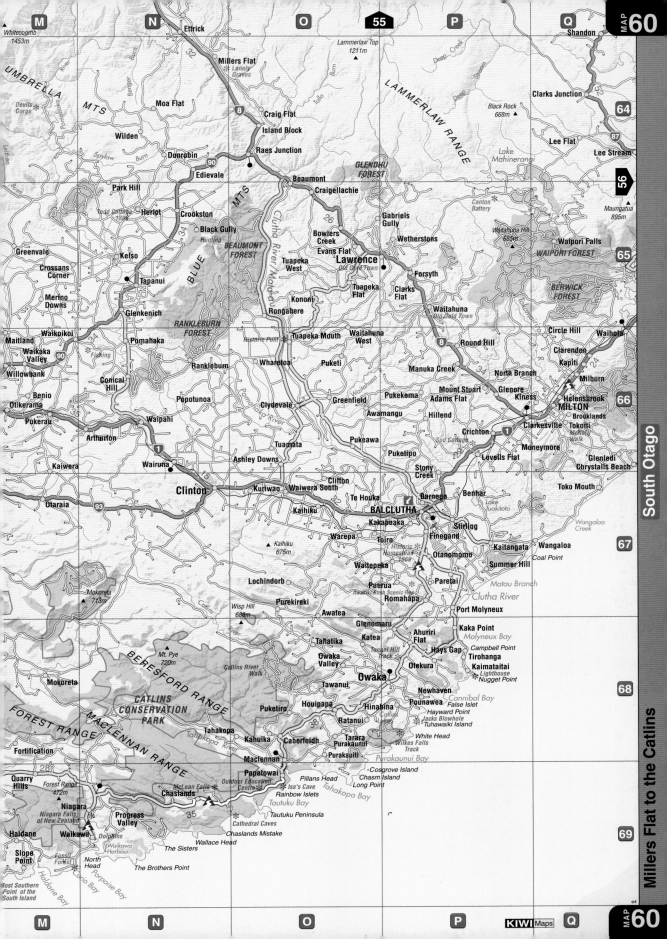

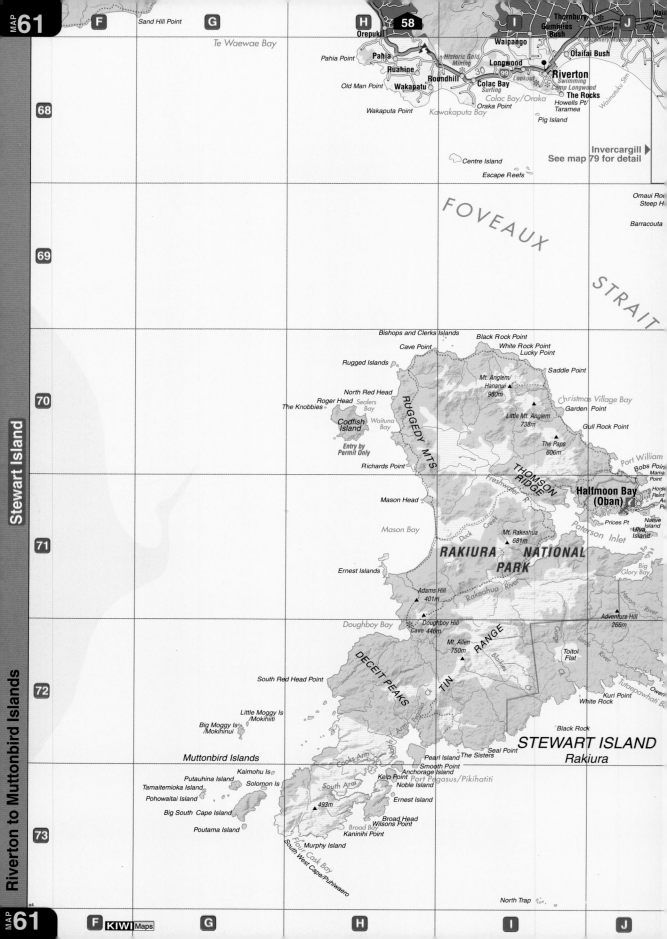

MAP
61

F   G   H   58   I   J

Sand Hill Point

Thornbury
Gummies
Bush
McKinery Museum

Te Waewae Bay

Orepuki

Waipango

Otaitai Bush

Pahia Point
Pahia
Ruahine
Old Man Point
Wakapatu
Roundhill
Wakaputa Point
Colac Bay/Oraka
Oraka Point
Kawakaputa Bay

Historic Gold
Mining

Longwood

Lookout
Camp Longwood

Riverton
Swimming
The Rocks
Howells Pt/
Taramea
Pig Island

Colac Bay
Surfing

68

Centre Island

See map 79 for detail
Invercargill ▶

Escape Reefs

F O V E A U X

Omaui Ro
Steep H

Barracouta

69

S T R A I T

Bishops and Clerks Islands
Cave Point
Rugged Islands

Black Rock Point
White Rock Point
Lucky Point

Saddle Point

North Red Head
Roger Head Sealers
The Knobbies Bay
Codfish
Island *Waituna*
Bay

Mt. Anglem/
Hananui ▲
980m

Little Mt. Anglem
738m

Christmas Village Bay
Garden Point

RUGGEDY MTS

Gull Rock Point

The Paps
606m

Port William

Bobs Poin
Mama
Point

70

Entry by
Permit Only

*THOMSON
RIDGE*

Richards Point

Freshwater R.

**Halfmoon Bay
(Oban)**

Horse
Point
A
P

Mason Head

Duck *Creek*

Prices Pt

Native
Island
Ulva
Island

Mason Bay

Mt. Rakeahua
681m

**RAKIURA   NATIONAL
PARK**

Paterson Inlet

71

Ernest Islands

Adams Hill
401m

Rakeahua *River*

Big
Glory Bay

Heron River

Doughboy Bay
Cave 446m

Doughboy Hill

Adventure Hill
266m

TIN *RANGE*

Mt. Allen
750m

Coop

Toitoi
Flat

South Red Head Point

DECEIT PEAKS

Blaikies

Tutaepawhati B

72

Little Moggy Is
/Mokihiiti

Kuri Point
White Rock

Big Moggy Is
/Mokihinui

Cooks Arm

Black Rock

Seal Point

STEWART ISLAND
Rakiura

Muttonbird Islands

Kaimohu Is

Pearl Island The Sisters
Smooth Point
Anchorage Island
Kelp Point
Noble Island

Putauhina Island
Tamaitemioka Island Solomon Is
Pohowaitai Island
Big South Cape Island
Poutama Island

South Arm

493m

Port Pegasus/Pikihatiti

Ernest Island

Broad Head
Wilsons Point
Kaninihi Point

73

Flour Cask Bay
South West Cape/Puhiwaero

Broad Bay
Murphy Island

North Trap

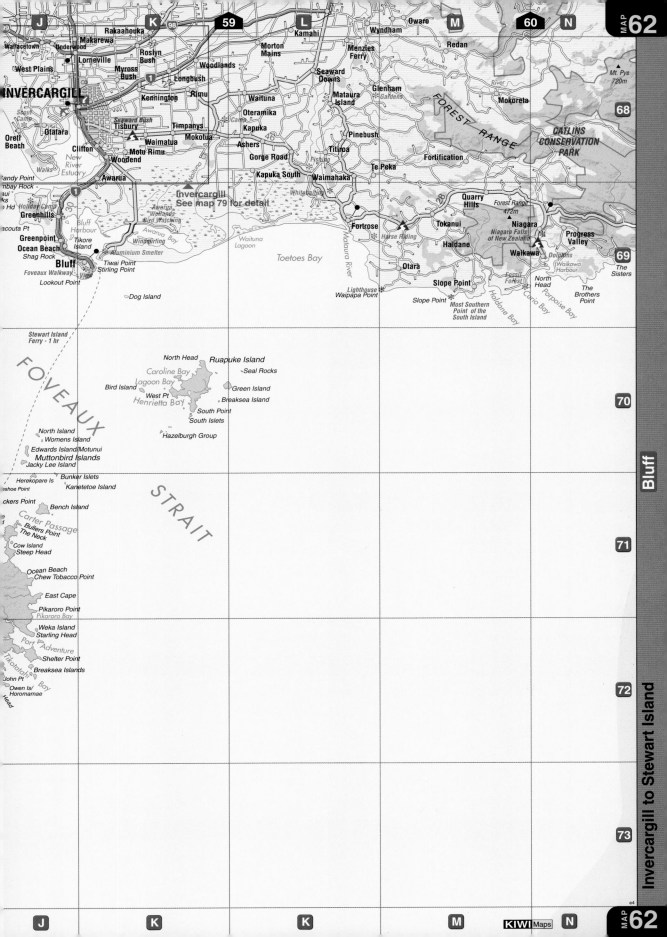

MAP 62

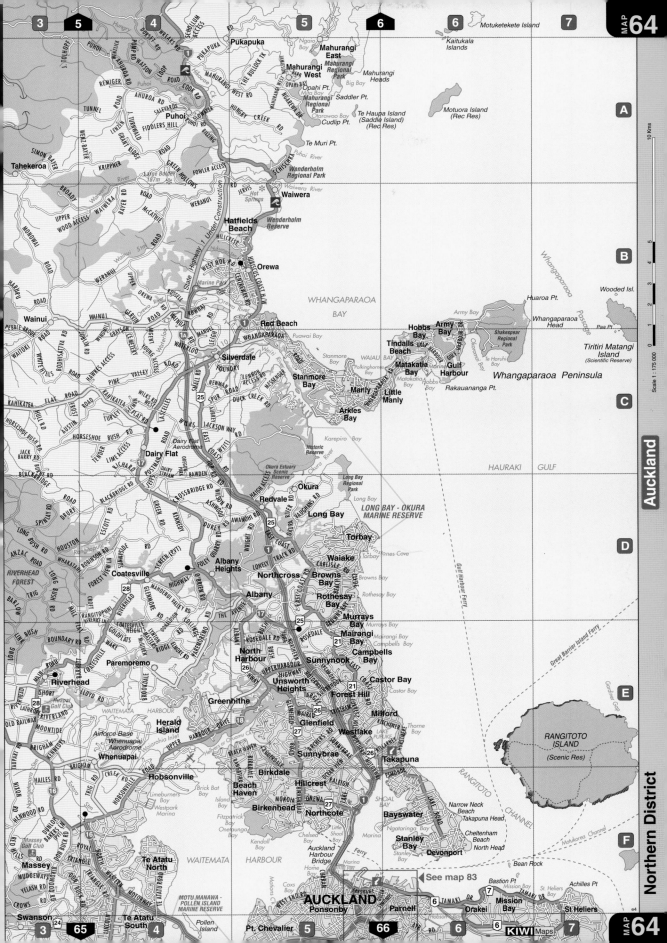

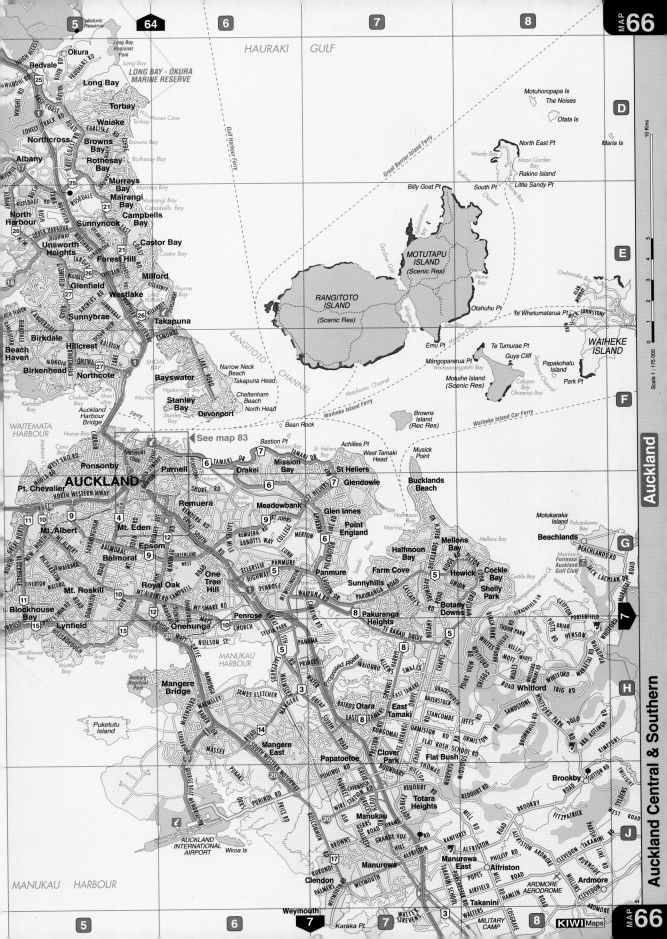

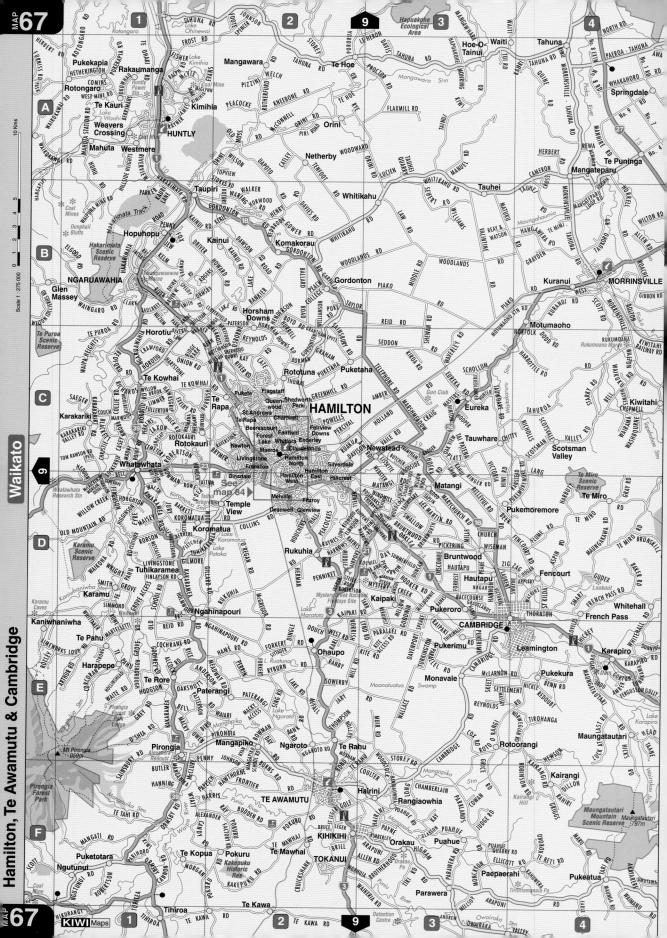

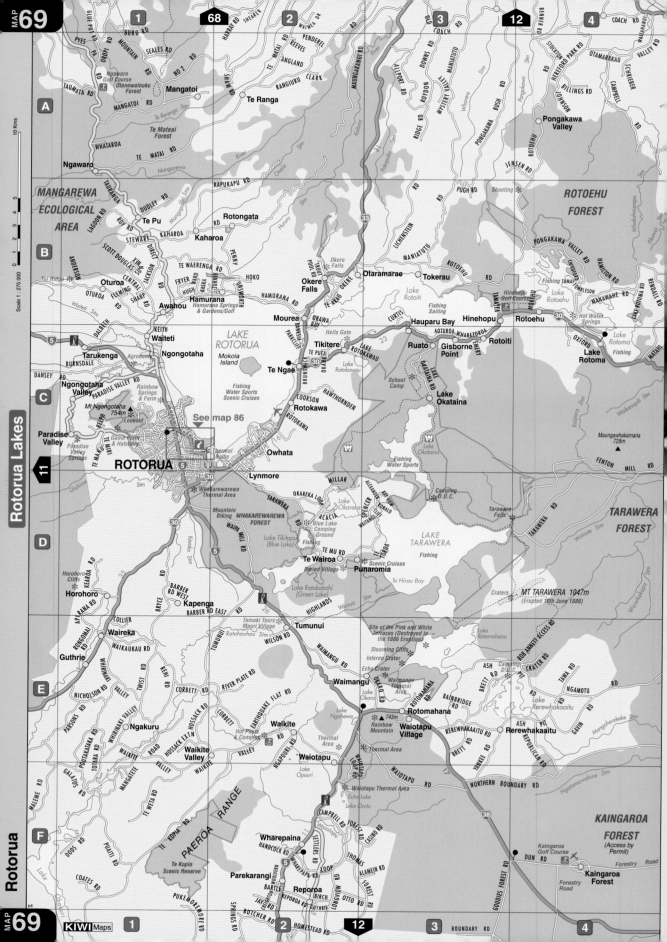

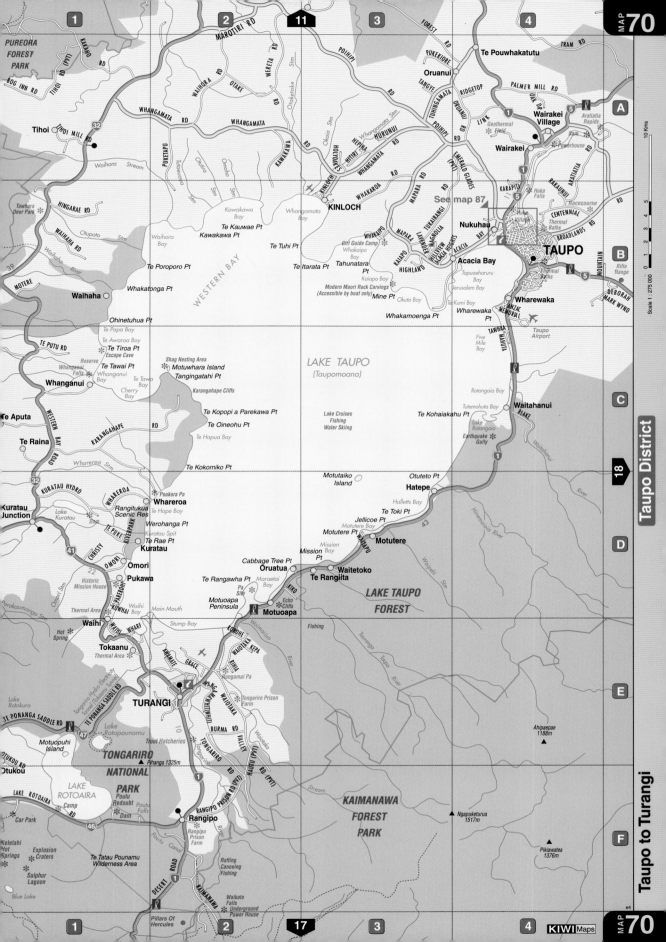

MAP 70

Taupo District

Taupo to Turangi

PUREORA FOREST PARK

BOG INN RD

TIHOI RD (PVT)

KAKAHO RD

Tihoi

TIHOI MILL RD

32

MAROTIRI RD

WAIHORA RD

WHANGAMATA RD

WHANGAMATA RD

WERETA RD

OTAKE RD

Otaketoke Stm

POIHIPI RD

FOREST RD

Te Pouwhakatutu

PUKEKIORE RD

Oruanui

TANGYE RD

TUHINGAMATA RD

ORUANU RD

RIDGETOP

PALMER MILL RD

TRAM RD

OAK DR

Wairakei Village

Aratiatia Rapids

A

HEPINA Stm

HURUNUI RD

POIHIPI RD

LINK

Geothermal Field

1

Wairakei

Powerhouse

Waihora Stream

PUKETAPU RD

Omoho Stm

Onuko Stm

KINLOCH RD

WHAKAROA RD

KAWAKAWA RD

MAPARA RD

Whangamata Stm

Whangamata Bay

KINLOCH

See map 87

EMERALD GLADES (PVT)

KARAPITI RD

Huka Falls

5

RAKAUNUI RD

ANATIATIA

Racecourse

CENTENNIAL DR

Thermal Baths

BROADLANDS RD

HINGARAE RD

Tawhara Deer Park

WAIHAHA RD

Otuputa Stm

Te Kauwae Pt

Kawakawa Bay

Kawakawa Pt

Te Tuhi Pt

WHAKAPO RD

TUKAIRANGI RD

KAIPO RD

Girl Guide Camp

Whakaipo Bay

Nukuhau

MAGNOLIA

LAVROCK

HILLVIEW

ACACIA HEIGHTS

HIGHLAND

Acacia Bay

TAUPO

B

39

MOTERE RD

Waihaha

Whakatonga Pt

Te Poroporo Pt

Ohinetuhua Pt

WESTERN BAY

Te Itarata Pt

Tahunatara Pt

Te Papa Bay

Modern Maori Rock Carvings (Accessible by boat only)

Mine Pt

Kaiapo Bay

Okuta Bay

Whakamoenga Pt

Tapuaeharuru Bay

Jerusalem Bay

Te Kumi Bay

Wharewaka Pt

ANZAC MEMORIAL

Wharewaka

Thermal Baths

5

Rifle Range

DEBORAH MARK WYND

MOUNTAIN RD

Te Awaroa Bay

Te Putu RD

Te Tiroa Pt

Escape Cave

Reserve

Te Tawai Pt

Whanganui Falls

Whanganui Bay

Te Tawa Bay

Cherry Bay

Shag Nesting Area

Motuwhara Island

Tangingatahi Pt

Karangahape Cliffs

Whanganui

Te Kopopi a Parekawa Pt

Te Oineohu Pt

Te Hapua Bay

LAKE TAUPO

(Taupomoana)

Lake Cruises Fishing Water Skiing

Te Kohaiakahu Pt

Five Mile Bay

Rotongaio Bay

Tutemohuta Bay

Lake Rotongaio

Waitahanui

BLAKE RD

Taupo Airport

TAWHAA RD

MAHUTA RD

C

Te Aputa

WESTERN BAY ROAD

KARANGAHAPE RD

Whareroa Stm

Te Kokomiko Pt

Motutaiko Island

Otuteto Pt

Hatepe

Earthquake Gully

1

Te Raina

32

KURATAU HYDRO RD

Kuratau Junction

Lake Kuratau

Dam

WHAREROA RD

RIVER PARK

Poukura Pa

Whareroa

Rangitukua Scenic Res

Werohanga Pt

Te Hape Bay

Halletts Bay

Te Toki Pt

Jellicoe Pt

Motutere Bay

WAITAHANUI RD

Motutere

Hirangaroa River

Waipehi Stm

43

LAKE TAUPO FOREST

Tongariro River

D

41

CHRISTY RD

OMORI RD

Kuratau Spit

Te Rae Pt

Kuratau

Cabbage Tree Pt

Oruatua

Mission Pt

Mission Bay

Waitetoko

Te Rangiita

22

Te PUKE RD

Omori

Pukawa

Historic Mission House

PAKEKAHI RD

Te Rangawha Pt

Maraetai Bay

Pa Site

KINO RD

Echo Cliffs

Parakaumanga Stm

Thermal Area

KOWHAI RD

Waihi Bay

Main Mouth

Motuoapa Peninsula

Motuoapa

Stump Bay

Waimarino

Fishing

KAIMANAWA FOREST PARK

Ngapuketurua 1517m

E

Waihi

Hot Spring

Tokaanu

Thermal Area

WAIHI WHARF RD

KOROHE RD

WAIOTAKA RD

KEPA RD

RIHA RD

Rangamai Pa

Tongariro Prison Farm

Ahipaepae 1188m

Te PONANGA SADDLE RD

TE PONANGA SADDLE RD

47

Motuopuhi Island

TURANGI

GRACE RD

KAHUI RD

WHAKAHIHIHI RD

WAIOTAKA RD

BURMA RD

VALLEY RD

HAUTU RD (PVT)

Tongariro Hydro Electricity Tunnel Tokaanu Tunnel

Lake Rotopounamu

Trout Hatcheries

10

Tongariro River

Waiotaka Stm

Lake Rotokura

Te PONANGA SADDLE RD

TONGARIRO NATIONAL PARK

Pihanga 1325m

Lake Rotoaira

1

OTUKOU RD

Otukou

Poutu Redoubt

Poutu Falls

Dam

Poutu Canal

Rangipo Prison Farm

RANGIPO PRISON RD (PVT)

Rangipo

46

LAKE ROTOAIRA

Camp RD

Car Park

Ketetahi Hot Springs

Explosion Craters

Sulphur Lagoon

Blue Lake

Te Tatau Pounamu Wilderness Area

DESERT ROAD

1

KAIMANAWA RD

Waikato Falls

Underground Power House

Rafting Canoeing Fishing

Pikiawatea 1376m

F

Pillars Of Hercules

Scale 1: 275 000

0   1   2   3   4   5

10 Kms

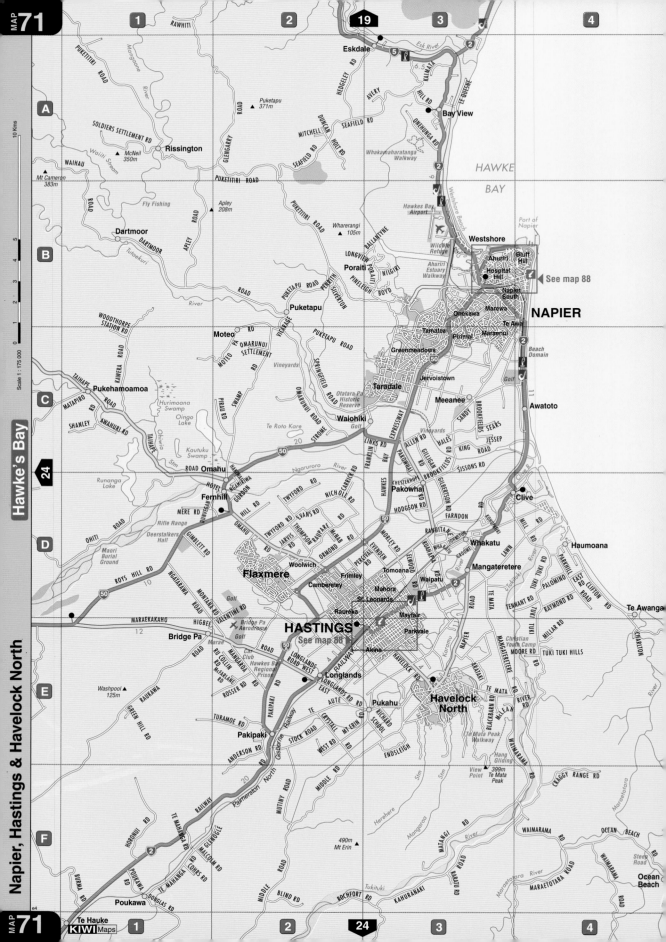

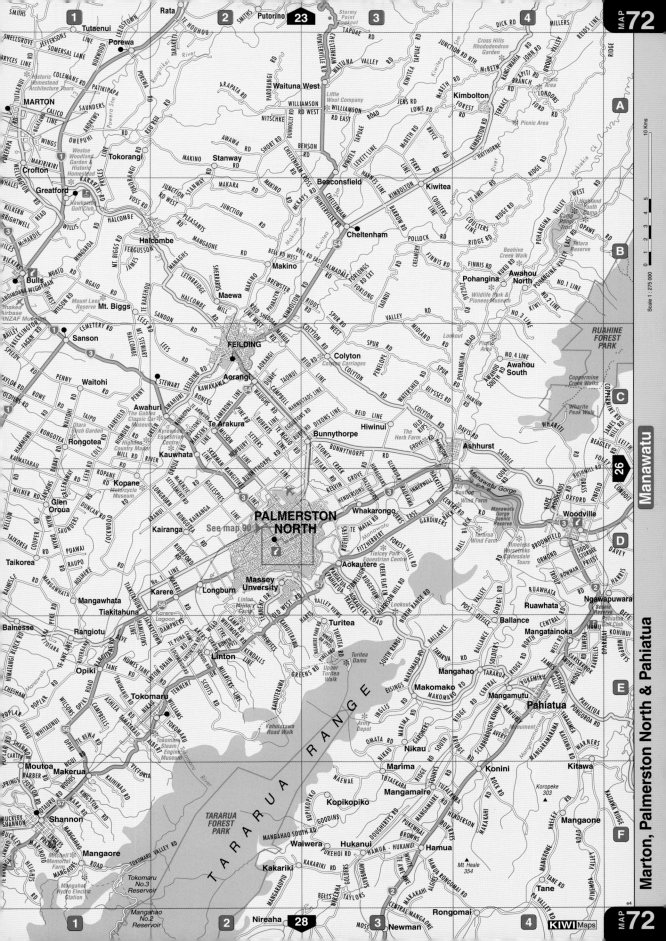

MAP 72

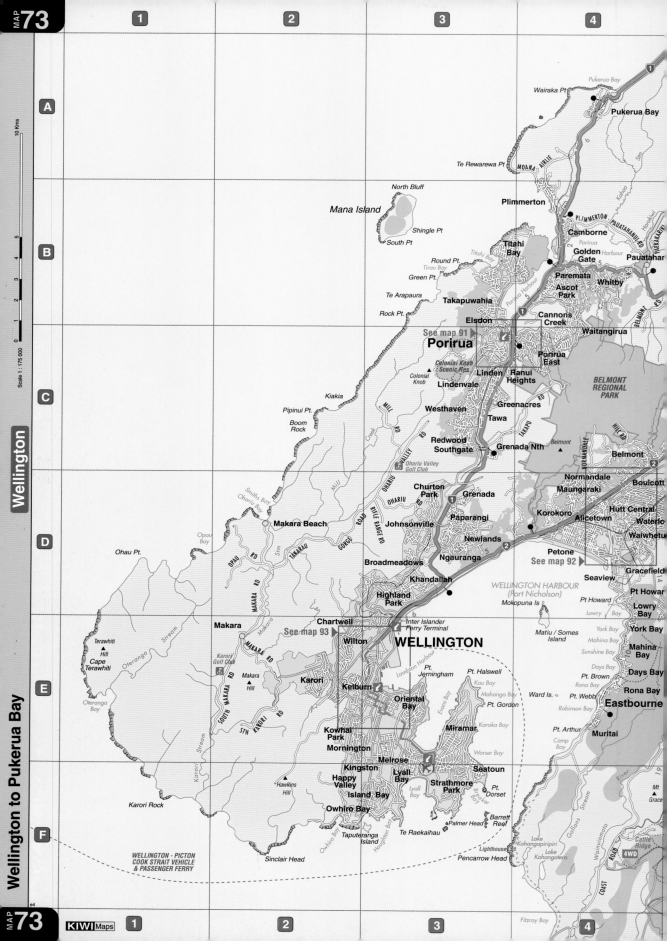

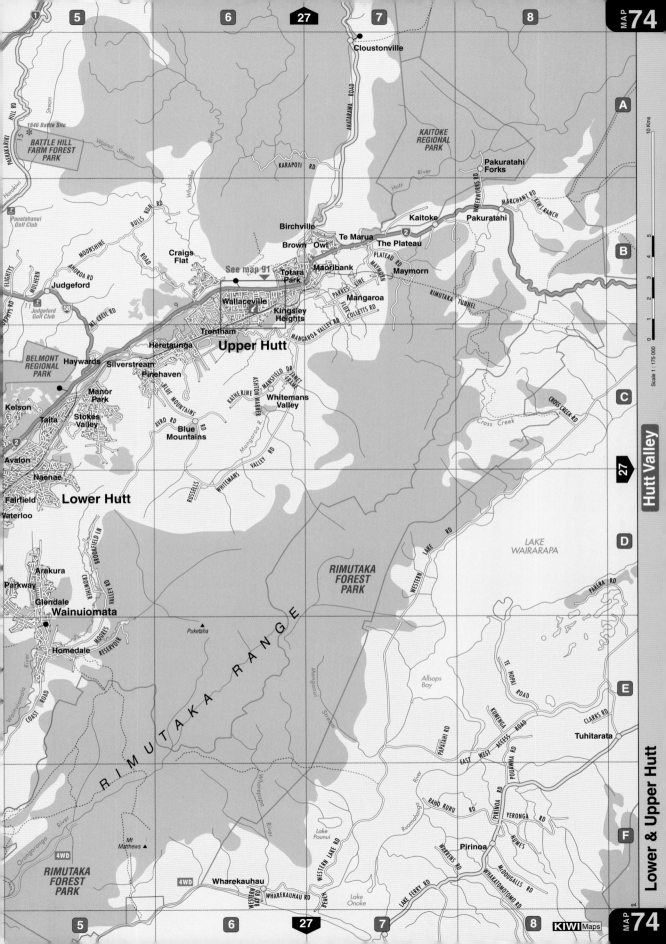

MAP **74**

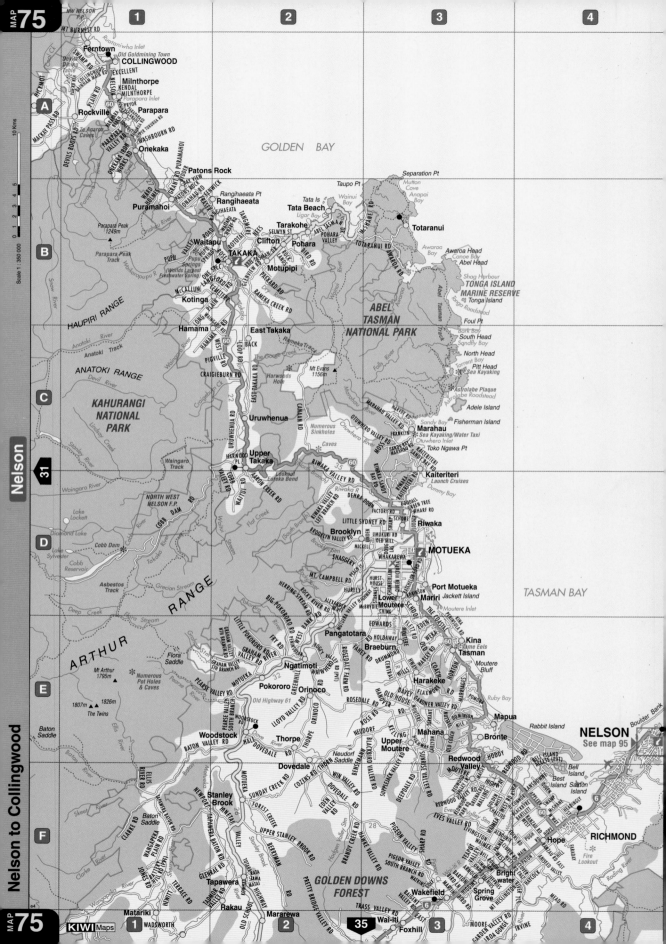

MAP 76

MAP 76
KIWI Maps

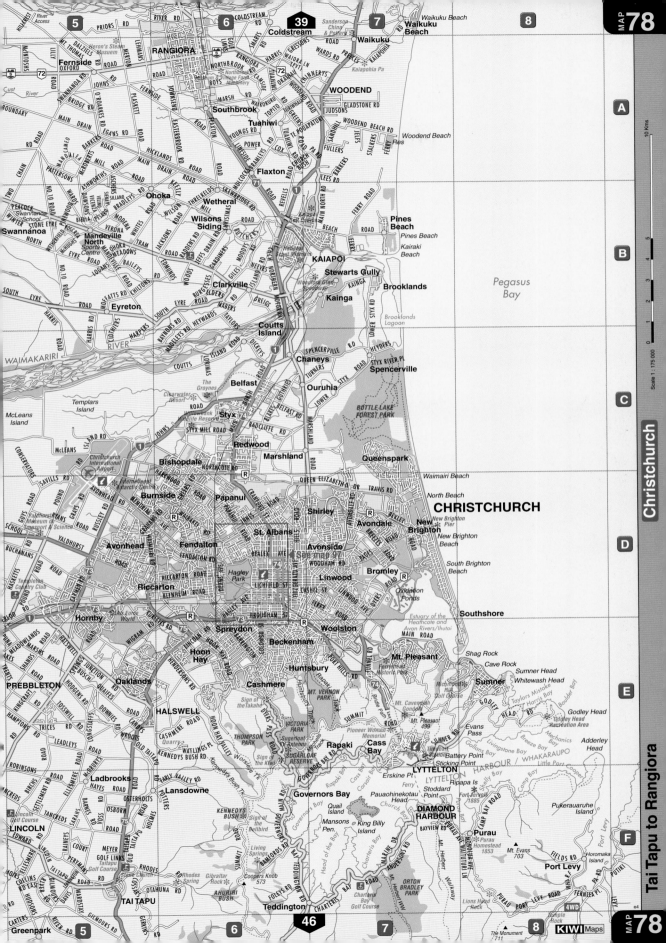

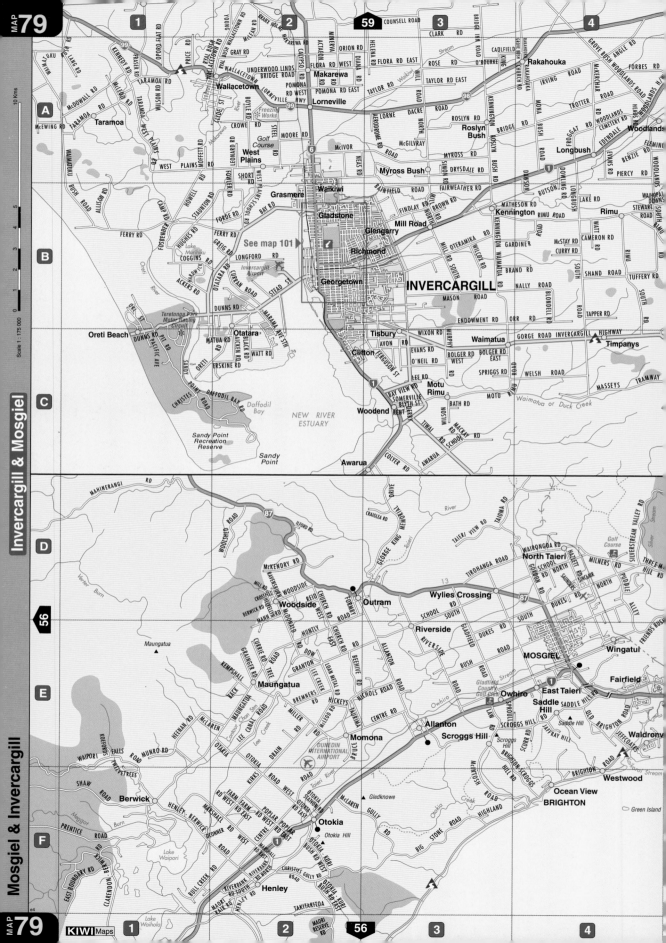

MAP 80

Scale 1: 175 000

10 Kms

5 4 3 2 1 0 1 2 3 4 5

SILVERPEAKS FOREST

Silver Peak

Pulpit Rock

Green Peak

Whare Flat

Flagstaff - Whare Flat Rd

Flagstaff

Swampy Summit

Abbotts Hill

Halfway Bush

Wakari

Brockville

Kaikorai

Roslyn

Bellknowes

Bradford

Kenmure

Balaclava

Abbotsford

Burnside

Sunnyvale

Green Island

Concord

Kew

St. Clair

St. Kilda

St. Kilda Beach

St. Clair Beach

Forbury Hill

Black Head

White Island

Helensburgh

Maori Hill

Mary Hill

DUNEDIN

See map 100

Burns Pt

Kensington

Vauxhall

Andersons Bay

Tamui

Ocean View

Tomahawk Beach

Lawyers Head

Bird Isl.

Smails Beach

Maori Head

Liberton

Dalmore

North East Valley

Burkes

North Dunedin

Opoho

Maia

Ravensbourne

Signal Hill

Black Jack Point

Waverley

Challis

Shiel Hill

Mt. Mera

St. Leonards

Sawyers Bay

Roseneath

Martins Hill

Curls Point

PORT CHALMERS

Careys Bay

Careys Bay

Blanket Bay

Grassy Pt.

Kilgour Pt.

Goat Island/Rakiriri

Quarantine Island/Kamau Taurua

Marine Research Aquarium

Harbour

Otago Harbour

Deborah Head

Acheron Head

Rocky Point

Dowling Bay

Pulling Point

Hamilton Bay

Lewis

Aramoana

Otafelo Pt.

Taylor Point

Te Rauone Beach

Whaling Stn

Otakou Point

Otekiho Beach

Pilots Beach

"Disappearing" Gun

Taiaroa Albatross Colony Head

Lighthouse

Rerewahine Point

Penguin Beach

Hautai Hill

Reids Beach

Pipikaretu Beach

Pipikaretu Pt.

Ryans Beach

OTAKOU GOLF COURSE RD

Harwood

HARWOOD

PIPIKARETU RD

The Pyramids

McArthny Hill

Wickliffe Bay

Victory Beach

Okia Flat

Papanui Inlet

McKAY RD

Mt. Charles/Poatiri

Papanui Beach

Allans Beach

Lighthouse

Cape Saunders

Sandy Mt.

Lovers Leap

The Chasm

Boulder Beach

Sandfly Bay

Harakehe Head

Seal Point

Harbour Cone

Broad Bay

Company Bay

Macandrew Bay

Glenfalloch

Colinswood

Highcliff

Yellow Head

Larnachs Castle

Raynbird Bay

Macandrew Bay

PORTOBELLO

Broad Bay

Challis Point

HIGHCLIFF

KARETAI

SOUTHDALE

CENTRE RD

McHEEKING

BRAIDWOOD RD

BUSHKIN

PARADISE RD

SEAL POINT RD

CAMP RD

LIME RD

SHADDON RD

SANDYMOUNT RD

SANDYMOUNT RIDGE

HOOPERS INLET

Papanui Inlet

WEIR RD

DICK RD

SHEPPARD RD

ALLANS RD

INLET RD

CAPE SAUNDERS RD

KAIMATA

HARINGTON RD

TIDEWATER

HARINGTON POINT RD TO

Carey's Bay

Whareakeake Bay

Purehurehu Pt.

Kaikai Beach

Heyward Point

Long Beach

MURDERING BEACH RD

Spit Beach Mole

Pilot Point

BEACH RD

DRIVER

Mihiwaka

HEYWARD POINT

HAMILTON BAY RD

BLUESKIN RD

PURAKANUI RD

Osborne

Purakanui

Mopanui

Purakanui Bay

Potato Point

MIHIWAKA STATION RD

MOPANUI RD (ALFS RD)

Main South Line

Mopanui

WHITE RD

Doctors Point

Blueskin Bay

Waitati

DOCTORS RD

THORNICROFT RD

KING QUEEN

JONES RD

MANSE RD

WRIGHT RD

DOUBLE HILL RD

CLARK RD

MILLER RD

KILPATRICK RD

SHORTCUT RD

DONALDS

DENIS VALLEY RD

HAZEL RD

McINTOSH RD

WEATHERSTONE RD

GREEN RD

MT. CARGILL RD

Wetherston Hill

Mt. Cargill

WAITATI VALLEY RD

O'CONNELL RD

Pigeon Flat

PIGEON FLAT RD

Evansdale

EVANSDALE GLEN RD

COAST RD

Warrington

RESERVOIR RD

WILSON RD

Coast Creek

DAWSON RD

DONALD RD

KILMOG CREEK

SEMPLE RD

MOUNTAIN ROAD

Waikouaiti River

Omimi

Seacliff

KILGOUR RD

PALMER RD

COAST RD STH

RUSSELL RD STH

PORTEOUS RD

PULLAR RD

PRYDE RD

STEEP HILL RD

WHITES RD

CHURCH ROAD

LAWSON RD

Gate

Gate

KOORE RD

MARKS ROAD

APES ROAD

ROUND HILL RD

McLACHLAN RD

Karitane

Puketeraki

Green Point

Brinns Point

RUSSELL RIVER RD

BLUCHER ROAD

LAMB HILL ROAD

South Branch Waikouaiti River

LONGRIDGE RD

CHALMERS RD

ROLLINSONS RD

HALFWAY BUSH RD

LEITH VALLEY RD

WHARE FLAT RD

THREE MILE HILL ROAD

88

88

1

1

56

7

56

MAP 80 KIWI Maps

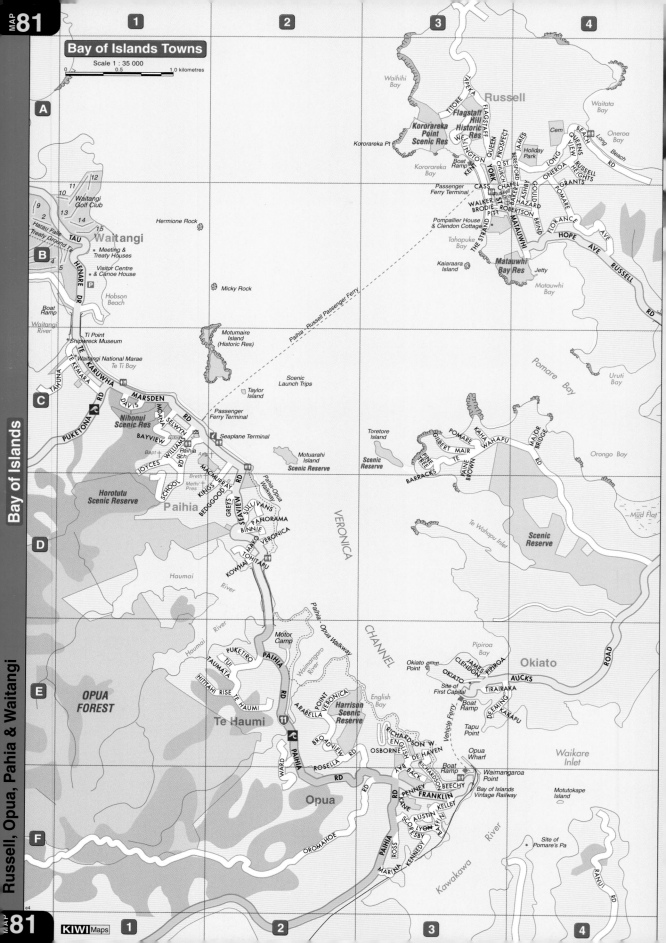

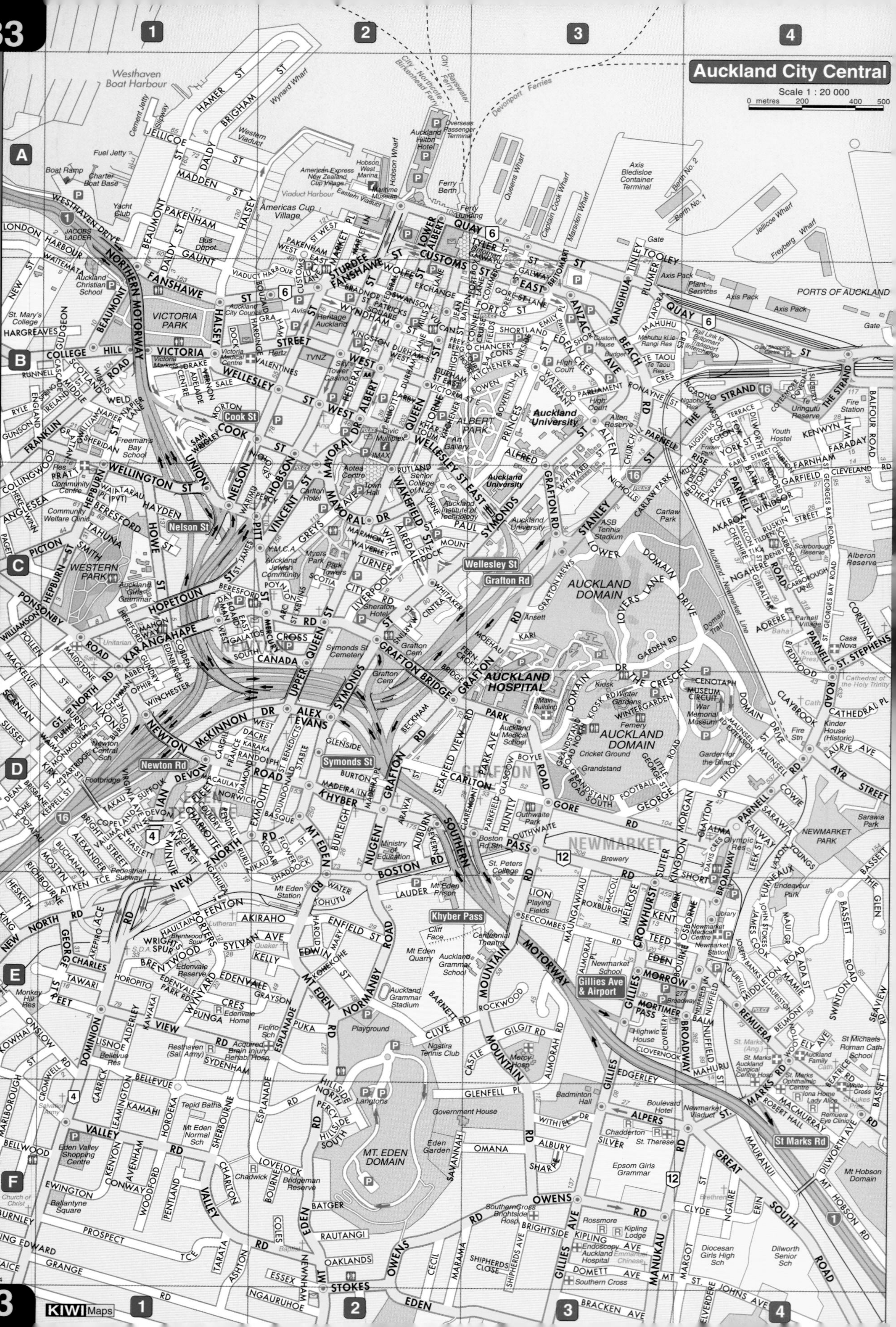

MAP 83

Auckland City Central

Scale 1 : 20 000

0 metres   200   400   500

Auckland City Central

Auckland Central

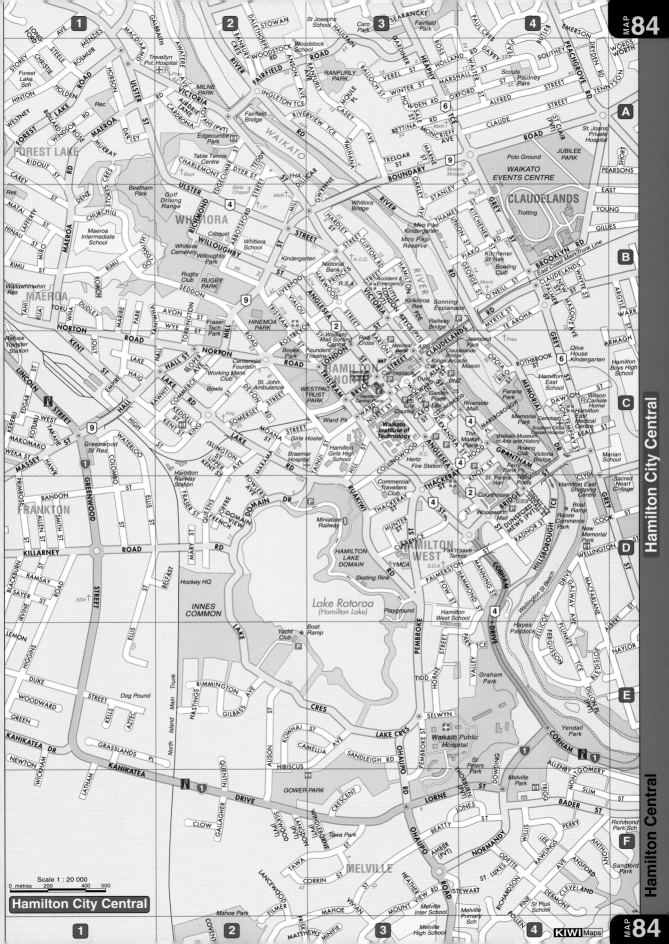

MAP
84
Hamilton City Central
Hamilton Central

Hamilton City Central

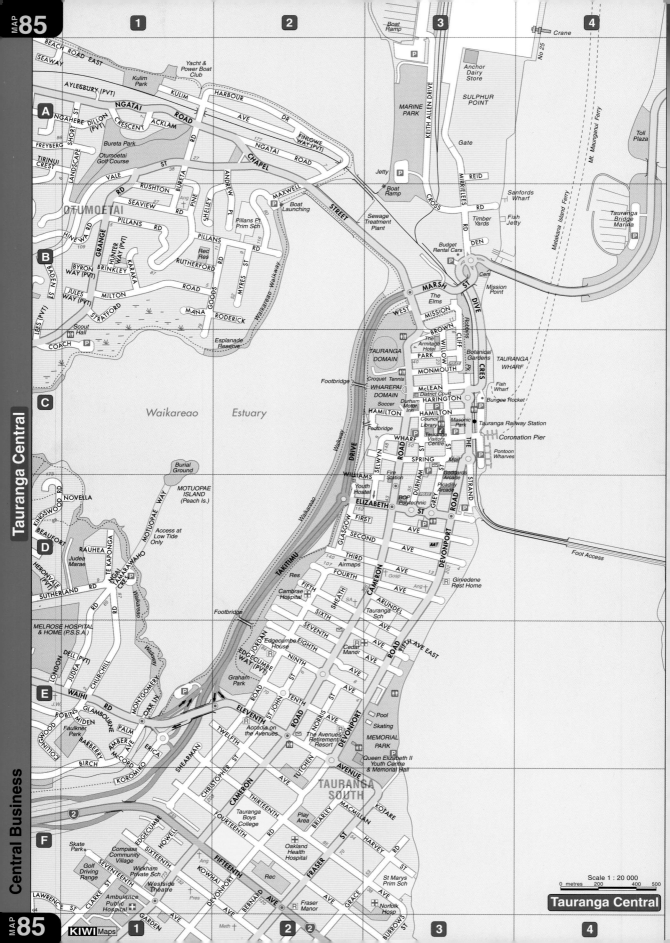

MAP 85

Tauranga Central

Central Business

MAP 85

KIWI Maps

Scale 1 : 20 000
0 metres 200 400 500

Tauranga Central

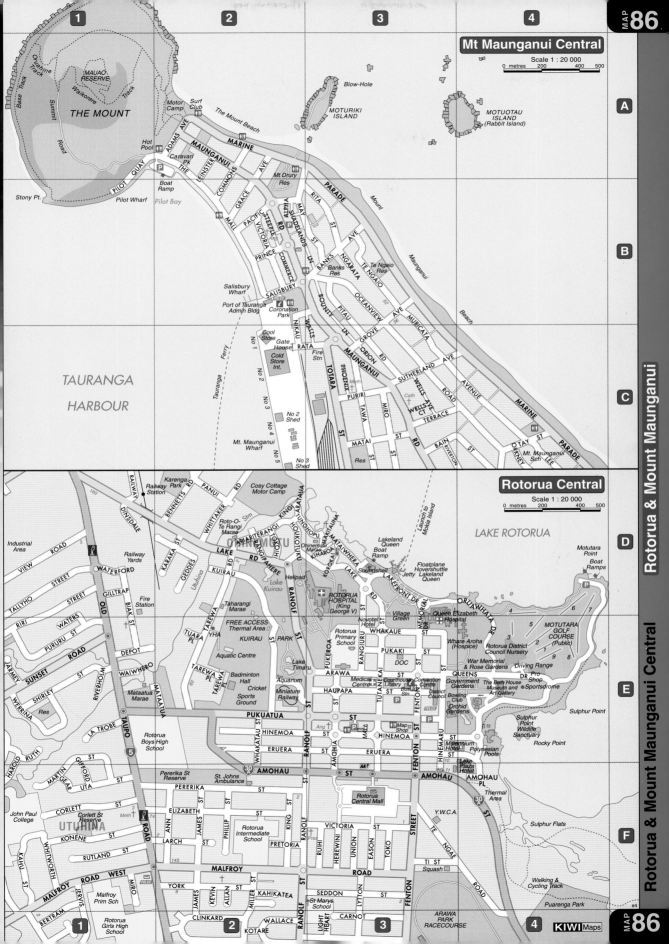

MAP 86

Mt Maunganui Central

Scale 1 : 20 000

0 metres 200 400 500

Rotorua Central

Scale 1 : 20 000

0 metres 200 400 500

KIWI Maps

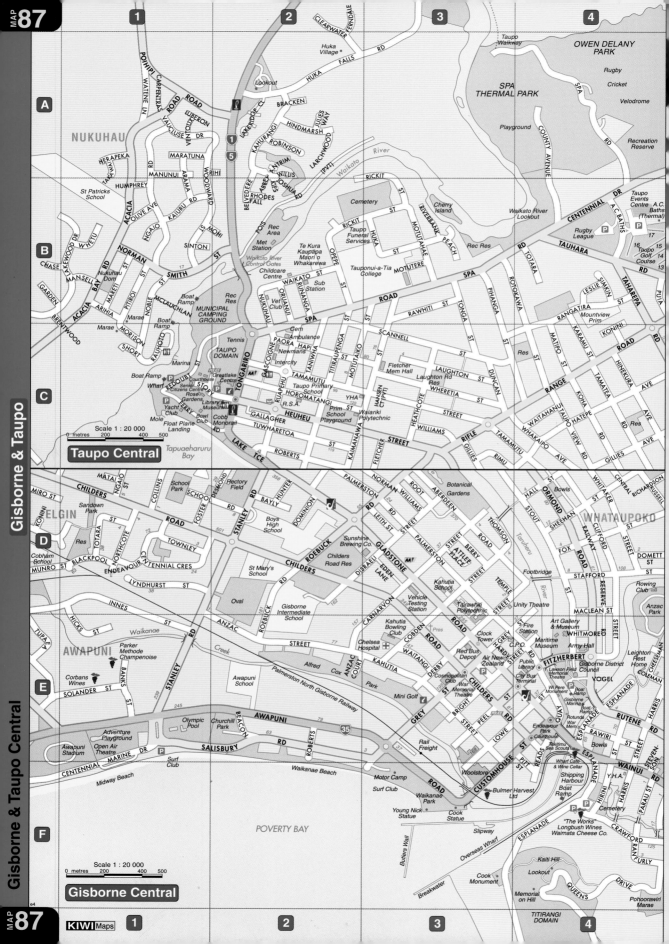

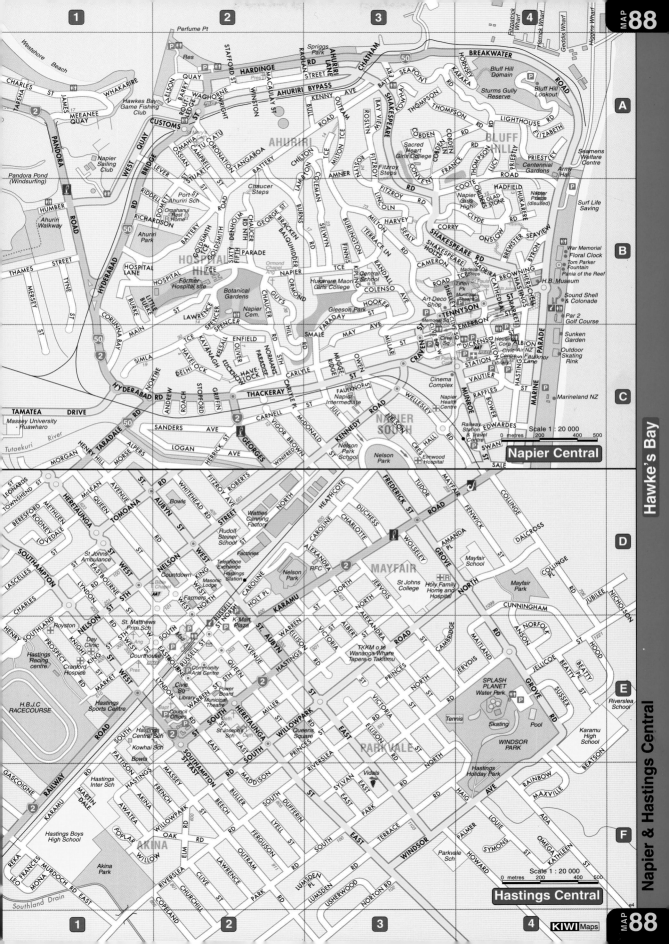

MAP 88

Napier Central

Scale 1 : 20 000
0 metres   200   400   500

Hastings Central

Scale 1 : 20 000
0 metres   200   400   500

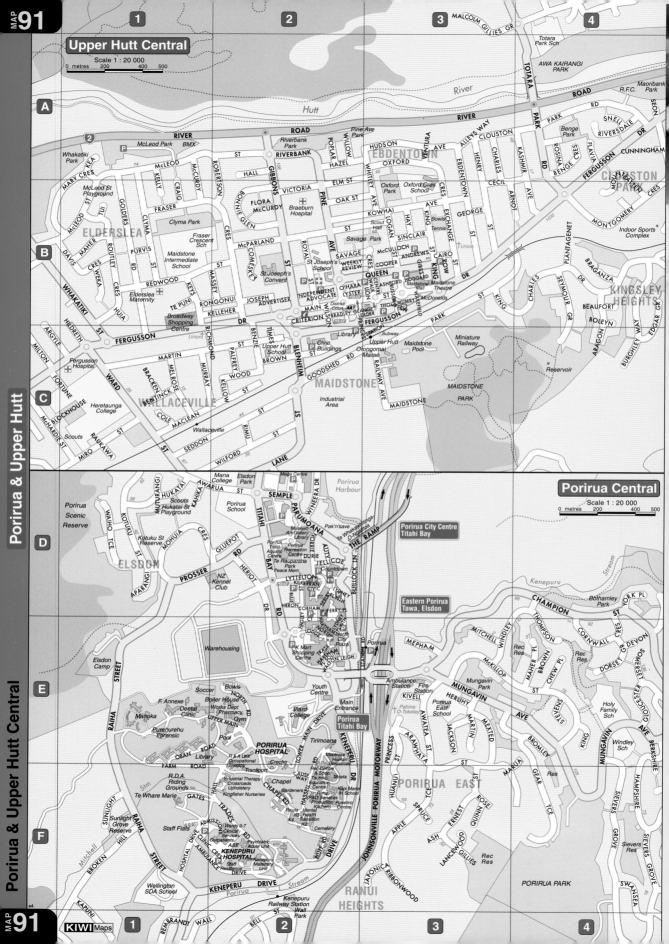

MAP 92

Lower Hutt Central

Scale 1 : 20 000
0 metres 200 400 500

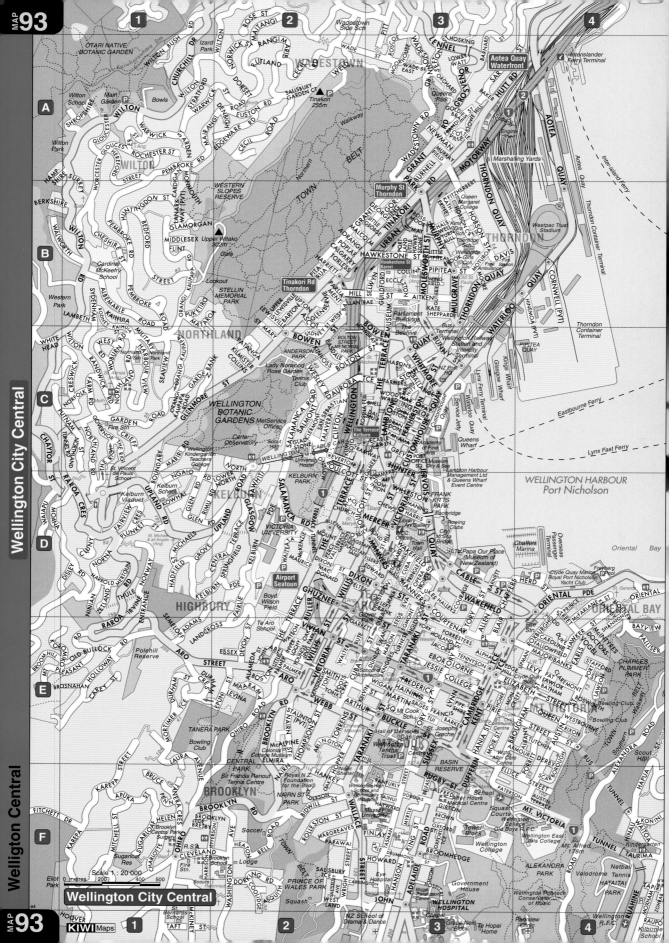

MAP
93

Wellington City Central

Scale 1 : 20 000
0 metres 200 400 500

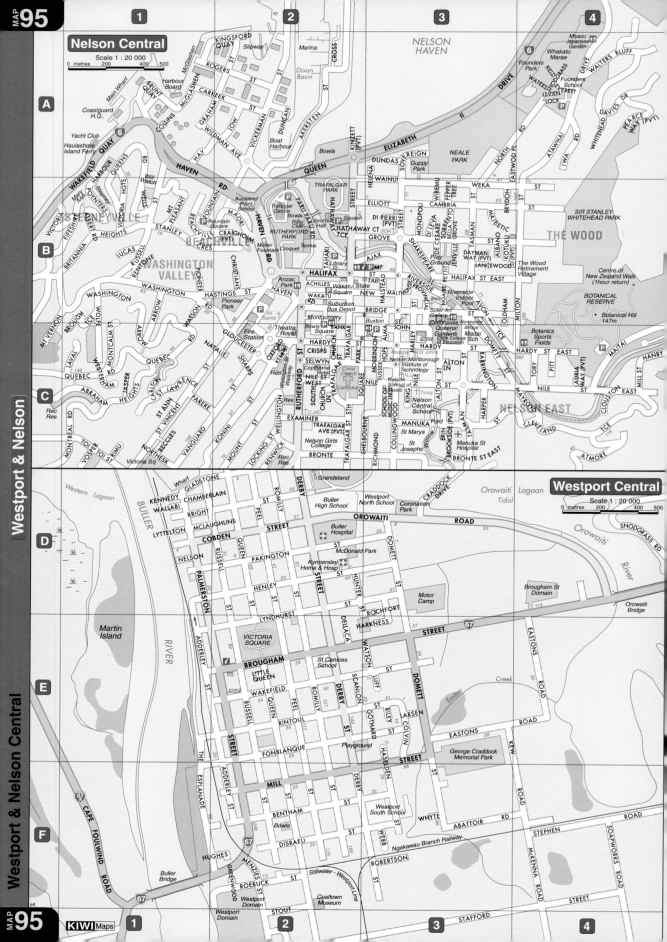

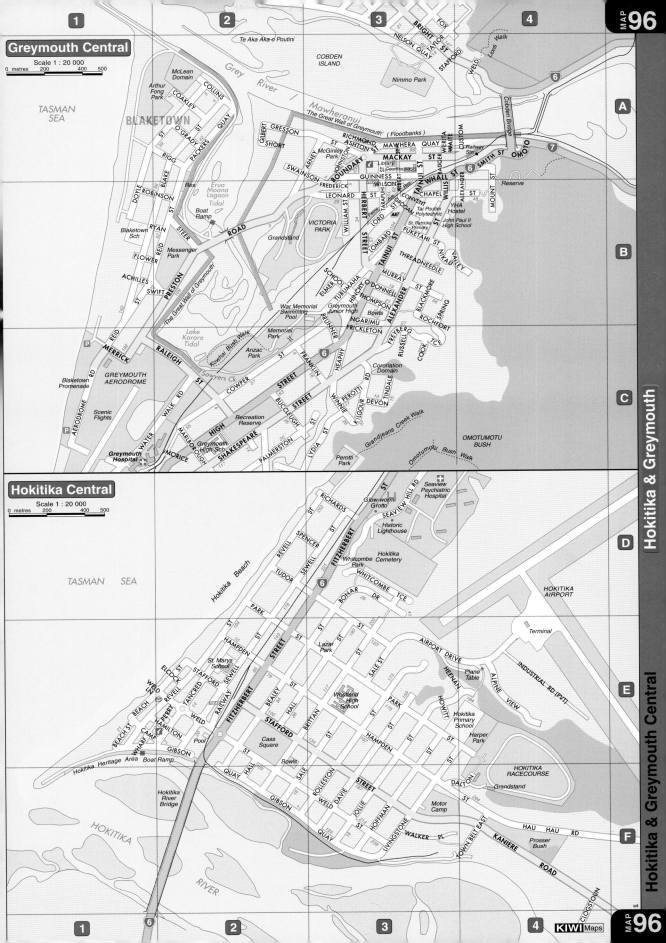

MAP 96

Greymouth Central

Scale 1 : 20 000

0 metres 200 400 500

TASMAN SEA

BLAKETOWN

Grey River / Mawheranui

'The Great Wall of Greymouth' (Floodbanks)

COBDEN ISLAND

Nimmo Park

Cobden Bridge

OMOTO

McLean Domain

Arthur Fong Park

Erua Moana Lagoon Tidal

Boat Ramp

Blaketown Sch

Messenger Park

Victoria Park

Grandstand

War Memorial Swimming Pool

Lake Karoro Tidal

Kowhai Bush Walk

Anzac Park

Memorial Park

Greymouth Junior High

Bowls

Coronation Domain

Blaketown Promenade

GREYMOUTH AERODROME

Scenic Flights

Sawyers Ck

Recreation Reserve

Greymouth High Sch

Greymouth Hospital

Perotti Park

Grandjeans Creek Walk

Omotomotu Bush Walk

OMOTUMOTU BUSH

Railway Stn

Reserve

Library
Courthouse

Tai Poutini Polytechnic

St Patricks Primary

YHA Hostel

John Paul II High School

Tai Poutini Polytechnic

Hokitika Central

Scale 1 : 20 000

0 metres 200 400 500

TASMAN SEA

Hokitika Beach

Glow-worm Grotto

Seaview Psychiatric Hospital

Historic Lighthouse

Whitcombe Park

Hokitika Cemetery

HOKITIKA AIRPORT

Terminal

Plane Table

Lazar Park

St. Marys School

Westland High School

Hokitika Primary School

Harper Park

HOKITIKA RACECOURSE

Grandstand

Cass Square

Bowls

Motor Camp

Prosser Bush

Hokitika Heritage Area

Boat Ramp

Pool

Hokitika River Bridge

HOKITIKA RIVER

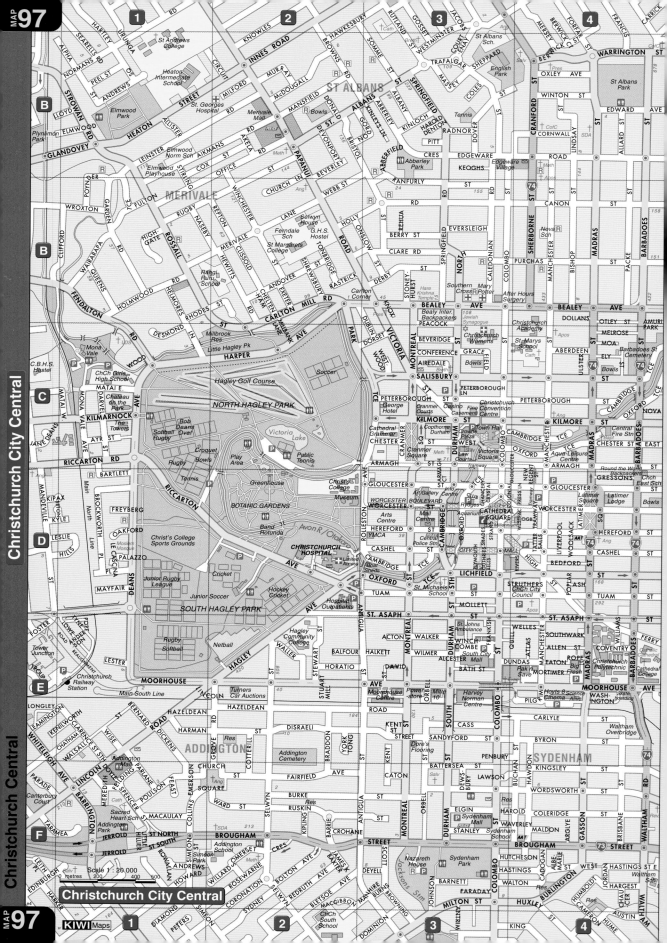

MAP 97
Christchurch City Central

MAP 97
Christchurch City Central
KIWI Maps

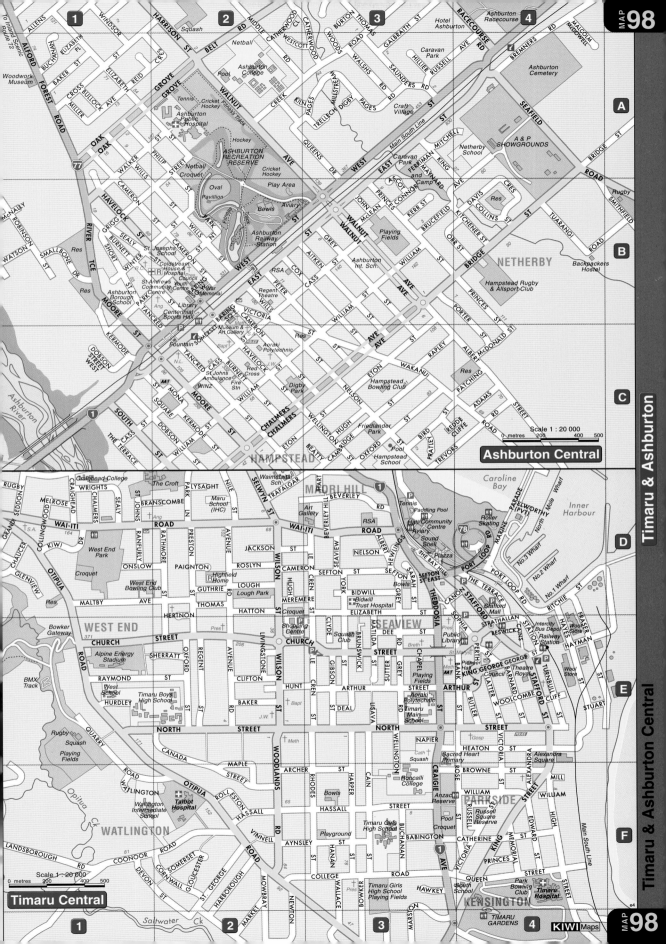

MAP 98

Ashburton Central

Scale 1 : 20 000

0 metres 200 400 500

Timaru Central

Scale 1 : 20 000

0 metres 200 400 500

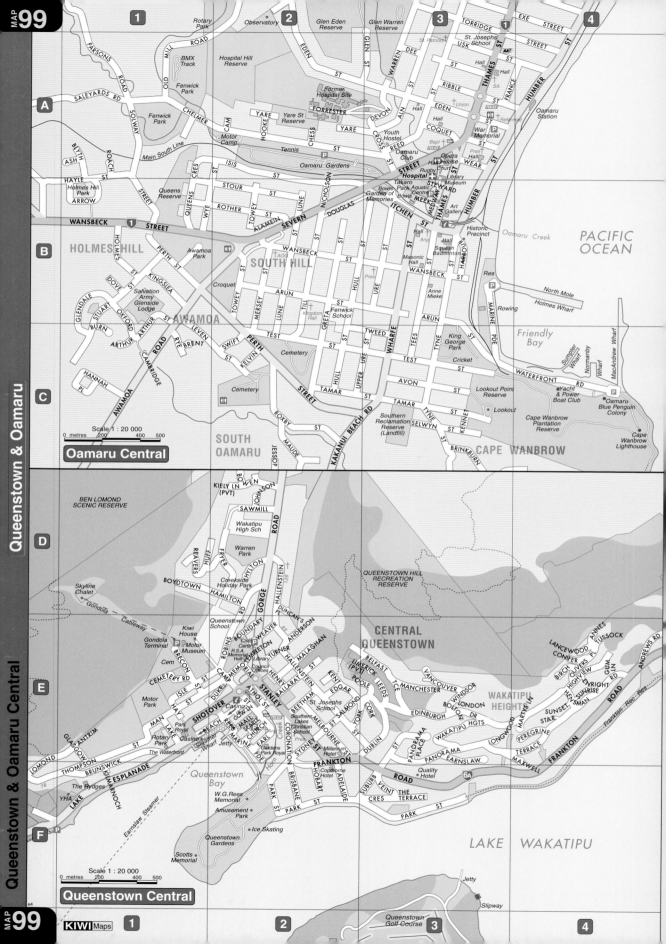

MAP
99

Queenstown & Oamaru

Queenstown & Oamaru Central

Oamaru Central

Scale 1 : 20 000

0 metres 200 400 500

Queenstown Central

Scale 1 : 20 000

0 metres 200 400 500

MAP
99

KIWI Maps

PACIFIC
OCEAN

LAKE WAKATIPU

MAP 100

Dunedin City Central

Scale 1 : 20 000

0 metres   200   400   500

KIWI Pathfinder
New Zealand
Travellers Road Atlas

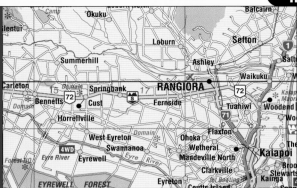

Important Index Information

All Cities, Towns and Localities for New Zealand have been indexed alphabetically with the geographical and tourist features following in separate sections.

The District street maps & City & Town centre maps (maps 63-101) are indexed alphabetically following the main map section. Note where a district & city centre map appear for the same region (e.g. Auckland Central & District) they are indexed within the same section (e.g. Auckland).

Cities Towns & Localities	Pages 2-9	Blenheim, Nelson & Picton Central Roads	Pages 27-28
Coastal & Water Features	Pages 9-15	Nelson & Marlborough District Roads	Pages 28-29
Mountains, Passes & Land Features	Pages 15-16	New Plymouth Central Roads	Page 29
Skifields, Tracks, Parks & Forests	Pages 16-17	Oamaru Central Roads	Pages 29-30
Ashburton Central	Pages 17-18	Palmerston North Central & District Roads	Pages 30-31
Auckland City & District Roads	Pages 18-20	Queenstown Central Roads	Page 31
Bay of Islands Towns & District Roads	Page 20	Rotorua Central & District Roads	Pages 31-32
Christchurch Central & District Roads	Pages 20-22	Taupo Central & District Roads	Page 32
Dunedin Central & District Roads	Pages 22-23	Tauranga & Mt Maunganui Roads	Pages 32-33
Gisborne & Greymouth Central Roads	Page 23	Timaru Central Roads	Page 33
Hamilton Central & District Roads	Pages 23-25	Wanganui, Lower Hutt & Porirua Central Roads	Page 34
Hokitika Central Roads	Page 25	Upper Hutt Central & District Roads	Page 35
Invercargill Central & District Roads	Pages 25-26	Wellington Central & District Roads	Pages 35-36
Masterton Central Roads	Page 26	Westport & Whangarei Central Roads	Page 36
Napier-Hastings Central & District Roads	Pages 26-27		

How to locate a town

TOWN NAME	MAP NO.	REFERENCE	NW NE / SW SE
Example: **KORERE**	**34**	A 40 SE	

Locate **KORERE** in the index. Note the reference and turn to the map number(**34**) -. The location will appear on this map in the square found by intersecting the letter **A** and the number **40** - these are in the border. To help you find the town quickly, each square can be further subdivided into 4 parts: NorthWest, NorthEast, SouthWest & SouthEast. **KORERE** will be found in the **S**outh**E**ast Corner.

Overlapping Page   Grid   Adjacent Map Number   Index Grid Reference   Map Number

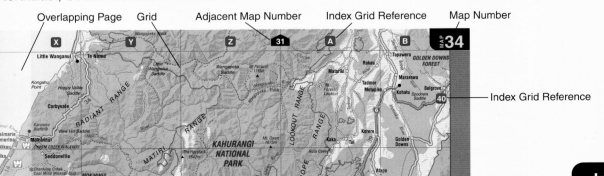

Index Grid Reference

Index 2

A

A - E Acacia Bay - Evans Flat

Cities, Towns & Localities

A

Location	Map No.	Ref
ACACIA BAY	11	P 25 NW
ADAIR	50	U 57 NE
ADAMS FLAT	55	P 66 NE
AHAURA	33	V 45 NE
AHIKIWI	3	F 8 SW
AHIPARA	1	C 5 SW
AHITITI	15	I 26 NE
AHURIRI FLAT	60	P 68 NW
AHUROA	5	I 12 SE
AICKENS	38	W 47 SW
AIREDALE	50	T 60 NW
AKA AKA	7	J 17 NE
AKAROA	42	B 53 NE
AKATARAWA	27	K 38 NE
AKATERE	2	E 4 SE
AKATORE	56	Q 66 SE
AKERAMA	4	H 7 NW
AKITIO	26	Q 35 SW
ALBANY	5	J 14 NW
ALBERT TOWN	48	M 58 SE
ALBURY	45	T 55 SW
ALEXANDRA	54	N 61 SE
ALFORD FOREST	41	V 52 SE
ALFREDTON	26	N 36 NE
ALFRISTON	7	K 15 SW
ALGIES BAY	6	J 12 SE
ALL DAY BAY	50	T 61 NW
ALLANDALE		
(BANKS PENINSULA)	42	A 52 SW
(MACKENZIE)	44	T 55 NW
ALLANTON	56	R 65 NW
ALMA	50	T 60 SE
ALTON	21	I 30 SW
AMBERLEY	42	A 49 SE
AMBERLEY BEACH	42	A 49 SE
AMODEO BAY	6	M 14 NE
ANAKIWA	29	F 39 NE
ANAMA	41	V 53 NW
ANAURA BAY	14	Z 23 NW
ANAWHATA	5	I 15 NW
ANIWANIWA	19	T 25 SE
ANNAT	41	X 51 NE
AOKAUTERE	23	N 34 SW
AONGATETE	10	O 19 NE
AORAKI/MT COOK	44	Q 53 NW
AORANGI		
(GISBORNE)	14	Y 21 SE
(MANAWATU)	23	M 33 SE
AORERE	31	A 36 NW
AOROA	3	F 10 NE
AOTEA	9	J 21 NE
APANUI	13	U 21 SE
APARIMA	58	I 66 SE
APATA	10	O 19 NE
APITI	23	O 32 NW
APONGA	4	G 8 NE
APOTU	4	H 8 NE
APUTEREWA	2	E 4 SW
ARAHIWI	10	O 22 NE
ARAHURA	38	T 47 NE
ARAMATAI	9	L 23 SW
ARAMIRO	9	K 20 SE
ARAMOANA		
(CENTRAL HAWKES BAY)	24	S 33 SW
(DUNEDIN CITY)	56	S 64 SE
ARANGA	3	E 8 SW
ARANGA BEACH	3	E 8 SW
ARAPAE	9	K 23 SE
ARAPAOA	4	H 11 NW
ARAPARERA	5	I 13 NW
ARAPITO	31	Y 39 NW
ARAPOHUE	4	G 10 NW
ARAPUNI	10	N 21 SW
ARARATA	21	H 29 SE
ARARIMU	7	K 16 SE
ARARUA	4	H 10 NW
ARATAKI	11	N 24 NE
ARATAPU	3	F 10 NE
ARATIATIA	11	P 24 SW
ARATIKA	38	V 46 SW
ARATORO	16	L 24 NW
ARAWHATA	48	K 55 NE
ARDGOUR	49	N 59 SE
ARDGOWAN	50	T 60 SE
ARDKEEN	19	U 26 SW
ARDMORE	7	K 15 SE
ARERO	14	Y 23 NE
ARGYLL EAST	24	Q 31 SE
ARIA	16	K 24 NW
ARIKI	34	Y 42 NE
ARNO	50	T 58 SE
AROHENA	10	N 22 NW
AROPAOANUI	18	T 28 SW
AROWHENUA	45	U 56 NE
ARROW JUNCTION	53	L 60 NE
ARROWTOWN	53	L 60 NE
ARTHUR'S PASS	41	V 48 SE
ARTHUR'S POINT	52	K 60 NE
ARTHURSTOWN	38	T 47 SE
ARTHURTON	55	N 66 SW
ARUNDEL	45	U 54 NE
ASHBURTON	41	W 54 NE
ASHBURTON FORKS	41	W 53 NW
ASHBURTON GORGE	45	U 52 SW
ASHCOTT	24	Q 32 NW
ASHERS	59	L 68 SW
ASHHURST	23	N 34 NE
ASHLEY	42	A 50 SW
ASHLEY CLINTON	24	P 32 NE
ASHLEY DOWNS	55	O 66 SW
ASHLEY GORGE	41	Y 50 NE
ASHTON	45	W 54 SE
ASHWICK FLAT	44	T 54 SW
ATAAHUA	42	A 53 NE
ATAPO	34	A 41 NE
ATARAU	33	V 45 NE
ATAU PAPARUA	29	F 37 NE
ATAWHAI	29	D 39 NW
ATHENREE	8	O 18 NE
ATHOL	52	K 63 NE
ATIAMURI	10	P 23 SW
AUCKLAND	7	J 14 NE
AUKOPAE	16	K 26 NE
AURERE	1	D 4 SE
AUROA	21	G 29 NW
AVOCA		
(KAIPARA)	3	F 9 NE
(SELWYN)	41	X 49 SW
AWAHOU	10	P 21 SE
AWAHOU NORTH	23	N 33 SE
AWAHOU SOUTH	23	N 33 SE
AWAHURI	23	M 34 NW
AWAITI	8	N 18 NW
AWAKAPONGA	12	S 21 NW
AWAKERI	12	S 21 SE
AWAKERI SPRINGS	12	S 21 SE
AWAKINO	15	I 24 SE
AWAKINO POINT	3	F 9 SE
AWAMANGU	55	O 66 SE
AWAMARINO	9	J 22 SE
AWAMOA	50	T 60 SE
AWAMOKO	50	T 59 SW
AWANUI		
(FAR NORTH)	1	C 4 SE
(GISBORNE)	13	W 20 SW
AWARIKI	23	P 33 SE
AWAROA	1	D 6 NW
AWARUA		
(FAR NORTH)	3	F 7 SE
(INVERCARGILL CITY)	59	K 68 SW
AWATEA	60	O 67 SE
AWATERE	14	Z 20 NW
AWATOITOI	28	O 37 SW
AWATOTO	18	S 30 NE
AWATUNA		
(SOUTH TARANAKI)	21	G 29 NW
(WESTLAND)	38	T 47 NE
AWHITU	7	I 16 NE
AWHITU CENTRAL	7	I 16 NE
AYLESBURY	41	Y 52 NE

B

Location	Map No.	Ref
BACK RIVER	2	E 4 SW
BAINESSE	23	L 34 SE
BAINHAM	31	Z 36 SE
BALCAIRN	42	A 50 NE
BALCLUTHA	60	P 67 NW
BALFOUR	59	K 65 NE
BALLANCE	23	N 34 SE
BALMORAL	39	A 48 NE
BANKSIDE	41	Y 52 SW
BANNOCKBURN	54	M 61 NE
BARNEGO	60	P 67 NW
BARRHILL	41	X 52 SW
BARRYTOWN	33	U 44 SE
BARTLETTS	20	X 26 SW
BATLEY	4	H 11 SE
BAY VIEW		
(NAPIER CITY)	18	S 29 NE
(NELSON CITY)	29	D 39 NW
BAYLYS BEACH	3	F 9 SW
BAYSWATER	58	I 66 SE
BEACHLANDS	7	K 15 NE
BEACONSFIELD	23	N 33 NW
BEALEY	41	W 49 NW
BEAUMONT	55	O 64 SE
BEAUTIFUL VALLEY	45	T 55 NE
BECKENHAM HILLS	40	C 48 NW
BECKS	49	P 60 NW
BELFAST	42	A 51 SE
BELFIELD	45	U 55 NE
BELGROVE	32	B 40 NE
BELL BLOCK	15	G 26 SE
BELL HILL	38	V 46 SE
BENDIGO	54	N 60 NW
BENHAR	60	P 67 NE
BENIO	55	M 66 NE
BENMORE		
(SOUTHLAND)	58	J 65 SE
(WAITAKI)	49	Q 57 SE
BENNETTS	42	Z 50 SW
BENNETTS SIDING	17	N 30 SE
BENNEYDALE	11	M 24 NW
BERLINS	33	W 42 SE
BERWICK	56	Q 65 SE
BETHLEHEM	10	P 19 SW
BEXLEY	41	Y 51 NW
BICKERSTAFFE	4	H 10 SE
BIDEFORD	26	N 37 NE
BIG BAY	7	J 15 SW
BIG OMAHA	5	J 12 NW
BIRCHFIELD	33	W 41 SE
BIRCHVILLE	30	K 38 SE
BIRCHWOOD	58	H 65 SE
BIRDLINGS FLAT	42	A 53 SE
BLACK FOREST	49	Q 57 NE
BLACK GULLY	55	N 65 NE
BLACK POINT	50	S 59 SE
BLACKBALL	33	V 45 SW
BLACKBURN	24	P 31 SE
BLACKHEAD	24	S 33 SW
BLACKMOUNT	58	H 65 NW
BLACKPOOL	6	K 14 SE
BLACKS POINT	33	X 44 NW
BLACKWATER	33	W 44 SE
BLANDSWOOD	45	U 54 NE
BLENHEIM	29	F 40 SE
BLIND RIVER	36	G 41 SE
BLUE CLIFFS	50	T 57 SE
BLUE MOUNTAINS	27	K 38 SW
BLUESKIN RIDGE	56	S 64 SW
BLUFF	59	J 69 SE
BLYTHE VALLEY	42	C 48 NW
BODDYTOWN	38	U 46 NW
BOMBAY	7	K 16 SE
BONNY GLEN	23	L 32 SE
BORTONS	50	T 59 SW
BOWENTOWN	10	P 18 SW
BOWLERS CREEK	55	O 65 NE
BRADLEYS LANDING	3	F 10 NE
BRAEBURN	32	B 38 SE
BRAIGH	4	I 10 NW
BRANXHOLME	58	J 67 SE
BRIDGE PA	18	R 30 SE
BRIGHTON	56	R 65 SE
BRIGHTWATER	32	C 39 SW
BRIXTON	15	H 26 SW
BROAD BAY	56	S 65 NE
BROAD GULLY	50	U 59 NW
BROADFIELD	42	Z 52 NE
BROADLANDS	12	Q 24 NW
BROADWOOD	1	D 6 NW
BRONTE	32	C 39 NW
BROOKBY	7	K 15 SE
BROOKLANDS		
(CHRISTCHURCH CITY)	42	A 51 NE
(CLUTHA DISTRICT)	56	Q 66 SW
BROOKLYN	32	B 38 NE
BROOKSIDE	41	Y 52 SE
BROWNS	59	K 66 SW
BROWNS BEACH	45	V 56 NE
BRUCE BAY	43	O 52 SW
BRUNSWICK	22	K 31 SW
BRUNTWOOD	9	M 20 SE
BRYDONE	59	L 67 NE
BRYNAVON	4	I 8 NW
BRYNDERWYN	4	I 10 SW
BUCKLAND		
(FRANKLIN DISTRICT)	7	K 17 NW
(MATAMATA PIAKO DISTRICT)	10	N 20 SW
BULLS	23	M 33 SW
BULWER	29	F 37 SE
BUNNYTHORPE	23	N 34 NW
BURKES PASS	44	S 55 NE
BURNBRAE	34	Y 43 SE
BURNHAM	42	Z 52 NW
BUSHEY	56	T 62 SW
BUTCHERS GULLY	54	N 62 NW

C

Location	Map No.	Ref
CABERFEIDH	60	O 68 SW
CABLE BAY	2	E 4 SW
CALDERVALE	31	Y 38 SW
CAMBRIANS	49	P 59 SW
CAMBRIDGE	9	M 20 SE
CAMDEN	36	E 42 SE
CAMERONS	38	U 46 SW
CAMP VALLEY	50	T 55 SW
CANNINGTON	50	T 56 SE
CANVASTOWN	29	E 39 SE
CAPE FOULWIND	33	V 42 NE
CAPE REINGA	1	A 1 NW
CARDIFF	15	H 28 SW
CARDRONA	53	M 59 SW
CAREW	41	V 54 NW
CARLETON	41	Y 50 SE
CARLUKE	29	E 39 NW
CARNARVON	23	L 34 NE
CAROLINE	59	J 65 NE
CARRINGTON	28	M 37 SW
CARTERS BEACH	33	V 42 NE
CARTERS MILL	48	L 54 SW
CARTERTON	28	M 38 NW
CASCADE CREEK	52	I 60 NE
CASS	41	W 49 NE
CASTLE HILL		
(SELWYN DISTRICT)	41	W 50 NE
(TARARUA DISTRICT)	26	O 36 SW
CASTLECLIFF	22	K 32 NW
CASTLEPOINT	28	P 37 SE
CASTLEROCK	58	J 64 SE
CATTLE CREEK	50	S 57 SW
CATTLE FLAT	53	K 64 NE
CATTLE VALLEY	45	T 55 NE
CAVE	45	T 56 NE
CAVENDISH	41	V 53 NW
CAVERHILL	40	D 47 SW
CECIL PEAK STATION	52	K 61 NE
CHAMBERLAIN	50	S 56 NE
CHANEYS	42	A 51 NE
CHARING CROSS	41	Y 52 NE
CHARLESTON	33	V 43 NW
CHARLTON	55	M 66 SW
CHARTERIS BAY	42	A 52 SE
CHASLANDS	60	N 69 NE
CHATTO CREEK	49	O 61 NW
CHATTON	55	M 65 SW
CHEDDAR VALLEY	13	T 21 SE
CHELTENHAM	23	N 33 NW
CHERTSEY	41	X 53 NE
CHESTERFIELD	38	T 47 NE
CHEVIOT	40	D 47 SW
CHORLTON	42	B 52 SE
CHRISTCHURCH	42	A 51 SE
CHRYSTALLS BEACH	56	Q 66 SE
CHURCHILL	7	K 18 NE
CIRCLE HILL	55	P 66 NE
CLANDEBOYE	45	V 55 SW
CLAREMONT	50	U 56 SW
CLARENCE	36	F 44 NE
CLARENDON	56	Q 66 NW
CLAREVILLE	28	M 38 NW
CLARIS	6	M 11 SE
CLARKESVILLE	55	P 66 SE
CLARKS BEACH	7	J 16 NW
CLARKS FLAT	55	P 65 NW
CLARKS JUNCTION	54	Q 64 NW
CLARKVILLE	42	A 51 NW
CLAVERLEY	40	D 46 SE
CLAYTON	44	T 54 NW
CLEARBURN	49	P 56 SE
CLEVEDON	7	K 15 SE
CLIFDEN	58	H 66 SW
CLIFTON		
(CLUTHA DISTRICT)	60	O 67 NE
(HASTINGS DISTRICT)	18	T 30 SW
(INVERCARGILL CITY)	59	K 68 SW
(TASMAN DISTRICT)	32	B 37 NW
CLINTON	60	N 67 NE
CLIVE	18	S 30 NE
CLOUSTONVILLE	27	K 38 NE
CLYDE	54	N 61 SW
CLYDESDALE	23	L 34 NW
CLYDEVALE	55	O 66 NW
COAL CREEK FLAT	54	N 63 NW
COALGATE	41	X 51 SE
COASTLANDS	12	T 21 NW
COATESVILLE	5	J 14 NW
COBDEN	38	U 45 SW
COLAC BAY	58	I 68 NW
COLDSTREAM	45	W 55 NW
COLLIERS JUNCTION	17	M 30 NE
COLLINGWOOD	31	A 36 NE
COLVILLE	6	M 13 SE
COLYTON	23	N 33 SW
CONICAL HILL	55	N 66 NW
CONROYS GULLY	54	N 61 SW
CONWAY FLAT	40	D 46 SE
COOKS BEACH	8	O 15 NW
COONOOR	26	P 34 SW
COOPERS BEACH	2	E 4 SW
COOPERS CREEK	41	Y 50 SW
COOPTOWN	42	B 53 NW
CORBYVALE	34	X 40 SE
CORNWALLIS	7	I 15 SE
COROGLEN	8	N 15 NE
COROMANDEL	6	M 14 SE
CORRIEDALE	50	T 60 NW
COURTENAY	41	Y 51 SE
COUTTS ISLAND	42	A 51 NW
COWES	6	L 14 SW
CRAIG FLAT	55	O 64 SW
CRAIGELLACHIE	55	O 65 NE
CRAIGIEBURN		
(GREY DISTRICT)	33	V 45 NE
(SELWYN DISTRICT)	41	X 49 SW
CRAIL BAY	29	F 38 SE
CRICHTON	55	P 66 SE
CRICKLEWOOD		
(MACKENZIE DISTRICT)	50	T 55 SW
(WAIROA DISTRICT)	19	U 27 NW
CRIPPLETOWN	54	N 60 NW
CROFTON	23	M 33 NW
CROMWELL	54	M 60 SE
CRONADUN	33	X 43 SW
CROOKSTON	55	N 65 NE
CROSS CREEK	27	K 38 SE
CROSSANS CORNER	55	M 65 SE
CROWN TERRACE	53	L 60 NE
CROWNTHORPE	18	R 30 NW
CROYDON	55	M 66 NW
CRUSHINGTON	33	X 44 NW
CULVERDEN	40	B 47 SW
CURIOUS COVE	29	G 39 NW
CUST	42	Z 50 SW

D

Location	Map No.	Ref
DACRE	59	L 67 SW
DAIRY FLAT	5	J 13 SW
DALEFIELD	28	M 38 NW
DANNEVIRKE	23	O 33 SE
DANSEYS PASS	50	R 60 NE
DARFIELD	41	Y 51 SW
DARGAVILLE	3	F 9 SW
DARTMOOR	18	R 29 SE
DASHWOOD	29	G 41 SW
DAWSON FALLS	15	G 28 SE
DEBORAH	50	T 60 SW
DEEP COVE	57	F 63 SW
DEEP CREEK	50	U 58 SW
DENNISTON	33	W 42 NE
DIAMOND HARBOUR	42	A 52 SE
DICKEYS LANDING	7	J 16 NW
DIGGERS VALLEY	1	D 5 SW
DILLMANSTOWN	38	U 47 NE
DIPTON	58	J 65 SE
DIPTON WEST	58	J 65 SE
DOBSON	38	U 46 NE
DOME VALLEY	5	J 12 NW
DOMETT	40	C 48 NE
DONNELLYS CROSSING	3	E 8 SE
DORIE	41	Y 53 SW
DOUGLAS		
(STRATFORD DISTRICT)	15	I 28 SW
(WAIMATE DISTRICT)	50	T 58 SE
DOVEDALE	32	B 39 NW
DOYLESTON	42	Z 53 NW
DREYERS ROCK	26	N 36 SE
DROMORE	41	X 53 SW
DRUMMOND	58	J 67 NW
DRURY	7	K 16 NE
DRYBREAD	49	O 60 NE
DUMBARTON	54	N 63 SW
DUNBACK	56	S 62 NW
DUNEARN	58	J 66 NW
DUNEDIN	56	S 65 NW
DUNGANVILLE	38	U 46 SE
DUNMORE	9	K 19 NW
DUNNOLLY	23	M 32 SE
DUNROBIN	55	N 64 SE
DUNSANDEL	41	Y 52 SW
DUNTROON	50	S 59 NE
DURIE HILL	22	K 32 NE
DUVAUCHELLE	42	B 53 NE
DYERVILLE	27	L 39 NE

E

Location	Map No.	Ref
EALING	45	V 54 SW
EARNSCLEUGH	54	N 61 SW
EAST CAPE	14	A 20 NW
EAST CHATTON	55	M 65 SW
EAST EGMONT	15	G 28 SE
EAST GORE	55	M 66 SW
EAST TAKAKA	32	B 37 NW
EASTERN BUSH	58	H 66 NE
ECHOLANDS	16	M 26 NW
EDENDALE	59	L 67 SE
EDGECUMBE	12	S 21 NE
EDIEVALE	55	N 64 SE
EGMONT VILLAGE	15	G 27 NE
EIFFELTON	45	W 54 SE
EIGHT MILE JUNCTION	9	L 23 SW
EKETAHUNA	25	N 36 NW
ELAINE BAY	29	F 38 NW
ELDERSLIE	50	T 60 NW
ELEPHANT HILL	50	T 59 NW
ELFIN BAY	52	J 60 NE
ELGIN	41	X 54 NW
ELLESMERE	42	Z 52 SW
ELSTHORPE	24	S 32 NW
ELSTOW	10	N 18 SW
ELTHAM	21	H 29 NW
ENDEAVOUR INLET	29	G 38 NE
ENFIELD	50	T 60 NW
EPWORTH	45	U 55 SE
EREWHON	17	O 29 SE
EREWHON PARK	44	T 52 NW
EREWHON STATION	44	T 51 SW
ERMEDALE	58	I 67 SE
ERUA	16	M 28 NW
ESK VALLEY	50	U 57 SW
ESKDALE	18	S 29 NW
ETHELTON	40	C 48 NW
ETTRICK	54	N 63 SE
EUREKA	9	M 20 NW
EVANS FLAT	55	O 65 NE

Location	Map No.	Ref
VANSDALE	56	S 64 NW
VERSLEY	44	T 55 NW
YRE CREEK	52	K 63 SW
YRETON	42	Z 51 NE
AIRBURN	1	D 5 NW
AIRDOWN	33	W 41 SW
AIRFAX	58	I 67 NE
AIRFIELD	56	R 65 NE
AIRHALL	29	F 40 SE
AIRLIE	44	T 55 NW
AIRLIGHT	53	K 62 SE
AIRTON	41	X 53 SW
AIRVIEW	50	U 56 SW
EATHERSTON	27	L 38 SW
EILDING	23	M 33 SE
ELDWICK	58	H 66 NE
ENCOURT	9	M 20 SE
ERGUSONS	37	S 49 NE
ERN FLAT		
(FAR NORTH DISTRICT)	2	E 5 NW
(RANGITIKEI DISTRICT)	23	L 32 SE
(TASMAN DISTRICT)	34	Y 42 NE
ERNDALE	59	M 67 NW
ERNHILL		
(HASTINGS)	18	S 30 NW
(QUEENSTOWN LAKES)	52	K 60 SE
ERNIEHURST	40	D 46 SW
ERNSIDE	42	Z 50 SE
ERNTOWN	31	A 36 NW
NEGAND	60	P 67 NW
VE FORKS	50	S 60 SE
VE RIVERS	53	K 64 NW
AG SWAMP	56	S 63 NE
AXMERE	18	S 30 NW
AXTON	42	A 51 NW
LEMINGTON		
(ASHBURTON)	45	W 54 SE
(CENTRAL HAWKES BAY)	24	Q 33 SE
ORDELL	22	L 32 NW
ORSYTH	55	P 65 SW
ORTIFICATION	59	M 68 SW
ORTROSE	59	L 69 NE
OUR PEAKS	45	U 54 SE
OUR RIVERS	34	Y 42 NE
OX GLACIER	44	P 51 SE
OXHILL	32	B 40 NE
OXTON	25	L 35 NE
OXTON BEACH	25	L 35 NE
RANKTON	53	L 60 SW
RANZ JOSEF	37	Q 51 NE
RASERTOWN	19	U 27 NE
RENCH FARM	42	B 53 NW
RENCH PASS		
(MARLBOROUGH)	29	F 37 NW
(WAIPA DISTRICT)	9	M 20 SE
RENCHMANS SWAMP	2	H 6 NW
RESHFORD	59	L 64 SE
RUITLANDS	54	N 62 NW
CHSIA CREEK	50	S 60 SE
ABRIELS GULLY	55	P 65 NW
ALATEA	12	S 23 SW
ALLOWAY	54	N 61 SE
APES VALLEY	45	U 55 NW
ARSTON	53	L 63 NW
EORGETOWN	50	T 59 SW
ERALDINE	45	U 55 NE
ERALDINE DOWNS	45	U 55 NE
ERALDINE FLAT	45	U 55 NE
BBSTON	53	L 60 SE
LLESPIES BEACH	43	O 51 NE
MMERBURN	49	Q 61 NW
SBORNE	20	X 25 SW
SBORNE POINT	12	Q 21 SE
ADFIELD	58	I 66 SE
ADSTONE		
(CARTERTON)	28	M 38 SE
(GREY)	38	V 46 SW
(HOROWHENUA)	25	L 36 NE
(MARLBOROUGH)	36	E 42 SW
(QUEENSTOWN LAKES)	48	N 58 NW
ASNEVIN	42	A 49 SE
EN AFTON	9	K 19 NE
EN MASSEY	9	K 19 SE
EN MURRAY	7	K 18 NW
EN OROUA	23	M 34 NW
ENAVY	50	U 59 SE
ENBERVIE	4	I 8 NW
ENBROOK	7	J 16 SE
ENBROOK BEACH	7	J 16 SE
ENBURN	41	Y 49 NE
ENCOE	59	L 67 NW
ENDHU	28	N 40 NW
ENDHU BAY	48	L 58 SE
ENDUAN	29	D 38 SW
ENGARRY	34	Y 42 SE
ENHAM	59	L 68 NE
ENHOPE	34	A 41 NW
ENITI	50	U 56 SW
ENKENICH	55	N 65 SW
ENLEDI	56	Q 66 SE
ENLEITH	56	R 64 SE
ENOMARU	60	P 68 NW
ENORCHY	52	J 59 SE
ENORE	55	P 66 NE
ENPARK	56	S 62 NE
ENROY	41	X 51 SW
ENTUI	41	Y 50 NE
ENTUNNEL	41	X 51 SW
ENURE	59	K 65 SE
INKS GULLY	3	F 10 SE
ORIT	5	I 12 SW
OLDEN CROSS	8	O 17 SW
OLDEN DOWNS	34	B 40 SW
OLDEN SPRINGS	12	Q 24 NW
OLDSBOROUGH	8	O 17 SE
OODWOOD	56	T 63 NE
ORDON	10	O 19 SW
ORDONS VALLEY	50	T 57 NE
ORDONTON	9	M 19 SW
ORE	55	M 66 SW
GORE BAY	40	D 48 NW
GORGE CREEK	58	N 62 SW
GORGE ROAD	59	L 68 SW
GOVERNORS BAY	42	A 52 NW
GOWANBRIDGE	34	Z 41 SE
GRAHAMS BEACH	7	J 16 NW
GRANITY	33	W 41 NE
GRAYS CORNER	50	U 59 NW
GRAYS HILL	49	R 56 SW
GREATFORD	23	M 33 NW
GREEN ISLAND	56	R 65 NE
GREEN VALLEY	56	S 61 SW
GREENDALE	41	Y 52 NW
GREENFIELD	55	O 66 NE
GREENHILLS	59	J 69 NE
GREENPARK	42	Z 52 SE
GREENPARK HUTS	42	Z 53 NE
GREENSTONE	38	U 47 NE
GREENSTREET	41	W 53 SW
GREENVALE	55	M 65 NE
GREIGS	33	U 45 NE
GRETA VALLEY	42	B 48 SE
GREYMOUTH	38	U 46 NW
GREYTOWN	28	M 38 NW
GROPERS BUSH	59	I 67 SE
GROVE BUSH	59	K 67 SE
GROVETOWN	37	F 40 SE
GUMMIES BUSH	58	I 67 SE
GUMTOWN	4	H 8 NW
GUTHRIE	10	P 23 NE
GWAVAS	24	Q 31 NE

H

Location	Map No.	Ref
HAAST BEACH	43	L 54 NE
HAAST VILLAGE	43	L 54 NE
HACKTHORNE	41	V 53 SE
HADFIELD	41	X 53 NE
HADLOW	50	U 56 SW
HAHEI	8	O 15 NW
HAIRINI	9	M 21 NW
HAKARU	4	I 11 NE
HAKATARAMEA	50	R 58 SE
HAKATARAMEA DOWNS	50	S 57 NW
HAKATERE		
(ASHBURTON)	46	X 54 SW
(CANTERBURY)	45	U 52 SW
HAKU	9	J 23 SE
HALCOMBE	23	M 33 NE
HALDANE	58	M 69 SW
HALDON	49	Q 56 SE
HALFMOON BAY	61	J 71 NW
HALFWAY BAY	52	K 61 SE
HALKETT	42	Z 51 SW
HALSWELL	42	A 52 NW
HAMAMA	31	A 37 NE
HAMILTON		
(CENTRAL OTAGO)	56	Q 61 SE
(HAMILTON CITY)	9	L 20 NE
HAMILTON BURN	58	J 64 SE
HAMPDEN	56	T 62 NW
HAMUA	26	N 35 SW
HAMURANA	10	Q 21 SW
HANGAROA	20	V 25 NE
HANGATIKI	9	L 22 SW
HANMER SPRINGS	40	B 46 NW
HAPPY VALLEY		
(FRANKLIN)	7	L 16 SW
(SOUTHLAND)	58	H 67 NE
HAPUKU	36	E 45 NE
HARAKEKE	32	B 39 NE
HARAPEPE	9	L 20 SW
HARIHARI	37	R 50 NE
HARIKI BEACH	13	W 20 NW
HAROTO BAY	9	K 20 NW
HARRISVILLE	7	K 17 NW
HARURU	2	G 6 NE
HARVEYS FLAT	56	Q 65 NE
HARWOOD	56	S 64 SE
HASTINGS	18	S 30 NE
HASTWELL	28	N 36 SW
HATEPE	17	O 26 NE
HATFIELDS BEACH	5	J 13 NW
HATUMA	24	Q 32 SE
HAUITI	24	Y 24 NE
HAUKAWAKAWA	29	F 37 NE
HAUMAKARIRI STREAM	23	M 31 SE
HAUMOANA	18	S 30 SE
HAUNUI	26	O 35 SE
HAUPARU BAY	10	Q 21 SE
HAUPIRI	38	W 46 SE
HAUTANOA	14	Z 22 SW
HAUTAPU	9	M 20 SE
HAUTURU	9	K 21 SW
HAUWAI	36	G 42 NE
HAVELOCK	28	E 39 NE
HAVELOCK NORTH	18	S 30 SW
HAWAI	13	V 21 NE
HAWARDEN	42	A 48 SW
HAWEA FLAT	48	N 58 SW
HAWERA	31	H 30 NW
HAWK HILLS	35	D 45 SW
HAWKENS JUNCTION	12	S 21 NW
HAWKESBURY BUSH	56	T 63 NE
HAWKSWOOD	40	D 47 NW
HAYS GAP	60	P 68 NW
HAZELBURN	50	T 55 SE
HAZLETTS	58	J 67 NE
HEATHERLEA	25	L 35 SW
HECTOR	33	X 41 NW
HEDDON BUSH	58	J 66 NE
HEDGEHOPE	59	K 67 NE
HEENANS CORNER	58	J 66 SW
HELENA BAY	4	H 7 NE
HELENSBROOK	56	Q 66 NW
HELENSVILLE	5	I 13 SW
HELVETIA	7	K 16 SW
HENLEY	56	Q 65 SE
HEPBURN CREEK	5	J 12 SW
HERBERT	56	T 61 NW
HERBERTVILLE	26	Q 35 NE
HEREKINO	1	C 6 NE
HEREPO	37	R 49 SE
HERIOT	55	N 65 NE
HEXTON	20	X 25 NE
HICKS BAY	14	Z 19 SW
HIGHBANK	41	W 52 NE
HIGHCLIFF	56	S 65 NE
HIHI	2	E 4 NW
HIHITAHI	17	N 30 NW
HIKUAI	8	O 16 NE
HIKUMUTU	16	L 26 SE
HIKURANGI	4	H 7 SE
HIKUTAIA	8	N 17 NE
HIKUWAI	14	Y 22 SE
HILDERTHORPE	50	U 60 NW
HILLEND	55	P 66 SW
HILLERSDEN	29	D 41 NE
HILLGROVE	56	T 62 NW
HILLSBOROUGH	15	G 27 NE
HILTON	45	U 55 NW
HIMATANGI	23	L 34 SE
HIMATANGI BEACH	25	L 34 SW
HINAHINA	60	P 68 SW
HINAKURA	28	M 39 SE
HINAU	23	N 32 NE
HINDON	56	Q 64 NE
HINDS	45	W 54 SW
HINEHOPU	12	R 21 SW
HINUERA	10	N 20 SE
HIRA	29	D 39 NW
HIRATA	16	N 26 NW
HIROKINO	9	M 23 SE
HIRUHARAMA	14	Y 21 NE
HIWINUI	23	N 34 NW
HMNZS IRIRANGI	17	N 29 SW
HOANGA	3	F 9 SE
HODDERVILLE	10	N 22 NE
HOE O TAINUI	9	M 18 SW
HOHONU	38	U 47 NE
HOKIO BEACH	25	L 35 SW
HOKITIKA	37	T 47 SW
HOKONUI	59	K 66 SE
HOLLYFORD	47	I 59 NE
HOMEBUSH		
(MASTERTON)	28	N 37 SW
(SELWYN)	41	Y 52 NW
HOMEWOOD	28	O 39 NW
HONEYMOON VALLEY	1	D 5 NE
HONIKIWI	9	L 22 NW
HOOK	50	U 58 NE
HOOPERS INLET	56	S 65 NE
HOPE	32	C 39 SE
HOPELANDS	23	O 34 SW
HOPEONE	13	T 23 SE
HOPUHOPU	9	L 19 NW
HOPURUAHINE LANDING	19	T 25 SE
HORAHIA	8	M 17 NE
HORAHORA		
(WAIPA)	10	N 21 NW
(WHANGAREI)	4	I 8 NE
HOREKE	2	E 6 SE
HOROERA	14	Z 19 SE
HOROHORO	10	P 22 SE
HOROMANGA	12	S 23 SW
HOROPITO	16	M 28 SW
HORORATA	41	X 52 NE
HOROTIU	9	L 19 SW
HORRELLVILLE	42	Z 50 SW
HORSHAM DOWNS	9	L 19 SE
HORSLEY DOWNS	39	A 48 NW
HOSPITAL HILL	13	U 21 SW
HOT WATER BEACH	8	O 15 NW
HOTEO	5	I 12 NE
HOTEO NORTH	5	I 11 SW
HOUHORA	1	C 3 NW
HOUHORA HEADS	1	C 3 SE
HOUIPAPA	60	O 68 SE
HOUPOTO	13	V 21 NE
HOUTO	4	G 8 SW
HOWARD	34	A 42 NW
HOWARD JUNCTION	34	A 41 SW
HUANUI	14	X 23 SE
HUAPAI	5	I 14 NE
HUARAU	4	H 10 SE
HUIA	7	I 15 SE
HUIAKAMA	15	I 28 NE
HUIARUA	14	X 22 NE
HUINGA	15	H 28 NE
HUIRANGI	15	H 27 NW
HUIROA	15	I 28 NE
HUKANUI	25	N 35 SW
HUKAPAPA	16	M 27 NW
HUKARERE	33	W 44 SW
HUKATERE		
(FAR NORTH)	1	C 3 SW
(KAIPARA)	4	H 11 NW
HUKERENUI	4	H 7 NW
HUMPHREYS	38	U 47 NE
HUNDALEE	40	D 46 SW
HUNGAHUNGA	10	N 19 SE
HUNTER	50	U 58 NW
HUNTERVILLE	23	M 32 NE
HUNTINGDON	45	W 54 SE
HUNTLY	9	L 18 SW
HUNUA	7	K 16 NE
HUPARA	2	G 6 SW
HURFORD	15	G 27 NW
HURLEYVILLE	21	I 30 NW
HURUNUI	39	A 48 NE
HURUNUI MOUTH	40	C 48 NE
HURWORTH	15	G 27 NW
HYDE	56	R 62 NW

I

Location	Map No.	Ref
IDA VALLEY	49	P 60 SW
IDABURN	49	P 60 NE
IHAKARA	25	L 35 SW
IHUNGIA	14	Y 22 NE
IHURAUA	26	N 36 SE
IKAMATUA	33	W 45 NW
IKAWAI	50	T 59 SW
INAHA	21	G 29 SE
INANGAHUA	33	X 42 SW
INANGAHUA JUNCTION	33	X 42 SW
INANGAHUA LANDING	33	X 43 NW
INCH VALLEY	56	S 62 SE
INCHBONNIE	38	V 47 SW
INCHOLME	50	T 60 SW
INGLEWOOD	15	G 27 SE
INVERCARGILL	59	J 68 NE
IRWELL	42	Z 52 SW
ISLA BANK	58	J 67 NW
ISLAND BLOCK	55	O 64 NE
ISLAND CLIFF	50	S 59 SE
ISLAND STREAM	50	T 61 NW
IVYDALE	2	E 6 SW
IWIKAU VILLAGE	16	M 28 NE
IWITAHI	18	Q 26 NW

J

Location	Map No.	Ref
JACKSON BAY	47	K 54 SW
JACKSONS	38	V 47 SE
JACOBS RIVER	43	O 52 NW
JERUSALEM	22	K 30 NE
JOSEPHVILLE	59	J 65 NE
JUDGEFORD	27	K 38 SW

K

Location	Map No.	Ref
KAAWA	9	K 18 SW
KAEO	2	F 5 NW
KAHAROA	10	Q 21 NW
KAHIKA	18	S 28 NE
KAHIKATOA	2	E 6 NW
KAHOE	2	E 4 SE
KAHUIKA	60	O 68 SW
KAHUTARA	27	L 39 NE
KAI IWI	22	K 31 SE
KAIAKA	1	D 5 NE
KAIAPOI	42	A 51 NE
KAIATA	38	U 46 NE
KAIATEA	4	I 8 NW
KAIAUA	7	L 16 NE
KAIHERE	8	M 17 SE
KAIHIKU	60	O 67 NE
KAIHINU	38	T 47 NW
KAIHU	3	F 8 SW
KAIKARANGI	23	M 32 NE
KAIKOHE	2	F 6 SW
KAIKOU	4	G 7 SW
KAIKOURA	36	E 45 SE
KAIMAI	10	O 20 NE
KAIMAMAKU	4	H 7 NE
KAIMARAMA	8	N 15 NE
KAIMATA		
(GREY)	38	V 46 SW
(NEW PLYMOUTH)	15	H 27 SW
KAIMATAITAI	60	P 68 NE
KAIMAUMAU	1	D 4 NW
KAIMIRO	15	G 27 SE
KAINGA	42	A 51 NE
KAINGAROA	1	D 4 NE
KAINGAROA VILLAGE	12	R 23 SW
KAINUI	9	L 19 NE
KAIPAKI	9	M 20 SW
KAIPARA FLATS	5	I 12 NE
KAIPARORO	25	M 36 NE
KAIPIKARI	15	H 27 NE
KAIRAKAU BEACH	24	S 32 NE
KAIRANGA	23	M 34 NW
KAIRANGI	9	M 21 NE
KAIRARA	3	F 9 NW
KAIRUA	10	Q 19 SW
KAITAIA	1	C 5 NE
KAITANGATA	60	P 67 NE
KAITARATAHI	14	X 24 SE
KAITAWA		
(TARARUA)	26	N 35 NE
(WAIROA)	19	T 26 NE
KAITEMAKO	10	P 20 NE
KAITERITERI	32	B 38 NE
KAITIEKE	16	L 27 NE
KAITOKE		
(TARARUA)	23	P 33 NE
(UPPER HUTT CITY)	27	K 38 NE
(WANGANUI)	22	K 32 NE
KAITUI	3	E 8 NW
KAITUNA		
(MARLBOROUGH)	29	F 40 NW
(MASTERTON)	25	M 37 NE
KAIWAKA	4	I 11 NW
KAIWERA	55	M 66 SE
KAIWHAIKI	22	K 31 SE
KAKA	34	A 40 SE
KAKA POINT	60	P 68 NE
KAKAHI	16	M 26 NW
KAKAHU	45	U 55 NW
KAKAHU BUSH	45	U 55 NW
KAKANUI		
(RODNEY)	5	I 13 NW
(WAITAKI)	50	T 61 NE
KAKANUI SOUTH	50	T 61 NW
KAKAPOTAHI	37	S 49 NW
KAKAPUAKA	60	P 67 NW
KAKARAMEA	21	H 30 SE
KAKARIKI		
(GISBORNE)	14	Z 21 NE
(MANAWATU)	23	M 33 NW
(TARARUA)	25	M 35 SE
KAKATAHI	17	L 30 SE
KAMAHI	59	K 67 NE
KAMAKA	33	V 45 SW
KAMO	4	H 8 NE
KANAKANAIA	14	X 24 NW
KANIERE	38	T 47 SE
KANIWHANIWHA	9	K 20 SE
KANOHI	5	I 13 SW
KAPENGA	10	P 22 SE
KAPIRO	2	F 5 SE
KAPITI	56	Q 66 NW
KAPONGA	21	G 29 NE
KAPOWAIRUA	1	B 1 NW
KAPUKA	59	K 68 SE
KAPUKA SOUTH	59	K 68 SE
KAPUNI	21	G 29 NE
KARA	4	H 8 SW
KARAHAKI	1	I 30 SE
KARAKA	7	K 16 NW
KARAKARIKI	9	K 20 SE
KARAMEA	31	Y 39 NW
KARAMU	9	L 20 SW
KARANGAHAKE	8	N 18 NE
KARANGARUA	43	P 52 NW
KARAPIRO	10	N 20 SE
KARATIA	1	B 2 NW
KAREKARE	7	I 15 SW
KAREPONIA	1	D 4 SW
KARERE	23	M 34 SE
KARETU	4	G 7 SW
KAREWAREWA	23	O 31 SW
KARIOI	17	M 29 NE
KARITANE	56	S 63 SE
KARORO	38	U 46 NW
KARUHIRUHI	3	D 7 NE

K

Location	Map No.	Ref

K

KATEA — 60 — O 68 NE
KATIKATI — 10 — O 18 SE
KATIKI — 56 — T 62 NW
KAUAERANGA — 8 — N 16 SW
KAUANA — 58 — J 66 NE
KAUANGAROA — 22 — L 32 NE
KAUKAPAKAPA — 7 — I 13 SW
KAUKAPAKAPA — 9 — G 29 SW
KAUPOKONUI — 21 — G 29 SW
KAURI — 4 — H 8 NE
KAURI FLAT — 9 — J 20 NE
KAURITUTAHI — 7 — J 16 NW
KAUROA — 9 — K 20 NW
KAURU HILL — 50 — S 60 SE
KAUWHATA — 23 — M 34 NW
KAWA — 6 — M 11 NW
KAWAKAWA — 3 — G 6 SE
KAWAKAWA BAY — 7 — L 15 SW
KAWARAU FALLS — 53 — L 60 SW
KAWATIRI — 34 — A 41 SW
KAWAUITAHI — 16 — L 27 NE
KAWERAU — 12 — R 22 NE
KAWERUA — 3 — D 8 NE
KAWHIA — 9 — J 21 SE
KAWITI — 2 — G 6 SW
KEKERENGU — 36 — G 63 NW
KELCHERS — 50 — T 58 SW
KELLYS BAY — 5 — G 11 SE
KELSO — 55 — N 65 NW
KELVIN HEIGHTS — 52 — K 60 SE
KENANA — 2 — E 4 SW
KENEPURU HEAD — 29 — G 38 SE
KENNEDY BAY — 6 — N 14 NW
KENNINGTON — 59 — K 68 NW
KEREONE — 10 — N 19 SW
KEREPEHI — 8 — M 17 SE
KERERU — 18 — O 30 SE
KERERUTAHI — 13 — T 22 NE
KERETA — 6 — M 15 NE
KERETU — 13 — V 24 NE
KERIKERI — 2 — G 5 SW
KERIKERI INLET — 2 — G 5 SE
KERRYTOWN — 45 — U 56 NE
KIA ORA — 50 — T 60 NE
KIHIKIHI — 9 — M 21 SW
KIHITU — 19 — U 27 SE
KIKIWA — 35 — B 41 SW
KILGRAM — 36 — F 42 NE
KILLINCHY — 41 — Y 53 NE
KIMBELL — 44 — S 54 SE
KIMBERLEY — 41 — Y 51 SW
KIMBOLTON — 23 — N 32 SE
KIMIHIA — 9 — L 18 SW
KINA — 32 — C 38 SW
KINESS — 55 — P 66 SE
KINGSDOWN — 50 — U 57 NE
KINGSEAT — 7 — J 16 SE
KINGSTON — 53 — L 62 SW
KINLEITH — 10 — O 23 NW
KINLOCH
  (QUEENSTOWN LAKES) — 52 — J 59 SW
  (TAUPO) — 11 — O 25 NE
KINOHAKU — 9 — J 22 NE
KIOKIO — 9 — L 22 NE
KIRETEHERE — 9 — J 23 NW
KIRIKAU — 16 — L 26 SW
KIRIOKE — 8 — F 7 NW
KIRIPAKA — 4 — I 8 NW
KIRIROKE — 63 — F 1 NE
KIRITAKI — 23 — O 33 SW
KIRWEE — 41 — Y 51 SE
KIWITAHI — 10 — N 19 SW
KIWITEA — 23 — N 33 SW
KNAPDALE — 55 — M 66 NW
KNOBS FLAT — 52 — I 60 SW
KOEKE JUNCTION — 17 — N 30 SW
KOHATU — 32 — B 40 NW
KOHE — 1 — D 6 NW
KOHEKOHE — 7 — I 16 SE
KOHI — 22 — I 30 SE
KOHIKA — 50 — U 57 SW
KOHINUI — 23 — O 34 SW
KOHUKOHU — 2 — E 6 SW
KOHUMARU — 2 — E 5 NW
KOHURATAHI — 15 — J 27 NE
KOITIATA — 25 — K 32 SE
KOKAKO — 19 — T 26 NE
KOKATAHI — 38 — T 48 NE
KOKIRI — 38 — V 46 NW
KOKOAMO — 50 — S 59 SE
KOKONGA — 49 — R 61 NW
KOKOPU — 4 — G 8 SE
KOMAKO — 23 — O 33 NW
KOMAKORAU — 9 — L 19 NE
KOMATA — 8 — N 17 SE
KOMATA NORTH — 8 — N 17 SW
KOMATA REEF — 8 — N 17 SE
KOMOKORIKI — 5 — I 12 SW
KONGAHU — 31 — X 39 SE
KONINI — 26 — N 35 NE
KONONI — 55 — O 65 SW
KOPAKI — 9 — L 23 SE
KOPANE — 23 — M 34 NW
KOPARA — 38 — W 46 SE
KOPIKOPIKO — 25 — N 35 NW
KOPU — 8 — N 16 SW
KOPUA — 24 — P 33 NE
KOPUARANGA — 25 — N 37 NW
KOPUAROA — 14 — Y 21 SE
KOPUAWHARA — 20 — W 27 SE
KOPUKU — 7 — L 17 NW
KOPURIKI — 12 — S 23 SW
KOPUTAROA — 25 — L 35 SE
KORAKONUI — 9 — M 22 NW
KORANGA — 13 — V 24 NW
KOREMOA — 3 — F 10 SE
KORERE — 34 — A 40 SE
KORINITI — 22 — L 30 NW
KORITO — 15 — J 27 SW
KOROMATUA — 9 — L 20 NW
KOROMIKO — 29 — F 39 SE
KORORA — 26 — P 35 NW
KORU — 15 — J 26 SW
KOTARE — 15 — J 26 NW
KOTEMAORI — 18 — T 27 SW
KOTINGA — 31 — A 37 NE

KOTUKU — 38 — V 46 SW
KOURAWHERO — 5 — I 12 SE
KOUTU — 3 — D 7 NE
KOWAI BUSH — 41 — X 50 SW
KOWHAI — 36 — E 45 SW
KOWHATU — 50 — S 57 SE
KOWHITIRANGI — 38 — T 48 NE
KUAOTUNU — 8 — N 14 NE
KUKU — 25 — L 36 NW
KUKUMOA — 13 — U 21 SW
KUMARA — 38 — U 47 NW
KUMARA JUNCTION — 38 — U 46 SW
KUMEROA — 23 — O 34 NW
KUMEU — 5 — I 14 NE
KUPE — 15 — H 28 NE
KURANUI — 18 — M 19 SE
KURATAU — 16 — N 26 NE
KURATAU JUNCTION — 16 — N 26 NW
KURIPAPANGO — 18 — Q 29 NW
KURITUNU STREAM — 6 — K 22 NW
KURIWAO — 60 — O 67 NW
KUROW — 50 — R 58 SE
KUTARERE — 13 — T 21 SE
KUTIA — 17 — N 20 NE
KYEBURN — 49 — Q 61 NE
KYEBURN DIGGINGS — 49 — R 60 NW
KYLE — 41 — Y 54 NW

L

LADBROOKS — 42 — Z 52 NE
LADY BARKLY — 58 — J 66 SE
LAGMHOR — 41 — W 53 SE
LAINGHOLM — 7 — J 15 SW
LAIRDVALE — 16 — L 26 NE
LAKE ALICE — 23 — L 33 NE
LAKE COLERIDGE — 41 — V 51 NE
LAKE FERRY — 27 — K 40 NE
LAKE GRASSMERE — 36 — G 41 SE
LAKE HAWEA — 48 — M 58 NE
LAKE HAYES — 53 — L 60 SE
LAKE KANIERE — 38 — U 48 NW
LAKE MOERAKI — 43 — M 53 NE
LAKE OHAU LODGE — 49 — P 56 NW
LAKE OHIA — 1 — D 4 NW
LAKE OKATAINA — 12 — Q 22 NE
LAKE PARINGA — 43 — N 53 NE
LAKE PUKAKI — 44 — Q 55 SE
LAKE ROTOMA — 12 — R 21 SW
LAKE TEKAPO — 44 — R 54 SE
LAKE WAITAKI — 50 — R 58 SE
LAKESIDE — 42 — Z 53 SW
LANGRIDGE — 36 — D 43 NE
LANGS BEACH — 4 — I 10 NE
LANSDOWN — 50 — T 58 NE
LANSDOWNE — 42 — A 52 NW
LARRYS CREEK — 33 — X 43 SW
LAUDER — 49 — O 60 SE
LAURISTON — 41 — W 53 NE
LAWRENCE — 55 — O 65 SE
LE BONS BAY — 42 — C 53 NE
LEAMINGTON
  (HURUNUI DISTRICT) — 40 — C 47 SE
  (WAIPA DISTRICT) — 9 — M 20 SE
LEE FLAT — 56 — Q 64 SW
LEE STREAM — 56 — Q 64 SE
LEES VALLEY — 42 — Z 53 NW
LEESTON — 42 — Z 53 NW
LEIGH — 6 — J 11 SE
LEITHFIELD — 42 — A 50 NE
LEITHFIELD BEACH — 42 — A 50 NE
LEPPERTON — 15 — H 27 NW
LETTS GULLY — 54 — N 61 SE
LEVELS — 45 — U 56 NW
LEVELS VALLEY — 45 — U 56 NW
LEVIN — 25 — L 36 NE
LICHFIELD — 10 — O 22 NW
LILYBANK STATION — 44 — S 53 NW
LIMEHILLS (CENTRE BUSH) — 58 — J 66 NE
LIMESTONE DOWNS — 7 — J 18 NW
LIMESTONE ISLAND — 4 — H 8 SE
LIMESTONE VALLEY — 44 — S 55 SE
LINCOLN — 42 — Z 52 SE
LINDIS VALLEY — 48 — N 59 NE
LINKWATER — 29 — F 39 NE
LINTLEY — 59 — K 64 SW
LINTON — 23 — M 34 SE
LISMORE — 41 — V 54 NE
LITTLE AKALOA — 42 — B 52 SE
LITTLE BAY — 6 — N 13 SW
LITTLE HUIA — 7 — J 15 SE
LITTLE RAKAIA — 41 — Y 53 SE
LITTLE RIVER — 42 — A 53 NE
LITTLE VALLEY — 54 — O 62 NW
LITTLE WAIHI — 12 — R 20 NW
LITTLE WANGANUI — 31 — X 40 NE
LIVINGSTONE
  (MANAWATU DISTRICT) — 23 — N 32 NW
  (WAITAKI DISTRICT) — 50 — S 60 NW
LOBURN — 42 — Z 50 NE
LOBURN NORTH — 42 — Z 50 NE
LOCH NORRIE — 5 — I 13 SW
LOCHIEL — 58 — J 67 NE
LOCHINDORB — 60 — O 67 NW
LONG BEACH — 56 — S 64 NE
LONGBEACH — 45 — W 55 NE
LONGBURN — 23 — M 34 SE
LONGBUSH
  (CARTERTON) — 28 — M 38 SE
  (INVERCARGILL CITY) — 59 — K 68 NE
LONGFORD — 34 — Z 42 NW
LONGLANDS — 18 — S 30 SW
LONGRIDGE NORTH — 59 — K 64 SE
LONGWOOD — 58 — I 68 NW
LORNEVILLE — 59 — K 68 NW
LOVELLS FLAT — 55 — P 66 SE
LOWBURN — 54 — M 60 SE
LOWCLIFFE — 45 — W 55 NW
LOWER HUTT — 27 — K 39 NW
LOWER KAIMAI — 10 — P 20 NW
LOWER KAWHATAU — 23 — N 31 NE
LOWER MOUTERE — 32 — B 38 SE
LOWER NEVIS — 53 — L 61 SE
LOWER SELWYN HUTS — 42 — Z 53 NE
LOWER SHOTOVER — 53 — L 60 SW
LOWER WAIHOU — 1 — D 6 SE
LOWGARTH — 15 — H 28 SW
LOWTHER — 53 — K 64 NW
LUGGATE — 48 — M 59 NE

LUMSDEN — 59 — K 64 SW
LYALLDALE — 50 — U 57 NW
LYELL — 34 — X 42 NE
LYNDHURST — 41 — W 52 SE
LYNTON DOWNS — 36 — D 45 NE
LYTTELTON — 42 — A 52 NE

M

MAATA — 21 — H 29 NE
MABEL BUSH — 59 — K 67 NE
MACANDREW BAY — 56 — S 65 NE
MACKAYTOWN — 8 — N 18 NE
MACLENNAN — 60 — O 68 SW
MACRAES FLAT — 56 — R 62 NE
MAERAWEKA — 50 — S 61 NE
MAEREWHENUA — 50 — S 59 SW
MAEWA — 23 — M 33 SE
MAHAKIRAU — 6 — N 15 NW
MAHANA — 32 — B 39 NE
MAHANGA — 20 — W 27 SE
MAHARAHARA — 23 — O 34 NW
MAHARAKEKE — 24 — Q 32 SW
MAHENO — 50 — T 61 NW
MAHIA — 20 — X 27 SW
MAHIA BEACH — 20 — W 27 SE
MAHINEPUA — 2 — F 4 SE
MAHITAHI — 43 — O 52 SW
MAHOE — 15 — G 28 SE
MAHOENUI — 9 — J 24 NE
MAHUNA — 14 — Z 21 NW
MAHURANGI — 6 — J 12 SE
MAHURANGI WEST — 5 — J 12 SW
MAHUTA
  (KAIPARA) — 3 — F 10 NW
  (WAIKATO) — 9 — L 19 NW
MAIHIIHI — 9 — M 22 SW
MAIMAI — 33 — W 44 NE
MAIORO — 7 — J 16 SW
MAIROA — 9 — K 23 NW
MAITAHI — 3 — F 9 NW
MAITLAND — 55 — M 66 NE
MAKAHU — 15 — I 28 NE
MAKAKA — 9 — J 21 NE
MAKAKAHO — 22 — K 29 SW
MAKAKAHO JUNCTION — 22 — J 30 NE
MAKARA — 27 — I 39 NE
MAKARA BEACH — 20 — X 25 NW
MAKARAKA — 20 — X 25 NW
MAKARANUI — 17 — L 29 NE
MAKARAU — 5 — I 13 NW
MAKAREWA — 59 — J 67 SE
MAKAREWA JUNCTION — 59 — J 67 SE
MAKARORA — 48 — M 56 NE
MAKAURI — 20 — X 25 NW
MAKERUA — 25 — M 35 NW
MAKETU — 12 — R 20 NW
MAKETU PA — 50 — U 58 NE
MAKIKIHI — 50 — U 58 NE
MAKINO — 23 — M 33 NE
MAKIRIKIRI SOUTH — 23 — L 32 SE
MAKOMAKO
  (OTOROHANGA) — 9 — K 21 NW
  (TARARUA) — 25 — N 35 NW
MAKORORI — 20 — Y 25 NW
MAKOTUKU — 24 — P 33 NE
MAKURI — 26 — O 35 SE
MAMAKU — 10 — P 22 NW
MAMARANUI — 3 — F 9 NW
MANAIA
  (SOUTH TARANAKI) — 21 — G 29 SE
  (THAMES COROMANDEL) — 6 — M 15 NE
MANAKAU — 27 — L 36 NW
MANANUI — 37 — T 47 SW
MANAPOURI — 58 — G 64 NE
MANAROA — 29 — G 38 SW
MANAWAORA — 2 — H 6 NW
MANAWARU — 10 — N 19 NE
MANDEVILLE — 59 — L 66 NE
MANDEVILLE NORTH — 42 — A 51 NW
MANGAETUROA — 22 — L 29 NW
MANGAHAO — 23 — N 34 SE
MANGAITI — 10 — N 18 SE
MANGAKAHU VALLEY — 16 — M 25 SW
MANGAKINO — 10 — N 23 SE
MANGAKURA — 5 — I 12 SW
MANGAKURI BEACH — 24 — S 32 SE
MANGAMAHU — 22 — L 31 NE
MANGAMAIRE — 25 — N 35 NW
MANGAMAUNU — 36 — E 45 NE
MANGAMINGI — 21 — I 29 NW
MANGAMUKA — 2 — E 5 SW
MANGAMUKA BRIDGE — 2 — E 5 SW
MANGAMUTU — 26 — N 35 NE
MANGAONE — 26 — O 35 SW
MANGAONOHO — 23 — N 31 SW
MANGAORAPA — 24 — Q 34 SE
MANGAORE — 25 — M 35 SW
MANGAORONGO — 9 — M 22 NW
MANGAOTAKI — 9 — K 23 SW
MANGAPA — 2 — E 5 SE
MANGAPAI — 4 — H 9 NE
MANGAPAPARO — 18 — K 26 NW
MANGAPEHI — 11 — L 24 NE
MANGAPIKO — 9 — L 21 NE
MANGAPIKO VALLEY — 8 — M 18 NW
MANGARAKAU — 31 — Z 35 SE
MANGARATA — 34 — Z 42 NW
MANGARAWA — 23 — O 34 NW
MANGARIMU — 23 — O 32 NW
MANGATAINOKA — 23 — N 34 SE
MANGATAIORE — 1 — D 5 NE
MANGATANGI — 7 — L 16 SW
MANGATARA — 3 — F 9 SW
MANGATARAIRE — 2 — E 6 SE
MANGATARATA
  (GISBORNE) — 14 — Y 22 SW
  (HAURAKI) — 8 — M 17 NW
MANGATAWHIRI — 7 — L 17 NW
MANGATEA — 11 — L 23 NW
MANGATEPARU — 10 — N 19 NE
MANGATERETERE — 18 — S 30 SE
MANGATOETOE — 1 — D 5 NE
MANGATOI — 10 — P 20 SE
MANGATOKI — 21 — G 29 NE
MANGATORO — 23 — P 34 NW

MANGATU — 3 — E 8 N
MANGATUNA
  (GISBORNE) — 14 — Y 23 S
  (TARARUA) — 24 — P 34 N
MANGATUPOTO — 11 — L 25 N
MANGAWARA — 9 — L 18 S
MANGAWEKA — 23 — N 31 N
MANGAWHAI — 4 — I 10 S
MANGAWHAI HEADS — 4 — J 10 S
MANGAWHARE — 3 — F 9 S
MANGAWHATA — 23 — M 34 S
MANGAWHERO
  (FAR NORTH) — 3 — E 7 N
  (OTOROHANGA) — 9 — L 22 S
MANGAWHIO — 22 — J 30 S
MANGLES VALLEY — 34 — Z 42 N
MANGONUI — 2 — E 4 S
MANGOREI — 15 — G 27 N
MANGUNGU — 2 — E 6 S
MANIATUTU — 12 — R 20 S
MANLY — 6 — J 13 S
MANOEKA — 10 — Q 20 N
MANSONS SIDING — 16 — M 27 N
MANUI — 23 — N 31 N
MANUKA CREEK — 55 — P 66 N
MANUNUI — 1 — C 5 S
MANUNUI — 16 — M 26 N
MANUTAHI — 21 — H 30 S
MANUTUKE — 20 — X 25 S
MAPAU — 4 — G 11 N
MAPIU — 16 — L 24 S
MAPUA — 32 — C 39 N
MARA — 26 — P 36 N
MARAEHARA — 14 — Z 20 S
MARAEKAKAHO — 24 — R 30 S
MARAEROA — 2 — E 6 S
MARAETAHA — 20 — X 26 N
MARAETAI
  (MANUKAU CITY) — 6 — K 15 S
  (TAUPO) — 10 — N 23 S
MARAHAU — 32 — B 37 S
MARAMARUA — 7 — L 17 S
MARAMARUA MILL — 7 — L 17 N
MARAREWA — 32 — B 40 N
MARATOTO — 8 — O 17 S
MARERETU — 4 — H 10 N
MARIMA — 25 — N 35 N
MARIRI — 32 — B 38 S
MARKET CROSS — 31 — Y 39 N
MARLOW — 6 — G 7 S
MAROHEMO — 4 — H 11 S
MAROKOPA — 9 — J 22 S
MAROMAKU — 3 — G 7 S
MARONAN — 41 — V 54 S
MAROPIU — 3 — F 9 N
MAROTIRI — 25 — L 35 S
MARSDEN
  (GREY) — 38 — U 46 S
  (WHANGAREI) — 4 — I 9 S
MARSDEN BAY — 4 — I 9 N
MARSDEN POINT — 4 — I 9 S
MARSHLANDS — 29 — G 40 N
MARTINBOROUGH — 28 — M 39 N
MARTON — 23 — L 32 S
MARTON BLOCK — 23 — O 32 N
MARUA — 4 — H 7 S
MARUIA — 34 — Y 44 S
MARUIA SPRINGS — 34 — Z 45 S
MARUMARU — 19 — U 26 S
MARYBANK
  (NELSON CITY) — 29 — D 39 S
  (WANGANUI) — 22 — K 32 S
MASONS FLAT — 42 — A 48 S
MASSEY — 5 — I 14 S
MASSEY UNIVERSITY — 23 — M 34 S
MASTERTON — 28 — M 37 S
MATA
  (FAR NORTH) — 2 — E 6 N
  (WHANGAREI) — 4 — I 9 N
MATAHANEA — 13 — U 22 S
MATAHAPA — 13 — T 22 S
MATAHI — 13 — T 23 N
MATAHINA — 13 — S 22 S
MATAHIWI
  (MASTERTON) — 25 — M 37 S
  (WANGANUI) — 22 — L 30 N
MATAHURU — 7 — L 18 S
MATAI
  (GREY) — 33 — V 45 S
  (MATAMATA PIAKO) — 10 — N 20 S
MATAIKONA — 26 — P 36 S
MATAKANA — 6 — J 12 S
MATAKANUI — 49 — O 60 S
MATAKAWAU — 7 — I 16 N
MATAKAWAU POINT — 7 — I 16 N
MATAKITAKI — 34 — Z 43 N
MATAKOHE — 4 — G 10 N
MATAMATA — 10 — N 20 N
MATAMAU — 23 — P 33 N
MATANGI — 9 — M 20 N
MATANGIRAU — 2 — E 5 N
MATAPIHI — 10 — P 19 S
MATAPOURI — 4 — I 7 S
MATAPU — 21 — H 29 N
MATARAE — 56 — Q 63 S
MATARANGI — 6 — N 14 S
MATARAU — 4 — H 8 N
MATARAUA — 3 — F 7 S
MATARAWA — 27 — L 38 S
MATARIKI — 31 — A 40 S
MATAROA — 17 — N 30 S
MATATA — 12 — S 21 N
MATATOKI — 8 — N 17 N
MATAU — 15 — I 27 S
MATAURA — 59 — L 67 S
MATAURA ISLAND — 59 — L 68 S
MATAURI BAY — 2 — G 4 S
MATAWAI — 13 — V 23 S
MATAWAIA — 3 — G 6 S
MATAWHERO — 20 — X 25 S
MATIERE — 16 — L 25 S
MATIHETIHE — 1 — D 5 N
MATINGARAHI — 7 — L 15 S
MATIRA — 9 — J 19 S
MATIRI — 34 — Z 41 S
MAUKU — 7 — J 16 S
MAUNGAKARAMEA — 23 — P 34 N

Location	Map No.	Ref

MAUNGAPOHATU .... 13 T 24 SE
MAUNGATAPERE .... 4 H 8 SW
MAUNGATAUTARI .... 10 N 21 NW
MAUNGATI .... 57 T 57 NE
MAUNGATIRO .... 50 S 58 NW
MAUNGATUA .... 56 R 65 NW
MAUNGATUROTO .... 4 H 10 SE
MAUNGAWERA .... 48 M58 SE
MAUNU .... 4 H 8 SE
MAURICEVILLE .... 25 M 36 SW
MAURICEVILLE WEST .... 25 N 36 NE
MAWARO .... 45 T 56 NE
MAWHERAITI .... 33 W 44 NE
MAXWELL .... 21 J 31 NE
MAYFIELD .... 41 V 53 SW
MAYTOWN .... 50 U 58 SW
MCLAREN .... 10 P 20 NW
MCLEANS ISLAND .... 42 Z 51 SE
MCLEOD BAY .... 4 I 9 NE
MCNAB .... 55 M66 SW
MEADOWBANK .... 56 S 62 SE
MEANEE .... 18 S 30 NE
MEDBURY .... 39 A 48 NE
MENIN REIKI .... 27 K 37 SE
MENZIES FERRY .... 59 L 68 NE
MERAEKAKAHO .... 8 R 30 SW
MERCER .... 7 K 17 NE
MEREMERE
 (SOUTH TARANAKI DISTRICT) .... 21 H 29 SE
 (WAIKATO DISTRICT) .... 7 K 17 SE
MERINGA .... 4 H 7 NW
MERINO DOWNS .... 55 M65 SE
MERITA .... 1 D 3 SE
MERRIVALE .... 58 I 66 SW
MERTON .... 56 S 63 SW
MESOPOTAMIA STATION .... 44 T 52 SW
METHVEN .... 41 W52 SW
MIDDLE VALLEY .... 45 T 55 NE
MIDDLEHURST .... 36 D 43 NE
MIDDLEMARCH .... 56 Q 63 NW
MIDHIRST .... 15 H 28 NW
MIHI .... 12 Q 24 NW
MIHIWAKA .... 56 S 64 NW
MIKIMIKI .... 25 M 37 NE
MIKO .... 33 X 41 NW
MILBURN .... 56 Q 66 NW
MILFORD .... 45 V 55 SW
MILFORD SOUND .... 47 H 58 SE
MILL CREEK .... 8 N 15 NE
MILLERS FLAT .... 54 N 64 NE
MILLERTON .... 33 X 41 NW
MILLTOWN .... 41 Y 53 NE
MILNTHORPE .... 31 A 36 NW
MILTON .... 56 Q 66 SW
MIMIHAU .... 59 L 67 SE
MIMIWHANGATA BAY .... 4 I 7 NW
MINA .... 40 C 47 SE
MINDEN .... 10 P 19 SW
MINGINUI .... 12 S 25 NW
MIRANDA .... 8 M 16 SW
MIRZA .... 36 G 42 SW
MITCHAM .... 41 X 53 NW
MITCHELLS .... 38 V 47 NW
MITIMITI .... 3 C 6 SE
MITITAI .... 3 F 10 NE
MOA CREEK .... 54 O 61 SE
MOA FLAT .... 54 N 64 NE
MOANA .... 38 V 46 SE
MOAWHANGO .... 17 O 30 NW
MOEATOA .... 9 J 23 NW
MOEAWATEA .... 22 I 29 SE
MOEHAU .... 8 E 7 NW
MOENGAWAHINE .... 4 G 8 NW
MOENUI .... 29 F 39 NW
MOERAKI .... 56 T 62 NE
MOERANGI
 (OTOROHANGA DISTRICT) .... 9 K 21 NW
 (TAUPO DISTRICT) .... 16 N 26 NW
MOEREWA .... 2 G 6 SW
MOEROA .... 22 I 29 NE
MOEWHARE .... 4 H 9 NW
MOHAKA .... 19 T 27 SE
MOHUITI .... 1 D 6 NE
MOKAI .... 11 Q 24 NW
MOKARA .... 18 S 27 SE
MOKAU
 (NEW PLYMOUTH DISTRICT) .... 15 I 25 NE
 (WHANGAREI DISTRICT) .... 2 H 6 SE
MOKAUITI .... 16 L 24 NW
MOKE CREEK .... 52 K 60 SW
MOKIHINUI .... 34 X 40 SW
MOKOIA .... 21 H 30 NE
MOKORETA .... 60 M68 NE
MOKOTUA .... 59 K 68 SE
MOLESWORTH .... 35 C 43 SE
MOMONA .... 56 Q 65 NE
MOMORANGI .... 29 F 39 NE
MONAVALE
 (MACKENZIE) .... 45 T 56 NW
 (WAIPA) .... 9 M 21 NW
MONEYMORE .... 55 P 66 SE
MONOWAI .... 58 G 65 NE
MONTALTO .... 41 V 53 NW
MOONLIGHT .... 38 R 62 SW
MORELAND .... 28 N 38 NE
MORERE .... 20 W27 NW
MORRINSVILLE .... 9 M 19 NE
MORRISONS .... 56 R 61 SE
MORRISONS BUSH .... 28 M 38 SW
MORTON MAINS .... 59 L 68 NW
MORVEN .... 50 U 59 NW
MOSGIEL .... 53 J 64 NW
MOSSBURN .... 58 J 66 NW
MOTAIREHE .... 8 M 10 SE
MOTAKOTAKO .... 9 J 20 SE
MOTATAU .... 4 G 7 NE
MOTEA .... 24 P 34 NE
MOTEO .... 18 R 30 NE
MOTU .... 13 V 23 NE
MOTU RIMU .... 59 K 68 SW
MOTUEKA .... 31 B 38 SE
MOTUKAIKA .... 50 T 56 NE
MOTUKARAKA .... 2 E 6 SW
MOTUKARARA .... 42 A 53 NW
MOTUKIORE .... 2 E 6 SW
MOTUMAOHO .... 9 M 19 SE

MOTUNAU BEACH .... 42 C 49 NW
MOTUNUI .... 15 H 26 SW
MOTUOAPA .... 17 O 26 SW
MOTUPIKO .... 32 B 40 NW
MOTUPIPI .... 32 B 38 SW
MOTUTANGI .... 1 C 3 SE
MOTUTERE .... 17 O 26 NE
MOTUTI .... 1 D 6 SE
MOTUTUA .... 3 D 7 NE
MOUMAHAKI .... 22 I 31 NE
MOUNT ALLAN .... 56 R 64 SE
MOUNT ASPIRING .... 48 L 57 SW
MOUNT BARKER .... 48 M59 NE
MT BIGGS .... 23 M 33 SW
MOUNT BRUCE .... 25 M 36 SE
MOUNT COOK/AORAKI .... 44 Q 53 NW
MT CREIGHTON .... 52 J 60 SE
MT CURL .... 22 M 32 NW
MT FURNEAUX .... 36 E 45 NW
MT FYFFE .... 36 E 45 NW
MT LYFORD VILLAGE .... 40 C 46 NW
MOUNT MAUNGANUI .... 10 P 19 SE
MOUNT NESSING .... 50 S 56 NE
MOUNT NICHOLAS .... 52 J 61 NE
MT PEEL .... 45 U 53 SE
MT PLEASANT .... 29 F 39 SE
MT PISA .... 54 M60 NE
MT POSSESSION .... 45 U 52 SE
MOUNT SOMERS .... 41 V 52 SW
MOUNT STOKER .... 56 R 63 SW
MOUNT STUART .... 55 P 66 NE
MT WESLEY .... 3 F 9 SE
MOUNT WHITE .... 41 X 49 NE
MOUREA .... 10 Q 21 SW
MOUTOA .... 25 L 36 SW
MOUTOHORA .... 13 V 23 NE
MOWHANAU BEACH .... 22 J 31 SE
MUHUNOA .... 25 L 36 NW
MUHUNOA EAST .... 25 L 36 NE
MUKAHANGA .... 29 F 36 SE
MURCHISON .... 34 Y 42 NE
MURIWAI .... 20 X 25 SW
MURIWAI BEACH .... 5 I 14 SW
MURUPARA .... 12 R 24 NE
MUTTONTOWN .... 54 N 61 SE
MYROSS BUSH .... 59 K 68 NW

N

NAIKE .... 9 K 18 SW
NAPIER .... 18 S 29 NE
NASEBY .... 49 Q 60 SE
NATIONAL PARK .... 16 M 27 SW
NAUMAI .... 4 G 10 SW
NEILS BEACH .... 47 K 55 NW
NELSON .... 32 C 39 NE
NELSON CREEK .... 33 V 45 SE
NENTHORN .... 56 R 62 SE
NESS VALLEY .... 7 L 15 SW
NETHERBY .... 9 L 19 NE
NETHERTON .... 8 N 17 SW
NEVIS CROSSING .... 53 M61 SW
NEW CREEK .... 34 X 42 NE
NEW PLYMOUTH .... 15 G 27 NW
NEWALL .... 21 F 28 NE
NEWHAVEN .... 60 P 68 SW
NEWLAND .... 41 X 53 SW
NEWMAN .... 25 N 35 SW
NEWSTEAD .... 9 M20 NW
NEWTON FLAT .... 34 Y 42 NW
NGAERE .... 21 H 29 NW
NGAHAPE .... 9 M 22 NW
NGAHERE .... 33 V 45 SW
NGAHINAPOURI .... 9 L 20 SW
NGAIOTONGA .... 2 H 6 NE
NGAKAWAU .... 33 X 41 NW
NGAKONUI
 (RUAPEHU) .... 16 L 25 SE
 (SOUTH WAIRARAPA) .... 28 M39 SE
NGAKURU .... 10 P 23 NE
NGAKUTA BAY .... 29 F 39 NE
NGAMATAPOURI .... 22 J 30 NE
NGAMOKO .... 23 P 32 SW
NGAPAENGA .... 9 K 23 NW
NGAPARA .... 50 S 59 SE
NGAPEKE .... 10 Q 19 SW
NGAPIPITO .... 3 F 7 NW
NGAPUHI .... 3 F 7 NW
NGAPUKE .... 16 M 26 NW
NGAPUNA
 (DUNEDIN CITY) .... 56 Q 62 SE
 (ROTORUA DISTRICT) .... 10 Q 22 NW
NGAPUTAHI .... 12 S 24 SE
NGARARATUNUA .... 4 H 8 NE
NGARIMU BAY .... 8 M 16 NE
NGAROMA .... 10 N 23 NW
NGAROTO .... 9 L 21 NE
NGARUA .... 10 N 19 SE
NGARUAWAHIA .... 9 L 19 SW
NGATAKI .... 1 B 3 NE
NGATAMAHINE .... 16 K 24 NE
NGATAPA .... 20 W25 NE
NGATEA .... 8 M 17 NE
NGATIMOTI .... 32 B 39 NW
NGATIRA .... 10 O 22 NW
NGATURI
 (TARARUA) .... 26 O 35 NW
 (WANGANUI) .... 22 L 31 SE
NGAWAKA .... 23 N 30 NE
NGAWAPURUA .... 23 O 34 SW
NGAWARO .... 10 P 21 NE
NGAWHA .... 2 F 6 SE
NGAWHA SPRINGS .... 2 F 6 SE
NGAWIHI .... 27 L 41 NW
NGONGOTAHA .... 10 P 21 NW
NGONGOTAHA VALLEY .... 10 P 22 NW
NGUNGURU .... 4 I 8 NE
NGUTUNUI .... 9 L 21 SW
NGUTUWERA .... 22 J 31 NE
NIAGARA .... 60 N 69 NW
NIGHTCAPS .... 58 I 66 NE
NIHONIHO .... 16 K 25 SE
NIKAU
 (BULLER) .... 33 X 40 SW
 (TARARUA) .... 25 N 35 NW
NIREAHA .... 25 M 35 SE
NOBLES .... 33 W 45 NW
NOKOMAI .... 53 K 63 NE
NOPERA .... 29 F 38 SE

NORMANBY
 (SOUTH TARANAKI) .... 21 H 29 SW
 (TIMARU) .... 50 U 57 NE
NORSEWOOD .... 23 P 33 NW
NORTH BRANCH .... 55 P 66 NE
NORTH EGMONT .... 15 G 28 NE
NORTH RIVER .... 4 I 9 SW
NORTH TAIERI .... 56 R 64 SE
NORTHOPE .... 58 J 67 NE
NORTON RESERVE .... 50 U 58 SW
NORWOOD .... 41 Y 52 SE
NOTOWN .... 38 V 46 NE
NUHAKA .... 20 W27 SW
NUKUHAU .... 11 P 25 NW
NUKUHOU NORTH .... 13 T 22 NE
NUKUMARU .... 22 J 31 SE
NUKUROA .... 50 U 58 SW
NUKUTAWHITI .... 3 F 8 NE

O

OAKLEIGH .... 4 H 9 NE
OAKURA
 (NEW PLYMOUTH) .... 21 F 27 NE
 (WHANGAREI) .... 2 H 6 SE
OAMARU .... 50 T 60 SE
OAMARU BAY .... 6 M 14 SE
OAONUI .... 21 F 28 SW
OARO .... 40 D 46 NE
OCEAN BEACH
 (HASTINGS) .... 24 T 31 NW
 (INVERCARGILL CITY) .... 59 J 69 NE
 (WHANGAREI) .... 4 I 9 NW
OCEAN VIEW .... 56 R 65 NE
OEO .... 21 F 29 SE
OHAAKI .... 12 Q 24 NW
OHAEAWAI .... 2 F 6 SE
OHAI .... 58 I 65 SW
OHAKEA .... 23 M 33 SW
OHAKUNE .... 17 M29 NW
OHAKURI .... 10 P 23 SW
OHANGAI .... 21 H 30 NE
OHAPI .... 45 U 55 SW
OHAU .... 25 L 36 NW
OHAUA .... 12 T 24 SW
OHAUITI .... 10 P 20 NE
OHAUPO .... 9 L 20 SE
OHAUTIRA .... 9 K 20 NE
OHAWE .... 21 G 30 NE
OHINEAKAI .... 14 Z 21 SW
OHINEPAKA .... 19 U 27 NW
OHINEPANEA .... 12 R 20 SE
OHINEWAI .... 9 L 18 SW
OHINGAITI .... 23 N 31 SW
OHIWA .... 13 U 21 SW
OHOKA .... 42 A 51 NW
OHOPE .... 13 T 21 NE
OHOTU .... 17 O 30 SW
OHUI .... 8 O 16 NE
OHUI SIDING .... 12 S 22 NW
OHUKA .... 19 U 26 NW
OHURA .... 16 K 26 NW
OHURI .... 3 E 7 NW
OIO .... 16 M 27 NW
OKAERIA .... 7 L 17 SE
OKAHU
 (KAITAIA) .... 1 D 5 NW
 (WHANGAREI) .... 16 L 25 SE
OKAHUKURA .... 16 L 25 NW
OKAHUNA .... 23 G 29 SE
OKAIHAU .... 2 F 6 NW
OKAINS BAY .... 42 C 52 SW
OKAKA .... 2 E 6 NE
OKAPU .... 9 J 21 SE
OKARAMIO .... 28 E 40 NE
OKARITO .... 37 Q 50 SW
OKATO .... 21 F 27 SW
OKAU .... 15 J 26 NW
OKAUIA .... 10 O 20 NW
OKAUIA PA .... 10 O 20 NW
OKERE FALLS .... 10 Q 21 SW
OKETE .... 9 K 20 NW
OKIATO .... 2 H 6 NW
OKIORE .... 13 U 22 SE
OKITU .... 20 X 25 SE
OKIWI .... 6 M 11 NE
OKIWI BAY .... 29 E 38 NE
OKOIA .... 22 K 32 NE
OKOKI .... 15 I 26 NW
OKORORE .... 42 Z 50 NW
OKUKU .... 5 J 13 SW
OKUPU .... 6 M 11 SE
OKURA .... 5 J 13 SW
OKURU .... 48 L 54 NE
OKUTI VALLEY .... 42 B 53 NW
OMAHA .... 5 J 12 NE
OMAHA FLATS .... 5 J 12 NW
OMAHU
 (HASTINGS) .... 18 S 30 SW
 (THAMES COROMANDEL) .... 8 N 17 NE
OMAHUTA .... 2 E 5 SE
OMAIO .... 13 W20 SW
OMAKAU .... 49 Q 60 SW
OMAKERE .... 24 R 32 SE
OMAMARI .... 3 E 9 NE
OMANA .... 4 G 9 SE
OMANAIA .... 3 E 7 NW
OMANAWA .... 10 P 20 NW
OMANAWA FALLS .... 10 Q 19 SW
OMANU BEACH .... 3 D 7 SE
OMAPERE .... 13 V 21 SW
OMATA .... 15 G 27 NW
OMATANE .... 23 O 31 NW
OMAUNU .... 2 F 5 NW
OMIHA .... 6 L 14 SW
OMIHI .... 42 B 49 NW
OMIMI .... 56 S 64 NE
OMOANA .... 22 I 29 NE
OMOKOROA .... 10 P 19 SW
OMORI .... 16 N 26 NE
OMOTO .... 38 U 46 NW
ONAERO .... 15 H 26 SE
ONE TREE POINT .... 4 I 9 NW
ONEKAKA .... 31 A 36 SE
ONEMANA .... 8 O 16 SE
ONEPOTO .... 19 T 26 NE
ONERAHI .... 4 H 8 SE

ONERIRI .... 5 H 11 SE
ONEROA .... 6 K 14 SE
ONETANGI .... 6 L 14 SW
ONEWHERO .... 7 K 17 SW
ONGAONGA .... 24 Q 32 NW
ONGARE POINT .... 10 P 18 SW
ONGARUE .... 11 L 25 NE
ONGARURU .... 14 Z 22 SW
ONOKE .... 1 D 6 SE
OPAEA .... 17 N 30 NE
OPAHEKE .... 7 K 16 NE
OPAHI .... 4 G 9 NW
OPAKI .... 25 N 37 NW
OPAKU .... 21 I 30 NE
OPAPA .... 24 R 31 SW
OPAPE .... 13 V 21 SW
OPARARA .... 31 Y 39 SW
OPARAU .... 9 K 21 SW
OPARURE .... 9 L 23 NW
OPATU .... 16 K 26 SE
OPHIR .... 49 O 61 NE
OPIHI .... 45 U 55 SW
OPIKI .... 25 M 35 NW
OPIO .... 58 I 66 SE
OPITO .... 8 O 14 NW
OPONAE .... 13 U 23 NE
OPONONI .... 3 D 7 NW
OPORO .... 58 J 67 SE
OPOTIKI .... 13 U 21 SE
OPOURIAO .... 12 T 22 NW
OPOUTAMA .... 20 W27 SE
OPOUTEKE .... 8 O 16 NE
OPUA .... 2 G 6 NE
OPUATIA .... 4 H 7 NE
OPUAWHANGA .... 4 H 7 NE
OPUHA .... 45 T 55 SE
OPUNAKE .... 21 F 29 NW
ORAKA BEACH .... 20 X 27 SW
ORAKAU .... 9 M 21 SW
ORAKEIKORAKO .... 11 P 24 NW
ORAKIPAOA .... 45 V 56 NW
ORANGAPAI .... 56 Q 61 SE
ORANGIMEA .... 22 J 30 SE
ORAORA .... 3 E 7 SW
ORAPIU .... 6 L 14 SW
ORARI .... 45 V 55 NW
ORARI BRIDGE .... 45 U 54 SE
ORAUTA .... 2 G 6 SW
ORAUTOHA .... 16 L 28 SW
ORAWAU .... 1 D 6 NE
ORAWIA .... 58 H 66 SE
OREPUKI .... 58 H 67 SE
ORERE .... 7 L 15 SE
ORERE POINT .... 7 L 15 SE
ORETI BEACH .... 58 J 68 SE
ORETI PLAINS .... 58 J 66 SW
OREWA .... 5 J 13 NW
ORINGI .... 23 O 34 SE
ORINI .... 9 M 18 SW
ORMOCO .... 32 B 39 NW
ORMOND .... 20 W 25 SW
ORMONDVILLE .... 24 P 33 NE
OROMAHOE .... 2 G 6 NW
ORONGO .... 8 N 16 SW
ORONGO BAY .... 2 H 6 NW
ORONGORONGO .... 27 J 40 NE
OROPI .... 10 P 20 SE
OROUA DOWNS .... 23 L 34 SE
ORTON
 (TIMARU) .... 45 V 55 SE
 (WAIKATO) .... 7 K 17 SE
ORUA BAY .... 7 I 15 SE
ORUAITI .... 2 E 4 SW
ORUAITI BEACH .... 14 X 19 SE
ORUAIWI .... 16 M25 SW
ORUANUI .... 11 Q 24 SW
ORUATUA .... 17 O 26 NW
ORUAWHARO .... 5 I 11 SW
ORURU .... 2 E 4 SW
OSBORNE .... 56 S 64 NE
OSTEND .... 6 K 14 SE
OTA CREEK .... 59 L 67 SE
OTAHA .... 2 G 5 NW
OTAHU FLAT .... 58 H 66 NW
OTAHUTI .... 58 J 67 SW
OTAIHANGA .... 25 K 37 NW
OTAIKA .... 4 H 8 SE
OTAIO .... 50 U 57 SW
OTAIO GORGE .... 50 T 57 SE
OTAIRI .... 23 M 31 NE
OTAITAI BUSH .... 58 I 68 NE
OTAKAIRANGI .... 4 H 8 NW
OTAKEHO .... 21 G 29 SW
OTAKI .... 25 K 36 SE
OTAKI BEACH .... 25 K 36 SE
OTAKI FORKS .... 25 L 37 NW
OTAKIRI .... 13 S 21 SW
OTAKOU .... 56 S 64 SE
OTAMA .... 58 L 65 SE
OTAMAKAPUA .... 23 N 31 SE
OTAMARAKAU .... 12 R 20 SE
OTAMAROA .... 14 X 19 SE
OTAMAURI .... 23 Q 29 SE
OTAMITA .... 59 L 66 NE
OTANA .... 57 T 24 NE
OTANE
 (CENTRAL HAWKES BAY) .... 24 R 32 NW
 (WHAKATANE) .... 13 T 24 NE
OTANGAROA .... 2 E 5 NE
OTANGIWAI .... 16 L 25 NW
OTANOMOMO .... 60 P 67 SW
OTAO .... 2 G 6 NE
OTAPIRI .... 59 K 66 NW
OTARA
 (OPOTIKI) .... 13 U 22 NE
 (SOUTHLAND) .... 59 M69 SW
OTARAIA .... 60 M67 NE
OTARAMARAE .... 10 Q 21 SE
OTATARA .... 23 J 68 SE
OTAUA
 (FAR NORTH) .... 3 F 7 NW
 (FRANKLIN) .... 7 J 17 NE
OTAUTAU .... 58 I 67 NE
OTATU .... 6 M 13 SE
OTEHEI BAY .... 2 H 5 SW
OTEHIRINAKI .... 13 W20 SW

Location	Map No.	Ref
OTEKAIEKE	50	S 59 NW
OTEKURA	60	P 68 NW
OTEMATATA	49	Q 58 NE
OTERAMIKA	59	L 68 SW
OTEWA	9	L 22 SE
OTIAKE	50	R 59 NE
OTIKERAMA	55	M 66 SE
OTIPUA	50	U 57 NW
OTIRA	38	V 48 NE
OTIRIA	2	G 6 SW
OTOKIA	56	R 65 SW
OTOKO	13	W 24 NW
OTONGA	4	H 7 SE
OTOROA	2	F 5 NE
OTOROHANGA	9	L 22 NW
OTUHI	4	H 9 NW
OTUKOU	16	N 27 NW
OTUNUI	16	L 26 NW
OTUREHUA	49	P 60 NE
OTUROA	10	P 21 SE
OTURU	1	D 5 NW
OTUWHARE	13	W 20 SW
OTWAY	10	N 18 SW
OUE	3	E 7 NW
OUEROA	24	R 33 NE
OURUHIA	42	A 51 SE
OUTRAM	56	R 65 NW
OVERDALE	41	X 53 NE
OWAHANGA	26	P 36 NE
OWAIRAKA VALLEY	9	M 22 NE
OWAKA	60	P 68 NW
OWAKA VALLEY	60	O 68 NE
OWARE	59	M 67 SW
OWEN JUNCTION	34	Z 41 NE
OWEN RIVER	34	Z 41 NW
OWHANGO	16	M 26 NW
OWHATA		
(FAR NORTH)	1	C 6 NE
(ROTORUA)	10	O 22 NW
OWHIWA	4	I 8 SW
OXFORD	41	Y 50 SE
P		
PAEKAKARIKI	27	J 37 SE
PAEMAKO	16	K 24 NW
PAENGA	34	Y 43 NW
PAENGAROA	10	Q 20 SE
PAEPAERAHI	9	M 21 SE
PAERATA	7	K 16 SW
PAERATA RIDGE	13	U 21 SW
PAERAU	54	P 62 SE
PAEROA	8	N 17 SE
PAEWHENUA	9	M 22 SW
PAHI	4	H 11 NW
PAHIA	58	H 68 NE
PAHIATUA	26	N 35 NE
PAHOIA	10	P 19 SW
PAHOU	12	T 21 SW
PAIAKA	2	G 7 NE
PAIHIA	2	G 6 SE
PAKANAE	3	G 7 NE
PAKARAE	14	Y 24 SE
PAKARAKA	2	G 6 SW
PAKAUTUTU	18	Q 28 NE
PAKEHO	9	K 23 NE
PAKIHIKURA	23	N 32 NW
PAKIPAKI	24	R 30 SE
PAKIRI	5	J 11 SE
PAKOTAI	3	F 8 NE
PAKOWHAI	18	S 30 NW
PAKURATAHI	27	L 38 NW
PAKURATAHI FORKS	27	L 38 NW
PALM BEACH	6	K 14 SE
PALMERSTON	56	S 62 SE
PALMERSTON NORTH	23	M 34 SE
PAMAPURIA	1	D 5 NW
PANETAPU	9	M 22 NE
PANGATOTARA	32	B 38 SW
PANGURU	1	D 6 SE
PAPAAROHA	8	M 14 NE
PAPAKAI	16	N 27 NW
PAPAKAIO	50	T 60 NE
PAPAKURA	7	K 16 NE
PAPAMOA	10	Q 20 NW
PAPAMOA BEACH	10	Q 19 SW
PAPANUI JUNCTION	17	M 30 SE
PAPARANGI	22	K 30 SW
PAPARATA	5	K 16 SE
PAPARIMU	7	L 16 SW
PAPAROA	4	H 10 SW
PAPARORE	1	C 4 NE
PAPATAWA	23	O 34 NW
PAPATEA	14	X 19 SW
PAPATOTARA	58	H 67 NW
PAPATOWAI	60	O 69 NW
PAPAWAI	28	M 38 SW
PAPAWERA	14	Y 21 NE
PAPONGA	1	D 6 NE
PAPUA	12	S 25 NE
PAPUERU	12	S 25 NE
PARA	29	F 39 SE
PARADISE	47	J 59 NE
PARAHAKA	4	H 9 SW
PARAHI	4	G 10 NE
PARAKAI	5	I 13 SW
PARAKAO	3	G 8 SW
PARAKIWAI	8	O 17 NW
PARANUI	1	D 4 SE
PARAOANUI	13	T 23 NE
PARAOANUI PA	13	T 23 NE
PARAPARA		
(FAR NORTH)	1	D 4 SE
(TASMAN)	31	A 36 NE
PARAPARAUMU	30	K 37 SW
PARAU	7	I 15 SE
PARAWA	53	K 63 SW
PARAWAI	8	N 16 SW
PARAWERA	9	M 21 SW
PAREKARANGI	10	Q 23 SW
PAREMATA	14	Y 24 NE
PAREMOREMO	5	J 14 NW
PAREORA	50	U 57 NE
PAREORA WEST	50	U 56 SW
PARETAI	60	P 67 SW
PAREWANUI	23	L 33 SE
PARIHAUHAU	22	L 31 NW
PARIKAWA	36	F 43 SE
PARIKINO	22	K 31 NW
PARIOKARA	13	W 20 SW
PARK HILL	55	N 65 NW
PARKHURST	5	H 13 SE
PARKVILLE	25	N 36 NW
PARNASSUS	40	D 47 NW
PAROA		
(GISBORNE)	12	S 21 NE
(GREY)	38	U 46 NW
PAROA BAY	2	H 6 NW
PARORE	3	F 9 SE
PARUA BAY	4	I 8 SW
PATANGATA	24	R 32 NE
PATAUA NORTH	4	I 8 SE
PATAUA SOUTH	4	I 8 SE
PATEA	21	I 31 NW
PATEAROA	54	Q 61 SW
PATERANGI	9	L 21 NE
PATETONGA	8	M 18 NE
PATOKA	18	R 29 NE
PATONS ROCK	31	A 36 SE
PATUKI	29	F 36 NE
PATUMAHOE	7	J 16 SE
PATURAU RIVER	31	Z 35 SW
PATUTAHI	20	X 25 NW
PAUA	1	B 2 NW
PAUANUI	8	O 16 NE
PAUATAHANUI	27	J 38 SE
PAURI VILLAGE	22	K 32 NE
PAWARENGA	1	C 5 SE
PEEBLES	50	T 60 NE
PEEL FOREST	45	U 54 NE
PEEP O DAY	23	N 32 NE
PEGGIOH	36	G 42 SW
PEHIRI	20	V 25 NE
PEKAPEKARAU	4	G 8 SW
PEKATAHI	12	T 21 SW
PEKERAU	1	D 4 SE
PEKETA	36	E 45 SW
PELORUS BRIDGE	29	E 39 SW
PEMBERTON	23	O 32 NW
PEMBROKE	15	H 28 SW
PENDARVES	41	X 53 SW
PENTLAND HILLS	50	S 58 SE
PENZANCE	29	E 38 NE
PEPEPE	9	K 19 NW
PERIA		
(FAR NORTH)	2	E 5 NW
(MATAMATA PIAKO)	10	N 20 NE
PHOEBE	40	C 47 SE
PIARERE	10	N 21 NE
PICTON	29	G 39 SW
PIGEON BAY	42	B 52 NW
PIGEON BUSH	27	L 38 SW
PIHA	5	I 15 NW
PIHAMA	21	F 29 SE
PIKES POINT	50	U 59 SW
PIKIWAHINE	4	G 9 SW
PIKOPIKO	58	H 66 SE
PIKOWAI	12	R 20 SE
PINE HILL	56	S 64 SW
PINEBUSH	59	L 68 SE
PINEDALE	10	O 21 SW
PIOPIO	9	K 23 SE
PIOS BEACH	10	P 18 SW
PIPIRIKI	22	K 29 SE
PIPIROA	8	M 17 NE
PIPIWAI	4	G 8 NW
PIRIAKA	16	M 26 SW
PIRINOA	27	K 39 SE
PIRIPAI	12	T 21 NW
PIRIPAUA	19	T 26 NE
PIRIPIRI		
(TARARUA)	23	P 33 SW
(WAITOMO)	9	K 22 SW
PIRONGIA	9	L 21 NW
PIROPIRO	11	M 24 SW
PIRORUA STREAM	9	K 22 NW
PISA MOORINGS	54	M 60 NE
PLEASANT POINT	45	U 56 NW
PLEASANT VALLEY	45	U 55 NW
PLECKVILLE	25	N 36 NE
POERUA	38	V 47 SE
POHANGINA	23	N 33 SE
POHARA	32	B 36 SW
POHARA MARAE	10	N 21 SW
POHATUKURA	14	Y 21 NE
POHOKURA	15	J 27 SW
POHONUI	23	M 31 NE
POHUEHUE	5	J 12 SW
POINT WELLS	6	J 17 NE
POKAKA	16	M 28 SW
POKAPU	4	G 6 SW
POKENO	7	K 17 NE
POKERE	4	G 7 NW
POKORORO	32	B 39 NW
POKURU	9	L 21 SE
POLLOK	7	I 16 NW
POMAHAKA	55	N 66 NW
POMARANGAI	9	J 23 NE
PONATAHI	28	M 38 SE
PONGA	7	K 16 NE
PONGAKAWA	12	R 20 SW
PONGAKAWA VALLEY	12	R 21 NW
PONGAROA	26	P 35 SW
POOLBURN	49	O 61 NE
POPOTUNOA	55	N 66 NE
PORAITI	18	S 29 SW
PORANGAHAU	24	R 34 NW
POREWA	23	M 32 SW
PORI	26	O 35 SW
POROOTARAO	11	L 24 NE
POROPORO	12	T 21 NW
POROTI	4	G 8 SE
POROUTAWHAO	25	L 35 SE
PORT ALBERT	5	I 11 SW
PORT AWANUI	14	Z 21 NE
PORT CHALMERS	56	S 64 SE
PORT CHARLES	6	M 13 NE
PORT FITZROY	6	M 11 NW
PORT JACKSON	6	M 13 NW
PORT LEVY	42	B 52 SW
PORT MOLYNEUX	60	P 67 SE
PORT MOTUEKA	32	B 38 SW
PORT OHOPE	13	T 21 SE
PORT PUPONGA	31	A 35 NE
PORT ROBINSON	40	D 48 NW
PORT WAIKATO	7	J 17 SW
PORTAGE	29	G 39 NW
PORTLAND	4	H 9 NE
PORTOBELLO	56	S 64 SE
POTAKA	14	Y 19 SW
POUAWA	20	Y 25 NW
POUKAWA	24	R 31 NE
POUKIORE	23	M 31 SE
POUNAWEAR	60	P 68 SW
POURERERE	24	S 33 NE
POUTO	5	H 11 NE
PREBBLETON	42	Z 52 NE
PROGRESS JUNCTION	33	X 44 SW
PROGRESS VALLEY	60	N 69 NW
PUAHA	42	B 53 NW
PUAHUE	9	M 21 SE
PUERUA	60	P 67 SW
PUHA	14	W 24 NE
PUHATA	1	C 6 NE
PUHIPUHI	4	H 7 NE
PUHOI	5	J 13 NW
PUKAHU	18	S 30 NE
PUKAPUKA	5	J 12 SW
PUKAWA	16	N 26 NE
PUKEARUHE		
(NEW PLYMOUTH)	15	I 26 NW
(SOUTHLAND)	58	H 66 NE
PUKEATUA	9	M 21 SE
PUKEAWA	55	O 66 SE
PUKEHAMOAMOA	18	R 30 NE
PUKEHIKI	56	S 65 NE
PUKEHINA	12	R 20 SW
PUKEHOU	4	G 9 NW
PUKEHUIA	4	G 9 NW
PUKEINOI	9	K 22 NW
PUKEKAPIA	9	L 18 SW
PUKEKARORO	4	I 10 SW
PUKEKAURI	8	O 18 NW
PUKEKAWA	7	K 17 SE
PUKEKOHE	7	K 16 SW
PUKEKOHE EAST	7	K 16 SW
PUKEKOMA	55	P 66 NW
PUKEKURA		
(WAIPA)	9	M 21 NE
(WESTLAND)	37	S 49 NW
PUKEMAORI	58	H 66 SE
PUKEMIRO		
(FAR NORTH)	1	D 6 NW
(WAIKATO)	9	K 19 NE
PUKEMOREMORE	9	M 20 NE
PUKEMUTU	58	J 66 NW
PUKENGAHU	15	H 28 SE
PUKENUI	1	C 3 SW
PUKEOKAHU	17	O 30 NE
PUKEOWARE	7	J 17 NE
PUKEPOTO	1	C 5 NE
PUKERANGI	56	R 63 SW
PUKERAU	55	M 66 SE
PUKERIMU	9	M 20 SW
PUKEROA	23	M 31 SE
PUKERORO	9	M 20 SW
PUKERUA BAY	27	J 38 NE
PUKETAHA	9	M 20 SW
PUKETAPU		
(HASTINGS)	18	S 29 SE
(WAITAKI)	56	T 63 NW
PUKETERAKI	56	S 63 SE
PUKETI		
(CLUTHA)	55	O 66 NE
(FAR NORTH)	2	F 5 NW
PUKETIPO	55	P 66 SW
PUKETIRO	60	O 68 SW
PUKETITIRI	18	R 28 SW
PUKETOI	26	P 35 NW
PUKETONA	2	G 6 NW
PUKETOTARA	9	L 21 SW
PUKETUI	8	O 16 NW
PUKETURUA	10	N 21 SE
PUKETUTU	9	L 23 SW
PUKEURI	50	U 60 NW
PUNAKAIKI	33	U 44 NE
PUNAKITERE	3	F 7 NW
PUNAKITERE VALLEY	3	F 7 NE
PUNAROMIA	10	Q 22 SE
PUNARUKU	4	H 7 SE
PUNAWAI	41	V 53 NE
PUNGAERE	2	G 5 NE
PUNGAPUNGA	16	M 26 NW
PUNGAREHU	21	F 28 NW
PUNGATAWA	17	O 30 NW
PUNI	7	J 17 NE
PUNIHO	21	F 27 SW
PUNIWHAKAU	15	I 28 SE
PUPONGA	31	A 35 NE
PUPUERU	12	S 25 NE
PUPUKE	2	F 5 NW
PURAKANUI	56	S 64 NE
PURAKAUITI	60	O 68 SW
PURAKAUNUI	60	O 68 SW
PURAMAHOI	31	A 36 SE
PURANGI	15	I 27 SW
PURAU	42	A 52 SW
PUREKIREKI	60	O 67 SW
PURERUA	2	G 5 NE
PURIRI	8	N 17 NE
PURUA	4	G 8 NE
PURURU	9	L 23 NE
PUTARA	25	M 36 NE
PUTARURU	10	N 21 SE
PUTERE	18	T 26 SW
PUTORINO		
(HASTINGS)	18	T 27 SW
(RANGITIKEI)	23	M 32 SE
PUWERA	4	H 9 NE
PYES PA	10	P 20 SE
PYRAMID	59	L 65 SE
PYRAMID VALLEY	42	A 48 SW
Q		
QUAILS RISE	53	L 60 NE
QUARRY HILLS	60	M 69 NE
QUEENS FLAT	50	S 60 NE
QUEENSBERRY	54	N 59 SW
QUEENSTOWN	52	K 60 SE
R		
RACECOURSE HILL	41	Y 51 SW
RAES JUNCTION	55	N 64 S
RAETIHI	17	L 29 N
RAGLAN	9	K 20 NW
RAHANUI	9	J 21 NW
RAHIRI		
(FAR NORTH)	2	E 6 N
(STRATFORD)	15	G 28 N
RAHOTU	21	F 28 SW
RAI VALLEY	29	E 39 NW
RAINCLIFF	45	T 55 S'
RAIO	1	C 3 SW
RAKAHOUKA	59	K 67 SW
RAKAIA	41	Y 53 NW
RAKAIA HUTS	41	Y 53 S
RAKAU	31	A 40 N
RAKAUMANGA	9	L 18 SW
RAKAUNUI		
(OTOROHANGA)	9	K 21 SW
(TARARUA)	26	P 35 SW
RAKAUROA	13	V 24 NW
RAKAUTAO	3	F 7 NW
RAKAUTARA	36	F 44 SW
RAKAUTATAHI	24	P 32 SW
RAMANUI	16	K 28 SW
RAMARAMA	7	K 16 SW
RANANA	22	K 30 NW
RANFURLY	49	Q 61 NW
RANGATAUA	17	M 29 NW
RANGATIRA VALLEY	45	U 55 SW
RANGI POINT	3	D 7 NW
RANGIAHUA		
(FAR NORTH)	2	E 6 NE
(WAIROA)	19	U 26 SW
RANGIAOWHIA	9	M 21 NW
RANGIATEA	9	M 22 SW
RANGIHAEATA	31	A 36 SE
RANGIKURA	21	I 31 NW
RANGIORA		
(FAR NORTH)	2	E 6 SW
(WAIMAKARIRI)	42	A 50 SW
RANGIOTU	23	M 34 SW
RANGIPO	17	O 27 NW
RANGIPU	9	J 20 NE
RANGIPUTA	1	D 3 SW
RANGIRIRI	7	L 18 NW
RANGITAIKI	18	Q 26 NW
RANGITATA	45	V 55 NW
RANGITATA ISLAND	45	V 55 NW
RANGITATAU	22	J 31 NE
RANGITIHI	1	D 5 NW
RANGITOTO	9	L 23 NE
RANGITUKIA	14	Z 20 SE
RANGITUMAU	25	N 37 NW
RANGIURU	10	Q 20 NE
RANGIWAEA JUNCTION	17	M 30 NE
RANGIWAHIA	23	O 32 NW
RANKLEBURN	55	N 66 NE
RANUI	9	K 20 NE
RAORAOKAUERE	9	J 21 NE
RAORIAKA	3	G 7 NW
RAPAHOE	33	U 45 SW
RAPAKI	42	A 52 NE
RAPANUI	45	K 31 SW
RAPAURA	29	F 40 NW
RAPUWAI	45	T 55 SE
RARANGI	29	G 40 NW
RAROA PA	12	T 22 SE
RATA	23	M 32 NE
RATANA	25	L 32 SW
RATAPIKO	15	H 27 SW
RAUKAWA	24	R 31 SE
RAUKOKORE	14	X 19 SW
RAUMAI	23	N 33 SE
RAUMATI		
(KAPITI COAST)	27	K 37 SW
(TARARUA)	23	P 33 SW
RAUPO	4	G 10 SW
RAUPUNGA	19	T 27 SE
RAURIMU	16	M 27 NW
RAWENE	3	E 6 NW
RAWHIA	2	E 6 NW
RAWHITI	2	H 5 SE
RAWHITIROA	21	H 29 NE
RAYMONDS GAP	58	I 66 SW
RED BEACH	5	J 13 SW
RED HILL	7	K 16 NE
REDAN	59	M 68 NW
REDHILL	3	F 10 SE
REDVALE	5	J 14 NW
REDWOOD VALLEY	32	C 39 SW
REEFTON	33	X 44 NW
REENA	3	D 7 NW
REHIA	4	G 10 NW
REHUTAI	3	F 10 NW
REIDSTON	50	T 61 NW
REIKORANGI	25	K 37 NW
REMUERA SETTLEMENT	2	F 6 SE
RENOWN	9	K 18 SE
RENWICK	29	F 40 SW
REOTAHI BAY	4	I 9 NE
REPIA	3	F 10 SE
REPOROA	10	Q 23 SW
REPORUA	14	Z 21 NW
RERE	13	V 24 SE
REREWHAKAAITU	12	R 23 NW
REREWHAKAATU	12	R 23 NW
RETARUKE	16	L 27 SW
REWA	23	N 32 NW
REWAREWA	9	L 22 SE
REWITI	5	I 14 NW
RICHMOND		
(TASMAN)	32	C 39 SW
(WAITAKI)	50	U 60 NW
RICHMOND DOWNS	10	N 20 NE
RIMU		
(SOUTHLAND)	59	K 68 SW
(WESTLAND)	38	T 47 SE
RINGWAY	58	I 67 NE
RIPONUI	4	H 7 SW
RIPPONVALE	54	M 60 SE
RISSINGTON	18	R 29 SE
RIVERHEAD	5	I 14 NE
RIVERLANDS	29	F 40 SE
RIVERLEA	21	G 29 NW

Location	Map No.	Ref
RIVERSDALE	59	L 65 SW
RIVERSDALE BEACH	28	O 38 SE
RIVERSIDE	46	X 54 SW
RIVERTON	58	I 68 NE
RIWAKA	32	B 38 NE
ROA	33	V 45 NW
ROCK AND PILLAR	56	Q 62 SE
ROCKFORD	41	X 50 SE
ROCKVILLE	31	A 36 NW
ROKEBY	41	X 53 NW
ROLLESTON	42	Z 52 NW
ROMAHAPA	60	P 67 SW
RONGAHERE	55	O 65 SW
RONGOITI JUNCTION	17	N 30 SW
RONGOKOKAKO	25	M 36 NE
RONGOMAI	26	N 35 SE
RONGOTEA	23	M 34 NW
ROSEWILL	50	U 56 NE
ROSLYN BUSH	59	K 68 NW
ROSS	37	S 48 SE
ROTHERHAM	40	B 47 NE
ROTOEHU	12	R 21 SW
ROTOITI	12	R 21 SW
ROTOKAKAHI	1	D 6 NW
ROTOKAURI	9	L 20 NW
ROTOKAUTUKU	14	Z 21 NW
ROTOKAWA		
(ROTORUA)	10	Q 22 NW
(TAUPO)	12	P 25 NE
ROTOKINO	37	R 50 NW
ROTOKOHU	33	X 43 NW
ROTOMAHANA	10	Q 23 NE
ROTOMANU	38	W 47 NW
ROTONGARO	9	K 18 SE
ROTONGATA		
(ROTORUA)	10	Q 21 NW
(WAIPA)	10	N 22 NW
ROTOORANGI	9	M 21 NE
ROTOROA	34	A 42 NW
ROTORUA	10	P 22 NE
ROTOTUNA		
(KAIPARA)	5	G 11 SW
(WAIKATO)	9	L 19 SE
ROTOWARO	9	K 19 NE
ROUND HILL	55	P 66 NE
ROUNDHILL	58	I 68 NW
ROWAN	21	G 29 NE
ROXBURGH	54	N 63 NW
ROXBURGH HYDRO	54	N 63 NW
RUAHINE		
(MANAWATU)	23	O 31 SW
(SOUTHLAND)	58	H 68 NE
RUAKAKA	4	I 9 SW
RUAKAKA BEACH	4	I 9 SW
RUAKITURI	19	U 26 NE
RUAKIWI	9	K 19 SW
RUAKOKOPUTUNA	27	L 39 SE
RUAKURA	9	M 20 NW
RUAMAHUNGA	8	M 15 SE
RUANUI	17	N 30 NW
RUAPEKAPEKA	4	H 7 NW
RUAPUKE	9	J 20 SE
RUAPUNA	41	V 53 SW
RUARANGI	4	H 9 SE
RUAROA	23	O 33 SE
RUATAHUNA	12	S 24 SE
RUATANGATA	4	H 8 NW
RUATANIWHA	24	Q 32 NE
RUATAPU	37	T 48 NW
RUATITI	16	L 28 SW
RUATO	10	Q 21 SE
RUATOKI NORTH	12	T 22 NW
RUATORIA	14	Z 21 NW
RUAWAI	4	G 10 SW
RUAWARO	9	K 18 SE
RUAWHATA	23	N 34 SE
RUBY BAY	32	C 39 NW
RUKUHIA	9	L 20 SE
RUKUWAI	4	I 8 SE
RUNANGA	33	U 45 SE
RUNARUNA	1	D 6 NW
RUNCIMAN	7	K 16 NE
RURU	38	V 46 SE
RUSSELL	2	G 6 NE
RUSSELLS FLAT	41	X 51 NW
RUTHERGLEN	38	U 46 SW
RYAL BUSH	58	J 67 SE
S		
SAIES	63	A 1 SW
ST ANDREWS	50	U 57 SE
ST ARNAUD	34	B 42 NW
ST BATHANS	49	P 59 SW
ST PATRICKS	59	K 65 NW
SALES	2	E 4 SE
SALISBURY	50	U 57 NE
SALTWATER CREEK	42	A 50 SE
SANDSPIT	5	J 12 NW
SANDY BAY	4	I 7 SE
SANDY KNOLLS	42	Z 52 NW
SANSON	23	M 33 SW
SANTOFT	25	L 33 NW
SAWYERS BAY	56	S 64 SW
SCARGILL	42	B 48 SE
SCOTSMAN VALLEY	9	M 20 NE
SCOTTS GAP	58	I 66 SW
SCROGGS HILL	56	R 65 NE
SEACLIFF	56	S 64 NE
SEADOWN	45	U 56 NE
SEAFIELD	41	X 54 NW
SEAFORD	31	A 35 SE
SEAFORTH	50	V 56 SW
SEAGROVE	7	J 16 NE
SEAVIEW	37	T 47 NW
SEAWARD DOWNS	59	L 68 NE
SEDDON	36	G 41 SW
SEDDONVILLE	34	X 41 NE
SEDGEMERE	42	Z 53 SW
SEFTON	42	A 50 NW
SELWYN		
(MATAMATA PIAKO)	10	O 20 SW
(SELWYN)	41	Y 52 SE
SELWYN HUTS	42	Z 53 NE
SENTRY HILL	15	G 27 NE
SERGEANTS HILL	33	W 42 NW
SHAFTESBURY	10	O 19 NW
SHAG POINT	56	T 62 SW
SHAG VALLEY	56	S 62 NW
SHANDON	54	Q 63 SW
SHANNON	25	M 35 SW
SHANTYTOWN	38	U 46 SW
SHEFFIELD	41	X 51 NE
SHELLY BEACH	5	H 13 NE
SHENANDOAH	34	Y 42 SE
SHERENDEN	18	R 29 SW
SHERWOOD DOWNS	44	T 54 SW
SILVERDALE	5	J 13 SW
SILVERHOPE	23	M 32 NE
SIX MILE	34	Z 42 SW
SLOPE POINT	59	M 69 SW
SMITHFIELD	50	U 56 SE
SNELLS BEACH	5	J 12 NW
SOUTH BAY	36	E 45 SE
SOUTH BEACH	38	U 46 NW
SOUTH HEAD	5	H 12 SW
SOUTH HILLEND	58	J 66 NW
SOUTH MALVERN	41	X 51 SW
SOUTHBRIDGE	41	Y 53 SE
SOUTHBURN	50	U 57 NW
SPAR BUSH	58	J 67 SE
SPEARGRASS FLAT	53	L 60 NW
SPENCERVILLE	42	A 51 NE
SPOTSWOOD	40	C 47 SE
SPRING CREEK	29	F 40 NE
SPRING GROVE	32	C 40 NW
SPRINGBANK	42	Z 50 SW
SPRINGBROOK	50	U 57 NW
SPRINGBURN	41	V 52 SE
SPRINGDALE	10	N 18 SW
SPRINGFIELD		
(SELWYN)	41	X 50 SW
(WHANGAREI)	4	H 9 SE
SPRINGHILL	24	Q 31 SW
SPRINGHILLS	59	K 67 NW
SPRINGS JUNCTION	34	Y 45 NE
SPRINGSTON	42	Z 52 SW
SPRINGSTON SOUTH	42	Z 52 SE
SPRINGVALE	54	N 61 SE
SPYE	42	B 48 SW
STAFFORD	38	T 47 NE
STAIRCASE	41	X 50 NE
STANLEY BROOK	32	B 39 SW
STANWAY	23	M 33 NE
STAVELEY	41	V 52 SW
STEWARTS GULLY	42	A 51 NE
STILLWATER		
(GREY)	38	V 46 NW
(RODNEY)	5	J 13 SW
STIRLING	60	P 67 NW
STOCKTON	33	X 41 NW
STOKE	32	C 39 SE
STONEBURN	56	S 62 SW
STRACHANS	50	R 59 NE
STRATFORD	15	H 28 SW
STRATHMORE	15	I 28 NE
STREAMLANDS	5	I 12 NE
STRUAN	50	S 57 SW
STUDHOLME	50	U 58 SE
SUMMER HILL	60	P 67 SE
SUMMERHILL	42	Z 50 SW
SUMMERLEA	33	X 40 SW
SUMNER	42	A 52 NE
SURFDALE	6	K 14 SE
SUTHERLANDS	45	U 56 NW
SUTTON	56	Q 63 NW
SWANNANOA	42	Z 51 NE
SWEETWATER	1	C 4 SE
SWYNCOMBE	36	D 45 NE
T		
TABLELANDS		
(OPOTIKI)	13	U 21 SE
(SOUTH WAIRARAPA)	28	M 39 NW
TADMOR	31	A 40 NE
TAHAIA	9	L 22 SE
TAHAKOPA	60	N 68 SE
TAHAROA	9	J 22 NW
TAHATIKA	60	O 68 NW
TAHAWAI	10	O 18 SE
TAHEKE	3	E 7 NE
TAHEKEROA	5	I 13 NE
TAHERE	4	I 8 NW
TAHORA		
(GISBORNE)	13	T 23 NE
(STRATFORD)	15	J 27 NE
(WHAKATANE)	13	T 23 NE
TAHORAITI	23	O 33 SE
TAHUNA	9	M 18 SE
TAHUNA SIDING	12	S 22 NW
TAHUNGA	20	V 25 NW
TAHUROA	9	M 19 SE
TAIERI BEACH	56	R 66 NW
TAIERI MOUTH	56	Q 66 NE
TAIHAPE		
(HASTINGS)	18	R 30 NE
(RANGITIKEI)	17	N 30 SE
TAIHARURU	4	I 8 SE
TAIHOA	10	O 20 NW
TAIKIRAU	4	G 7 NE
TAIKO	50	U 56 NW
TAIKOREA	23	M 34 SW
TAIMATE	36	G 42 NE
TAINGAEHE	4	G 11 NW
TAIPA	1	D 4 SE
TAIPUHA	4	H 10 NW
TAIRUA	8	O 15 SE
TAITAPU	42	Z 52 SE
TAKAHIWAI	4	I 9 NW
TAKAHUE	1	D 5 SW
TAKAKA	31	A 36 SE
TAKAMATUA	42	B 53 NE
TAKAMORE	14	Y 21 NE
TAKAPAU		
(CENTRAL HAWKES BAY)	24	Q 32 SW
(GISBORNE)	14	Y 22 NE
TAKATU	6	J 12 NE
TAKOU BAY	2	G 5 NW
TAKUTAI	37	T 47 SW
TAMAHERE	9	M 20 NW
TAMATERAU	4	I 8 SW
TAMUMU	24	R 32 NW
TANATANA	13	T 22 SE
TANE	26	N 35 SE
TANEATUA	12	T 22 NW
TANEHOPUWAI	9	L 23 NW
TANEKAHA	4	H 7 SW
TANGIHUA	4	G 9 NE
TANGIMOANA	25	L 34 NW
TANGITERORIA	4	G 9 NE
TANGITU	16	L 24 SW
TANGIWAI	17	M 29 SE
TANGOAKE	1	B 2 SE
TANGOIO	18	S 28 SE
TANGOWAHINE	4	G 9 NW
TANIWHA	7	L 18 NE
TANOA	4	H 11 NE
TANUPARA	22	L 29 SE
TAOROA JUNCTION	17	O 30 SE
TAOTAOROA	10	N 20 SW
TAPANUI	55	N 65 SW
TAPAPA	10	O 21 NW
TAPATU	14	Y 20 NE
TAPAWERA	32	B 40 NW
TAPORA	5	H 12 NE
TAPU	8	M 15 SE
TAPUHI	4	H 7 NW
TAPUI	50	S 60 NE
TAPUWAE		
(FAR NORTH)	1	D 6 SE
(WAITOMO)	11	M 24 NW
TARA	4	I 10 SE
TARADALE	18	S 30 NW
TARAKOHE	32	B 36 SW
TARAMAKAU	38	U 47 NE
TARAPATIKI	19	U 26 NW
TARARA	60	O 68 SE
TARARU	8	N 16 NW
TARATA	15	H 27 SE
TARAUNUI	4	I 8 SE
TARAWERA	18	R 27 NW
TARIKI	15	H 28 NW
TARINGAMOTU	16	L 26 NE
TARINGAMOTU VALLEY	16	M 26 NW
TARONUI BAY	2	G 5 NW
TARRAS	49	N 59 SE
TARUKENGA	10	P 21 SW
TARURUTANGI	15	G 27 NE
TASMAN	32	B 38 SE
TATA BEACH	32	B 36 SW
TATAIAHAPE PA	13	T 22 SE
TATAPOURI	20	Y 25 NW
TATAPUTAHI	13	V 22 NE
TATARAIMAKA	21	F 27 SE
TATARAMOA	23	P 33 NW
TATARE	37	Q 51 NW
TATARIKI	3	F 10 NE
TATU	16	K 26 NW
TATUANUI	10	N 19 NW
TAUAKIRA	22	L 30 SE
TAUHEI	9	M 19 NE
TAUHERENIKAU	27	L 38 SE
TAUHOA	5	I 12 NW
TAUMARERE	2	G 6 SE
TAUMARUITI	16	L 26 NE
TAUMARUNUI	16	L 26 NE
TAUMUTU	42	Z 53 SW
TAUPAKI	5	I 14 SE
TAUPIRI	9	L 19 NW
TAUPO	11	P 25 NW
TAUPO BAY	2	E 4 SE
TAURANGA	10	P 19 SE
TAURANGA BAY	2	F 4 SW
TAURANGA VALLEY	2	F 4 SW
TAURANGANUI	7	J 17 SE
TAURANGARURU	7	J 17 NW
TAURAROA		
(OTOROHANGA)	9	M 22 SW
(WHANGAREI)	4	H 9 NW
TAUREWA	16	N 27 NW
TAURIKO	10	P 20 NW
TAURIKURA	4	I 9 NE
TAUTORO	3	F 7 NW
TAUWERU	28	N 37 SE
TAUWHARE		
(WAIKATO)	9	M 20 NE
(WHAKATANE)	13	T 23 NE
TAUWHAREPARAE	14	Y 23 NW
TAWAI	50	U 59 SW
TAWANUI	60	O 68 NE
TAWAPATA	20	X 28 SW
TAWATAIA	26	N 36 NE
TAWHAI	33	W 44 NE
TAWHANA	13	T 24 NE
TAWHARANUI	6	J 12 NE
TAWHAREMANUKA	13	T 23 SE
TAWHATA	16	K 27 NE
TAWHITI	21	H 30 NW
TAYLORVILLE	38	U 45 SE
TE AHUAHU	2	F 6 NE
TE AKATARAWA	49	Q 58 NE
TE AKATEA	9	K 19 NE
TE AKAU	9	J 19 SE
TE AKAU SOUTH	9	K 19 SW
TE ANAU	52	H 63 NW
TE ANAU DOWNS	52	H 61 SE
TE ANGA	9	J 22 SE
TE APUTA	16	N 25 SW
TE ARAI	4	I 11 NE
TE ARAI POINT	4	I 11 NE
TE ARAKURA	23	M 34 NE
TE ARAROA	14	Z 19 SW
TE ARIURU	14	Z 22 SW
TE AROHA	10	N 18 SE
TE AROHA WEST	10	N 19 NE
TE AWA	45	U 55 SE
TE AWAMUTU	9	L 21 NE
TE AWANGA	18	S 30 SE
TE HANA	5	I 11 SE
TE HAPUA	1	B 1 SW
TE HAROTO	18	R 27 SW
TE HAUKE	24	R 31 NW
TE HAUMI	63	D 4 NW
TE HENGA	5	I 15 NW
TE HIHI	7	J 16 NE
TE HOE	9	M 18 SW
TE HORO	25	K 36 SE
TE HORO BEACH	25	K 36 SE
TE HOUKA	60	O 67 NE
TE HUA HUA	1	D 6 SE
TE HUTEWAI	9	J 20 NE
TE IRINGA	3	F 7 NW
TE KAHA	13	W 20 NE
TE KAO	1	B 2 SE
TE KARAE	2	E 6 NW
TE KARAKA		
(FAR NORTH)	1	D 6 SE
(GISBORNE)	14	X 24 NW
TE KAURI	9	L 18 SW
TE KAUWHATA	7	L 18 NW
TE KAWA	9	L 21 SE
TE KAWA WEST	9	L 21 SE
TE KINGA	38	V 46 SE
TE KIRI	21	F 29 NE
TE KOHANGA	7	K 17 SW
TE KOPUA		
(OPOTIKI)	14	W 20 NE
(WAIPA)	9	L 21 SE
TE KOPURU	3	F 10 NE
TE KORAHA	9	K 22 SW
TE KOUMA	6	M 14 SE
TE KOURA	16	L 25 SE
TE KOWHAI		
(KAIPARA)	4	G 11 NE
(WAIKATO)	9	L 19 SW
TE KUHA	33	W 42 NW
TE KUITI	9	L 23 NW
TE KUMI	9	L 23 NW
TE MAHIA	29	F 39 NE
TE MAHOE	12	S 22 NE
TE MAIKA	9	J 21 SW
TE MAIRE		
(KAIPARA)	3	F 10 SE
(RUAPEHU)	16	L 26 SW
TE MAPARA	16	K 24 NE
TE MARUA	29	F 36 SE
TE MATA		
(THAMES COROMANDEL)	8	M 15 SE
(WAIKATO)	9	K 20 SW
TE MATAI	10	Q 20 NW
TE MAWHAI	9	L 21 SE
TE MIRO	10	N 20 NW
TE MOANA	45	U 54 SW
TE MOANANUI	8	N 18 NE
TE NAMU	31	Y 40 NW
TE NGAE	10	Q 22 NW
TE NGAIRE	2	F 4 SE
TE OHAKI PA	10	O 20 NW
TE ORE ORE	28	N 37 SW
TE PAHU	9	L 20 SW
TE PAKI	1	A 1 SE
TE PAPATAPU	9	J 21 NE
TE PEKA	59	L 68 SE
TE PENE	2	F 4 SE
TE PIRITA	41	X 52 SW
TE POHUE	18	R 28 SE
TE POI	10	O 20 SW
TE POPO	15	H 28 NE
TE POUWHAKATUTU	11	P 24 SW
TE PU	10	P 21 NE
TE PUA	5	I 13 SW
TE PUIA SPRINGS	14	Z 22 NW
TE PUKA	14	Z 22 SW
TE PUKE		
(GISBORNE)	10	Q 20 NW
(WESTERN BAY OF PLENTY)	10	Q 20 SW
TE PUNA	10	P 19 SW
TE PUNINGA	10	N 19 NW
TE PURU	8	N 16 NW
TE RAHU	9	M 21 NW
TE RAINA	16	N 26 NW
TE RANGA		
(TAURANGA)	10	P 20 NE
(WESTERN BAY OF PLENTY)	10	Q 20 SW
TE RANGIITA	17	O 26 NE
TE RAPA		
(MARLBOROUGH)	36	G 42 SW
(WAIKATO)	9	L 20 NE
TE RAUAMOA	9	K 21 SE
TE RAUMAUKU	9	L 22 NW
TE RAUPO	1	C 3 NW
TE REINGA	20	V 26 NW
TE RERENGA	6	N 14 NW
TE RORE		
(FAR NORTH)	1	D 5 SE
(WAIPA)	9	L 21 NW
TE ROTI	21	H 29 SW
TE ROU	29	D 40 SE
TE TAHO	37	R 50 NE
TE TEKO	12	S 21 SW
TE TII	2	G 5 NW
TE TIPUA	59	L 67 NE
TE TOI STREAM	9	K 22 NW
TE TOKE	12	Q 24 SW
TE TORO	7	J 16 SW
TE TUA	58	H 67 NW
TE TUHI JUNCTION	22	K 30 NW
TE TUMU	10	Q 20 NE
TE UKU	9	K 20 NW
TE URI	24	Q 34 NW
TE WAEWAE	58	H 67 SW
TE WAIITI	12	T 25 NW
TE WAIROA	10	Q 22 SW
TE WAITERE	9	J 22 NE
TE WERA		
(GISBORNE)	13	V 24 NW
(STRATFORD)	15	I 28 NE
TE WHAITI	12	S 24 SW
TE WHANGA	28	N 38 NW
TE WHARAU		
(CARTERTON)	28	N 39 NE
(KAIPARA)	3	F 9 SE
TE WHAU	2	F 5 SE
TE WHETU	10	O 22 NW
TEDDINGTON	42	A 52 SE
TEKAPO MILITARY CAMP	44	R 54 SW
TEMPLE VIEW	9	L 20 NE
TEMPLETON	42	Z 52 NE
TEMUKA	45	V 55 SW
TENNYSON INLET	29	F 38 SW
TESCHEMAKERS	50	T 61 NE
TEVIOT	54	N 63 SE
THAMES	8	M 16 SE
THE FIVE BRIDGES	14	Y 23 SW
THE FORKS	37	Q 50 SE
THE KEY	58	H 63 SE
THE PINES BEACH	42	A 51 NE
THE PLATEAU	27	K 38 SE
THE POINT	41	W 51 SE
THE ROCKS	58	I 68 NE
THE THREE BRIDGES	14	Y 23 NE

R - T Riversdale - The Three Bridges

Index 7

Location	Map No.	Ref
THOMSONS CROSSING	58	J 67 NE
THORNBURY	58	I 67 NE
THORNTON	12	S 21 NE
THORNTON BAY	8	M 16 NE
THORPE	32	B 39 NW
THREE MILE BUSH	4	H 8 SW
THREE STREAMS	9	K 20 NW
TI POINT	6	J 11 SE
TI TREE POINT	26	Q 35 NW
TIAKITAHUNA	25	M 34 SW
TIHIROA	9	L 21 SW
TIHOI	11	N 24 SE
TIKINUI	4	G 10 SW
TIKITERE	10	Q 21 SW
TIKITIKI	14	Z 20 SE
TIKOKINO	24	Q 31 SE
TIKORANGI	15	H 27 NW
TIKOTIKO	7	K 18 NE
TIMARU	50	U 56 SE
TIMPANYS	59	K 68 SE
TINIROTO	20	V 26 NE
TINOPAI	5	H 11 SW
TINUI	26	O 37 NE
TINWALD	41	W 54 NE
TIPAPAKUKU	23	P 33 SW
TIRATU	23	P 33 SW
TIRAU	10	N 21 NE
TIRAUMEA	26	O 36 NE
TIRIRAUKAWA	23	N 31 NW
TIROA	11	M 24 NE
TIROHANGA		
(CLUTHA)	60	P 68 NE
(GISBORNE)	13	U 21 NE
TIROHIA	8	N 18 SW
TIROITI	56	R 61 SW
TIROMOANA	33	V 43 SW
TISBURY	59	K 68 SW
TITIRANGI BAY	29	G 37 SW
TITIROA	59	L 68 SE
TITOKI	4	G 8 SE
TITRI	56	L 65 NE
TIWAI POINT	59	K 69 NW
TOATOA	13	V 22 NW
TOHUNGA JUNCTION	16	L 28 SE
TOI FLAT	24	P 34 SE
TOIRO	60	O 67 NE
TOKAANU	16	N 26 SE
TOKANUI		
(OTOROHANGA)	9	M 21 SW
(SOUTHLAND)	59	M 69 NW
TOKAORA	21	H 30 NW
TOKARAHI	50	S 60 NE
TOKATA	14	Z 19 SW
TOKATOKA	4	G 10 NW
TOKERAU	10	Q 21 SE
TOKERAU BEACH	1	D 3 SW
TOKIRIMA	16	K 26 NW
TOKO	15	H 26 SE
TOKO MOUTH	60	O 67 NW
TOKOITI	56	Q 66 SW
TOKOMARU	25	M 35 NE
TOKOMARU BAY	14	Z 22 SW
TOKORANGI	23	M 33 NE
TOKOROA	10	O 22 SW
TOLAGA BAY	14	Y 23 SE
TOMARATA	4	J 11 NW
TONGAPORUTU	15	I 25 SE
TONGARIRO	16	N 27 NW
TOPHOUSE	34	B 42 NW
TOPUNI	4	I 11 NW
TORA	28	M 40 SW
TOREHAPE	8	M 17 SE
TORERE	13	V 21 NW
TOTARA		
(THAMES COROMANDEL)	8	N 16 SW
(WAITAKI)	50	T 60 SW
TOTARA FLAT	33	V 45 NE
TOTARA NORTH	2	F 4 SW
TOTARA VALLEY	45	T 56 NE
TOTARANUI	32	B 36 SE
TOWAI	4	G 7 NE
TRENTHAM	44	T 54 SW
TRIPP SETTLEMENT	45	U 54 SE
TRYPHENA	6	N 12 NW
TUAHIWI	42	A 50 SW
TUAI	19	T 26 NE
TUAKAU	7	K 17 NW
TUAMARINA	29	F 40 NE
TUAMATA	55	O 66 SW
TUAPEKA FLAT	55	O 66 SW
TUAPEKA MOUTH	55	O 66 NE
TUAPEKA WEST	55	O 65 SW
TUATAPERE	58	H 67 NW
TUATEAWA	6	N 13 SW
TUATINI	14	Z 22 SW
TUHARA	20	V 27 NW
TUHIKARAMEA	9	L 20 SW
TUHIPA	2	G 6 SW
TUHITARATA	27	L 39 SW
TUHUA	16	L 25 SW
TUI	34	A 40 SE
TUKEMOKIHI	20	V 26 SE
TUMAHU	21	F 28 NE
TUMAI	56	S 63 NE
TUMUNUI	10	Q 22 SW
TUNA	15	H 28 NW
TUNAKOTEKOTE	16	L 26 NE
TUPAROA	14	Z 21 SE
TURAKINA	25	L 32 SW
TURANGAOMOANA	10	O 20 NW
TURANGARERE	17	N 30 NE
TURANGI	16	N 26 SE
TURITEA	23	N 34 SW
TURIWHATE	38	U 47 SE
TURIWIRI	3	F 9 SE
TURUA	8	N 17 NW
TUSSOCK CREEK	59	K 67 SW
TUTAEMATAI	2	H 6 NE
TUTAENUI	23	M 32 NW
TUTAKI	34	Z 42 NE
TUTAMOE	3	E 8 NE
TUTEKEHUA	2	E 6 NW
TUTIRA	18	S 28 NE
TUTUKAKA	4	I 8 NE
TUTURAU	59	L 67 NE
TUTURUMURI	28	M 40 NW

Location	Map No.	Ref
TUTUTAWA	15	I 28 SW
TWIN BRIDGES	3	F 8 NE
TWIZEL	49	Q 56 NW
TWYFORD	18	S 30 NE
U		
UMAWERA	2	E 6 NE
UMERE	31	Y 39 NW
UMUTAOROA	23	O 33 NE
UMUTOI	23	O 32 SW
UNDERWOOD	58	J 68 NE
UPOKONGARO	22	K 31 SE
UPOKORAU	2	F 5 NE
UPPER ATIAMURI	10	O 23 NE
UPPER HUTT	27	K 38 SE
UPPER JUNCTION	56	S 64 SW
UPPER KAWHATAU	23	O 31 SW
UPPER MATAKITAKI	34	Z 43 SW
UPPER MOUTERE	32	B 39 NE
UPPER RETARUKE	16	L 27 SE
UPPER TAKAKA	31	A 38 NE
UPPER WAITATI	56	S 64 SW
UPPER WAITOHI	45	U 55 SW
URAWHITIKI POINT	9	J 21 SW
URENUI	15	H 26 SE
URETANE	50	U 59 NW
URETITI BEACH	4	I 9 NE
URQUHARTS BAY	4	I 9 NE
URUTI	15	I 26 NW
URUTI POINT	28	O 38 SE
URUWHENUA	32	B 37 SW
UTAKURA	2	E 6 SE
UTIKU	23	O 31 NW
UTUWAI	23	O 32 SW
V		
VALLETTA	41	V 53 NE
VICTORIA VALLEY	1	D 5 NE
VIEW HILL	41	Y 50 SW
VINEGAR HILL	23	N 32 NW
W		
WADDINGTON	41	X 51 NE
WAERENGA	7	L 17 SE
WAERENGAAHIKA	20	X 25 NW
WAERENGAOKURI	20	W 25 SW
WAHAROA	10	N 20 NE
WAI-ITI	32	B 40 NE
WAIANAKARUA	56	T 61 SW
WAIANIWA	58	J 67 SW
WAIAPI	45	U 56 NE
WAIARE	2	F 5 NW
WAIAREKA JUNCTION	50	T 60 SE
WAIARIARI	50	U 58 NW
WAIARIKIKI	59	M 67 SW
WAIARO	6	M 13 SE
WAIARUHE	23	O 34 NE
WAIATARUA	5	I 15 NE
WAIATOTO	48	K 55 NE
WAIAU	40	C 47 NW
WAIAU BEACH	7	J 16 SE
WAIAU PA	7	J 16 NE
WAIAUA	13	V 21 SW
WAIHAHA		
(FAR NORTH)	2	H 6 NW
(TAUPO)	11	N 25 NE
WAIHAO DOWNS	50	T 59 NW
WAIHAO FORKS	50	T 59 NE
WAIHAORUNGA	50	T 58 SW
WAIHAPA	2	F 5 NW
WAIHARAKEKE		
(HAURAKI)	8	O 17 NE
(WAITOMO)	9	J 22 NE
WAIHARARA	1	C 4 NE
WAIHAU BAY	14	X 19 SW
WAIHI		
(HAURAKI)	8	O 18 NE
(TAUPO)	16	N 26 SE
WAIHI BEACH	8	O 18 NE
WAIHI GORGE	45	U 54 SE
WAIHI VILLAGE	16	N 26 SE
WAIHIRERE	20	X 25 NW
WAIHOAKA	58	H 67 SW
WAIHOKI VALLEY	26	P 36 NW
WAIHOLA	56	Q 66 NE
WAIHOPO	1	C 3 NW
WAIHOU	10	N 20 NE
WAIHOU VALLEY	2	F 6 NW
WAIHUA	19	U 27 SW
WAIHUE	3	F 9 NE
WAIHUKA	2	F 5 NW
WAIKAIA	59	L 64 SE
WAIKAKA	55	M 65 SW
WAIKAKA VALLEY	55	M 66 NE
WAIKAKAHI	50	T 59 NE
WAIKANA	59	M 67 NW
WAIKANAE	25	K 37 SE
WAIKANAE BEACH	25	K 37 SW
WAIKARAKA	4	I 8 SW
WAIKARE	2	H 6 SW
WAIKAREMOANA	19	T 25 SE
WAIKARETU	9	J 18 SE
WAIKARI	42	A 48 SE
WAIKATO	31	A 35 SE
WAIKAWA		
(MARLBOROUGH)	29	G 39 NW
(SOUTHLAND)	60	M 69 NW
WAIKAWA BEACH	25	K 36 NE
WAIKAWAU		
(COLVILLE)	8	N 13 SW
(THAMES)	8	M 15 SE
(WAITOMO)	9	J 23 SW
WAIKERIA	9	M 22 NW
WAIKIEKIE	4	H 9 SW
WAIKINO	8	O 18 NW
WAIKIRIKIRI	12	T 22 SW
WAIKITE VALLEY	10	P 23 NE
WAIKOAU	18	S 28 NW
WAIKOIKOI	55	M 66 NE
WAIKOKOPU	20	W 27 SE
WAIKOKOWAI	9	K 19 NE
WAIKOREA	9	K 18 SW
WAIKOUAITI	56	S 63 SE
WAIKOURO	58	I 66 SE
WAIKUKU	42	A 50 SE
WAIKUKU BEACH	42	A 50 SE

Location	Map No.	Ref
WAIKUNE	16	M 28 NW
WAIMA		
(FAR NORTH)	3	E 7 NW
(GISBORNE)	14	Z 22 SW
WAIMA VALLEY	3	E 7 NW
WAIMAHAKA	59	L 68 SE
WAIMAHANA	12	Q 24 NW
WAIMAHORA	9	M 23 NW
WAIMAIRE	33	X 40 SW
WAIMAMAKU	3	E 7 SW
WAIMANA	13	T 22 NE
WAIMANGAROA	33	W 41 SW
WAIMANGU	10	Q 23 NW
WAIMANONI	1	D 4 SW
WAIMARAMA	24	S 31 SE
WAIMATA		
(GISBORNE)	14	X 24 SE
(HAURAKI)	8	O 18 NE
WAIMATE	50	T 58 SE
WAIMATE NORTH	2	F 6 NE
WAIMATENUI	3	F 8 NW
WAIMATUA	59	K 68 SE
WAIMATUKU	58	J 67 SW
WAIMAUKU	5	I 14 NW
WAIMAUNGA	33	W 44 SW
WAIMIHA	11	L 24 SE
WAIMIHIA	18	Q 26 NW
WAIMIRO	26	P 35 NE
WAIMOTU	50	T 61 NW
WAIMUMU	59	L 66 SE
WAINGAKE	20	W 26 NE
WAINGARARA	13	T 21 SW
WAINGARO	9	K 19 SE
WAINGAWA	28	M 37 SE
WAINIHINIHI	38	U 47 SE
WAINUI		
(BANKS PENINSULA)	42	B 53 SW
(FAR NORTH)	2	F 4 SE
(GISBORNE)	20	X 25 SE
(OPOTIKI)	13	T 21 SE
(RODNEY)	1	I 13 SE
WAINUI JUNCTION		
(FAR NORTH)	1	C 5 NE
(RANGITIKEI)	17	O 30 SW
WAINUIORU	28	N 38 NE
WAIOEKA PA	13	U 22 NE
WAIOHAU	12	S 22 SE
WAIOHIKI	18	S 30 NW
WAIOMATATINI	14	Z 20 SW
WAIOMIO	2	G 6 SE
WAIOMOU	10	O 21 NW
WAIOMU	8	M 16 NE
WAIONE	26	P 35 NE
WAIONEKE	5	H 13 NW
WAIONGANA	15	H 27 NW
WAIORONGOMAI	10	O 19 NW
WAIORORE	13	W 20 NW
WAIOTAHI	13	U 21 SW
WAIOTAHI BEACH	13	U 21 SW
WAIOTAHI PA	13	U 21 SW
WAIOTAHI VALLEY	13	U 22 NW
WAIOTAMA	4	G 9 NE
WAIOTAPU	10	Q 23 NE
WAIOTAPU VILLAGE	10	Q 23 NE
WAIOTEPUE	1	D 5 SW
WAIOTEMARAMA	3	D 7 SE
WAIOTIRA	4	H 9 SW
WAIOTU	4	H 7 SW
WAIOURU	17	N 29 SW
WAIPA VALLEY	9	M 23 NW
WAIPAHI	55	N 66 SW
WAIPAIPAI	4	I 7 SE
WAIPANGO	58	I 67 SE
WAIPAOA	14	X 24 SW
WAIPAPA		
(FAR NORTH)	2	F 5 SE
(SOUTH WAIKATO)	10	N 23 NE
WAIPAPAKAURI	1	C 4 SE
WAIPAPAKAURI BEACH	1	C 4 SE
WAIPARA	42	A 49 NE
WAIPARERA	4	I 8 SE
WAIPARU	59	L 65 NE
WAIPATIKI	24	P 34 SE
WAIPATIKI BEACH	18	S 28 SE
WAIPAWA	24	R 32 NW
WAIPIATA	56	Q 61 NE
WAIPIPI	7	J 16 SW
WAIPIRO BAY	14	Z 22 NW
WAIPOPO	45	V 56 NW
WAIPORI FALLS	56	Q 65 NW
WAIPOUA FOREST	3	E 8 NW
WAIPOUA SETTLEMENT	3	D 8 NE
WAIPOUNAMU	59	L 65 NW
WAIPU	4	I 10 NW
WAIPU CAVES	4	H 9 SE
WAIPU COVE	4	I 10 NE
WAIPUKU	15	H 28 NW
WAIPUKURAU	24	R 32 SW
WAIPUNA	33	W 45 NW
WAIPURU	23	N 31 SW
WAIRAKAU	10	O 19 NW
WAIRAKEI	11	P 24 NW
WAIRAKEI VILLAGE	11	P 24 SW
WAIRAMARAMA	7	J 18 NE
WAIRATA	13	U 23 NE
WAIRAU BAR	29	G 40 SW
WAIRAU PA	29	G 40 SW
WAIRAU VALLEY	29	E 41 NW
WAIREIA	1	D 6 SW
WAIREKA	10	P 22 SE
WAIRERE	8	H 10 SE
WAIRIO	58	I 66 NE
WAIROA		
(GISBORNE)	14	Z 20 SW
(WAIROA)	19	U 27 SE
(WESTERN BAY OF PLENTY)	10	P 20 NW
WAIROA PA	10	P 19 SE
WAIRUNA	55	N 66 SW
WAIRUNGA	56	T 63 NE
WAITAANGA	15	J 25 SE
WAITAHA	37	S 49 NE
WAITAHANUI	17	P 26 SW
WAITAHORA	23	P 34 NW
WAITAHU	33	W 43 SE
WAITAHUNA	55	P 65 NW
WAITAHUNA WEST	55	O 66 NE
WAITAKARURU	8	M 17 NW
WAITAKERE	5	I 14 SE

Location	Map No.	Ref
WAITAKI	50	U 59 SW
WAITANE	59	L 67 NW
WAITANGI		
(FAR NORTH)	2	G 6 NE
(WAIMATE)	49	R 58 NW
WAITANGURU	9	K 23 NY
WAITAO	10	Q 20 NV
WAITAPU		
(FAR NORTH)	3	D 7 NV
(TASMAN)	31	A 37 NV
WAITARA	15	H 26 SW
WAITARERE	25	L 35 SW
WAITARIA BAY	29	G 38 SW
WAITARUKE	2	F 5 NW
WAITATI	56	S 64 NW
WAITAWA	45	U 56 NV
WAITAWHETA	8	O 18 NW
WAITEITEI	5	I 11 SW
WAITEKAURI	8	O 18 NV
WAITEPEKA	60	O 67 SE
WAITERIMU	7	L 18 NE
WAITETE BAY	6	M 13 SE
WAITETI		
(ROTORUA)	10	P 21 SE
(WAITOMO)	9	L 23 NW
WAITETOKI	2	E 4 NV
WAITETOKO	17	O 26 NE
WAITETUNA	9	K 20 NE
WAITI	9	M 18 SE
WAITIKI LANDING	1	B 1 SW
WAITOA	10	N 19 NV
WAITOETOE	15	I 26 SW
WAITOHI		
(MANAWATU)	23	M 33 NW
(TIMARU)	45	U 55 SE
WAITOITOI	6	M 13 NW
WAITOKI		
(MATAMATA PIAKO)	10	N 18 SE
(RODNEY)	5	I 13 SE
WAITOMO CAVES	9	L 22 SW
WAITOMO VALLEY	9	L 22 SW
WAITORIKI	15	H 27 SV
WAITOTARA	22	J 31 NV
WAITUHI	20	X 25 NV
WAITUI	15	H 27 SV
WAITUNA		
(SOUTHLAND)	59	L 68 NW
(WAIMATE)	50	T 58 SE
WAITUNA WEST	23	N 32 SW
WAIUKU	7	J 17 NW
WAIUTA	33	W 45 NE
WAIWAKA	25	N 36 NW
WAIWERA		
(RODNEY)	5	J 13 NW
(TARARUA)	25	M 35 SE
WAIWERA SOUTH	60	O 67 NW
WAIWHARE	18	Q 29 SE
WAIWHIU	5	J 12 NW
WAKANUI	41	X 54 NW
WAKAPATU	58	H 68 NE
WAKAPUAKA	29	D 38 SW
WAKARARA	24	P 31 NE
WAKEFIELD	32	B 40 NE
WALDRONVILLE	56	R 65 NE
WALLACETOWN	58	J 68 NE
WALLINGFORD	24	R 33 SW
WALTER PEAK STATION	52	K 61 NW
WALTON	10	N 19 SE
WANAKA	48	M 58 SW
WANGALOA	60	O 67 SW
WANGANUI	22	K 32 NW
WANGANUI EAST	22	K 32 NE
WANSTEAD	24	Q 33 NE
WAOTU	10	N 22 SE
WARD	36	G 42 NE
WARDVILLE	10	O 19 SW
WAREA	21	F 28 NW
WAREPA	60	O 67 NE
WARKWORTH	5	J 12 SW
WARO	4	H 7 SE
WARRINGTON	56	S 64 NE
WASHDYKE	50	U 55 SE
WATERTON	45	W 54 SE
WATTLE BAY	7	I 16 NE
WAVERLEY	22	I 31 NE
WAWA	10	O 23 NW
WAYBY	5	I 12 NE
WAYBY VALLEY	5	I 11 SE
WEAVERS CROSSING	9	L 19 NW
WEBER	24	P 34 SE
WEDDERBURN	56	Q 60 NW
WEEDONS	42	Z 52 NW
WEKAWEKA	3	E 7 SW
WELCOME BAY	10	P 20 NE
WELDS HILL	36	F 42 NW
WELLINGTON	27	I 39 SE
WELLSFORD	5	I 11 SE
WENDON	59	L 65 NE
WENDON VALLEY	55	M 65 NW
WENDONSIDE	59	L 64 SW
WEST ARM	57	F 63 SW
WEST EYRETON	42	Z 51 NW
WEST MELTON	42	Z 51 SW
WEST PLAINS	58	J 68 NE
WEST WANAKA	48	L 58 SE
WESTERFIELD	41	W 53 NW
WESTMERE		
(WAIKATO)	9	L 19 NW
(WANGANUI)	22	K 31 SW
WESTON	50	T 60 SE
WESTPORT	33	W 42 NW
WESTSHORE	18	S 29 SE
WETHERAL	42	A 51 NW
WETHERSTONS	55	P 65 NW
WHAKAANGIANGI	14	Z 20 NW
WHAKAHUWHAKA	22	L 31 NW
WHAKAKI	19	V 27 SE
WHAKAMARA	21	H 30 NE
WHAKAMARAMA	10	O 19 NE
WHAKAMARU	10	O 23 SW
WHAKAMARU HYDRO VILLAGE	10	O 23 SW
WHAKAPAPA	16	M 28 NE
WHAKAPARA	4	H 7 SE
WHAKAPIRAU	4	H 11 NW
WHAKAPOURANGI	14	Y 21 SE
WHAKARAE	13	T 23 NE
WHAKARAU	13	T 23 NE
WHAKAREWAREWA	10	P 22 NE

Location	Map No.	Ref
WHAKARONGO	23	N 34 NW
WHAKATAKI	26	P 37 NE
WHAKATANE	12	T 21 NW
WHAKATETE BAY	8	M 16 NE
WHAKATIWAI	7	L 16 NE
WHAKATU	18	S 30 SE
WHAKAWHITIRA	14	Z 20 SW
WHANANAKI	4	I 7 NW
WHANANAKI SOUTH	4	I 7 SW
WHANARUA BAY	14	W 20 NE
WHANAWHANA	18	Q 30 NW
WHANGAE	2	G 6 SW
WHANGAE BRIDGE	2	G 6 NE
WHANGAEHU		
(MASTERTON)	28	N 37 SE
(RANGITIKEI)	17	L 31 NE
WHANGAIMOANA	27	K 40 NE
WHANGAMARINO	7	L 17 SW
WHANGAMATA	8	O 17 NW
WHANGAMOMONA	15	J 27 SW
WHANGANUI	16	N 25 SE
WHANGAPARAOA		
(OPOTIKI)	14	X 19 SE
(RODNEY)	6	J 13 SE
WHANGAPARAPARA	6	M 11 SW
WHANGAPE	1	C 6 NE
WHANGAPOROTO	16	M 26 NW
WHANGAPOUA	6	N 14 NE
WHANGARA	20	Y 25 NE
WHANGAREI	4	H 8 SE
WHANGARIPO	5	J 11 SW
WHANGAROA	2	H 6 SE
WHANGARURU	2	H 6 SE
WHANGARURU NORTH	2	H 6 SE
WHANGARURU SOUTH	6	J 11 SE
WHANGATEAU	6	K 17 NE
WHANGERATA	7	G 43 NW
WHARE FLAT	56	R 64 SE
WHAREAMA	28	O 37 SW
WHAREATA	27	F 36 SE
WHAREHINE	5	I 12 NW
WHAREHUANUI	53	L 60 NW
WHAREHUIA	15	H 28 SE
WHAREKAKA	14	Y 23 SE
WHAREKAUHAU	27	K 40 NW
WHAREKAWA	6	O 16 SW
WHAREKOHE	4	G 8 SE
WHAREKOPAE	13	V 24 SW
WHAREORA	4	H 8 NE
WHAREPAINA	10	O 23 SW
WHAREPAPA		
(RODNEY)	5	I 14 NW
(WAIROA)	9	M 22 NE
WHAREPOA	8	N 17 NW
WHAREPONGA	14	Z 21 SW
WHAREPUHUNGA	9	M 22 SE
WHAREROA		
(SOUTH TARANAKI)	21	H 30 NW
(TAUPO)	16	N 26 NE
WHAREROA BEACH	27	K 37 SW
WHARETOA	55	O 66 NW
WHAREWAKA	17	P 25 NW
WHARUA	50	R 58 SE
WHATAROA	37	Q 50 SE
WHATATUTU	14	W 23 SE
WHATAWHATA	9	L 20 NW
WHATIPU	7	I 15 SW
WHATITIRI	4	H 8 SW
WHATORO	3	E 8 SE
WHATUWHIWHI	1	D 3 SE
WHAWHARUA	9	L 22 SE
WHEATSTONE	45	W 54 SE
WHEKI VALLEY	4	G 9 NE
WHENUAHOU	24	P 33 NE
WHENUAKITE	8	O 15 NW
WHENUAKURA	21	I 30 SW
WHENUANUI	4	G 10 SW
WHENUAPAI	5	I 14 SE
WHETUKURA	24	P 33 SE
WHIRINAKI		
(FAR NORTH)	3	D 7 NE
(HASTINGS)	18	S 29 NE
WHIRITOA	8	O 17 NE
WHIRIWHIRI	7	J 17 NW
WHITE PINE BUSH	12	T 21 SW
WHITE ROCK		
(SOUTH WAIRARAPA)	27	L 41 NE
(WAIMAKARIRI)	42	Z 49 SE
WHITECLIFFS	41	X 51 SW
WHITEHALL	10	N 20 SW
WHITEMANS VALLEY	27	K 38 SE
WHITERIGG	55	M 66 SE
WHITFORD	6	K 15 NE
WHITIANGA		
(OPOTIKI)	13	W 20 SW
(THAMES COROMANDEL)	8	N 14 SE
WHITIKAHU	9	M 19 NW
WHITIKAU	13	V 22 SW
WILDEN	55	N 64 SW
WILDER SETTLEMENT	24	Q 34 NE
WILLOW FLAT	18	S 27 NE
WILLOWBANK	55	M 66 NW
WILLOWBRIDGE	50	U 58 SW
WILLOWBY	45	W 54 SW
WILLOWFORD	18	Q 29 SE
WILSONS CROSSING	58	J 67 SE
WILSONVILLE	4	H 7 SW
WILTSDOWN	10	N 22 NE
WIMBLEDON	26	Q 35 NE
WINCHESTER	45	V 55 SW
WINCHMORE	41	W 53 SE
WINDERMERE	41	W 54 NW
WINDSOR	50	T 60 NW
WINDSOR PARK	50	T 60 NE
WINDWHISTLE	41	W 51 SE
WINDY HILL	4	G 9 SW
WINGATUI	56	R 65 NE
WINIATA	17	N 30 SE
WINSCOMBE	44	T 55 NW
WINSLOW	41	W 54 NW
WINTON	58	J 67 NE
WOODBOURNE	29	F 40 SE
WOODBURY	45	U 54 SE
WOODCOCKS	5	I 12 SE

WOODEND		
(INVERCARGILL CITY)	59	K 68 SW
(WAIMAKARIRI)	42	A 50 SE
WOODEND BEACH	42	A 50 SE
WOODHILL		
(RODNEY)	5	I 14 NW
(WHANGAREI)	7	I 14 NW
WOODLANDS		
(OPOTIKI)	13	U 21 SE
(SOUTHLAND)	59	K 68 NE
(WESTERN BAY OF PLENTY)	10	O 18 SE
WOODLAW	58	I 66 NE
WOODLEIGH	9	K 18 SW
WOODSIDE	56	Q 65 NE
WOODSTOCK		
(TASMAN)	32	B 39 NW
(WESTLAND)	38	T 47 SW
WOODVILLE	23	O 34 NW
WOOLLEYS BAY	4	I 7 SE
WREYS BUSH	58	I 66 NE
WRIGHTS BUSH	58	J 67 SW
WYLLIES CROSSING	56	R 65 NE
WYNDHAM	59	L 67 SE

Y

| YALDHURST | 42 | Z 51 NE |

Coastal & Water Features

ABBEY ROCKS	43	M 53 NW
ABBOTS STREAM	27	L 38 SW
ABUT HEAD	37	Q 49 SE
ACHERON HEAD	80	C 7 SE
ACHERON LAKES	52	I 61 SE
ACHERON PASSAGE	57	D 64 SE
ACHERON RIVER	35	C 44 SW
ACHILLES POINT	64	F 7 SW
ACKERS POINT	61	J 71 NE
ADDERLEY HEAD	78	E 8 SE
ADELE ISLAND	32	C 37 SW
ADMINISTRATION BAY	66	E 7 NE
ADMIRALTY BAY	29	F 37 SW
AHAURA RIVER	33	W 45 SW
AHIKOPUA POINT	8	O 13 SW
AHIPARA BAY	1	C 5 NE
AHUAHU STREAM	22	K 30 SE
AHURIRI POINT	20	W 28 SE
AHURIRI RIVER	48	O 56 SW
AIGUILLES ISLAND	6	M 10 SE
AIREDALE REEFS	15	H 26 SW
AKAROA HARBOUR	42	B 53 SE
AKAROA HEAD	42	B 53 SE
AKATARAWA RIVER	27	K 37 SE
AKATORE CREEK	56	R 66 NW
AKITIO RIVER	26	Q 35 SW
ALBATROSS POINT	9	J 21 SE
ALBERT BAY	48	L 56 SE
ALL DAY BAY	50	T 61 NE
ALLANS BEACH	80	E 7 NE
ALLEN STRAIT	76	B 4 SW
ALLIGATOR HEAD	29	G 37 SE
ALLPORTS ISLAND	29	G 39 NW
ALLSOPS BAY	27	K 39 SE
ALMA RIVER	35	B 44 SE
ANAKAHA BAY	76	B 4 SW
ANAKAKATA BAY	30	H 38 NW
ANAKOHA BAY	29	H 38 NW
ANAPAI BAY	32	B 36 SE
ANARAKE POINT	8	N 14 NE
ANATAKUPU ISLAND	29	F 37 NE
ANATOKI RIVER	31	A 34 NE
ANAURA BAY	14	Z 23 NW
ANAWHATA STREAM	65	G 2 SW
ANCHOR BAY	6	K 12 NW
ANCHOR ISLAND	57	C 65 NE
ANCHORAGE ISLAND	61	H 73 NE
ANNIE BAY	76	B 4 NW
ANXIETY POINT	51	E 61 SW
AORANGI ISLAND	4	J 7 NE
AORANGI STREAM	17	O 29 SE
AORERE RIVER	31	Z 37 SE
AOTEA HARBOUR	9	J 21 NE
APARIMA RIVER	58	I 67 NE
APITI STREAM	12	T 23 NW
ARAHURA RIVER	38	U 47 SW
ARAPAOA RIVER	4	H 11 NW
ARAPAWA ISLAND	30	H 38 SE
ARAPAWAITI POINT	25	J 37 NE
ARGYLE BURN	59	L 65 NE
ARIMAWHAI POINT	8	O 13 SW
ARMY BAY	64	B 6 SE
AROMAIRE STREAM	22	L 30 SW
AROPAOANUI RIVER	18	T 28 SW
ARROW RIVER	53	L 59 NW
ARTHUR RIVER	52	H 59 SW
ASHBURTON RIVER	46	X 54 SW
ASHBURTON RIVER NORTH BRANCH	41	V 51 NW
ASHBURTON RIVER SOUTH BRANCH	45	T 51 NE
ASHLEY RIVER	42	A 50 SE
ASTROLABE ROADSTEAD	75	C 3 NE
ATAHAUA CREEK	76	E 1 SE
ATIU ISLAND	8	O 13 SE
ATIWHAKATU STREAM	28	M 37 NW
AUROA POINT	20	X 27 SW
AVOCA RIVER	41	V 49 SE
AVON RIVER	36	E 41 SW
AWAKINO RIVER	15	J 24 SW
AWAKINO STREAM	3	F 9 SE
AWANA BAY	6	N 11 NW
AWAPATU STREAM	17	N 29 NE
AWARAU RIVER	33	X 43 SW
AWAROA BAY	32	B 36 SE
AWAROA RIVER	32	C 37 NW
AWAROA ROCK	1	C 6 NE
AWATERE RIVER		
(GISBORNE)	14	Z 19 SE
(KAIKOURA)	36	E 42 SE
AWATURE STREAM		
(WAIKATO)	9	K 18 SU
(WAITAKERE CITY)	65	D 2 NW
AWARAU BAY	59	K 69 NE
AWARUA RIVER	47	I 56 NW
AWE BURN	51	F 63 NE
AWHEA RIVER	28	M 40 SW
AWHEAITI STREAM	28	M 40 NW

BANKS PENINSULA	42	B 54 NE
BANNOCK BURN	54	M 61 SE
BAR POINT	31	Z 35 SE
BARE ISLAND	24	T 31 SW
BARING HEAD	27	J 40 NE
BARK BAY	75	C 3 NE
BARN ISLANDS	47	J 55 SW
BARRACOUTA POINT	59	J 69 NE
BARRETT REEF	73	F 3 NE
BARTLETTS CREEK	76	F 1 NW
BARTRUM BAY	65	F 1 SE
BASTION POINT	6	J 14 SE
BATON RIVER	31	A 39 NW
BAUZA ISLAND	51	E 62 SW
BAY OF ISLANDS	2	H 5 SW
BAY OF MANY COVES	76	D 4 NE
BAY OF PLENTY	10	Q 19 NE
BEACON POINT	65	J 2 SE
BEAN ROCK	64	F 6 SE
BEATRIX BAY	29	G 38 NW
BELL POINT	51	G 59 NW
BELLS ISLAND	32	C 39 NW
BENCH ISLAND	62	J 71 NE
BENGER BURN	54	N 64 NW
BERGHAN POINT	2	E 4 NW
BESTS ISLAND	32	C 39 NW
BETHELLS BEACH	5	I 15 NW
BIG BAY		
(SOUTHLAND)	47	I 56 SW
(TASMAN)	31	Y 37 NW
BIG GLORY BAY	61	J 71 SW
BIG HOPWOOD BURN	48	N 56 SW
BIG LAGOON	29	G 41 NW
BIG MOGGY ISLAND	61	G 72 SE
BIG MUDDY CREEK	65	H 4 SW
BIG RIVER		
(BULLER)	33	V 44 SE
(SOUTHLAND)	57	E 66 SE
(TASMAN)	31	Y 37 NE
BIG SOUTH CAPE ISLAND	61	G 73 NE
BILLY GOAT POINT	66	E 7 NE
BIRD ISLAND		
(CENTRAL HAWKES BAY)	24	T 31 NE
(DUNEDIN CITY)	56	S 65 NW
(SOUTHLAND)	62	K 70 NW
BISCUIT STREAM	28	O 37 SW
BISHOP & CLERKS ISLANDS	61	H 70 NE
BLACK HEAD		
(DUNEDIN CITY)	56	R 65 NE
(MARLBOROUGH)	29	G 38 NE
BLACK JACK POINT	80	E 6 NE
BLACK REEF	18	T 30 SW
BLACK ROCK	61	J 72 SE
BLACK ROCK POINT	61	I 70 NE
BLACK ROCKS		
(SOUTH WAIRARAPA)	27	L 41 NW
(THAMES COROMANDEL)	8	O 14 NE
BLACKHEAD POINT	24	R 33 SE
BLACKWATER RIVER	33	W 43 NE
BLACKWOOD BAY	76	D 4 NW
BLAIKIES CREEK	61	I 72 NW
BLANCHARDS BLUFF	37	P 50 SE
BLANKET BAY	80	D 7 NW
BLIGH SOUND	51	G 59 SW
BLIND BAY	6	M 11 SE
BLUE CREEK	53	M 63 NW
BLUE LAKE		
(QUEENSTOWN LAKES)	53	L 63 NE
(TAUPO)	16	N 27 SW
BLUESKIN BAY	56	S 64 NE
BLUFF HARBOUR	59	K 69 NW
BLUMINE ISLAND	29	G 38 SE
BOAT BAY	66	H 5 NE
BOBBYS HEAD	56	T 63 NW
BOBS POINT	61	J 70 SW
BOMBAY ROCK	59	J 69 NE
BONAR KNOB	47	I 56 NE
BOOM ROCK	27	J 38 SW
BOTTLE POINT	27	F 36 SW
BOULDER BANK	29	G 40 SE
BOULDER BAY	78	E 8 SE
BOULDER BEACH	80	E 7 NW
BOULDER LAKE	31	A 37 NW
BOULDER STREAM	35	C 41 SW
BOUNDARY CREEK	49	Q 59 SE
BOUNTY HAVEN	51	G 59 SW
BOWEN CHANNEL	57	D 65 NW
BOWENTOWN HEADS	68	B 2 NW
BOYLE RIVER	39	Z 45 SE
BRADSHAW SOUND	51	E 62 SE
BRANCH RIVER	35	C 42 NW
BREAKER BAY	73	F 3 NE
BREAKSEA ISLAND	57	D 64 NW
BREAKSEA ISLANDS	62	J 72 NE
BREAKSEA SOUND	57	C 64 NE
BREAM BAY	4	I 9 SE
BREAM HEAD	4	J 9 NW
BREAM ISLANDS	4	J 9 NW
BREAM TAIL	4	I 10 NE
BREAST CREEK	48	N 58 NE
BREEZE BAY	78	E 8 SE
BRICK BAT BAY	64	F 4 NE
BRIG ROCK	47	H 58 NW
BRINNS HEAD	56	S 64 NE
BROAD BAY	80	E 7 NW
BROAD HEAD	61	H 73 NE
BROKEN ISLANDS	6	L 11 SE
BROKEN RIVER	41	W 50 NE
BROOKLANDS LAGOON	78	B 7 SE
BROOKLYN STREAM	75	D 2 NE
BROUGHTON ARM	57	E 64 NW
BROWNE ISLAND	47	I 55 SE
BROWNS BAY	65	G 2 SE
BROWNS BAY	80	D 5 SE
BROWNS ISLAND	6	K 14 SW
BRUCE BAY	43	O 52 NW
BRUCE ROCKS	56	R 65 NE
BRYCE BURN	53	G 66 NE
BULLER BAY	33	V 42 NE
BULLER RIVER	33	W 42 SW
BULLERS POINT	62	J 71 NE
BULRUSH LAKE	1	B 3 NE
BUNKER ISLETS	62	K 71 NE
BURGESS BAY	6	K 12 SW
BURGESS ISLAND	6	G 11 NE
BURNS POINT	80	E 6 NW
BURNT PATH	66	S 53 NE
BUSH CREEK	44	S 53 NE
BUSHY POINT	30	H 39 NW

CABLE BAY	29	D 38 SW
CALYPSO BAY	66	F 8 NW
CAMELOT RIVER	51	E 62 SE
CAMERON RIVER	45	T 51 NE
CAMP BAY		
(BANKS PENINSULA)	78	F 8 NW
(FAR NORTH)	63	A 1 NW
CAMP CREEK	48	N 58 SE
CAMPBELL POINT	60	P 68 NE
CAMPBELLS BAY	64	E 5 NE
CANNIBAL BAY	60	P 68 SW
CANNIBAL CREEK	65	G 2 SW
CANTERBURY BIGHT	46	Z 55 NW
CAPE BARRIER	6	N 12 NW
CAPE BRETT	2	H 5 SE
CAPE CAMPBELL	36	H 41 SW
CAPE COLVILLE	6	M 12 SW
CAPE EGMONT	21	F 28 NW
CAPE FAREWELL	31	A 35 NW
CAPE FOULWIND	33	V 42 NW
CAPE JACKSON	30	H 37 SE
CAPE KARIKARI	1	D 3 NE
CAPE KIDNAPPERS	18	T 30 SW
CAPE KOAMARU	30	H 38 NE
CAPE LAMBERT	30	H 37 SW
CAPE MARIA VAN DIEMEN	1	A 1 SW
CAPE PALLISER	27	L 41 NE
CAPE PROVIDENCE	57	C 66 SE
CAPE REINGA	1	A 1 NW
CAPE RIVER	27	L 40 SE
CAPE RODNEY	6	K 11 SW
CAPE RUNAWAY	14	X 19 SE
CAPE SAUNDERS	56	T 65 NW
CAPE SOUCIS	29	E 38 NW
CAPE STEPHENS	29	F 36 NE
CAPE TERAWHITI	27	I 39 SE
CAPE TURNAGAIN	26	R 35 NW
CAPE WIWIKI	2	H 5 SE
CAPLES RIVER	52	J 59 SW
CARDRONA RIVER	53	M 59 SW
CAREYS BAY	80	C 7 SW
CAROLINE BAY		
(SOUTHLAND)	62	K 70 NE
(TIMARU)	50	U 56 SE
CAROLINE BURN	57	F 66 NW
CARTER PASSAGE	62	J 71 NE
CARTERS BEACH	9	J 19 SE
CASCADE POINT	47	J 55 NW
CASCADE RIVER	47	J 56 NE
CASS BAY	78	E 7 SW
CASS RIVER	44	R 53 NW
CASTLE ISLAND	29	G 39 NW
CASTLE POINT	28	P 37 SW
CASTLE RIVER	27	L 40 SE
CASTOR BAY	6	J 14 SE
CASWELL SOUND	51	E 60 NE
CATHERINE COVE	76	A 3 SW
CATLINS LAKE	60	P 68 SW
CATLINS RIVER	30	N 67 SE
CAVALLI ISLANDS	2	G 4 NW
CAVE POINT	61	H 70 NE
CAVE ROCK	78	E 8 NW
CAVE STREAM	38	W 50 NE
CENTRE ISLAND	58	I 68 SW
CHALKY INLET	57	C 66 SE
CHALKY ISLAND	57	C 67 NE
CHALLIS POINT	80	E 6 NE
CHANNEL ISLAND	6	M 12 SW
CHARLES SOUND	51	E 61 NE
CHARWELL RIVER	35	D 45 SW
CHASLANDS MISTAKE	60	O 69 NE
CHASM ISLAND	60	O 69 NE
CHATTO CREEK	49	O 61 NW
CHELSEA BAY	47	F 5 NE
CHELTENHAM BEACH	64	F 6 NE
CHERRY BAY	16	N 25 SE
CHETWODE ISLANDS	29	G 37 NW
CHEW TOBACCO POINT	61	J 71 SE
CHRISTMAS VILLAGE BAY	61	I 70 SE
CHURCH BAY	78	F 7 NE
CLARENCE RIVER	36	F 44 NE
CLARK POINT	30	H 38 SW
CLARKE RIVER		
(GREY)	33	X 45 SW
(TASMAN)	31	A 40 NW
(WESTLAND)	43	N 54 NE
CLAY POINT	29	F 37 NE
CLEAR STREAM	49	Q 59 NW
CLIFFORD BAY	36	G 41 SE
CLINTON RIVER	52	H 60 NE
CLIVE RIVER	18	S 30 NE
CLOUDY BAY	29	G 40 NW
CLUDEN STREAM	48	O 56 NW
CLUTHA RIVER	55	O 65 NW
CLYDE RIVER	37	S 51 NE
COAL CREEK	53	M 62 NW
COAL ISLAND	57	C 67 NW
COBB RESERVOIR	31	A 38 SW
COCHRANES GAP	7	I 16 SE
COCKLE BAY	66	G 8 SW
CODFISH ISLAND	61	H 70 SW
COLAC BAY	58	I 68 NW
COLINS BAY	53	K 61 NE
COLLINS BAY	65	F 1 SE
COLONIAL HEAD	51	E 61 SW
COLVILLE BAY	6	M 13 SE
COLVILLE BAY	6	M 12 NW
COLVILLE CHANNEL	80	D 6 SE
COMPANY BAY	61	H 2 SW
COMPANY STREAM	65	H 2 SW
CONE ISLAND	2	F 4 NW
CONTOUR CHANNEL STREAM	79	E 2 SW
CONWAY RIVER	40	D 46 NW
COOK CHANNEL	57	D 65 NW
COOK RIVER	43	P 51 SW
COOK STRAIT	27	I 40 NW
COOKS ARM	61	H 72 SE
COOKS BAY	8	N 14 SE
COOMBE BEACH	29	G 39 SE
COOPER ISLAND	57	D 65 NE
COPLAND RIVER	43	O 52 SW
CORALIE BAY	57	D 66 SE
CORDING ISLAND	58	S 63 SE
CORNISH HEAD	56	S 63 SE
CORNWALLIS BEACH	7	I 15 SE
COROMANDEL HARBOUR	6	M 14 SE
COROMANDEL PENINSULA	8	O 15 NE
CORSAIR BAY	78	F 7 NW
COSGROVE ISLAND	60	O 69 NE
COSSEYS RESERVOIR	7	L 15 SW

Location	Map No.	Ref
COW ISLAND	62	J 71 NE
COX RIVER	39	X 48 NE
COXS BAY	64	F 5 SW
CRADDOCK CHANNEL	6	L 11 SE
CRAIGIEBURN CREEK	75	C 1 SE
CRAIL BAY	29	F 38 SE
CRATER LAKE	16	M 28 NE
CROISILLES HARBOUR	29	E 38 NW
CROMBIE HEAD	57	F 67 NW
CROMEL STREAM	53	J 63 SE
CROOKED ARM	51	E 63 NW
CROW RIVER	31	Z 39 SE
CROWLES BAY	63	C 3 NE
CUDLIP POINT	64	A 5 SE
CULDAFF POINT	29	G 37 NW
CULLEN CREEK	76	E 2 NE
CUNARIS SOUND	57	D 66 NE
CURIO BAY	60	M 69 SE
CURLS POINT	80	D 6 NE
CURRENT BASIN	29	F 37 SW
CUTTER ROCK	65	J 2 SW
CUTTER ROCKS	47	I 56 NE
CUVIER ISLAND	8	O 12 SW
D'URVILLE PENINSULA	29	F 37 NE
D'URVILLE RIVER	34	A 43 NW
DAGG SOUND	51	D 63 NW
DARK RIVER	51	G 60 NE
DART RIVER	47	J 59 NW
DAYS BAY	73	E 4 NE
DEADMANS POINT	6	M 15 NW
DEAN BURN	58	G 65 SE
DEBORAH BAY	80	C 7 SW
DEEP CREEK		
(CENTRAL OTAGO)	54	P 64 NE
(TASMAN)	75	D 1 SW
DEEP STREAM		
(CENTRAL OTAGO)	50	R 57 SE
(TIMARU)	75	P 64 NE
DEEPDALE RIVER	34	Y 43 NW
DELAWARE BAY	29	D 38 SE
DEVIL RIVER	75	C 1 NW
DIAMOND LAKE	47	J 59 NW
DILLON RIVER	35	C 45 NW
DINGLE BURN	48	N 57 NE
DIP CREEK	48	O 58 NW
DIPTON STREAM	58	J 65 NE
DIVIDE HEAD	57	D 66 NW
DOBSON RIVER	43	P 55 NW
DOCTORS POINT	80	B 6 SE
DOG ISLAND	58	K 69 SW
DOLOMITE POINT	33	U 44 NE
DOME BURN	53	L 64 NW
DONALD RIVER	18	Q 28 SE
DOOLANS CREEK	53	L 61 NE
DOON RIVER	51	G 61 SW
DOUBLE BAY	76	D 3 NW
DOUBLE LAKE	8	O 13 SE
DOUBTFUL RIVER	39	Y 46 NE
DOUBTFUL SOUND	51	D 62 NE
DOUBTLESS BAY	1	D 4 NE
DOUGHBOY BAY	4	H 72 NE
DOVEDALE CREEK	54	P 61 SW
DOWLING BAY	80	C 7 SE
DRY RIVER	27	L 39 SE
DRYDEN BAY	48	M 58 SW
DUBLIN BAY	48	M 58 SW
DUCK CREEK	61	I 71 NW
DUMMY BAY	75	D 3 NW
DUNSDALE STREAM	59	K 66 SE
DUNSTAN CREEK	49	O 59 NE
D'URVILLE ISLAND	29	F 36 SW
DUSKY SOUND	57	C 65 NW
EARTHQUAKE LAKES	31	Z 39 NE
EAST BAY		
(FAR NORTH)	2	F 4 SE
(MARLBOROUGH)	30	H 38 SW
EAST BEACH	1	C 3 SE
EAST CAPE		
(GISBORNE)	14	A 20 NW
(SOUTHLAND)	62	J 71 SE
EAST HEAD	30	H 39 NE
EAST ISLAND	14	A 20 NW
EASTERN PASSAGE	57	C 67 NE
ECHO LAKE	10	Q 23 SW
EDWARDS ISLAND	62	J 70 SE
EDWARDS RIVER	34	A 45 SW
EDWARDSON SOUND	57	D 66 NW
EGG ISLAND	68	C 2 NW
EGLINTON RIVER	52	H 61 SE
ELECTRIC RIVER	57	F 65 SE
ELLIS RIVER	75	E 1 SW
EMELIUS ARM	51	E 61 NE
EMERALD LAKES	16	N 27 SW
EMU BAY	66	E 7 SE
EMU POINT	66	F 7 NE
ENDEAVOUR INLET	29	G 38 SE
ENGLISH BAY	81	E 3 SW
ENTRY ISLAND	57	D 64 NW
ERANGI POINT	5	I 15 NW
ERNEST ISLAND	61	H 73 NE
ERNEST ISLANDS	61	H 71 SE
ERSKINE POINT	78	F 7 NE
ESCAPE REEFS	58	I 68 SW
ESK RIVER	18	S 29 NE
ETAL STREAM	58	I 65 NE
ETTRICK BURN	51	G 62 NE
EVES VALLEY STREAM	75	D 1 NE
EYRE RIVER		
(QUEENSTOWN LAKES)	52	K 63 SW
(WAIMAKARIRI)	42	Z 51 NE
FAIRCHILD REEF	6	K 12 NW
FAIRY BAY	76	C 2 SE
FALLS DAM	49	P 59 SE
FALLS RIVER	75	C 3 NW
FALSE ISLET	60	P 68 SW
FANTAIL BAY	6	M 13 NW
FAREWELL SPIT	31	A 35 NE
FARLEY POINT	65	H 2 SW
FARMER PT	1	C 3 NE
FEBRERO POINT	51	D 62 SE
FINGER POINT	6	L 14 SW
FIRST ARM	51	E 62 SW
FIRTH OF THAMES	8	M 16 NE
FISHERMAN ISLAND	32	C 37 SW
FISHERMANS ROCK	65	H 1 NE
FITZPATRICK BAY	64	F 5 NW
FITZROY BAY		
(LOWER HUTT)	27	J 40 NW
(MARLBOROUGH)	76	B 2 SW
FIVE FINGERS PENINSULA	57	C 64 SE
FIVE FINGERS POINT	57	C 65 NW
FIVE MILE BAY	70	C 4 NW
FIVE MILE BEACH	37	P 50 SE
FLAT CREEK	75	D 2 NW
FLAT ISLAND		
(FAR NORTH)	2	F 4 SE
(THAMES COROMANDEL)	8	O 14 NE
FLAT POINT		
(MASTERTON)	28	O 39 NW
(SOUTHLAND)	51	F 59 SE
FLAXBOURNE RIVER	36	G 42 NW
FLEA BAY	42	B 53 SE
FLETCHER BAY	6	M 12 SE
FLORA STREAM	75	E 1 NE
FLOUR CASK BAY	61	H 73 SW
FOOT ARM	51	E 62 NE
FOREST CREEK	44	T 53 NW
FORK STREAM	44	R 53 SW
FORSYTH BAY	29	G 37 SE
FORSYTH ISLAND	29	G 37 SW
FOUL POINT	32	C 37 NW
FOVEAUX STRAIT	61	I 69 NW
FOX RIVER	33	V 43 SW
FRASER RIVER	54	M 61 SE
FREAR BAY	63	A 1 NW
FRENCH BAY	65	H 4 NE
FRESHWATER RIVER	61	I 71 NE
GABLE END FORELAND	14	Y 24 SE
GABLE ISLET	14	Y 24 SE
GARDEN POINT	61	I 70 SE
GARDINER GAP	66	F 7 SE
GARNOCK BURN	58	G 64 NW
GEAR ARM	51	E 62 SE
GEORGE RIVER	51	F 60 SE
GEORGE SOUND	51	F 60 NW
GEORGES STREAM	65	H 3 SW
GIBSON BEACH	9	J 19 SE
GILBERT ISLANDS	57	D 64 NW
GILLESPIES POINT	43	O 51 SE
GLASGOW BAY	30	H 39 SW
GLEESON STREAM	65	G 2 SE
GLENCOE RIVER	39	A 47 NW
GLENDHU ROCKS	28	N 40 NW
GLENRAE RIVER	39	Z 47 SE
GLENROY RIVER	34	Z 44 NW
GOAT ISLAND		
(DUNEDIN CITY)	80	D 7 NW
(RODNEY)	6	J 11 SE
GODLEY HEAD	78	E 8 SE
GODLEY RIVER	44	R 52 SE
GOLD ARM	51	E 61 SE
GOLDEN BAY	32	B 36 NW
GOLLANS BAY	78	E 8 SW
GOLLANS STREAM	73	F 4 NW
GORGE CREEK	61	I 72 NE
GORGE ISLANDS	47	I 56 NE
GORGE RIVER	47	I 56 NE
GOUGHS BAY	42	C 53 SW
GOVERNORS BAY	78	F 6 NE
GOW BURN	53	L 63 NE
GOWAN RIVER	34	A 41 SW
GRAHAM STREAM	75	E 1 NE
GRAHAMS POINT	29	E 38 NW
GRANNYS BAY	66	H 5 NE
GRASSY POINT	80	D 7 SW
GRAYS RIVER	44	R 55 SE
GREAT BARRIER ISLAND	6	N 11 SW
GREAT EXHIBITION BAY	1	C 2 SE
GREAT ISLAND		
(SELWYN)	41	Y 53 SE
(SOUTHLAND)	57	D 66 SW
GREAT MERCURY ISLAND	8	O 13 SW
GREBE RIVER	57	F 64 SE
GRECIAN STREAM	75	D 1 SE
GREEN BAY	65	H 4 NE
GREEN GULLY	49	R 59 SW
GREEN ISLAND		
(DUNEDIN CITY)	56	R 65 NE
(SOUTHLAND)	62	L 70 NW
(THAMES COROMANDEL)	8	O 13 SE
GREEN LAKE	58	G 65 NW
GREEN POINT		
(DUNEDIN CITY)	80	A 7 SE
(PORIRUA CITY)	27	J 38 SW
GREENLAND RESERVOIR	54	O 62 SE
GREENSTONE RIVER	52	I 60 NE
GRENVILLE POINT	1	C 3 NE
GREVILLE HARBOUR	29	F 36 SW
GREY RIVER	33	V 45 SW
GUARDS BAY	76	B 4 NW
GULCHES HEAD	57	D 67 NW
GULL ROCK POINT	61	I 70 SE
GUYS CLIFF	66	F 8 NW
HAAST RIVER	43	M 54 SE
HAAST SPIT	43	L 54 NE
HAKATARAMEA RIVER	50	S 58 NW
HALDANE BAY	60	M 69 SE
HALF WAY POINT	57	F 36 SE
HALFMOON BAY	36	F 44 SW
HALL ARM	57	E 63 SE
HALLETTS BAY	18	O 26 NE
HAMENGA STREAM	4	G 8 NW
HAMILTON BAY	80	C 7 SE
HAMILTONS GAP	7	I 16 NE
HANGAROA RIVER	13	U 24 SE
HANMER RIVER	38	B 46 SW
HAPAKAPAPA STREAM	17	L 30 NE
HAPARAPARA RIVER	14	W 20 SE
HAPOKAPAPA STREAM	13	L 30 NE
HARAKEHE HEAD	56	S 65 NE
HARAKEKE ISLAND	5	H 5 NW
HARAWEKA ISLAND	63	A 2 NE
HARBOUR ISLAND	57	D 64 NE
HARIHARI BEACH	9	J 22 NW
HARPER RIVER	44	V 50 NE
HARRIS BAY	78	E 8 SW
HARWICH ISLAND	29	M 58 NW
HATEA RIVER	82	E 4 SE
HATUMA LAKE	24	Q 32 SE
HAUMI RIVER	81	D 1 SE
HAUPARA POINT	14	Z 19 SW
HAUPARUA INLET	25	C 3 SE
HAUPIRI RIVER	38	W 46 SE
HAURAKI GULF	6	L 13 SE
HAURERE POINT	13	V 21 SW
HAUROKO BURN	57	F 65 NW
HAUTAPU CHANNEL	6	M 14 NW
HAUTAPU POINT	6	M 14 NW
HAUTAPU RIVER		
(HASTINGS)	18	R 26 SW
(RANGITIKEI)	17	N 30 NE
HAUTURU ISLAND	8	O 17 NE
HAVELOCK RIVER	44	S 51 SE
HAWAI RIVER	13	V 21 NE
HAWES HEAD	51	E 61 NE
HAWKE BAY	19	U 28 NW
HAWKINS RIVER	46	Y 52 NW
HAYWARD POINT	60	P 68 SW
HAZELBURGH GROUP	62	K 70 SE
HEAD OF THE BAY	78	F 7 SW
HEAO STREAM	16	K 27 SW
HEAPHY BLUFF	31	X 37 SE
HEAPHY RIVER	31	Y 37 NW
HEDGEHOPE RIVER	59	L 67 NW
HEIMAMA STREAM	21	F 29 NW
HEKERANGI POINT	20	W 28 SE
HELLYERS CREEK	64	E 4 SE
HEN AND CHICKEN ISLANDS	4	J 9 SE
HENDERSON BAY	1	C 3 NE
HENDERSON POINT	1	C 3 NW
HENRIETTA BAY	62	K 70 NE
HEREHERE STREAM	71	C 3 NW
HEREKINO HARBOUR	1	C 6 NW
HEREKOPARE ISLAND	62	J 71 NE
HERETANIWHA POINT	43	N 52 SE
HERMIONE ROCK	81	J 1 SE
HERON RIVER	8	J 71 SW
HEYWOOD POINT	56	S 64 SE
HICKORY BAY	42	C 53 NW
HICKS BAY	14	Z 19 SW
HIDDEN LAKE	51	F 62 NE
HIKAPU REACH	76	D 2 NE
HIKAUAE CREEK	64	A 4 NE
HIKUAI RIVER	8	O 16 NW
HIKUWAI RIVER	14	Y 23 NE
HINDS RIVER	45	W 55 NE
HINEMAIAIA RIVER	17	P 26 NW
HINGAIA POINT	6	L 11 NW
HOBBS BAY	6	C 6 NW
HOBSON BAY	66	C 6 NW
HOBSON BEACH	81	B 1 SW
HODGEN VALLEY STREAM	75	F 2 NE
HOG BURN	49	Q 60 NE
HOKIANGA HARBOUR	3	D 7 NE
HOKIO STREAM	25	K 35 SE
HOKITIKA RIVER	37	T 48 SW
HOLLYFORD RIVER	47	I 58 SW
HOME BAY		
(AUCKLAND CITY)	64	F 5 SE
(MOTUTAPU ISLAND)	66	E 8 SE
(RAKINO ISLAND)	66	E 8 NW
HOME POINT	4	I 6 NW
HOMUNGA BAY	8	O 17 SE
HONEYCOMB ROCK	28	N 40 NE
HONGIORA ISLAND	8	P 15 SW
HOOPER POINT	1	B 1 NW
HOOPERS INLET	80	D 7 SE
HOPE RIVER	39	Y 46 SW
HOPKINS RIVER	43	P 54 SW
HOROERA POINT	14	A 19 SW
HOROKIWI STREAM	73	B 4 NE
HOROMAKA ISLAND	78	F 8 SE
HORORATA RIVER	46	X 52 NE
HOROROA POINT	63	A 2 NW
HORSESHORE POINT	61	J 71 NW
HOUGHTON BAY	27	J 39 SW
HOWE PT	2	G 5 SE
HOWELLS POINT	58	I 68 NE
HUANGARUA RIVER	28	M 39 SE
HUAPE STREAM	13	T 22 SE
HUAROA POINT	64	B 7 SW
HUATOKITOKI STREAM	24	R 33 SE
HUEHUE STREAM	63	F 1 NW
HUIA BAY	65	J 3 NW
HUIA RESERVOIR	65	H 3 SW
HUIA STREAM	65	H 3 SW
HUMP BURN	58	G 66 SW
HUNTER RIVER	48	N 56 NE
HUNTERS CREEK	68	C 3 SW
HURIMOANA SWAMP	71	C 1 SE
HURUHI HARBOUR	8	O 13 SW
HURUNUI RIVER	40	D 48 SW
HURUNUI RIVER SOUTH BRANCH	39	Y 47 SE
HURUNUI STREAM	68	E 1 SE
HURURU STREAM	69	B 2 NW
HUTIWAI STREAM	15	I 25 SE
HUTT RIVER	27	K 38 NE
IDA BURN	49	P 60 SW
IHUMOANA ISLAND	65	G 1 NE
IHUNGIA RIVER	14	Y 21 SE
IKAWATEA STREAM	18	P 30 NE
INANGAHUA RIVER	34	X 44 SE
INDIAN ISLAND	57	D 65 NW
INNER CHANNEL	6	J 12 SE
INUMIA STREAM	63	C 1 NE
IOTA BLUFF	47	J 55 NW
IRENE RIVER	51	F 61 SE
IRIS BURN	51	G 63 NE
IRTHING RIVER	52	J 63 NE
ISLAND BAY	64	F 4 NE
ISLAND LAKE		
(SOUTHLAND)	57	F 65 NE
(TASMAN)	31	Z 38 NE
ISLAND STREAM	65	H 3 SE
ISLET POINT	51	E 61 NE
ISLINGTON BAY	66	E 7 SE
JACKETT ISLAND	32	C 38 SW
JACKSON BAY	47	K 54 SW
JACKSON HEAD	47	K 54 SW
JACKSON RIVER	47	K 55 SW
JACKY LEE ISLAND	62	J 70 SE
JAG ROCKS	29	G 36 SW
JELLICOE CHANNEL	6	K 11 NW
JELLICOE POINT	17	O 26 NE
JENKINS BAY	65	H 4 SW
JERUSALEM BAY	70	B 4 SW
JOHN ISLAND	57	D 64 NW
JOHN POINT	62	J 72 NE
JOHNSON CREEK	76	E 1 NW
JOLLIE RIVER	44	Q 53 SE
JONKERS ROCK	65	G 1 NE
KAHAO STREAM	27	J 38 NE
KAHAROA STREAM	13	U 23 NW
KAHUA POINT	9	J 21 SW
KAHUNUI STREAM	13	U 24 NW
KAHURANGI POINT	31	Y 36 SW
KAHUTARA RIVER	36	D 45 NE
KAHUWERA STREAM	4	G 7 SW
KAI IWI LAKES	3	E 9 NE
KAI IWI STREAM	22	K 31 NE
KAIARAARA ISLAND	81	B 3 SE
KAIAUA BAY	14	Z 23 SW
KAIAUAI STREAM	15	G 28 NE
KAIHAKA LAKES	31	A 35 NW
KAIITI POINT	6	M 12 SW
KAIKAI BEACH	80	C 7 NE
KAIKAIKURI STREAM	28	M 39 SE
KAIKORAI STREAM	79	E 4 SE
KAIKOURA ISLAND	6	M 11 NW
KAIKOURA PENINSULA	36	E 45 SE
KAIMOHO POINT	14	Z 21 SE
KAIMOHU ISLAND	61	I 73 SE
KAIPAKATI POINT	33	U 43 SE
KAIPARA ENTRANCE	5	G 12 SE
KAIPARA HARBOUR	5	H 12 SE
KAIPARA HEAD	5	G 12 NE
KAIPARA RIVER	65	E 2 NW
KAIPARA STREAM	72	R 22 NW
KAIPATIKI STREAM	6	D 3 NE
KAIPO RIVER	47	H 57 SE
KAIRA CREEK	5	H 11 SE
KAITARAKIHI POINT	65	J 3 NW
KAITEKE POINT	65	J 3 SE
KAITORETE SPIT	42	A 53 SW
KAITUKALA ISLANDS	6	J 12 SE
KAITUNA RIVER		
(MARLBOROUGH)	29	E 39 SE
(ROTORUA)	10	Q 21 NE
KAIWHATA RIVER	28	O 39 NW
KAIWHITU POINT	5	G 11 NE
KAKAMATUA INLET	65	H 3 NE
KAKANUI POINT	50	T 61 NE
KAKANUI RIVER	50	T 61 NE
KANAE BAY	76	D 4 SE
KANETOETOE ISLAND	62	J 71 NE
KANGAROO LAKE	38	V 46 SE
KANIHI STREAM	13	T 23 SW
KANINIHI POINT	61	H 73 SW
KANIWHANIWHA STREAM	67	D 2 NW
KAPITI ISLAND	25	J 36 SE
KAPOAIAIA STREAM	21	F 28 NW
KAPOWAI RIVER	8	O 15 SW
KAPUAPOUNAMU RIVER	14	Y 20 NE
KAPAKA BAY		
(GISBORNE)	14	Z 23 SW
(MARLBOROUGH)	29	G 39 SE
KARAKA POINT	29	G 39 NW
KARAKATUWHERO RIVER	14	Y 20 SE
KARAMEA BIGHT	33	W 40 SW
KARAMEA ISLAND	24	S 31 SE
KARAMEA RIVER	31	X 39 NE
KARAMU RIVER	71	E 2 SE
KARAMU STREAM	22	K 31 NW
KARAMURAMU ISLAND	6	L 15 NE
KARANGARUA RIVER	43	O 52 NE
KARAUI PT	2	F 4 NW
KAREKARE POINT	65	H 2 SW
KAREKARE STREAM	65	H 2 SW
KAREPIRO BAY	64	C 5 SE
KARERE LAGOON	72	D 2 SW
KAREWA ISLAND	10	P 18 SE
KARIKARI BEACH	1	D 3 SW
KARIKARI MOANA	1	D 3 NW
KARIKARI PENINSULA	1	D 3 SE
KARIOITAHI BEACH	7	J 17 NW
KARIPARIPA PT	1	H 5 SE
KARORI ROCK	27	I 39 SE
KARORI STREAM	73	F 1 NE
KATHERINE BAY	6	M 10 SW
KATIKATI ENTRANCE	10	P 18 SW
KATIKI POINT	56	T 62 NW
KATIRAEA	29	G 37 SW
KAU BAY	73	E 3 NE
KAUAKA STREAM	69	D 1 NE
KAUMINGI STREAM	28	O 38 NW
KAUPOKONUI STREAM	21	G 30 NW
KAURI POINT PONUI	6	L 15 NW
KAURI POINT WAIHEKE	6	L 14 SE
KAURU RIVER	50	S 61 NE
KAUTUKU SWAMP	71	C 1 SE
KAUWAHAIA ISLAND	65	G 1 NE
KAWAKAPUTA BAY	58	I 68 NW
KAWAKAWA BAY	11	O 25 NW
KAWAKAWA POINT	11	O 25 NW
KAWAKAWA RIVER	81	F 3 SE
KAWARAU RIVER	53	L 60 SE
KAWAU BAY	6	J 12 NE
KAWAU ISLAND	6	K 12 SW
KAWAU POINT	6	K 12 SW
KAWAUTAHI STREAM	16	L 27 NE
KAWHATAU RIVER	23	O 31 SE
KAWHIA HARBOUR	9	J 21 SE
KELP POINT	61	H 73 NE
KEMPE POINT	30	H 38 NW
KENDALL BAY	6	J 12 NW
KENEPURU SOUND	29	F 39 NE
KENNEDY BAY	8	N 14 NW
KENT PASSAGE	63	C 2 NE
KEREO RIVER	14	W 20 NE
KERIKERI INLET	2	G 5 SE
KERIKERI RIVER	2	F 5 SE
KERR POINT	1	B 1 NE
KETU BAY	76	B 3 NE
KIAKIA	29	G 37 SW
KIKOWHERO STREAM	13	Q 30 NE
KILGOUR POINT	80	D 7 NW
KING BILLY ISLAND	78	F 7 NW
KIRETEHERE BEACH	9	J 23 NW
KIRIKIRI BAY	65	F 1 SE
KIRIKIRI STREAM	6	E 1 SW
KIRIKIRITOKI STREAM	82	E 1 SW
KIRITA BAY	8	M 15 NE
KIWI BURN	57	D 67 SE
KIWITEA STREAM	23	M 33 SE
KNIGHTS POINT	43	M 53 NE
KNOBBY CREEK	53	L 63 SE
KNUCKLE POINT	1	D 3 SE
KOHAIHAI BLUFF	31	X 38 NE
KOHAIHAI RIVER	31	Y 38 NW
KOHAKAWA BEACH	1	A 2 NW

Coastal & Water Features

Coastal & Water Features

Location	Map No.	Ref
OHIOAWA BEACH	12	R 20 SE
OHUNUI BAY	65	H 1 NE
OITIATA STREAM	25	L 33 NW
OKATAHI RIVER	38	U 48 SW
ONGAHU POINT	31	X 40 NE
ONINI STREAM	12	T 23 SW
OPONGATAHI POINT	14	X 29 NE
OPUAWHARA STREAM	20	W 27 NE
OPUERA STREAM	7	L 17 NW
ORANGA RIVER	13	U 24 NE
ORAPUKI ISLAND	8	O 14 NE
OROMATUA STREAM	65	G 2 NE
OROPOTIKI STREAM	65	G 2 SE
ORORAREKA BAY	81	A 3 SE
ORORAREKA POINT	81	A 3 SW
OTI STREAM	22	J 30 SE
OUKOUPO RIVER	17	M 30 NE
OUTUAMOA POINT	14	Z 21 NE
OUTUNUI HEAD	14	Z 22 SW
OUTUNUI POINT	14	Z 22 SW
OWAI RIVER	42	A 50 NE
OWHAI BEACH	1	C 3 NE
OWHATUHURI PT	2	G 5 NE
OUAMAHANGA STREAM	28	N 38 SE
OUATA PT	1	D 4 NW
OUATAIKA STREAM	65	G 2 NE
OUMEU RIVER	76	D 4 NW
OUMUTOTO BAY	61	J 72 SW
OURI POINT	61	J 72 SW
OURI STREAM	15	J 28 NE
OUROW RIVER	50	R 59 NE
OURUKOHATU POINT	29	K 37 NW
KYE BURN	49	N 60 SW
LADY LAKE	38	W 46 SW
LAGOON BAY	62	K 70 NE
LAINGHOLM POINT	7	J 15 SW
LAKE ADA	47	H 59 NE
LAKE ADELAIDE	47	I 59 NW
LAKE AHAURA	38	W 46 SE
LAKE ALABASTER	47	I 58 NE
LAKE ALEXANDRINA	44	R 54 NE
LAKE ALICE (MANAWATU)	23	L 33 NE
LAKE ALICE (SOUTHLAND)	60	G 60 SW
LAKE ARAPUNI	10	N 22 SE
LAKE ATIAMURI	10	P 23 SW
LAKE AVIEMORE	49	R 58 NW
LAKE BEATTIE	49	Q 57 NE
LAKE BENMORE	49	Q 57 NE
LAKE BLOXHAM	57	G 61 SW
LAKE BRIGHT	57	F 64 SW
LAKE BROWN	57	E 63 NE
LAKE BRUNNER	38	V 47 NW
LAKE CADMAN	57	D 65 SE
LAKE CARRICK	57	D 65 SE
LAKE CHALICE	29	D 40 SW
LAKE CHRISTABEL	34	Y 45 SE
LAKE CLEARWATER	45	T 52 NE
LAKE COBB	31	Z 38 NE
LAKE COLERIDGE	41	V 50 SE
LAKE CONSTANCE	34	A 43 SW
LAKE DANIELLS	34	Y 45 NE
LAKE DORA	51	E 62 NE
LAKE DOUGLAS	43	M 54 SW
LAKE DUNCAN	57	F 62 NE
LAKE DUNSTAN	54	N 60 NW
LAKE ELLERY	47	K 55 NW
LAKE ELLESMERE (TE WAIHORA)	42	Z 53 NE
LAKE ELMER	31	Y 38 NE
LAKE EMMA	45	U 52 SW
LAKE ERSKINE	52	I 59 SW
LAKE FORSYTH	42	A 53 NE
LAKE FRASER	57	C 66 NE
LAKE GRASMERE	41	W 49 NE
LAKE GRAVE	51	G 59 SE
LAKE GUNN	52	I 60 NW
LAKE GUYON	34	A 44 SW
LAKE HAKAPOUA	57	E 67 NE
LAKE HALL	51	F 62 SE
LAKE HANKINSON	51	G 61 NW
LAKE HARIHARI	9	J 22 SW
LAKE HARRIS	47	I 59 NE
LAKE HAUPIRI	38	W 46 SW
LAKE HAUROKO	57	F 66 NE
LAKE HAWEA	48	N 57 NW
LAKE HAY	57	E 65 NE
LAKE HEATON	25	L 33 NW
LAKE HENDERSON	31	Z 38 NE
LAKE HERENGAWE	22	I 31 NE
LAKE HERON	45	U 51 SW
LAKE HERRIES	51	F 62 SE
LAKE HILDA	51	F 62 NE
LAKE HOCHSTETTER	33	W 45 SW
LAKE HOROWHENUA	25	L 35 SW
LAKE HUMUHUMU	5	G 11 SE
LAKE IANTHE	37	S 49 NW
LAKE IDA	41	V 50 NE
LAKE INNES	57	E 67 SE
LAKE JEWELL	31	Z 38 SW
LAKE KAIKOKOPU	25	L 34 SE
LAKE KAITOKE	22	K 32 NE
LAKE KAKAPO	57	E 66 NE
LAKE KANIERE	38	U 48 NW
LAKE KANONO	5	G 12 NE
LAKE KARAPIRO	10	N 21 NW
LAKE KATHERINE	51	G 60 SW
LAKE KAURAPATAKA	38	W 47 SW
LAKE KAWAUPAKA	65	G 2 NW
LAKE KERETA	5	H 13 SE
LAKE KIMIHIA	9	L 18 SW
LAKE KOHANGAPIRIPIRI	73	F 4 SW
LAKE KOHANGATE	73	F 4 SW
LAKE KOITIATA	25	L 33 NW
LAKE KOPUERA	7	L 18 NW
LAKE KOPUTARA	25	L 34 SW
LAKE KOROMATUA	9	L 20 NE
LAKE KURATAU	17	N 26 NE
LAKE LOCKETT	31	A 38 NW
LAKE LUNA	52	K 60 NW
LAKE LYNDON	41	W 50 SW
LAKE MACKINNON	51	F 61 SE
LAKE MAHINAPUA	37	T 47 NW
LAKE MAHINERANGI	55	P 64 SE
LAKE MANAPOURI	58	G 63 SW
LAKE MANGAWHIO	22	J 30 NE
LAKE MANUWAI	2	F 5 NE
LAKE MAPOURIKA	37	Q 50 SE
LAKE MARAETAI	10	N 23 NE
LAKE MARATOTO	9	L 20 SE
LAKE MARCHANT	52	I 59 SW
LAKE MARIAN	52	I 59 SW
LAKE MASON	39	Y 47 NW
LAKE MATAHINA	12	S 22 NE
LAKE MATHESON	44	P 51 SE
LAKE MAUNGARATANUI	23	M 32 NE
LAKE MAUNGAROTOITI	23	M 32 NE
LAKE MCIVOR	51	G 61 NW
LAKE MCKERROW	47	I 57 NW
LAKE MCRAE	35	D 44 NW
LAKE MIKE	57	E 65 SW
LAKE MINERVA	51	F 62 SE
LAKE MOAWHANGO	17	N 29 NE
LAKE MOERAKI	43	M 53 NE
LAKE MOKENO	5	G 12 NW
LAKE MONK	57	E 67 SW
LAKE MONOWAI	58	G 65 SW
LAKE MOREHUREHU	1	B 2 SE
LAKE MORETON	47	G 59 NE
LAKE MOUMAHAKI	22	J 30 SW
LAKE NAMUNAMU	22	M 31 SW
LAKE NGAHEWA	10	Q 23 NW
LAKE NGAKEKETA	1	A 1 SE
LAKE NGAROTO	9	L 21 NE
LAKE NGARURU	22	M 31 SW
LAKE OHAKURI	10	P 23 SW
LAKE OHAU	43	P 55 SW
LAKE OHINEWAI	9	L 18 SW
LAKE OKAIHAU	65	F 1 NE
LAKE OKAREKA	10	Q 22 NW
LAKE OKARO	10	Q 23 NW
LAKE OKATAINA	10	Q 22 NE
LAKE OMAPERE	2	F 6 SW
LAKE ONOKE	27	K 40 NE
LAKE ONSLOW	54	O 63 NE
LAKE OPOURI	10	Q 23 NW
LAKE OPUHA	44	T 54 NW
LAKE ORATU	10	Q 23 SW
LAKE OTAMANGAKAU	16	N 26 SW
LAKE OTOTOA	5	H 13 NW
LAKE OTUHIE	31	Z 36 NW
LAKE OWHAREITI	2	G 5 SW
LAKE PAEKAWAU	65	E 1 SE
LAKE PAPAITONGA	25	L 36 NW
LAKE PARADISE	57	D 63 SE
LAKE PARINGA	43	N 53 NW
LAKE PATAKA	9	L 20 SE
LAKE PEARSON	41	W 49 SE
LAKE POERUA	38	V 47 NE
LAKE POKORUA	7	I 16 SE
LAKE POTERITERI	57	F 66 SW
LAKE POUARUA	18	Q 26 SW
LAKE POUKAWA	24	R 31 NE
LAKE POUNUI	27	K 39 SE
LAKE PUKAKI	44	Q 55 NE
LAKE PUPUKE	64	E 5 SE
LAKE PURSER	57	D 65 SE
LAKE RAKATU	58	G 64 NE
LAKE RASSELAS	43	N 53 NW
LAKE RATAPIKO	15	H 27 SE
LAKE REPONGAERE	20	W 25 NE
LAKE REREWHAKAAITU	12	R 23 NW
LAKE RIMMER	57	D 66 NW
LAKE ROE	57	F 64 SW
LAKE RONALD	47	G 58 SE
LAKE ROTOAIRA	16	N 27 NE
LAKE ROTOEHU	12	R 21 SW
LAKE ROTOITI (ROTORUA)	10	Q 21 SE
LAKE ROTOITI (TASMAN)	34	B 42 NW
LAKE ROTOKAKAHI	10	Q 22 SW
LAKE ROTOKARE	21	H 29 NE
LAKE ROTOKAWA (FAR NORTH)	1	D 3 SW
LAKE ROTOKAWA (ROTORUA)	12	P 25 NE
LAKE ROTOKAWAU (KAIPARA)	5	G 12 NE
LAKE ROTOKAWAU (ROTORUA)	10	Q 21 SE
LAKE ROTOKAWAU (WAIKATO)	9	L 18 NW
LAKE ROTOKINO	37	R 50 NW
LAKE ROTOKURA	16	N 27 NW
LAKE ROTOMA	12	R 21 SE
LAKE ROTOMAHANA	12	Q 23 NE
LAKE ROTONGARO	9	L 18 SW
LAKE ROTONGAROITI	7	L 18 SW
LAKE ROTONUIAHA	18	T 26 SW
LAKE ROTOPOUNAMU	16	N 27 NE
LAKE ROTOROA (FAR NORTH)	1	C 4 SE
LAKE ROTOROA (TASMAN)	34	A 42 SW
LAKE ROTORUA	10	Q 21 SW
LAKE ROXBURGH	54	N 62 SE
LAKE RUATANIWHA	49	Q 56 NW
LAKE RUATUNA	9	L 20 SE
LAKE SHEPPARD	39	Y 47 SE
LAKE STANLEY	31	A 39 NE
LAKE STREAM	45	U 51 NW
LAKE SUMNER	39	Y 47 NW
LAKE SWAN	57	D 63 SE
LAKE SYLVAN	47	I 59 NE
LAKE SYLVESTER	31	A 38 NW
LAKE TAEORE	1	B 2 SE
LAKE TAHAROA (KAIPARA)	3	E 8 SE
LAKE TAHAROA (WAIKATO)	9	J 22 NW
LAKE TAMURENUI	12	S 21 SW
LAKE TARAWERA	10	Q 22 SE
LAKE TAUPO	17	O 25 SE
LAKE TAYLOR	39	Y 47 SE
LAKE TE ANAU	52	H 62 NW
LAKE TE AU	51	F 62 NE
LAKE TE KAHIKA	1	B 2 SE
LAKE TEKAPO	44	R 54 NE
LAKE TENNYSON	34	A 44 SE
LAKE THOMAS	52	I 63 NE
LAKE THOMPSON	52	I 59 SW
LAKE THOMSON	51	G 61 NW
LAKE TIKITAPU	10	Q 22 SE
LAKE TUAKITOTO	60	P 67 NE
LAKE TUTIRA	18	Q 28 NE
LAKE UNKNOWN	47	J 58 SE
LAKE VICTOR	57	D 66 NE
LAKE VIPAN	25	L 33 NE
LAKE WAAHI	9	L 18 SW
LAKE WADE	51	G 61 NW
LAKE WAHAKARI	1	B 2 SW
LAKE WAHAPO	37	Q 50 SE
LAKE WAIATARU	65	I 1 SW
LAKE WAIAU	22	J 31 NE
LAKE WAIKARA	56	Q 65 SE
LAKE WAIKAROMA	1	C 4 NE
LAKE WAIKARE (RODNEY)	7	L 18 SE
LAKE WAIKARE (WANGANUI)	22	J 30 SE
LAKE WAIKAREITI	19	T 25 SE
LAKE WAIKAREMOANA	19	T 25 SW
LAKE WAINAMU	65	G 2 NW
LAKE WAIPARA	10	N 23 NE
LAKE WAIPARERA	1	C 4 NE
LAKE WAIPORI	56	Q 65 SE
LAKE WAIRARAPA	27	L 39 NW
LAKE WAITAKI	50	R 58 SE
LAKE WAKATIPU	52	K 61 NW
LAKE WAKANA	48	M 57 NE
LAKE WAPITI	51	E 60 SE
LAKE WHAKAMARU	10	O 23 NW
LAKE WHANGAPE	9	K 18 SE
LAKE WIDGEON	57	E 66 NW
LAKE WILMOT	47	I 57 NE
LAKE WIRITOA	22	K 32 NE
LAMBTON HARBOUR	73	E 3 NE
LANDSBOROUGH RIVER	43	O 54 NW
LAUDER CREEK	49	O 59 SE
LAWRENCE RIVER	37	T 51 NW
LAWRY POINT	7	J 15 SW
LAWYERS HEAD	80	E 6 SW
LE BONS BAY	42	C 53 NW
LEADER RIVER	40	C 46 SE
LEE CREEK	79	E 2 SW
LEE RIVER	35	C 40 NE
LEITHEN BURN	55	M 64 SE
LEWIS RIVER	39	Z 46 NW
LILL BURN	58	G 66 NE
LIMEBURNERS BAY	64	F 4 NE
LIMEBURNERS CREEK	82	F 3 SE
LINDIS RIVER	48	O 59 NW
LINDSAY CREEK	75	C 1 SW
LINN BURN	54	P 62 SW
LION ROCK	65	H 2 NW
LITTLE AKALOA BAY	42	B 52 SE
LITTLE BARRIER ISLAND	6	K 11 NE
LITTLE GLASS BAY	57	D 66 SW
LITTLE KYE BURN	49	O 60 NE
LITTLE MOGGY ISLAND	61	G 72 SE
LITTLE MUDDY CREEK	65	H 4 SW
LITTLE PORT COOPER	78	F 8 NE
LITTLE SANDY POINT	66	E 5 NE
LITTLE SHOAL BAY	64	F 5 NE
LIVINGSTONE BAY	78	E 8 SW
LOCH KATRINE	39	Y 47 SE
LOCH MAREE	57	E 64 SE
LOCHNAGAR	47	K 58 NW
LOCHY RIVER	52	K 61 SE
LONG BAY	42	B 53 SW
LONG BEACH (DUNEDIN CITY)	80	C 7 NE
LONG BEACH (FAR NORTH)	81	A 4 SE
LONG BURN (QUEENSTOWN LAKES)	52	K 62 NE
LONG BURN (SOUTHLAND)	57	E 65 SW
LONG ISLAND (MARLBOROUGH)	30	H 38 SW
LONG ISLAND (SOUTHLAND)	57	D 65 NW
LONG POINT (CLUTHA)	20	W 28 NE
LONG POINT (MARLBOROUGH)	57	F 67 SW
LONG POINT (SOUTHLAND)	60	O 69 NE
LONG POINT (WAIROA)	36	G 42 NE
LONG REEF (SOUTHLAND)	57	D 67 SE
LONG REEF (WESTLAND)	47	H 57 NE
LONG SOUND	57	D 66 SE
LONGRIDGE POINT	47	I 56 NW
LOOKING GLASS BAY	51	F 60 SW
LOOKOUT BLUFF	56	T 61 SE
LOOKOUT POINT	59	J 69 NW
LORD ASHLEY BAY	29	G 37 NW
LORDS RIVER	61	I 72 NE
LOTTIN POINT	14	Y 19 NE
LOWER HUIA RESERVOIR	65	H 3 SW
LOWER NIHOTUPU RESERVOIR	65	H 3 SE
LOWRY BAY	73	D 4 SE
LUCKY POINT (MARLBOROUGH)	30	H 39 NW
LUCKY POINT (SOUTHLAND)	61	I 70 NE
LYALL BAY	27	J 39 SW
LYTTELTON HARBOUR	42	A 52 NE
MACANDREW BAY	80	D 6 SE
MACAULAY RIVER	44	S 52 NW
MAGNET BAY	42	A 53 SE
MAHAKIPAWA ARM	76	D 2 SE
MAHAKIRAU RIVER	6	N 15 NW
MAHANGA BAY	73	E 3 NE
MAHARAKEKE STREAM	24	Q 33 SW
MAHAU SOUND	29	F 39 NW
MAHIA PENINSULA	20	X 28 NW
MAHINA BAY	73	E 4 NE
MAHINEPUA BAY	63	A 2 NW
MAHITAHI RIVER	43	O 53 NW
MAHUNGARAPE ISLAND	8	O 14 SW
MAHURANGI HARBOUR	5	J 12 SW
MAHURANGI HEADS	64	A 5 NE
MAHURANGI ISLAND	8	O 14 SW
MAIKAKATOA STREAM	15	J 27 NW
MAIRANGI BAY	64	E 5 NE
MAITAI BAY	1	D 3 SE
MAKAHIKA STREAM	28	N 39 SW
MAKAHIKATOA STREAM	16	N 28 SW
MAKARA STREAM	24	R 31 SW
MAKARORA RIVER	48	M 56 NE
MAKATOTE STREAM	14	Y 26 SE
MAKAURA STREAM	20	O 36 NE
MAKAWHIO POINT	43	O 52 NW
MAKAWHIO RIVER	43	O 53 NE
MAKERETU STREAM	20	V 26 SE
MAKIEKIE CREEK	23	O 33 NW
MAKINO RIVER	18	Q 28 NW
MAKINO STREAM	24	R 31 NE
MAKIRIKIRI STREAM (TARARUA)	26	O 37 NE
MAKIRIKIRI STREAM (WANGANUI)	22	O 31 SW
MAKOHINE STREAM	23	N 31 SW
MAKORORI POINT	20	Y 25 SW
MAKOTUKUTUKU STREAM	27	L 40 SW
MAKUKUPARA STREAM	26	P 35 NE
MAKURI STREAM	26	O 35 NE
MALASPINA REACH	51	E 62 SE
MAMAKU POINT	61	J 70 SW
MANA ISLAND	27	J 38 NW
MANAIA HARBOUR	6	M 15 NE
MANAWAORA BAY	1	H 6 NW
MANAWAPAU RIVER	21	H 30 SE
MANAWATU RIVER	23	O 34 NE
MANGAARUHE STREAM	19	U 26 NE
MANGAEHU STREAM	15	I 28 SW
MANGAEHUEHU STREAM	17	M 29 NW
MANGAETOROA STREAM	22	L 29 SE
MANGAHAO RIVER	25	M 36 NW
MANGAHAWHI STREAM	22	L 31 NE
MANGAHEREKEKE STREAM	12	R 23 NE
MANGAIHE STREAM	15	K 29 SE
MANGAIO STREAM (TAUPO)	17	N 29 NE
MANGAIO STREAM (WANGANUI)	22	K 29 NE
MANGAITI STREAM	26	K 31 NE
MANGAKAHIA STREAM	4	G 9 NE
MANGAKAHU STREAM	11	L 25 NE
MANGAKARA STREAM	16	N 25 SW
MANGAKINO STREAM	10	N 18 SE
MANGAKOTAHA STREAM	10	O 22 NE
MANGAKURI RIVER	24	S 32 SW
MANGAMAHU STREAM	22	M 31 NW
MANGAMAIA STREAM	13	W 23 NW
MANGAMAIO STREAM	15	I 26 SW
MANGAMAIRE RIVER	17	P 28 NW
MANGAMAIRE STREAM	24	Q 34 SE
MANGAMAUKU STREAM	24	Q 31 SW
MANGAMAUNU BEACH	36	E 45 NE
MANGAMAUNU RIVER	14	X 22 SE
MANGAMOEAHU STREAM	15	H 27 SE
MANGANUI RIVER	4	G 9 SW
MANGANUI STREAM	27	K 39 SE
MANGANUIATEAO RIVER	16	L 28 SW
MANGANUIOHOU RIVER	18	S 26 NE
MANGANUIOTAHU STREAM	22	K 30 SW
MANGAOHOI STREAM	67	F 3 NW
MANGAOKEWA RIVER	9	L 23 NE
MANGAONE RIVER	18	R 28 SE
MANGAONE STREAM (RUAPEHU)	22	K 29 NW
MANGAONE STREAM (TARARUA)	26	P 35 SE
MANGAONE STREAM (WAIROA)	19	T 26 SW
MANGAONE STREAM (WANGANUI)	22	J 31 NE
MANGAONUKU STREAM	24	Q 31 NE
MANGAOPARO RIVER	14	Y 20 SE
MANGAORAPA STREAM	24	Q 34 SE
MANGAOTAKI RIVER	9	K 23 SW
MANGAOTUKU STREAM	15	I 28 NE
MANGAPAI STREAM	7	J 18 NW
MANGAPAKA STREAM	13	J 27 NW
MANGAPAPA RIVER	10	P 21 NW
MANGAPAPA STREAM (FRANKLIN)	7	K 18 NW
MANGAPAPA STREAM (TAUPO)	22	K 25 NE
MANGAPAPA STREAM (WANGANUI)	22	J 30 NE
MANGAPIKO STREAM	9	K 18 SE
MANGAPOIKE RIVER	20	V 26 SE
MANGAPOURI STREAM	69	B 1 NE
MANGAPUKA STREAM	24	P 34 SE
MANGAPURUA STREAM	16	K 28 NW
MANGARA STREAM	14	L 32 NE
MANGARANGIORA STREAM	20	V 26 NE
MANGARARA STREAM	24	R 32 NE
MANGAREWA STREAM	10	N 22 SE
MANGAROA RIVER	74	C 6 SE
MANGAROA STREAM	16	K 26 NE
MANGAROUHI STREAM	24	R 33 NW
MANGATAINOKA RIVER	25	M 36 NE
MANGATAPU STREAM	10	O 21 SW
MANGATAWA STREAM (FAR NORTH)	3	E 7 NE
MANGATAWA STREAM (WAITOMO)	15	J 26 NW
MANGATE STREAM	18	R 22 NE
MANGATEWAI RIVER	24	P 32 SE
MANGATIPONA STREAM	22	L 31 SE
MANGATITI STREAM	16	K 28 NE
MANGATOETOE STREAM	1	L 41 NW
MANGATOETOENUI STREAM	16	N 28 NE
MANGATOI CREEK	58	N 39 SW
MANGATOTE STREAM	15	J 26 NW
MANGATU RIVER	14	W 23 NE
MANGATU STREAM	3	E 8 SE
MANGATUKUTUKU STREAM	11	M 25 NW
MANGATURUTURU RIVER	16	L 28 SE
MANGATUTARA STREAM	14	W 21 NE
MANGATUTU STREAM (HASTINGS)	18	Q 28 SE
MANGATUTU STREAM (OTOROHANGA)	9	M 22 NW
MANGAUIKA STREAM	67	F 1 NE
MANGAWARA STREAM	9	M 18 SW
MANGAWHARO STREAM	10	O 20 SW
MANGAWHAU STREAM	23	O 31 SW
MANGAWHERARIKI RIVER	23	O 31 SW
MANGAWHERO RIVER	17	L 30 SE
MANGAWHERO STREAM	20	O 33 SE
MANGITITI STREAM	26	O 35 SE
MANGLES RIVER	34	Z 42 NE
MANGOIWA STREAM	17	N 30 NW
MANGONUI HARBOUR	1	D 3 SE
MANGOPARERUA POINT	66	F 8 NW
MANGOREWA RIVER	10	Q 21 NW
MANOR BURN	54	O 61 SW
MANORBURN RESERVOIR	54	O 62 SE
MANSON CREEK	18	P 28 SE
MANSONS PENINSULA	78	F 7 NW
MANUHERIKIA RIVER	49	O 61 NW
MANUKAU ENTRANCE	7	I 16 NE
MANUKAU HARBOUR	7	J 15 SW
MANUREWA POINT	28	M 40 SE
MANUWHAKAPAKAPA BAY	29	F 37 NE
MANY ISLANDS	57	C 65 NE
MAORI BAY	65	F 1 SE
MAORI CREEK	37	P 61 SW
MAORI GARDEN BAY	66	D 8 SW
MAORI HEAD	58	S 65 NW
MAPARA STREAM	16	K 24 NE
MARAEHARA RIVER	14	Z 20 NE
MARAEKAKAHO RIVER	24	R 31 NE
MARAETAHA RIVER	20	X 26 NW
MARAETAI BAY	17	O 26 SW
MARAETOTARA RIVER	24	S 31 NE

Coastal & Water Features

Location	Map No.	Ref
MARAEWHITI PT	1	D 3 SW
MARAHAU RIVER	75	C 2 SE
MARANGAE RIVER	15	J 27 SE
MARAROA RIVER	52	I 63 NE
MARAU POINT	14	Z 23 SW
MARAWHARA STREAM	65	H 2 NW
MARE BURN	56	R 61 SW
MARIA ISLAND	6	K 14 NE
MAROA STREAM	23	O 34 SE
MAROKOPA RIVER	9	J 23 NW
MAROTERE ISLANDS	4	J 9 SE
MARSHALL ROCKS	57	D 67 SE
MARTINS BAY	47	H 57 NE
MARUARUA STREAM	4	H 8 NW
MARUIA RIVER	34	Y 45 SE
MARY BURN	44	R 55 NW
MARY ISLAND	57	F 66 NE
MASON BAY	61	H 71 NE
MASON HEAD	61	H 71 NE
MATA RIVER	14	Y 21 SW
MATAHUI POINT	68	C 2 NW
MATAIKONA RIVER	26	P 36 SW
MATAKANA ISLAND	10	P 19 NW
MATAKANA POINT	10	P 19 NW
MATAKAOA POINT	14	Z 19 SW
MATAKATIA BAY	64	C 6 NW
MATAKITAKI RIVER	34	Y 43 NE
MATAKUHIA STREAM	18	R 26 SW
MATAORA BAY	8	O 17 SE
MATAPAUA BAY	8	O 14 NE
MATATAPU ROCKS	12	Q 19 SE
MATAU BRANCH	60	P 67 SE
MATAURA RIVER	52	K 62 SW
MATAURI BAY	2	G 4 SW
MATAUWHI BAY	81	B 4 SW
MATAWHEROHIA PT	1	D 3 SE
MATHIAS RIVER	38	U 50 NW
MATIHE POINT	5	G 11 SE
MATIRANGI STREAM	15	I 27 NE
MATIRI RIVER	34	Z 41 NW
MATUKITUKI RIVER	48	L 57 SW
MAUD ISLAND	29	F 38 NW
MAUKUTEA BEACH	9	J 21 NE
MAUNGAKOTUKUTUKU STREAM	27	K 37 SW
MAUNGAMAUNGAROA CREEK	66	G 2 SW
MAUNGAPARERUA STREAM	63	C 2 SW
MAWHAI POINT	14	Z 22 SW
MAWHERAITI RIVER	33	W 44 NE
MCCORMICKS CREEK	56	S 62 NW
MCKAY BLUFF	29	D 38 SW
MECHANICS BAY	78	E 8 SE
MEDLANDS BEACH	6	N 11 SW
MEGGAT BURN	79	F 1 NW
MELLONS BAY	66	G 8 NW
MEMORY ROCK	6	N 11 SW
MERCER BAY	65	H 2 SW
MERCURY BAY	8	O 14 NW
MERCURY ISLANDS	8	O 13 SE
MICKY ROCK	81	B 2 SW
MID POINT	31	X 38 NE
MIDDLE BRANCH BORLAND BURN	58	G 64 SW
MIDDLE FIORD	51	G 61 SE
MIDDLE ISLAND		
(ALDERMAN ISLANDS)	8	P 15 SE
(MERCURY ISLANDS)	8	O 13 SE
MIDWAY POINT	14	Y 19 NE
MIKIMIKI STREAM	25	M 37 NE
MILFORD SOUND	47	H 58 NW
MILL BAY	65	J 3 NE
MILL CREEK	27	J 39 NW
MIMI RIVER	15	I 26 SW
MIMIHA STREAM	12	R 21 NE
MIMIHAU STREAM	59	M 67 SW
MINE POINT	70	B 3 SE
MINERS HEAD	6	M 10 SW
MINZION BURN	54	O 64 NW
MISSION BAY	17	O 26 NE
MISSION POINT	17	O 26 NE
MITA BAY	64	A 5 SE
MITRE ROCKS	14	Z 24 NW
MOA CREEK	54	O 61 SE
MOANATUATUA SWAMP	67	E 3 NW
MOAWHANGO HYDRO TUNNEL	17	N 29 NE
MOAWHANGO RIVER	17	O 30 SW
MOERAKI RIVER	43	N 53 SW
MOHAKA RIVER	19	T 27 SE
MOKAIHAHA STREAM	10	O 22 NE
MOKAU RIVER		
(OTOROHANGA)	9	L 23 SW
(WAITOMO)	15	J 25 NW
MOKAUITI STREAM	16	K 24 NE
MOKI STREAM	15	I 26 SE
MOKIHINUI RIVER	33	X 40 NW
MOKOIA ISLAND	10	P 22 NE
MOKOIWI STREAM	14	Y 21 NW
MOKOPUNA ISLAND	73	D 4 SW
MOKORETA RIVER	59	M 68 NW
MOKOROA STREAM	65	F 2 SW
MOKURI RIVER	26	O 35 SW
MOLYNEUX BAY	60	P 68 SE
MOMORI POINT	65	G 1 SE
MONKEY ROCK	65	H 1 NE
MOTATAPU RIVER	48	L 59 NE
MOTIAKATINO RIVER	15	I 25 NE
MOTIONS CREEK	64	F 5 SW
MOTITI ISLAND	10	Q 19 NE
MOTOKORUENGA ISLAND	8	O 14 NE
MOTU RIVER	13	V 20 SE
MOTUAIURI ISLAND	14	Z 22 NW
MOTUANAURU ISLAND	29	E 38 NW
MOTUARA ISLAND	30	H 38 NW
MOTUARAHI ISLAND	81	C 2 SE
MOTUEKA ISLAND	8	O 14 NW
MOTUEKA RIVER	32	B 38 SE
MOTUEKAITI ISLAND	63	A 2 NW
MOTUHOA ISLAND	68	D 3 NW
MOTUHORA ISLAND	13	T 20 SW
MOTUHOROPAPA ISLAND	6	K 14 NE
MOTUHUA POINT	6	K 14 NE
MOTUIHE ISLAND	6	K 14 SW
MOTUKAERE ISLAND	7	K 18 NE
MOTUKAHA ISLAND	12	R 19 SW
MOTUKAHAKAHA BAY	6	E 4 NE
MOTUKAHAUA	6	M 13 SW
MOTUKARAKA ISLAND	6	K 15 NE
MOTUKARAMARAMA	6	M 14 SW
MOTUKAWAITI ISLAND	2	G 4 SW
MOTUKAWANUI ISLAND	2	G 4 SW
MOTUKAWAO GROUP	6	M 13 SE
MOTUKIEKIE ROCKS	33	U 45 NE
MOTUKOPAKE ISLAND	6	M 14 NE
MOTUKORANGA ISLAND	8	O 14 NE
MOTUKOREA CHANNEL	64	F 7 NW
MOTUKORURE ISLAND	8	O 14 SW
MOTUMAIRE ISLAND	81	C 2 NW
MOTUNAU ISLAND		
(HURUNUI)	42	C 49 NW
(WESTERN BAY OF PLENTY)	12	R 19 SE
MOTUNGAIO ISLAND	68	C 3 SW
MOTUOAPA PENINSULA	17	O 26 SW
MOTUOPAO ISLAND	1	A 1 SW
MOTUOPUHI ISLAND	70	E 1 SW
MOTUORA ISLAND	6	J 13 NE
MOTUOROI ISLAND	14	Z 23 NW
MOTUORUHI ISLAND	6	M 14 NW
MOTUOTAU ISLAND	10	P 19 NE
MOTUPIA ISLAND	1	A 2 NE
MOTUPIKO RIVER	34	B 41 SW
MOTUREMU ISLAND	6	H 12 NE
MOTURERE POINT	17	O 26 NE
MOTURIKI ISLAND	10	P 19 SE
MOTUROA ISLAND		
(BAY OF ISLANDS)	2	G 5 SE
(FAR NORTH)	1	D 3 NW
(KAIPARA)	5	H 11 SW
MOTURUA	2	M 14 NW
MOTURUA ISLAND	2	H 5 SW
MOTUTAIKO ISLAND	17	O 26 NE
MOTUTAPERE ISLAND	6	M 14 SE
MOTUTAPU ISLAND	6	K 14 NE
MOTUTARA PT	4	I 7 SE
MOTUTOKAPE ISLAND	81	F 4 NW
MOTUWAIREKA STREAM	28	O 38 SE
MOTUWHARA ISLAND	17	O 25 SW
MOTUWI	6	M 14 NW
MOUMAHAKI STREAM	22	J 30 SW
MOUNTAIN CAMP CREEK	76	E 1 NE
MOUREESES BAY	4	I 7 NW
MOUTAHIAURU ISLAND	14	Z 22 NW
MOUTERE BLUFF	32	C 39 NW
MOUTERE INLET	75	D 3 SE
MOUTOA FLOODWAY	25	L 35 NE
MOUTOHORA ISLAND	12	T 20 SW
MOUTOKI ISLAND	12	S 20 SE
MUKAKA BAY	65	J 2 SE
MURCHISON RIVER	44	Q 52 NE
MURIMOTU ISLAND	1	C 1 NW
MURIWAI BEACH	5	H 14 NE
MURPHY ISLAND	61	H 73 SW
MURRAYS BAY	64	E 5 NE
MUSICK POINT	64	F 7 NW
MUSKET BAY	47	H 57 SW
MUSSEL POINT	36	G 41 SE
MUTTON COVE	75	B 3 NW
MUTTONBIRD ISLANDS		
(NTH STEWART ISLAND)	62	J 70 SE
(STH STEWART ISLAND)	61	G 72 SE
MYTH TARN	51	F 61 SW
NANCY SOUND	51	E 61 SW
NARROW NECK BEACH	64	F 6 NE
NATIVE ISLAND	61	J 71 NW
NEE ISLAND	51	D 62 NE
NEEDLE ROCK	8	O 14 SW
NELSONS MONUMENT	29	F 36 NE
NENTHORN STREAM	56	R 63 NW
NEVIS RIVER	53	L 62 NE
NEW RIVER ESTUARY	59	J 68 SE
NEWTON RIVER	57	C 66 NE
NGAIO BAY	64	A 5 NE
NGAKAUAU STREAM	28	P 37 SW
NGAKAUTUAKINA POINT	10	P 19 NW
NGAMUWAHINE RIVER	68	E 2 SW
NGARARA STREAM	28	M 39 SE
NGARUNUI BEACH	9	J 20 NE
NGARURARA RIVER	18	P 28 NE
NGARUROURO RIVER	18	S 30 NE
NGATAMAWAHINE RIVER	12	R 23 NW
NGATARINGA BAY	64	F 6 NW
NGATURI CREEK	26	O 35 NW
NGATUTURA POINT	9	J 18 SW
NGONGOTAHA STREAM	69	C 1 NW
NGUNGURU BAY	4	I 8 NE
NGUROA BAY	31	A 35 NW
NIHOTUPU AUXILIARY RESERVOIR	65	H 3 NW
NIHOTUPU STREAM	65	H 3 NE
NILE HEAD	29	F 36 NW
NINE MILE BEACH	33	V 42 NW
NINETY MILE BEACH	1	B 3 NE
NOBLE ISLAND	61	H 73 NE
NOKOMAI RIVER	53	K 63 SE
NORTH ARM	61	H 72 SE
NORTH BLUFF	27	J 38 NW
NORTH CAPE	1	C 1 NW
NORTH CHANNEL	6	K 12 NW
NORTH EAST POINT	66	D 8 SW
NORTH ESK RIVER	39	V 47 SW
NORTH FIORD	52	H 61 NW
NORTH HEAD		
(CLUTHA)	60	N 69 SW
(FAR NORTH)	3	D 7 NW
(KAIPARA)	5	G 12 NW
(NORTH SHORE CITY)	64	F 6 NE
(SOUTHLAND)	65	K 70 NE
(TASMAN)	32	C 37 NW
NORTH ISLAND	62	J 70 SE
NORTH MAVORA LAKE	52	J 61 SW
NORTH OPUHA RIVER	44	T 53 SW
NORTH PIHA BEACH	65	H 1 NE
NORTH RED HEAD	61	H 70 NE
NORTH TARANAKI BIGHT	15	G 25 NE
NORTH TRAP	61	I 73 SE
NORTH WEST BAY	76	C 2 NE
NORWEST LAKE	57	F 63 SE
NUGGET POINT		
(CLUTHA)	60	P 68 NE
(SOUTHLAND)	55	E 61 NE
NUHAKA RIVER	20	W 26 SE
NUKUTAUNGA ISLAND	2	G 4 NW
NUKUWAIATA ISLAND	29	G 37 NW
NUN ROCK	65	H 2 NW
NYDIA BAY	76	C 2 SW
O'NEILL BAY	65	G 1 NE
OAIA ISLAND	5	H 14 SE
OAOITI STREAM	21	F 28 SW
OAONUI STREAM	21	F 28 SW
OCEAN BEACH		
(SOUTHLAND)	62	J 71 SE
(THAMES COROMANDEL)	8	O 15 SE
OEO STREAM	21	F 29 SE
OHAKA HEAD	65	J 2 NW
OHANE STREAM	13	T 23 SW
OHAO POINT	1	B 1 SE
OHARA STREAM	18	P 30 SE
OHARIU RIVER	73	D 4 SW
OHAU CANAL	49	P 56 NE
OHAU POINT	27	I 39 NE
OHAU RIVER		
(HOROWHENUA)	49	Q 56 NW
(MACKENZIE)	25	K 36 NE
OHAUPARA STREAM	10	P 21 NE
OHIKANUI RIVER	33	W 43 NW
OHINAU ISLAND	8	O 14 NE
OHINAUITI ISLAND	8	O 14 NE
OHINE STREAM	10	N 18 SW
OHINERAU BAY	66	F 8 NW
OHINETUHUA POINT	17	N 25 SE
OHIWA HARBOUR	13	U 21 NW
OHOTE STREAM	67	C 1 SE
OHURA RIVER	16	L 25 SW
OHUTUTEA BAY	2	H 5 SE
OINGO LAKE	18	R 30 NE
OIO STREAM	16	L 27 NE
OKAHAU POINT	1	T 62 NW
OKAHU ISLAND	2	F 28 SE
OKAHU POINT	21	F 28 SE
OKAHUKURA PENINSULA	5	H 12 NE
OKAIA STREAM	11	O 24 SE
OKAINS BAY	42	C 52 SW
OKARAMIO RIVER	76	E 2 SW
OKARI LAGOON	33	V 42 SW
OKARITO LAGOON	37	Q 50 NW
OKARO CREEK	5	H 11 SW
OKAU STREAM	26	P 37 NE
OKE ISLAND	57	D 64 SE
OKIATO POINT	81	E 3 NW
OKIRITOTO STREAM	65	F 1 NE
OKIWI BAY	75	C 1 NE
OKOROMAI BAY	64	C 6 NE
OKOROPUNGA STREAM	28	M 40 SE
OKUKU RIVER	42	Z 49 SW
OKUPATA STREAM	9	K 21 SE
OKURA RIVER	64	C 5 SE
OKUREI POINT	10	R 20 NW
OKURI BAY	29	F 37 SW
OKURU RIVER	43	L 54 SE
OKUTA BAY	17	O 25 SE
OLD MAN POINT	58	H 68 NE
OLD MANS HEAD	29	F 36 SE
OLIVER POINT	57	D 64 NW
OMAHAKI STREAM	18	Q 29 SW
OMAHINE STREAM	22	J 30 SW
OMAIO BAY	13	W 20 SW
OMAKA RIVER	29	E 41 NE
OMARAE STREAM	17	M 29 NE
OMARAMA STREAM	49	P 58 NW
OMARU RIVER	4	G 10 NE
OMARU STREAM	22	J 29 NE
OMATA STREAM	22	J 30 SW
OMAUI ROCKS	59	J 69 NW
OMOEROA RIVER	37	P 51 NE
OMOHO STREAM	11	O 24 SW
OMORI STREAM	70	D 1 SE
ONAERO RIVER	15	H 26 SE
ONAHAU BAY	76	D 3 NE
ONAHAU RIVER	75	B 1 NE
ONAIA STREAM	10	Q 21 NW
ONAMALUTU STREAM	76	F 2 NW
ONEROA BAY	81	A 4 SE
ONETANGI BAY	6	L 14 SW
ONETAUNGA BAY	64	F 5 NW
ONEWHERO BAY	63	C 3 SE
ONGARUE RIVER	11	L 25 NE
ONGOHI STREAM	6	M 13 NW
ONUKUTAUIRA STREAM	10	O 22 NE
OPAHEKEHEKE ISLAND	5	H 13 SE
OPAHI POINT	64	A 5 NE
OPAKAU STREAM	10	O 22 SE
OPANI-APUTA POINT	29	G 38 NW
OPARAU RIVER	9	K 21 NW
OPATO STREAM	13	U 23 NE
OPAU BAY	73	D 1 NE
OPAWA RIVER	76	E 2 NW
OPIHI BAY	76	D 4 SW
OPIHI RIVER	45	V 56 NW
OPITO BAY	8	O 14 NW
OPORAE STREAM	23	P 34 SW
OPOUAWE RIVER	27	L 41 NE
OPOUTERE BEACH	8	O 16 NE
OPUATIA RIVER	7	J 17 SE
OPUATIA STREAM	7	K 18 NE
OPUIAKI RIVER	68	F 2 NW
ORAKA POINT	58	I 68 NW
ORAKA STREAM	10	O 21 SW
ORAKEI BASIN	66	G 6 NE
ORARI RIVER	45	U 53 SW
ORAUEA RIVER	58	I 65 SW
ORCHARD BAY	76	A 4 NW
ORERE POINT	50	T 61 NE
ORETE POINT	14	X 19 SW
ORETI RIVER	52	J 62 SW
OREWA RIVER	64	B 4 SE
ORIKAKA RIVER	33	X 42 SW
OROKAWA BAY	8	O 18 NE
ORONGO BAY	81	C 4 SE
ORONGO POINT	5	H 12 NE
ORONGORONGO RIVER	27	J 40 NE
ORONUI STREAM	14	X 21 NE
OROUA RIVER	23	N 33 SE
ORUATEMANU STREAM	63	A 1 NE
ORUAWHARO RIVER	5	H 11 SE
ORUTUA RIVER	14	Z 19 SE
OTAKETAKE STREAM	11	O 24 SW
OTAKI RIVER	25	L 37 SW
OTAKOU POINT	80	C 8 SE
OTAMA CREEK	59	L 65 SW
OTAMATAPAIO RIVER	49	P 58 NE
OTAMATEA CHANNEL	5	H 12 NW
OTAMATEA RIVER		
(HASTINGS)	18	Q 25 SW
(WHANGAREI)	4	H 11 SE
OTAMATEANUI RIVER	17	O 28 NE
OTAMITA STREAM	59	L 66 NW
OTAMURE BAY	4	I 7 NW
OTANERITO BAY	42	C 53 SE
OTAPIRI STREAM	59	K 66 NW
OTARA RIVER	13	U 22 SE
OTARAWAIRERE BAY	13	T 21 NE
OTARAWAO BAY	64	A 5 NE
OTARAWHATA ISLAND	14	X 19 NE
OTATA ISLAND	6	K 14 NE
OTAWHAO STREAM	23	O 34 NE
OTEHE POINT	9	J 19 NE
OTEKAIEKE RIVER	50	R 59 SE
OTEKE STREAM	9	J 22 NE
OTEKIHO BEACH	80	C 8 NW
OTEMATATA RIVER	49	Q 58 SE
OTERANGA BAY	27	I 39 SE
OTERANGA STREAM	73	E 1 NE
OTEREI RIVER	28	M 40 NE
OTIRA RIVER	38	W 48 NW
OTIRIA STREAM	3	E 3 SW
OTOKI STREAM	21	H 30 NE
OTOKIA CREEK	79	F 3 NE
OTOKO RIVER	43	O 53 SW
OTONGA POINT	8	O 17 SE
OTONGA PT	2	E 4 NE
OTOROKUA POINT	43	O 51 SE
OTUHAEREROA ISLAND	29	E 38 NW
OTUKOROITI POINT	31	Y 36 SW
OTUNUI STREAM	16	L 26 NE
OTUPOTO STREAM	11	N 25 NE
OTURERE STREAM	16	N 27 SE
OTUTETO POINT	17	O 26 NE
OTUWHERO INLET	75	C 3 SW
OTUWHERO RIVER	75	C 2 SE
OWAHANGA RIVER	26	P 35 SE
OWAIRAKA STREAM	9	M 21 SE
OWEN HEAD	61	J 72 NW
OWEN ISLAND	62	J 72 NE
OWEN RIVER	34	Z 41 NE
OWHANAKE BAY	66	E 8 SE
OWHIRO BAY	27	J 40 NW
OWHIRO STREAM	79	E 3 NE
OYSTER POINT	26	I 36 NW
PA CREEK	26	N 36 NE
PA ISLAND	2	F 4 NW
PAERAU POINT	14	Z 23 SW
PAHAOA RIVER	28	N 39 NE
PAHARAKEKE STREAM	27	L 39 SW
PAHAU RIVER	39	A 47 NW
PAHIA POINT	58	H 68 NW
PAHURUHURE INLET	7	K 16 NW
PAIAKARAHI STREAM	8	N 17 SE
PAIKEA BAY	65	H 1 NE
PAKARAE RIVER	14	Y 24 NW
PAKATOA ISLAND	6	L 14 SE
PAKIHI ISLAND	6	L 15 NW
PAKIHI STREAM	13	V 22 SW
PAKOWHAI RIVER	26	P 36 SW
PALLISER BAY	27	K 40 NW
PALMER HEAD	73	F 3 NE
PALNOON BURN	48	L 58 SW
PANAKI ISLAND	63	A 3 NW
PANANEHE ISLAND	1	B 1 NW
PANETIKI ISLAND	6	K 11 SW
PAOANUI POINT	24	S 33 NW
PAPAKOHATU ISLAND	66	F 8 NE
PAPANUI BEACH	56	T 65 NW
PAPANUI INLET	80	D 8 SW
PAPANUI POINT	9	J 20 SE
PAPATEA BAY	14	X 19 SW
PAPAWAI BAY	29	E 37 SE
PARAKAU RIVER	8	O 15 SW
PARAKAUMANGA STREAM	70	D 1 SW
PARAOANUI POINT	6	G 11 NE
PARAPARA INLET	75	A 1 NW
PARAPARA RIVER	75	B 1 NW
PARARAHA BAY	65	J 2 NW
PARARAHA POINT	5	H 12 SW
PARARAKI STREAM	27	L 39 SW
PARATAHI ISLAND	65	J 2 NW
PARATUTAE ISLAND	65	J 2 SE
PARENGARENGA HARBOUR	1	B 1 SE
PAREOHA BAY	8	O 14 NW
PAREORA RIVER	50	U 57 NE
PARERA POINT	65	G 1 SE
PARINGA RIVER	43	N 53 SE
PARIOKARIWA POINT	15	I 26 NW
PARIOKONOHI POINT	20	Y 25 NW
PARK BURN	54	M 60 NE
PARK POINT	66	F 8 NE
PARROT ISLAND	57	C 65 NE
PARRY CHANNEL	4	J 9 SW
PARUA BAY	63	A 2 SE
PASCOE POINT	65	J 2 SW
PASSAGE ISLAND	57	C 66 SE
PASSAGE POINT	57	D 65 NE
PATANUI STREAM	20	O 38 SW
PATEA RIVER	21	I 30 SW
PATERSON INLET	61	I 71 NE
PATITI POINT	50	U 56 SE
PATUHAMOKO POINT	8	O 16 SE
PATUNUI BAY	63	C 3 NE
PATUROA BAY	65	H 4 SE
PAUAOHINEKOTAU HEAD	78	F 7 NE
PAWHETAU POINT	6	L 15 NE
PAXTON PT	1	C 2 SW
PEACHGROVE BAY	8	O 13 SW
PEARL ISLAND	61	H 72 SE
PEARSE RIVER	75	E 1 NE
PEEL STREAM	31	A 38 SW
PEGASUS BAY	38	B 51 NE
PEGASUS CREEK	61	H 72 SE
PEKAPEKA BAY	63	A 1 SW
PELORUS RIVER	29	E 39 NW
PELORUS SOUND	76	F 38 SE
PENCARROW HEAD	27	J 40 NE
PENGUIN BAY	76	C 2 SE
PENGUIN BEACH	80	C 8 SE

Location	Map No.	Ref

ENGUIN ISLAND ... 8 O 16 NE
EPIN ISLAND ... 29 D 38 SE
ERAKI BAY ... 42 B 53 SW
ERANO HEAD ... 30 H 38 SE
ERFORATED PT ... 1 C 3 NE
EPPENDICULAR POINT ... 33 U 44 NE
EPPENDICULAR PT ... 1 C 3 SE
ERTH RIVER ... 43 R 51 NE
IAKATU POINT ... 8 N 52 SW
IAKO RIVER ... 67 B 4 NE
ICKERSGILL ISLAND ... 30 H 38 SW
ICTON HARBOUR ... 76 D 3 SE
IG BAY ... 8 B 4 SE
IG BURN ... 56 Q 61 SE
IG ISLAND
  (QUEENSTOWN LAKES) ... 52 J 60 NE
  (SOUTHLAND) ... 58 I 68 NE
IGEON BAY ... 42 B 52 NE
IGEON CREEK ... 75 F 3 SW
IGEON ISLAND ... 52 J 60 NE
IHAKOA PT ... 1 D 3 SE
IKARORO BAY ... 62 J 71 SE
IKARORO POINT ... 62 J 71 SE
IKOWAI STREAM ... 12 R 21 NE
ILCH POINT ... 31 A 35 NW
ILLANS HEAD ... 60 O 69 NE
ILLOW LAVA BAY ... 65 F 1 SE
ILOT POINT ... 80 C 7 NE
ILOTS BEACH ... 80 C 8 SW
IPIKARETU BEACH ... 80 C 8 SE
IPIKARETU POINT ... 80 C 8 SE
IPINUI POINT ... 27 J 38 SW
IPIROA BAY ... 81 E 3 NE
ITT HEAD ... 32 C 37 SW
LEASANT RIVER ... 56 T 63 NW
OERUA RIVER ... 37 R 49 SW
OHANGINA RIVER ... 23 O 33 NW
OHOWAITAI ISLAND ... 61 G 73 NW
OHUTUKAWA BAY ... 66 E 8 NE
OINT ARTHUR ... 73 E 4 SW
OINT BROWN ... 73 E 4 NW
OINT BURN ... 51 G 62 NE
OINT DORSET ... 27 J 39 SE
OINT ELIZABETH ... 33 U 45 SW
OINT GORDON ... 27 J 39 SE
OINT HALSWELL ... 73 E 3 SE
OINT HOWARD ... 27 J 39 NE
OINT JERNINGHAM ... 73 E 3 NE
OINT WEBB ... 73 E 4 SW
POISON BAY ... 51 G 58 SW
POKAIROA STREAM ... 12 R 23 NE
POKAITU STREAM ... 10 P 23 NW
POKEKO STREAM ... 22 J 29 SE
POKOHINU POINT ... 13 W 20 SW
POKOPOKO STREAM
  (ROTORUA) ... 10 Q 21 NE
  (TAUPO) ... 17 O 30 NE
POLEY BAY ... 8 M 12 SE
POLEY STREAM ... 27 L 40 SE
POLKINGHORNES BAY ... 64 C 5 NE
POMAHAKA RIVER ... 54 M 64 SW
POMARE BAY ... 81 C 4 NW
PONGAKAWA STREAM ... 12 R 21 NW
PONGAROA RIVER ... 26 P 35 SW
PONUI HEAD ... 6 L 14 SW
PONUI ISLAND ... 6 L 15 NE
POOL BURN ... 54 P 61 SW
POOLBURN RESERVOIR ... 54 P 62 NW
POOR KNIGHTS ISLANDS ... 4 J 7 NE
POPORANGI STREAM ... 24 Q 30 SW
POPORO STREAM ... 45 K 17 SW
PORAENUI POINT ... 63 C 4 NW
PORANGAHAU RIVER ... 24 R 34 NE
POREWA STREAM ... 23 N 31 SW
PORIRUA HARBOUR ... 73 B 3 SE
POROPORO RIVER ... 14 Z 20 SW
PORORARI RIVER ... 33 V 44 NW
PORPOISE BAY ... 60 N 69 SW
PORPOISE POINT ... 57 D 65 NW
PORT ABERCROMBIE ... 6 M 11 NW
PORT ADVENTURE ... 62 J 72 NE
PORT CHARLES ... 6 M 13 NE
PORT GORE ... 30 H 37 SW
PORT HARDY ... 29 F 36 NE
PORT JACKSON ... 6 M 12 SW
PORT LEVY ... 42 B 52 NW
PORT LIGAR ... 29 F 37 SE
PORT PEGASUS ... 61 H 73 NE
PORT UNDERWOOD ... 29 G 39 SW
PORT WILLIAM ... 61 J 70 SW
PORTLAND ISLAND ... 20 W 29 NE
POTAHI RIVER ... 9 J 21 NE
POTATO POINT ... 56 S 64 NE
POTATOE POINT ... 80 B 7 SE
POTIKI BAY ... 6 N 13 NE
POTTS RIVER ... 45 T 51 SE
POUARUA CANAL ... 8 M 16 NE
POULTER RIVER ... 39 X 48 NW
POUPOU STREAM ... 68 D 1 NE
POURANGAKI RIVER ... 23 O 31 SE
POUREWA ISLAND ... 14 Z 24 NW
POUTAMA ISLAND ... 61 G 73 NE
POUTO CANAL ... 70 F 2 SW
POVERTY BAY ... 20 X 25 SE
POWELL BAY ... 65 F 1 SE
PREECE POINT ... 6 M 14 SE
PRESERVATION INLET ... 57 D 67 NW
PRICES POINT ... 61 J 71 NW
PRINCESS BURN ... 57 E 65 SE
PROVIDENCE ROCKS ... 57 C 66 SE
PUAWAI BAY ... 64 C 5 NW
PUEREHUREHU POINT ... 80 C 7 NE
PUHOI RIVER ... 64 A 5 SE
PUKAKA STREAM ... 76 E 3 SE
PUKAKI CREEK ... 66 J 6 NW
PUKAKI RIVER ... 49 Q 56 NE
PUKEHINA BEACH ... 12 R 20 NW
PUKEKOWHAI POINT ... 65 G 1 SE
PUKEPUKE LAGOON ... 25 L 34 NW
PUKERAU POINT ... 29 E 38 NW
PUKEAURUHE ISLAND ... 78 F 8 NE
PUKERIMU STREAM ... 10 O 22 SE
PUKERUA BAY ... 73 A 4 NE
PUKETAI POINT ... 65 G 1 SE
PUKETAKAHIA PT ... 2 E 4 NW

PUKETI POINT ... 29 D 38 SE
PUKETOTARA PENINSULA ... 5 H 11 SE
PUKETOTARA STREAM ... 63 C 2 SW
PUKETUTU ISLAND ... 7 J 15 SE
PULLING POINT ... 80 C 7 SE
PUNAKAIKI RIVER ... 33 V 44 NW
PUNAKITERE RIVER ... 3 F 7 NW
PUNGAPUNGA RIVER ... 16 M 26 NE
PUNGATIKI STREAM ... 9 J 18 SW
PUNIU RIVER ... 67 F 2 NW
PUNIWHAKAU STREAM ... 15 I 28 SE
PUPONGA POINT
  (TASMAN) ... 31 A 35 NE
  (WAITAKERE CITY) ... 7 J 15 SW
PUPUIA ISLAND ... 4 G 11 NE
PURAKANUI BAY ... 80 B 7 SW
PURAKAUNUI POINT ... 60 P 68 SW
PURATOTO STREAM ... 22 K 29 NW
PURERUA PENINSULA ... 2 G 5 NE
PURIMU LAKE ... 24 Q 33 NE
PUTATAUA BAY ... 63 A 2 SE
PUTAUHINA ISLAND ... 61 G 73 NE
PUYSEGUR POINT ... 57 D 67 NW
QUAIL ISLAND ... 78 F 7 NW
QUARANTINE ISLAND ... 80 D 7 NW
QUEEN CHARLOTTE SOUND ... 29 G 39 NW
QUOIN POINT ... 56 Q 66 SE
RABBIT ISLAND
  (NELSON) ... 32 C 39 NW
  (OPITO) ... 8 O 14 NW
  (PAUANUI) ... 8 O 16 NE
RAEAKIAKI POINT ... 65 G 1 SE
RAETAHINGA POINT ... 5 H 15 NE
RAGGED POINT ... 29 F 36 SW
RAGLAN HARBOUR ... 9 K 20 NW
RAI RIVER ... 76 D 1 SW
RAINBOW ISLETS ... 60 O 69 NW
RAINBOW RIVER ... 34 X 43 SW
RAKAIA RIVER ... 41 X 52 NW
RAKAUANANGA POINT ... 64 C 6 NW
RAKEAHUA RIVER ... 61 I 71 NW
RAKINO CHANNEL ... 66 D 8 SW
RAKINO ISLAND ... 6 K 14 NE
RAKITU ISLAND ... 6 N 11 NW
RANGATAUA BAY ... 68 D 4 SW
RANGATIRA BAY ... 25 K 37 NW
RANGAUNU BAY ... 1 D 3 SW
RANGAUNU HARBOUR ... 1 D 3 SW
RANGIHAEATA POINT ... 32 B 36 NW
RANGIHOUA BAY ... 63 C 4 NW
RANGIORA BAY ... 1 B 1 SE
RANGIPUKEA ISLAND ... 6 J 14 SE
RANGITAIKI RIVER ... 12 S 23 SW
RANGITATA RIVER ... 45 U 53 NW
RANGITIKEI RIVER ... 17 O 29 SE
RANGITIKEI RIVER ... 17 O 28 NE
RANGITIRA BEACH ... 5 H 13 NW
RANGITOTO CHANNEL ... 6 J 14 SE
RANGITOTO ISLAND ... 6 K 14 SW
RANGITOTO ISLANDS ... 29 G 36 SW
RANGITUKIA STREAM ... 9 L 21 NW
RANGIWAEA ISLAND ... 68 D 3 NW
RANGIWHAKAEA BEACH ... 6 M 11 NE
RAPAKI BAY ... 78 F 7 NW
RAPARAHI STREAM ... 10 N 22 SE
RAUKOKORE RIVER ... 14 X 20 NW
RAUKURA POINT ... 6 L 15 NE
RAUMANGA STREAM ... 82 F 1 SE
RAUOTERANGI CHANNEL ... 25 K 37 SW
RAUPOROA BAY ... 6 N 13 NW
RAYNBIRDS BAY ... 80 D 6 SE
RED MERCURY ISLAND ... 8 O 13 SE
REDCLIFF CREEK ... 58 H 64 SW
REEF POINT ... 29 F 37 SE
REES RIVER ... 53 J 58 SE
REIDS BEACH ... 80 C 8 SE
REREWAHINE POINT ... 80 C 8 SE
REREWHAAITU RIVER ... 28 N 40 NW
RERETARUKE RIVER ... 16 L 27 NE
RETFORD STREAM ... 52 H 61 SE
RICHARDS POINT ... 61 H 70 SE
RICHMOND BAY ... 29 F 37 SE
RIMARIKI ISLAND ... 4 I 6 SW
RIPAPA ISLAND ... 78 F 8 NW
RIPIA RIVER ... 18 Q 27 NE
RIPIRO BEACH ... 3 E 9 SE
RIWAKA RIVER ... 75 D 2 NE
ROARING LION RIVER ... 31 Z 38 NW
ROARING MEG ... 53 M 60 NW
ROBERTSON POINT ... 29 G 39 SE
ROBIN HOOD BAY ... 76 E 4 NW
ROBINSON BAY ... 73 E 4 SW
ROBINSON RIVER ... 39 X 46 NE
ROCK POINT ... 27 J 38 SW
ROCKS POINT ... 31 Y 37 SW
ROCKY BAY ... 8 O 13 SW
ROCKY POINT
  (DUNEDIN CITY) ... 80 C 7 SW
  (SOUTH WAIRARAPA) ... 27 L 41 SE
ROCKY PT ... 2 G 5 NE
ROCKY RIVER ... 75 D 2 SE
RODGER INLET ... 58 G 65 NW
RODING RIVER ... 75 F 4 SE
ROE STREAM ... 65 F 2 NW
ROGER HEAD ... 61 H 70 SW
ROIMATA PT ... 4 I 7 NW
RONA BAY ... 73 E 4 NW
RONGA RIVER ... 76 D 1 NW
ROROKAKO STREAM ... 28 N 37 NE
ROSALIE BAY ... 6 N 12 NW
ROTAROA STREAM ... 68 F 1 NE
ROTHESAY BAY ... 64 D 5 SE
ROTOHOUHOU STREAM ... 68 E 2 NW
ROTONGAIO BAY ... 70 C 4 NW
ROTOROA ISLAND ... 6 L 14 SE
ROUGH RIVER ... 33 W 44 NW
ROUND HEAD ... 51 F 60 NW
ROUND POINT ... 73 B 3 SW
ROYS BAY ... 48 M 58 NW
RUAKAKA BAY ... 76 E 4 SE
RUAKITURI RIVER ... 19 U 25 NE
RUAKOKOPUTUNA RIVER ... 27 L 40 NE
RUAKORORA STREAM ... 22 K 31 NW
RUAMAHANGA RIVER ... 28 M 39 NW
RUAMAHUAITI ISLAND ... 8 P 15 SW
RUAMAHUANUI ISLAND ... 8 P 15 NW

RUAMAHUNGA RIVER ... 25 M 36 SE
RUANGIANGI ISLAND ... 29 F 36 SE
RUAPUKE BEACH ... 9 J 20 SE
RUAPUKE ISLAND ... 62 K 70 SE
RUATAHUNA STREAM ... 12 T 25 NW
RUATANIWHA INLET ... 31 A 36 NW
RUATITI RIVER ... 16 L 28 NE
RUATO STREAM ... 2 E 6 SE
RUGGED ISLANDS ... 61 H 70 NE
RUMBLING RIVER ... 48 L 57 SE
RUNANGA LAKE ... 18 R 30 NE
RUNUNDER POINT ... 30 H 39 SW
RYANS BEACH ... 80 D 8 NE
SADDLE POINT ... 61 I 70 NE
SADDLE ROCKS ... 29 F 36 NE
SADDLER POINT ... 64 A 5 NE
ST ANNE POINT ... 47 G 58 SE
ST CLAIR BEACH ... 80 E 5 SE
ST HELIERS BAY ... 64 F 7 SW
ST KILDA BEACH ... 80 E 5 SE
SALTWATER LAGOON ... 37 Q 49 SE
SAND HILL POINT ... 57 F 67 SE
SANDFLY BAY
  (DUNEDIN CITY) ... 80 E 7 NE
  (TASMAN) ... 75 C 3 NE
SANDROCK BLUFF ... 47 I 55 SE
SANDY BAY
  (FAR NORTH) ... 1 A 1 NW
  (TASMAN) ... 32 B 37 SE
  (WHANGAREI) ... 4 I 7 SE
SANDY POINT ... 58 J 68 SE
SAUVAGE POINT ... 29 E 37 SE
SAWDON STREAM ... 44 S 55 NW
SAWYERS BAY ... 80 D 7 NW
SAXTON ISLAND ... 32 C 39 SE
SAXTON RIVER ... 35 C 43 SE
SCENERY NOOK ... 42 B 54 NE
SCHNACKENBERG BAY ... 9 J 21 NE
SCHOOLHOUSE CREEK ... 53 L 61 SE
SCOTT POINT ... 1 A 1 NW
SEABREEZE POINT ... 51 G 58 SW
SEAFORTH RIVER ... 57 E 64 SE
SEAL ISLANDS ... 57 C 65 NE
SEAL POINT
  (DUNEDIN CITY) ... 80 E 7 NW
  (SOUTHLAND) ... 61 I 72 SW
SEAL ROCKS ... 47 I 55 NE
SEALERS BAY ... 61 H 70 SE
SECRETARY ISLAND ... 51 E 62 NW
SELWYN RIVER ... 46 Z 52 SW
SENTINEL ROCK ... 4 J 10 SW
SEPARATION POINT ... 32 B 36 SE
SERGEANT CHANNEL ... 66 F 8 NE
SERPENTINE CREEK ... 54 O 62 SE
SHAG POINT
  (THAMES COROMANDEL) ... 6 M 12 NE
  (WAITAKI) ... 56 T 62 SW
SHAG RIVER ... 59 J 69 NE
SHAG ROCK ... 31 J 35 SE
SHARKS HEAD ... 56 Q 63 NE
SHEEPWASH CREEK ... 56 Q 63 NE
SHELLY BAY ... 78 F 8 NW
SHELTER ISLAND ... 51 D 62 SE
SHELTER POINT ... 62 J 72 NE
SHERRY RIVER ... 75 F 1 SE
SHINGLE CREEK ... 54 N 62 SW
SHINGLE POINT ... 27 J 38 NW
SHIPWRECK BAY ... 1 C 5 NW
SHOAL BAY ... 64 F 6 NW
SHOE ISLAND ... 8 O 15 SE
SHOTOVER RIVER ... 52 K 59 NE
SILVER STREAM ... 80 D 7 NW
SIMMONDS ISLAND ... 1 C 3 NE
SINCLAIR HEAD ... 27 I 40 NE
SKEET RIVER ... 75 F 1 NW
SLATER POINT ... 6 K 12 NW
SLIPPER ISLAND ... 8 O 16 NE
SLOPE POINT ... 62 M 69 SE
SMAILS BEACH ... 80 E 6 SE
SMALL CRAFT HARBOUR ISLAND ... 57 D 66 NW
SMITHS BAY ... 73 D 2 NW
SMOOTH POINT ... 61 H 73 NE
SMOOTHWATER POINT ... 47 J 54 SE
SMUGGLERS BAY ... 4 I 9 NE
SOLOMON ISLAND ... 61 G 73 NE
SOMES ISLAND ... 27 J 39 NE
SOUTH ARM ... 61 H 73 NW
SOUTH CAPE ... 61 J 73 SE
SOUTH CHANNEL ... 6 J 12 SE
SOUTH FIORD ... 51 G 62 SE
SOUTH HEAD
  (FAR NORTH) ... 3 D 7 SW
  (RODNEY) ... 5 H 12 SW
  (TASMAN) ... 32 C 37 NW
SOUTH HEAD CONE ... 31 C 37 NW
SOUTH ISLETS ... 62 K 70 SE
SOUTH MAVORA LAKE ... 52 I 62 NE
SOUTH OPUHA RIVER ... 44 S 54 NE
SOUTH POINT
  (KAPITI COAST) ... 27 J 38 SW
  (RAKINO ISLAND) ... 66 E 8 NW
  (RUAPUKE ISLAND) ... 62 K 70 SE
  (SOUTHLAND) ... 57 C 65 SW
SOUTH RED HEAD POINT ... 61 H 72 NW
SOUTH TARANAKI BIGHT ... 21 G 31 SE
SOUTH WEST ARM ... 51 G 61 SW
SOUTH WEST CAPE ... 61 H 73 SW
SOUTH WEST POINT ... 51 D 62 NE
SPHINX LAKE ... 57 F 65 SW
SPIRITS BAY ... 1 A 1 NW
SPIT BEACH ... 8 O 8 NW
SPRAY RIVER ... 36 D 42 NE
SPYLAW BURN ... 55 N 64 SW
SQUALLY COVE ... 76 C 1 NE
SQUARE TOP ISLAND ... 6 M 12 SE
STACE CREEK ... 76 E 4 NW
STANLEY BAY ... 64 F 6 SW
STANLEY BROOK RIVER ... 32 B 39 SW
STANLEY PT ... 1 C 3 SE
STANLEY POINT ... 75 C 1 SW
STANMORE BAY ... 5 J 11 NE
STARLING ISLAND ... 62 J 72 NE
STEEP HEAD
  (INVERCARGILL CITY) ... 59 J 69 NW
  (SOUTHLAND) ... 62 J 71 NE
STEEP POINT ... 31 Y 37 NW
STEEPLE BURN ... 53 L 64 NE
STEEP-TO ISLAND ... 57 D 67 NW

STEPHENS ISLAND ... 29 G 35 SW
STEPHENSON ISLAND ... 2 F 4 NW
STEVENSONS ARM ... 48 M 58 NW
STEWART ISLAND ... 61 I 72 SE
STILLWATER RIVER ... 51 F 61 NE
STIRLING POINT ... 59 K 69 SW
STODDARD POINT ... 78 F 7 NE
STONY BAY ... 6 M 13 NE
STONY RIVER
  (MACKENZIE) ... 49 R 56 SW
  (NEW PLYMOUTH) ... 21 F 27 SW
STORM BEACH ... 8 O 16 NE
STRIPE HEAD ... 57 D 66 SW
STRIPE POINT ... 47 H 58 NW
STUMP BAY ... 17 O 26 SW
STYX CREEK ... 54 P 62 SE
STYX RIVER ... 38 U 48 NE
SUGAR LOAF ISLANDS ... 21 G 27 NW
SUGARLOAF ISLAND ... 1 D 3 NW
SUGARLOAF ROCK ... 4 J 7 SE
SUMNER HEAD ... 57 E 8 NW
SUNSHINE BAY ... 73 E 4 NE
SUPPER COVE ... 57 E 64 SW
SURVILLE CLIFFS ... 1 B 1 NE
SUTHERLAND SOUND ... 51 G 59 NW
SUTTON STREAM ... 54 O 63 SW
SWAN LAGOON ... 49 P 56 SE
SWAN LAKE ... 1 B 1 NE
TABLE CAPE ... 20 X 27 NE
TADMOR RIVER ... 34 A 40 SE
TAEMARO BAY ... 2 E 4 NW
TAHAENUI RIVER ... 20 V 27 NE
TAHAKOPA BAY ... 60 O 69 NE
TAHAKOPA RIVER ... 60 N 68 SE
TAHAPUKE BAY ... 81 B 3 NE
TAHARUA RIVER ... 18 Q 26 SW
TAHEKEROA RIVER ... 5 I 13 NE
TAHIRIMANGO POINT ... 25 J 37 NE
TAHUNATARA POINT ... 70 B 3 SW
TAHURUA POINT ... 14 Y 19 NW
TAIAROA HEAD ... 56 T 64 SW
TAIAUE BAY ... 63 A 2 SW
TAIERI ISLAND ... 56 R 66 NW
TAIERI RIVER ... 56 R 64 NW
TAIHARURU HEAD ... 4 I 8 SE
TAIKIRAU STREAM ... 4 G 7 NW
TAIPARE BAY ... 76 B 2 SW
TAIPO RIVER ... 38 V 48 NE
TAIRUA HARBOUR ... 8 O 15 SE
TAIRUA RIVER ... 8 N 16 SE
TAITA STREAM ... 63 C 1 NE
TAITOMO ISLAND ... 65 H 1 SE
TAKAHUE RIVER ... 1 D 5 SE
TAKAKA RIVER ... 31 A 38 NE
TAKAPUNA HEAD ... 64 F 6 NE
TAKATU HEAD ... 7 I 15 SW
TAKERAU BAY ... 2 E 4 NW
TAKOU BAY ... 2 G 5 NW
TAKOU RIVER ... 63 B 3 SW
TALLA BURN ... 54 O 64 NE
TAMA LAKES ... 16 N 28 NW
TAMAITEMIOKA ISLAND ... 61 G 73 NW
TAMAKI RIVER ... 7 K 15 NW
TAMAKI STRAIT ... 6 K 14 SE
TANGAHOE RIVER ... 11 H 30 SE
TANGAHOE STREAM ... 16 K 28 SW
TANGARAKAU RIVER ... 24 Q 34 NW
TANGARUHE STREAM ... 17 O 25 SW
TANGINGATAHI POINT ... 4 G 11 NE
TANGITIKI BAY ... 15 I 27 NE
TANGITU STREAM ... 15 I 27 NE
TANGOHOE STREAM ... 21 H 29 SE
TANGOIO BLUFF ... 18 S 29 NE
TANIWHANUI POINT ... 6 L 14 SE
TANUTANU STREAM ... 1 C 5 SW
TAONUI RIVER ... 16 M 28 SW
TAPARAMAPUA STREAM ... 6 K 21 NW
TAPEHAHAE STREAM ... 10 N 20 NW
TAPU POINT ... 81 E 3 SE
TAPUAEHARURU BAY ... 11 P 25 NW
TAPUAEROA RIVER ... 14 Y 21 NE
TAPUTERANGA ISLAND ... 73 F 3 NE
TARAERE BAY ... 1 B 2 NE
TARAMAKAU RIVER ... 38 U 47 NE
TARAMOUKOU STREAM ... 15 H 27 SE
TARANAKI BAY ... 65 J 2 SW
TARANAKI POINT ... 9 J 21 NE
TARANGA ISLAND ... 4 J 10 NE
TARATUIA POINT ... 14 X 19 SW
TARAWERA RIVER ... 13 S 21 NW
TARONUI BAY ... 63 B 3 SW
TARUARAU RIVER ... 17 P 28 SW
TASMAN BAY ... 32 C 38 NE
TASMAN RIVER ... 44 Q 53 SW
TASMAN SEA ... 37 R 46 NE
TATA ISLAND ... 32 B 36 SW
TATAPOURI POINT ... 20 Y 25 SW
TATARE STREAM ... 37 Q 51 NE
TAUGIHAU POINT ... 65 G 1 NE
TAUHERENIKAU RIVER ... 27 L 38 NW
TAUHOA CHANNEL ... 5 H 12 NW
TAUHOA RIVER ... 5 I 12 NW
TAUKARA STREAM ... 22 L 31 NE
TAUMAIHI ISLAND ... 10 O 19 SE
TAUMATARA PT ... 1 D 3 NW
TAUPIRI BAY ... 4 H 6 NE
TAUPO RIVER ... 63 A 1 NW
TAUPO POINT ... 32 B 36 SE
TAURANGA BAY ... 33 V 42 NW
TAURANGA ENTRANCE ... 10 P 19 NE
TAURANGA HARBOUR ... 10 P 19 NW
TAURANGA RIVER ... 13 T 24 NE
TAURANGA TAUPO RIVER ... 17 O 26 SE
TAURANGAKOUTUKU RIVER ... 14 Y 20 SE
TAUREKAITAI STREAM ... 24 Q 33 NW
TAUROA PENINSULA ... 1 B 5 SE
TAUROA POINT ... 1 C 5 SW
TAUTARAKOPUA STREAM ... 16 K 27 SE
TAUTEREI STREAM ... 9 J 19 NE
TAUTUKU PENINSULA ... 60 O 69 NW
TAUTUKU RIVER ... 60 O 69 NW
TAUWERU RIVER ... 28 N 38 NW
TAWERO POINT ... 29 F 38 NE
TAWHARANUI PENINSULA ... 5 K 12 NW
TAWHITI RAHI ISLAND ... 4 J 7 NE
TAWHITI STREAM ... 22 I 30 NE
TAWHITINUI ISLAND ... 29 F 38 NW

Coastal & Water Features

Coastal & Water Features

Location	Map No.	Ref
TAWHITINUI REACH	29	F 38 NW
TAYLOR ISLAND	81	C 2 NW
TAYLOR POINT	80	C 7 SE
TAYLORS MISTAKE	42	B 52 NE
TAYLORS STREAM	41	V 52 NW
TE AHUA POINT	65	H 2 SW
TE AKAROA	29	G 37 SW
TE ANAPUTA POINT	6	N 13 NW
TE ARAI RIVER	20	W 26 NE
TE ARAPAURA	27	J 38 SW
TE AWAROA BAY	70	C 1 NE
TE HAPE BAY	17	O 26 NW
TE HAPUA BAY	17	O 25 SW
TE HARA BAY	9	J 19 SE
TE HARUHI BAY	64	C 6 NE
TE HAUA BAY	17	O 25 SW
TE HAUPA ISLAND	64	A 5 SE
TE HERUOTARAIA POINT	20	W 28 NE
TE HIRAU BAY	69	D 3 SW
TE HOE RIVER	18	S 26 NW
TE HUE POINT	5	K 11 NE
TE HUMENGA POINT	27	K 40 SE
TE IKAARONGOMAI BAY	14	Y 24 NE
TE ITARATA POINT	11	O 25 NW
TE KAHA POINT		
(OPOTIKI)	13	W 20 NW
(WAIKATO)	9	J 20 NE
TE KAIAHORAWARU POINT	7	L 15 SE
TE KAKAHO ISLAND	29	G 37 SE
TE KARAE STREAM	2	E 6 NW
TE KARAKA ISLAND	8	O 15 NW
TE KAUKAU POINT	27	L 41 NE
TE KAUWAE POINT	11	O 25 NE
TE KAWAU POINT		
(RODNEY)	5	H 12 SW
(THAMES COROMANDEL)	6	M 13 SE
TE KOHIAKAHU POINT	70	C 4 SW
TE KOKOMIKO POINT	17	O 26 NW
TE KOPOPI A PAREKAWA POINT	17	O 25 SW
TE KUMI BAY	70	B 4 SW
TE MAIKA POINT	9	J 21 SE
TE MARA STREAM	25	M 36 SE
TE MURI POINT	64	A 5 SE
TE NGATO POINT	5	H 12 NE
TE OINEOHU POINT	17	O 25 NW
TE OKA BAY	42	A 53 SE
TE OPAI LAGOON	27	L 39 SW
TE OROROA POINT	9	O 15 SE
TE PAKI STREAM	5	K 19 SE
TE PAPA BAY	16	N 25 SE
TE POROPORO POINT	11	N 25 NE
TE PUNA INLET	2	E 5 NW
TE PUNE INLET	63	C 3 NE
TE PURU STREAM	8	N 16 NW
TE RAE POINT	17	N 26 NE
TE RAEKAIHAU	73	F 3 NW
TE RAKAUWHAKAMATUKU POINT	27	L 41 NE
TE RAUONE BEACH	80	C 8 SW
TE RERENGA STREAM	68	F 3 SE
TE REWAREWA POINT	27	J 38 NW
TE ROA BAY	9	H 5 SE
TE ROTO KARE	18	S 30 NW
TE TAMUITI POINT	6	L 15 NE
TE TAWA BAY	70	C 1 NE
TE TAWAI POINT	16	N 25 SE
TE TI BAY	81	C 1 NW
TE TIROA POINT	16	N 25 SE
TE TITOKI POINT	5	K 11 NE
TE TOTIPO HEAD	1	A 1 SW
TE TUHI POINT	11	O 25 NW
TE TUMURAE POINT	66	F 8 NW
TE UMAKURI PT	1	C 6 SE
TE UPOKOOHINEPAKI POINT	14	Z 21 NE
TE WAEWAE BAY	58	G 67 SE
TE WAHA POINT	5	I 15 NW
TE WAHAORA BAY	65	G 1 NE
TE WAHAPU INLET	81	D 3 NE
TE WAHAROA STREAM	65	G 1 NE
TE WAKATEHAUA ISLAND	1	B 2 SW
TE WERAHI BEACH	1	A 1 SW
TE WHAU POINT	6	M 13 SE
TE WHETUMATARUA POINT	66	E 8 SE
TE WI BAY	2	H 5 SE
TEHEPOUTU PT.	1	A 1 SW
TEKAPO HYDRO CANAL	44	R 55 NW
TEKAPO RIVER	44	R 55 NE
TELFORD BURN	58	H 64 SE
TENGAWAI RIVER	45	T 56 NE
TEVIOT RIVER	54	N 63 NE
THE ALDERMEN ISLANDS	8	P 15 SE
THE BLUFF		
(FAR NORTH)	1	B 2 SW
(RODNEY)	5	H 11 SW
THE BROTHERS	30	H 38 NE
THE BROTHERS POINT	60	N 69 SE
THE GAP	65	H 1 SE
THE GORGE CREEK	75	C 2 NW
THE GUT	51	E 62 SW
THE HAYSTACK	29	G 37 NE
THE ISLAND	44	R 53 NE
THE ISLANDS	29	G 37 SW
THE KNOBBIES	61	H 70 SW
THE NECK	62	J 71 NE
THE NOISES	6	K 13 SE
THE PINNACLES	4	J 7 SE
THE SISTERS		
(CLUTHA)	60	N 69 SE
(SOUTHLAND)	61	I 72 SW
THE TWINS	8	O 14 SW
THE WATCHMAN	65	H 2 SW
THOMAS RIVER	43	M 54 NE
THOMPSON SOUND	51	E 62 NW
THORNE BAY	64	E 6 SW
THREE O'CLOCK STREAM	56	R 64 NW
THUMB POINT	6	L 14 NE
TI POINT	81	C 1 NW
TIKIERE STREAM	17	N 30 SE
TIKOKOPU STREAM	56	D 2 NE
TIKORAKI POINT	58	T 62 NE
TIKORE ISLAND	59	K 69 NW
TIKOTATAHI BAY	62	J 72 NE
TIKOTIKO STREAM	7	K 18 NE
TILBY POINT	11	P 19 SE
TIMARU RIVER	48	N 57 SE
TINUI ISLAND	29	F 36 SE
TINUI RIVER	26	O 37 NE
TIRAU BAY	27	J 38 SW
TIRAUMEA RIVER		
(BULLER)	34	Z 42 SE
(TARARUA)	26	N 35 SE
TIRIKOHUA POINT	5	I 14 SW
TIRITIRI MATANGI ISLAND	6	K 13 SW
TIROHANGA POINT	10	P 19 NW
TIROHANGA STREAM	15	J 28 NW
TIRUA POINT	15	I 23 NE
TITAHI BAY	73	B 3 SE
TITI ISLAND	29	G 37 SE
TITIPUA STREAM	59	K 67 SE
TITITIRA HEAD	43	N 52 SW
TOETOE POINT	5	H 11 SW
TOETOES BAY	59	L 69 NW
TOKARAHU POINT	8	O 14 NW
TOKAROA POINT	8	O 15 SE
TOKATA POINT	13	V 20 SE
TOKATEA ROCKS	14	Z 23 SE
TOKATOKA PT	1	B 1 NE
TOKATU POINT	6	K 12 NW
TOKERAU BEACH	1	D 4 NW
TOKIAHURU STREAM	17	M 29 NE
TOKO NGAWA POINT	32	B 37 SE
TOKOMAIRIRO RIVER	56	Q 65 SW
TOKOMARU BAY	14	Z 22 SW
TOKOMARU RIVER	25	M 35 NE
TOKOTOROTO POINT	5	H 12 SE
TOLAGA BAY	14	Z 23 SE
TOM BOWLING BAY	1	B 1 NW
TOMAHAWK BEACH	80	C 8 SW
TOMATEA POINT	31	A 35 SW
TOMMY POINT	51	G 59 SW
TOMOGALAK STREAM	59	K 64 SE
TONGA ISLAND	32	C 37 SW
TONGA ROADSTEAD	32	C 37 NW
TONGARIRO RIVER	17	N 28 NE
TOREA BAY	76	D 3 SW
TORERE RIVER	13	V 21 SE
TORETORE ISLAND	81	C 3 SW
TOROPAPA STREAM	18	Q 27 NE
TORRENT BAY	32	C 37 SW
TORY CHANNEL	30	H 39 NE
TOTARA RIVER	22	J 29 NW
TOWER ROCKS	29	F 36 NE
TOWING HEAD	51	G 63 NW
TRANSIT RIVER	47	H 58 SW
TRAVERS RIVER	34	B 42 SW
TRENT RIVER	38	X 47 NW
TRIG POINT	25	J 32 NE
TRIO ISLANDS	29	G 37 NW
TRYPHENA HARBOUR	6	M 12 NE
TUAHENI POINT	20	X 25 SE
TUAMOTU ISLAND	20	X 25 SE
TUAPIRO CREEK	68	B 1 SE
TUHAWAIKI ISLAND	60	P 68 SW
TUHAWAIKI POINT	50	U 57 NE
TUKEMOKIHI STREAM	20	W 26 SW
TUKITUKI RIVER	24	Q 32 NW
TUNAKINO STREAM	76	D 1 NW
TUPUTUPUNGAHAU ISLAND	1	D 3 NW
TURAKINA RIVER	22	M 31 SW
TURAKIRAE HEAD	27	J 40 NE
TURANGA CREEK	66	H 8 NE
TURANGANUI RIVER	27	L 40 NW
TURIHAUA POINT	20	Y 25 NW
TURIPEKA POINT	6	M 13 SE
TURNBULL RIVER	43	L 55 NE
TUTAEKURI RIVER	18	R 29 SE
TUTAEPAWHAITI BAY	61	J 72 NW
TUTAETOKO STREAM	13	U 22 NE
TUTEMOHUTA STREAM	70	C 4 SW
TUTUKAKA HARBOUR	4	I 8 NE
TWO THUMB BAY	51	E 60 SE
UGLY RIVER	31	Y 38 SE
ULVA ISLAND	61	J 71 SW
UMAREAREA STREAM	9	L 22 NW
UPOKONUI STREAM	22	K 30 NW
UPPER GREY RIVER	34	X 45 SE
UPPER NIHOTUPU RESERVOIR	65	H 3 NW
UPUKERORA RIVER	52	H 62 SE
UPUKONGARO STREAM	22	L 31 NW
URENUI RIVER	15	I 27 NW
URUKOKOMUKE STREAM	13	W 23 SW
URUPUKAPUKA ISLAND	2	H 5 SW
URUROARAHI POINT	8	O 13 SW
URUTI BAY	81	C 4 NE
UTUHINA STREAM	69	D 1 NW
UWHIROA STREAM	1	C 5 SE
VANCOUVER ARM, BREAKSEA SOUND	57	E 63 SW
VERONICA CHANNEL	2	G 6 NE
VERTER BURN	79	D 1 SW
VICTORY BEACH	80	D 8 NW
VICTORY ISLAND	27	F 36 NE
VON RIVER	52	J 61 NE
WAERENGA STREAM	8	M 17 SW
WAIAEKA RIVER	13	U 22 SW
WAIANAKARUA RIVER	56	T 61 SE
WAIAPU RIVER	14	Z 20 SE
WAIAROHIA INLET	64	E 4 SW
WAIAROHIA STREAM	82	B 1 NE
WAIARUHE RIVER	63	D 2 SE
WAIATA STREAM	13	U 22 SW
WAIATATOTO RIVER	48	L 55 NW
WAIAU BAY	64	C 5 NE
WAIAU RIVER		
(GISBORNE)	14	Y 23 NW
(HASTINGS)	18	S 26 NE
(HURUNUI)	40	D 47 SW
(SOUTHLAND)	58	H 67 NW
WAIAU STREAM	22	I 31 SE
WAIAUA BAY	2	G 4 SW
WAIAUA RIVER		
(OPOTIKI)	13	V 22 NW
(SOUTH TARANAKI)	21	F 29 NE
WAIAUTE STREAM	12	R 22 SW
WAIHAHA RIVER	16	N 25 NE
WAIHAO RIVER	50	U 58 SE
WAIHAO RIVER NORTH BRANCH	50	T 57 NE
WAIHAO RIVER SOUTH BRANCH	50	T 58 NW
WAIHAORANGATAHI BAY	27	F 58 NW
WAIHARA RIVER	14	X 24 NW
WAIHARAKEKE STREAM	63	E 3 SW
WAIHAREHARE BAY	14	Y 24 SE
WAIHAU BAY		
(GISBORNE)	14	Y 24 NE
(OPOTIKI)	14	X 19 SE
WAIHAU BEACH	14	Y 24 NE
WAIHEKAU STREAM	10	N 19 SE
WAIHEKE ISLAND	6	K 13 NW
WAIHEKE RIVER	39	X 46 SE
WAIHI BAY	17	N 26 SE
WAIHI ESTUARY	12	R 20 NW
WAIHI POINT	30	H 38 NW
WAIHI STREAM	19	T 26 NE
WAIHIHI BAY	81	A 3 NW
WAIHINAU BAY	76	B 3 NE
WAIHINGAIA STREAM	28	N 40 NW
WAIHO RIVER	37	Q 50 SW
WAIHOANGA STREAM	63	E 1 NW
WAIHOHONU STREAM	16	N 28 NE
WAIHOKI STREAM	26	P 36 NW
WAIHOPAI RIVER	29	E 41 NE
WAIHORA BAY	11	N 25 NE
WAIHORA STREAM		
(MASTERTON)	28	O 38 NW
(TAUPO)	11	N 25 NE
WAIHOU RIVER	8	N 16 SW
WAIHOU STREAM	10	O 21 SW
WAIHUA RIVER	19	U 27 NW
WAIHUKA RIVER	13	W 24 NW
WAIITI BEACH	15	I 26 NW
WAIITI STREAM	17	M 29 SE
WAIKAHAWAI POINT	14	Z 21 SE
WAIKAIA RIVER	53	M 64 NW
WAIKAKAHO RIVER	76	E 2 SE
WAIKAKARIKI RIVER	14	W 20 SE
WAIKAMIHI STREAM	12	R 21 SE
WAIKANAE STREAM	1	B 2 NW
WAIKANAPITI STREAM	69	C 4 NE
WAIKARAKA STREAM	28	O 39 NE
WAIKARE INLET	2	H 6 NW
WAIKARE RIVER	12	T 24 NW
WAIKARETAHEKE RIVER	19	U 26 SW
WAIKARI RIVER		
(HASTINGS)	18	S 27 SE
(HURUNUI)	42	A 48 SE
WAIKATO RIVER	7	J 17 SE
WAIKATO STREAM	16	N 28 SW
WAIKAWA HARBOUR	60	N 69 SW
WAIKAWA POINT	14	W 19 SE
WAIKAWA STREAM	25	L 36 NW
WAIKAWAU BAY	6	N 13 SW
WAIKAWAU BEACH	15	I 23 SE
WAIKAWAU POINT	8	M 15 SE
WAIKINO STREAM	19	T 26 NW
WAIKITI RIVER	38	X 46 SW
WAIKIWI STREAM	79	A 3 NW
WAIKONINI STREAM	18	Q 29 SE
WAIKOPUA CREEK	66	G 8 SE
WAIKOREA STREAM	9	J 19 SE
WAIKOROPUPU RIVER	75	F 3 NW
WAIKOUAITI RIVER	56	S 63 NE
WAIKOUKOU STREAM	65	D 2 SE
WAIKOWHEWHE RIVER	12	R 22 SE
WAIKUKU BEACH	1	B 1 NE
WAIKURA RIVER		
(GISBORNE)	20	W 25 NW
(OPOTIKI)	14	Y 20 NW
WAIMA RIVER		
(FAR NORTH)	3	E 8 NE
(MARLBOROUGH)	36	G 42 SW
WAIMAHANA BAY	2	E 4 NE
WAIMAI STREAM	9	J 19 NE
WAIMAKARIRI RIVER	41	Y 51 NW
WAIMAMA BAY	8	O 17 NE
WAIMANA RIVER	12	T 22 NW
WAIMANGARO RIVER	81	E 2 NE
WAIMANGAROA POINT	81	F 3 NE
WAIMANGO STREAM	1	D 3 NW
WAIMARINO RIVER	17	O 26 SW
WAIMATA RIVER	20	X 24 SE
WAIMATE ISLAND	6	M 14 SW
WAIMATUA CREEK	79	C 4 NW
WAIMATUKU STREAM	58	J 68 NW
WAIMEA RIVER	59	L 65 SW
WAINGARO RIVER		
(TASMAN)	31	A 38 NW
(WAIKATO)	9	K 19 SE
WAINGAROMIA RIVER	14	X 23 SW
WAINGOKIA STREAM	17	O 26 NW
WAINGONGORO POINT	21	G 30 NE
WAINGONGORO STREAM	28	N 38 NW
WAINGUKIA STREAM	14	Y 21 SW
WAINONO LAGOON	50	U 58 SE
WAINUI BAY	63	A 2 SW
WAINUI BEACH	22	J 31 SE
WAINUI CREEK	49	N 59 SE
WAINUI INLET	32	B 36 SE
WAINUI RIVER	26	Q 35 NE
WAINUI STREAM	64	B 4 NW
WAINUIOMATA RIVER	27	J 40 NE
WAINUIORU RIVER	28	N 38 SW
WAINUIOTOTO BAY	8	N 14 NE
WAIOEKA RIVER	13	U 23 SE
WAIOHINE RIVER	27	L 38 NE
WAIOHOTU RIVER	10	O 21 NW
WAIOMOKO RIVER	20	Y 25 NE
WAIONE STREAM	16	M 27 NE
WAIONGANA STREAM	15	G 26 SE
WAIORUA BAY	25	K 37 NE
WAIOTAHI RIVER	13	U 22 NW
WAIOTAKA RIVER	17	O 27 NW
WAIOTIRA STREAM	4	H 10 NW
WAIPA RIVER	67	F 1 NE
WAIPAHIHI STREAM	10	N 21 NE
WAIPAKIHI RIVER	17	O 28 NW
WAIPAOA RIVER	14	W 23 SE
WAIPAPA POINT	59	L 69 SE
WAIPAPA STREAM	68	D 2 SW
WAIPARA POINT	42	A 49 NW
WAIPARE STREAM	10	O 21 SW
WAIPATUKAHU STREAM	65	E 1 SE
WAIPAUA STREAM	26	P 36 SE
WAIPAWA RIVER	24	Q 31 SE
WAIPAWA RIVER	28	N 38 NE
WAIPEHI STREAM	17	O 26 NW
WAIPIRO BAY	14	Z 22 NW
WAIPORI STREAM	26	O 36 NW
WAIPOUA RIVER	25	M 37 NE
WAIPUNA BAY	80	C 7 SE
WAIPUNGA RIVER	18	R 27 SE
WAIRAKA POINT	3	J 38 NE
WAIRAKAU STREAM	67	F 4 NE
WAIRAKI RIVER	58	H 65 NE
WAIRAU RIVER	29	E 40 SE
WAIRAURAHIRI RIVER	57	F 67 SE
WAIRERE STREAM	65	F 2 SW
WAIROA BAY	63	C 4 NE
WAIROA RESERVOIR	7	L 16 NW
WAIROA RIVER		
(HASTINGS)	19	U 26 SE
(MANAKAU CITY)	6	L 15 NW
(TASMAN)	32	C 40 NW
(WHANGAREI)	4	G 9 SW
WAIROA STREAM	68	B 1 SE
WAIRUA STREAM	69	D 2 SE
WAITA BEACH	43	M 53 SW
WAITAHA RIVER	37	S 49 SE
WAITAHAIA RIVER	14	X 22 SE
WAITAHANUI RIVER	17	P 26 NW
WAITAHORA STREAM	1	A 1 SE
WAITAHU RIVER	33	V 44 NW
WAITAHUNA RIVER	55	O 66 NE
WAITAIA BAY	6	O 14 SW
WAITAKARURU STREAM	9	M 19 SE
WAITAKERE RESERVOIR	65	G 2 SE
WAITAKERE RIVER		
(BULLER)	33	V 43 SE
(WAITAKERE CITY)	65	G 2 NE
WAITAKERE STREAM	65	G 2 NE
WAITAKI RIVER	50	U 59 SW
WAITANGI RIVER	2	D 3 NE
WAITANGIRUA STREAM	13	W 23 NW
WAITANGITAONA RIVER	37	Q 50 NE
WAITARA RIVER	15	I 27 NE
WAITARIA BAY	76	C 3 SE
WAITATA BAY	76	B 3 NE
WAITAWHITI STREAM	26	O 36 NE
WAITEKOHE STREAM	68	C 1 SW
WAITEMATA HARBOUR	6	J 14 SW
WAITENGAUE STREAM	10	O 18 SW
WAITETI STREAM	69	B 1 SW
WAITETUNA RIVER	9	K 20 NE
WAITETUNA STREAM	28	N 39 SW
WAITEWHENA RIVER	16	K 25 SW
WAITI STREAM		
(HASTINGS)	18	R 29 NW
(WAITAKERE CITY)	65	G 2 NW
WAITOA RIVER	10	N 19 NW
WAITOHI RIVER	39	Z 48 NE
WAITOMO STREAM	9	L 22 SW
WAITOTARA RIVER	22	J 31 NE
WAITUI BAY	76	B 4 SE
WAITUI STREAM	75	D 2 NW
WAITUNA BAY	61	H 70 SE
WAITUNA CREEK	65	K 69 NE
WAITUNA LAGOON	59	L 69 NW
WAITUTU RIVER	57	F 67 SW
WAIUKU RIVER	7	J 16 NW
WAIUNA LAGOON	47	I 56 NW
WAIWAWA RIVER	8	N 15 SE
WAIWERA RIVER	6	J 13 NE
WAIWHAKAIHO RIVER	15	G 26 SW
WAIWHAKAPA STREAM	69	D 4 SE
WAIWHERO STREAM	24	R 33 NE
WAKAMARINA RIVER	29	E 39 SW
WAKAPUTA POINT	58	H 68 NE
WALLACE HEAD	60	N 69 NE
WANGALOA CREEK	60	Q 67 NW
WANGANUI BLUFF	37	R 49 NW
WANGANUI RIVER	37	R 49 NE
WANGAPEKA RIVER	31	Z 40 NE
WAPAPA RIVER	63	C 1 SW
WARD ISLAND	73	E 4 SW
WATCHMAN ROCK	8	O 16 NE
WATERFALL BAY	25	I 37 NE
WEDGE POINT	29	G 39 NW
WEITI RIVER	64	C 5 NW
WEKA ISLAND		
(FIORDLAND)	57	D 67 SW
(STEWART ISLAND)	62	J 72 NE
WEKAKURA POINT	31	X 37 NE
WEKARUA ISLAND	6	M 14 SW
WELLINGTON HARBOUR	27	J 39 SE
WEST CAPE	57	C 66 NW
WEST HEAD	30	H 39 NE
WEST POINT	62	K 70 NE
WEST TAMAKI HEAD	66	F 7 SW
WESTERN BAY	17	O 25 NW
WESTERN PASSAGE	57	C 66 SE
WESTSHORE BEACH	21	B 3 NE
WET JACKET ARM	57	D 64 SE
WHAKAHAUPAPA STREAM	12	R 21 NE
WHAKAIPO BAY	70	B 3 SW
WHAKAKAIWHARA POINT	6	L 15 NW
WHAKAKI LAGOON	20	V 27 SE
WHAKAKI RIVER	5	H 11 SE
WHAKAMOENGA POINT	70	B 3 NW
WHAKANGAROMANGA STREAM	6	K 30 SE
WHAKAPAPA RIVER	16	M 27 NW
WHAKAPOAI POINT	1	X 37 SE
WHAKAPUNI STREAM	28	M 40 NW
WHAKARUA STREAM	14	M 39 NE
WHAKATAKAHE HEAD	20	W 27 SE
WHAKATAKI RIVER	26	P 37 NW
WHAKATANE RIVER	12	T 24 NW
WHAKATAUTUNA POINT	6	N 11 NW
WHAKATEREPAPANUI ISLAND	29	G 36 SW
WHAKATIKEI RIVER	27	K 38 NW
WHAKATONGA POINT	11	N 25 NE
WHALE BAY	63	C 4 NW
WHANGAEHU RIVER		
(TARARUA)	25	N 37 NW
(WANGANUI)	22	L 32 NW
WHANGAIHE BAY	63	A 1 NE
WHANGAIREHE STREAM	16	L 27 SE
WHANGAMARINO STREAM	1	L 17 SW
WHANGAMATA BAY	70	B 2 NE
WHANGAMATA HARBOUR	8	O 16 NW
WHANGAMOA HEAD	29	D 38 NE
WHANGANUI INLET	31	Z 35 SE
WHANGANUI ISLAND	6	M 14 SW
WHANGANUI RIVER	16	K 27 NE
WHANGAPARAOA BAY		
(OPOTIKI)	14	X 19 SE
(RODNEY)	6	J 13 SE
WHANGAPARAOA PASSAGE	64	B 7 SW
WHANGAPARAOA PENINSULA	6	J 13 SE
WHANGAPARAOA RIVER	14	Y 19 SW
WHANGAPARAPARA HARBOUR	6	M 11 SW

Location	Map No.	Ref
WHANGAPE HARBOUR	1	C 6 SE
WHANGAPOUA HARBOUR	8	N 14 NE
WHANGARA ISLAND	20	Y 25 NE
WHANGAREI HARBOUR	4	I 9 NW
WHANGAROA BAY	2	F 4 NW
WHANGAROA HARBOUR	2	F 4 SW
WHANGARURU HARBOUR	4	I 6 SW
WHANGATEAU HARBOUR	6	J 12 NE
WHARE CREEK	58	H 64 NW
WHAREAKEAKE	80	C 7 NE
WHAREAMA RIVER	28	O 37 SE
WHAREANA BAY	1	B 1 NE
WHAREKAWA HARBOUR	8	O 16 SE
WHAREKAWA RIVER	8	O 17 NW
WHAREKOPAE RIVER	13	W 24 SW
WHAREKURA POINT	13	W 20 NW
WHAREPAPA RIVER	27	K 39 SW
WHAREWAKA POINT	70	B 4 SW
WHAROWHARO STREAM	82	D 1 SW
WHATAROA RIVER	37	R 49 SW
WHATAUMU STREAM	22	K 30 NE
WHAU BAY	63	A 2 SE
WHAUWHAU BEACH	8	O 14 SW
WHAWANUI RIVER	27	L 41 NE
WHEAO RIVER	12	R 25 NW
WHENUAKURA ISLAND	8	O 17 NE
WHENUAKURA RIVER	22	I 30 SE
WHIRINAKI RIVER	12	R 25 NE
WHITCOMBE RIVER	38	T 49 SE
WHITE BLUFFS	29	G 40 SE
WHITE CLIFFS	15	I 26 NW
WHITE HEAD	60	P 68 SW
WHITE ISLAND		
(BAY OF PLENTY)	13	U 19 NW
(DUNEDIN CITY)	56	S 65 NW
WHITE ROCK	61	I 72 SE
WHITE ROCK POINT	61	I 70 NW
WHITE ROCKS	30	H 38 NW
WHITES BEACH	5	I 15 NW
WHITESTONE RIVER	52	I 62 SW
WHITEWASH HEAD	78	E 8 NW
WHITIANGA BAY	13	V 20 SE
WHITIKAU STREAM	17	O 27 SW
WHITIPIRORUA POINT	8	O 16 SE
WICKLIFFE BAY	80	D 8 NE
WIGMORE BAY	65	G 1 SE
WILBERFORCE RIVER	41	V 49 SW
WILKIN RIVER	48	M 56 NW
WILLS RIVER	43	N 55 NE
WILSON RIVER	57	D 67 NE
WILSONS BAY	6	M 15 NE
WILSONS POINT	61	H 73 NE
WINDLEY RIVER	53	J 63 NW
WINDON BURN	52	I 61 NE
WINDSOR POINT	57	D 67 SE
WINDY POINT	65	J 2 SW
WINSTONES COVE	64	D 5 NE
WIROA ISLAND	7	J 15 SE
WOMENS ISLAND	62	J 70 SE
WOOD BAY	65	H 4 NE
WOODY BAY	66	D 3 SE
WOODY HEAD	9	J 20 SE
WOOLWASH CREEK	17	P 29 NW
WORSER BAY	27	J 39 SW
WORSLEY STREAM	52	H 60 NW
WYE RIVER	35	D 41 SW
YATES POINT	47	H 58 NW
YELLOW HEAD	80	D 7 SW
YORK BAY	73	E 4 NE
YOUNG NICKS HEAD	20	X 26 NW

Mountains, Passes & Land Features

Location	Map No.	Ref
ADAMS HILL	61	H 71 SE
ADVENTURE HILL	61	J 71 SW
AHIMANAWA RANGE	18	O 27 NE
AHIPAEPAE	70	E 4 SE
AHIWEKA	24	O 33 SW
AILSA MOUNTAINS	52	I 59 SE
AMURI PASS	39	Y 46 NW
AMURI PLAIN	40	B 47 SW
ANATOKI PEAK	31	Z 37 SE
ANATOKI RANGE	31	A 37 SE
AORANGI MOUNTAINS	27	L 40 SE
ARAKIHI	14	X 23 SE
AROWHANA	14	X 22 NW
ARTHUR RANGE	31	A 39 NW
ARTHUR'S PASS	38	V 48 NE
ATOA	4	G 9 NE
ATTEMPT HILL	29	F 36 SW
BALD HILL	58	H 67 NE
BANNOCK BRAE RANGE	43	O 53 NE
BARE CONE	51	G 60 NW
BARE HILL	59	K 66 NE
BARRIER RANGE	43	O 55 NE
BATON SADDLE	31	A 39 NW
BEAUMONT	58	I 65 NE
BEEHIVES	15	G 28 SE
BEN LOMOND	52	K 60 SE
BEN MCLEOD	45	T 53 NE
BEN MCLEOD RANGE	44	S 54 NE
BEN MORE	44	W 50 SE
BEN NEVIS	53	L 61 NW
BEN OHAU RANGE	44	P 55 SE
BENMORE PEAK	49	Q 57 NW
BENMORE RANGE	52	Q 56 SW
BERESFORD RANGE	60	N 68 SE
BIRDWOOD RANGE	41	V 49 NW
BLACK PEAK	48	L 58 NW
BLACK RANGE	41	V 49 NE
BLACK ROCK	55	P 64 SE
BLACK UMBRELLA	54	M 64 SW
BLAIRICH	36	F 41 SW
BLUE MOUNTAIN	53	D 42 SW
BLUE MOUNTAINS	55	N 65 SE
BODDINGTON RANGE	44	B 44 SW
BROWNING PASS	38	V 48 SW
BRUCES HILL	34	X 43 NE
BRUNNER RANGE	34	D 39 NE
BRYANT RANGE	4	H 10 SE
BUNKER HILL	4	H 10 SE
BURNT HILL	7	Y 51 NW
CAMERON MOUNTAINS	57	E 66 NW
CAROLINE PEAK	57	F 66 NW
CASTLE MOUNTAIN	52	H 59 SW
CASTLE ROCK	6	N 14 SW
CATHEDRAL PEAKS	51	G 63 NW
CECIL PEAK	52	K 61 NE
CENTAUR PEAK	52	K 58 SW
CHEST PEAK	41	X 49 SE
CLEUGHEARN PEAK	58	G 65 SW
CLIMAX PEAK	47	J 57 SE
CLOUDY PEAK RANGE	44	S 51 NE
COLLYER	47	K 56 NW
COLONIAL KNOB	27	J 38 SW
COMMAND PEAK	51	E 61 SE
CONE PEAK	57	E 65 SE
CONICAL PEAK		
(RODNEY)	5	J 11 SW
(WAIMATA)	56	S 61 SW
COOK SADDLE	44	P 51 SE
COOPERS CASTLE	6	M 11 NE
COPLAND PASS	44	Q 52 SW
COROMANDEL RANGE	8	N 15 NW
CORONET PEAK	53	L 60 NW
CRAIGIEBURN RANGE	39	X 47 SE
CRAWFORD RANGE	48	M 59 NE
CRIFFEL PEAK	48	M 59 NE
CRIFFEL RANGE	53	M 60 NW
CROWN RANGE	53	L 59 SE
DAGON	47	K 56 NW
DALGETY RANGE	38	S 56 NW
DAMPIER RANGE	39	V 48 NW
DARK SUMMIT	2	J 12 SW
DARRAN MOUNTAINS	47	I 58 NW
DECEIT PEAKS	61	H 72 NE
DEVIL RIVER PEAK	31	A 37 SW
DEVILS BACKBONE	36	D 41 SE
DILLON CONE	35	C 44 SE
DINGWALL MOUNTAINS	57	E 64 NE
DOMETT RANGE	31	Y 38 NE
DOUBLE CONE	53	L 61 NW
DOUGHBOY HILL	61	H 72 SE
DOUGLAS RANGE	31	Z 37 SE
DUFFERS SADDLE	53	M 61 SW
DUN FIUNARY	44	P 54 SE
DUN MOUNTAIN	29	D 39 SW
DUNSTAN	49	N 60 SE
DUNSTAN MOUNTAINS	49	N 60 NE
EARL MOUNTAINS	52	H 61 NE
ELIE DE BEAUMONT	44	R 51 SW
ESK HEAD	39	V 48 NE
EYRE MOUNTAINS	52	J 63 NE
EYRE PEAK	52	K 62 NW
FANTHAMS PEAK	21	G 28 SW
FENIAN RANGE	31	Y 39 NE
FLAT MOUNTAIN	58	G 64 NW
FLEETWOOD PEAK	51	F 61 NW
FLORA SADDLE	31	A 38 SE
FOG HILL	2	N 15 NW
FORBES MOUNTAINS	47	J 58 NE
FOREST RANGE	59	M 68 NW
FOUR PEAKS RANGE	45	T 54 NE
FOX PEAK	45	S 53 SE
FRANKLIN MOUNTAINS	51	G 60 NE
GAMACK RANGE	44	Q 53 NE
GARIBALDI RANGE	31	Z 39 NW
GARVIE MOUNTAINS	53	L 63 NE
GLYNN WYE RANGE	52	Z 47 NW
GOAT HILL	7	I 15 SE
GODLEY GLACIER	44	R 51 SE
GORDON RANGE	35	B 41 NE
GOULAND DOWNS	31	Y 37 NE
GOULAND SADDLE	31	Z 37 SW
GRAMPIAN MOUNTAINS	50	R 56 NE
GRANDVIEW MOUNTAIN	48	N 58 NE
GRANGE RANGE	31	Z 38 SW
GRINDLEY RANGE	31	Y 38 NE
GUNN PEAK	37	R 51 NW
GUNNER DOWNS	31	Y 38 NE
HAAST PASS	43	N 55 NW
HAAST RANGE	48	K 56 NE
HALL RANGE	44	R 52 SE
HANMER RANGE	39	A 46 NE
HAPPY VALLEY SADDLE	34	X 40 NE
HARPER PASS	38	V 47 SW
HARPER RANGE	45	T 52 SE
HARRIS MOUNTAINS	48	L 58 NW
HAUHUNGAROA	16	M 25 SE
HAUHUNGAROA RANGE	11	M 25 NE
HAUPIRI RANGE	31	A 37 NW
HAUTURU	6	M 15 NE
HAWKDUN RANGE	49	O 58 SW
HAWKINS HILL	27	I 39 SE
HEATH MOUNTAINS	57	E 65 NE
HECTOR MOUNTAINS	53	L 63 NW
HELMET HILL	58	G 66 SW
HERANGI	15	J 24 NW
HERANGI RANGE	15	J 24 SW
HERBERT RANGE	31	Z 39 NE
HEREKAREAO	1	D 5 SW
HIHITAHI	17	N 29 SE
HIKURANGI		
(FAR NORTH)	3	F 7 SE
(GISBORNE)	14	Y 21 NW
HIRAKIMATA	6	M 11 NE
HIWI	22	J 30 NW
HOKONUI HILLS	59	K 65 SE
HOOKER GLACIER	44	Q 52 SW
HOPE PASS	39	Y 46 SW
HOPE RANGE	34	A 41 NW
HOPE SADDLE	34	A 41 NE
HOROMANGA	6	N 15 NW
HORSE RANGE	56	S 61 SE
HOWITT PEAKS	51	G 61 NE
HUARUA	4	H 9 SE
HUIA	2	F 5 NE
HUIARAU RANGE	17	T 25 SW
HUKARAHI	8	N 14 SE
HUMBOLDT MOUNTAINS	52	J 59 NW
HUMMOCK	56	R 63 NE
HUNTER MOUNTAINS	57	F 64 SE
HUNUA RANGES	7	L 16 NW
IDA RANGE	49	O 59 SW
IKAWHENUA RANGE	12	S 23 SE
INLAND KAIKOURA RANGE	36	D 43 SE
ISLAND SADDLE	34	A 44 NE
ISOLATED HILL	36	F 42 SE
IWITUAROA RANGE	31	Y 37 NW
JACKS PASS	40	B 46 NW
JACKSONS PEAKS	51	G 63 NE
JANE PEAK	52	J 62 SE
JOLLIES PASS	40	B 46 NW
KAHAAROA RANGE	21	I 29 NW
KAHAROA	13	U 23 SW
KAHEREKOAU MOUNTAINS	57	F 65 SE
KAHIKATEA RANGE	13	U 24 NW
KAHUPUTOI	2	E 6 SE
KAHURANAKI	24	S 31 NW
KAIHIKU	60	O 67 SW
KAIIWI	3	E 9 NE
KAIMAI RANGE	10	O 19 NE
KAIMANAWA MOUNTAINS	17	O 28 NW
KAIPARORO	25	M 36 NE
KAIPAUA	1	D 5 SW
KAIRANGI	2	E 4 NE
KAITAKE RANGE	21	F 27 SE
KAKANUI	27	K 37 SE
KAKANUI MOUNTAINS	50	R 60 SE
KAOKAOROA RANGE	24	R 31 SE
KARANGARUA SADDLE	44	P 53 NE
KAURI HILL	4	G 10 NE
KAWAKAWA	2	G 6 NE
KAWEKA	18	Q 28 SW
KAWEKA RANGE	18	P 28 NE
KELVIN PEAK	59	L 66 NE
KEPLER MOUNTAINS	51	F 62 SE
KEY SUMMIT	52	I 59 SE
KIRKLISTON RANGE	50	R 58 NE
KNOBBY RANGE	54	N 63 NE
KOHEKOHE	3	D 7 SE
KOHURAU	49	R 59 NW
KOHURONAKI	1	A 1 SE
KOROPEKE	26	N 35 NE
KOTIPU	1	D 5 SE
KOWHAIROA	2	F 4 NW
KUKUNUI	4	I 9 SW
LAMMERLAW RANGE	55	P 64 NW
LAMMERLAW TOP	54	O 64 NE
LAMMERMORE RANGE	54	P 64 NW
LEAD HILLS	31	Z 37 SE
LEES PASS	42	Z 49 NW
LEWIS PASS	34	Z 45 SE
LIEBIG RANGE	44	Q 52 SE
LINDIS PASS	49	O 58 NW
LINDIS PEAK	48	N 58 SE
LITTLE MT ANGLEM	61	I 70 SE
LITTLE WANGANUI SADDLE	34	Y 40 NE
LIVINGSTONE MOUNTAINS	52	I 61 NE
LOCKETT RANGE	31	A 38 NW
LONGWOOD RANGE	58	H 67 NE
LOOKOUT RANGE	34	A 40 SW
LOWRY PEAKS RANGE	40	B 47 SE
LYELL GLACIER	37	T 50 SW
LYELL RANGE	34	X 42 NE
MACKAY DOWNS	31	Y 37 SE
MACKENZIE PASS	44	S 55 SW
MACLENNAN RANGE	60	N 68 SW
MAHARAHARA	23	O 33 SW
MAKINO	21	H 29 SE
MAKOROKO	17	O 27 SE
MALCOLM RANGE	47	I 56 NE
MALTE BRUN	44	Q 52 NE
MANAIA	4	I 9 NE
MANAKAU	36	E 42 NW
MANGAOWATA	15	J 27 NW
MANGAREWA WEST	22	J 28 NW
MANGATANGI	7	L 16 SW
MANGAWEKA	23	P 31 SW
MANUKA	23	N 31 SE
MANUOHA	19	T 25 NE
MARSHALL RANGE	31	Z 38 SW
MATAIKOKAKO	7	L 15 SE
MATAKETAKE RANGE	43	M 54 NE
MATAKUHIA RANGE	19	U 25 SW
MATEMATEAONGA	15	J 24 SW
MATEMATEAONGA RANGE	15	J 28 SW
MATIRI RANGE	34	Y 41 NE
MAU	8	N 16 SW
MAUMAUPAKI	8	N 15 SW
MAUNGAHARURU RANGE	18	R 28 NE
MAUNGAHAUMI	13	W 23 NW
MAUNGAHEREMONA	1	C 5 NE
MAUNGAHOTOA	2	E 5 NE
MAUNGAMANGERO	9	J 23 NE
MAUNGANUI	3	E 8 SW
MAUNGAPOHATU	13	T 24 SE
MAUNGARAI	22	J 29 NE
MAUNGATANIWHA		
(FAR NORTH)	2	E 5 NW
(WAIROA)	18	S 26 NW
MAUNGATAUTARI	10	N 21 SW
MAUNGATUA	56	Q 65 NE
MAUNGAWHAKAMANA	12	R 22 NE
MEIKLEBURN SADDLE	45	T 53 SW
MERRIE RANGE	57	F 65 NW
MID DOME	53	K 63 SW
MINARET PEAKS	48	L 57 NE
MIROMIRO	39	A 46 NW
MITRE	25	M 36 SW
MITRE PEAK	47	H 58 SW
MOANA	22	J 30 NW
MOEHAU	6	M 13 NW
MOEHAU RANGE	6	M 13 NE
MOFFAT PEAK	52	I 60 SE
MOIR HILL	5	J 12 SE
MOKORETA	60	N 67 SW
MOLE SADDLE	34	A 43 NW
MONS SEX MILLIA	39	Z 46 NE
MORGAN RANGE	31	Z 38 SW
MOTATAU	4	G 7 SE
MOTUTERE	6	N 14 SW
MOUKAHU	22	K 30 SW
MT ADAMS		
(MASTERTON)	28	N 39 SW
(WESTLAND)	37	R 50 SE
MT AITKEN	57	E 67 NE
MT AJAX	39	X 46 SE
MT ALBA	43	L 55 SE
MT ALBERT		
(BULLER)	34	X 44 SE
(QUEENSTOWN LAKES)	48	M 56 SW
MT ALEXANDER	38	W 47 SW
MT ALGIDUS	41	V 50 NE
MT ALLA	61	I 72 NW
MT ALLEN	61	I 70 NW
MT ALTA	48	L 57 SE
MT ANGLEM	61	I 70 NW
MT ARNOLD	48	N 56 SE
MT ARROWSMITH	45	T 51 NE
MT ARTHUR	31	A 39 NW
MT ASPIRING	48	K 57 NE
MT BAKER	25	N 36 NE
MT BEALEY	41	V 48 SE
MT BECK	47	I 56 SE
MT BINSER	41	X 49 NW
MT BLACKBURN	44	Q 53 NE
MT BONPLAND	52	J 59 SW
MT BRAXTON	53	I 64 NE
MT BREWSTER	43	N 55 NE
MT BRYCE	38	U 49 NW
MT CAMPBELL	52	J 62 NW
MT CARDRONA	53	L 59 SE
MT CHRISTINA	52	I 59 SW
MT CLARA	34	A 45 NE
MT CLERKE	57	D 64 SW
MT COOK	44	Q 52 SW
MT CRAWFORD	25	L 37 NE
MT CROSSLEY	39	X 48 NE
MT CROWFOOT	57	E 64 NE
MT D'ARCHIAC	44	S 51 SW
MT DAMPER	15	J 26 NE
MT DOMETT	31	Y 38 NE
MT DONALD	51	F 61 NE
MT DONALD MCLEAN	65	J 3 NW
MT DORA	34	A 44 NE
MT DUNCAN	48	K 55 SE
MT DUNDAS	25	M 36 SW
MT EARNSLAW	47	J 58 NE
MT EDWARD	47	K 57 SW
MT EDWARDS	44	S 54 SW
MT EGLINTON	52	I 60 SW
MT EGMONT	15	G 28 NW
MT ELIZABETH	38	W 47 NE
MT ELLA	34	A 43 SW
MT ELLIOT	52	H 59 SW
MT ENYS	41	W 50 NW
MT ERIN	24	S 31 NW
MT EVANS	33	V 43 SE
MT FARADAY	33	V 43 SE
MT FISHTAIL	29	D 40 NE
MT FORBES	51	D 62 SE
MT FORSTER	37	R 50 SE
MT FRANKLIN	34	A 43 SE
MT FYFFE	36	E 45 NW
MT GLADSTONE	36	E 43 NW
MT GLENCAIRN	43	P 54 SW
MT GORGE	57	F 63 NW
MT GOULAND	31	Z 37 NW
MT GRACE	27	J 39 SE
MT GREENLAND	37	S 48 SE
MT HALL	36	E 42 NW
MT HARPER	45	U 52 SW
MT HAUITURU	6	L 11 NW
MT HEALE	26	N 35 SE
MT HECTOR	27	L 37 SW
MT HIWIROA	10	O 21 NE
MT HOCHSTETTER	39	X 46 NE
MT HOLDSWORTH	25	L 37 NE
MT HOPELESS	34	A 42 SE
MT HOPKINS	43	P 53 SW
MT HUMPHRIES	15	J 28 SW
MT HUTT RANGE	41	V 51 NE
MT HUXLEY	43	O 55 NE
MT IDA	49	O 59 SW
MT IRENE	51	F 61 SE
MT ISOBEL	40	B 46 NW
MT JERVOIS	34	A 45 SW
MT KARIOI	9	J 20 SE
MT KELLARD	57	D 63 SE
MT KENDALL	31	Z 39 SW
MT KINNAIRD	43	N 53 SE
MT KYEBURN	49	R 59 SW
MT LARKINS	52	J 60 NE
MT LATHROP	38	U 48 SE
MT LONGFELLOW	39	Y 47 NE
MT LONGSIGHT	51	G 59 NW
MT LUXMORE	51	G 62 SE
MT LYALL	51	G 62 NE
MT MALING	34	Z 44 SE
MT MANTELL	34	Y 43 NE
MT MARCHANT	26	O 35 SW
MT MARSH	26	O 36 NW
MT MATTHEWS	27	K 39 SW
MT MAUNGANUI	10	P 19 SE
MT MCDONALD	43	O 52 SE
MT MCDOUGALL	51	G 60 SE
MT MCFARLANE	43	N 54 NW
MT MELINA	48	O 57 NW
MT MESSENGER	15	I 26 NE
MT MISERY		
(KAIKOURA)	36	F 42 SW
(SELWYN)	41	W 49 NE
MT MUNRO	36	E 42 SE
MT MURCHISON		
(ASHBURTON)	41	V 49 NW
(BULLER)	34	Z 42 NE
MT MUSGRAVE	44	S 53 SE
MT NESSING	50	S 56 SE
MT NEWTON	34	Y 41 SE
MT NGAURUHOE	16	N 27 SW
MT NGONGOTAHA	10	P 22 NE
MT NIMROD	50	T 57 NW
MT ORR	34	Z 40 SE
MT OWEN	34	Z 40 NE
MT OXFORD	41	Y 50 NW
MT PARNASSUS	40	C 47 NE
MT PATRIARCH		
(NELSON)	35	C 41 NE
(TASMAN)	31	Z 40 NE
MT PEEL	45	U 53 SE
MT PEMBROKE	47	H 58 NE
MT PERCY	26	P 37 NE
MT PHILLIPS	35	D 41 SW
MT PISA	54	M 59 SE
MT PISGAH		
(SOUTH CANTERBURY)	51	G 61 SW
(SOUTHLAND)	60	R 60 SE
MT POTTS	45	T 51 SE
MT PUTEKETEKE	57	F 65 NE
MT PYE	60	N 68 SE
MT RADOVE	44	R 53 NE
MT RAKEAHUA	61	I 71 NE
MT RAMESES	33	X 45 SW
MT RICHARDSON	41	Y 50 NE
MT RICHMOND	29	D 40 SW
MT RINTOUL	35	C 40 SE
MT ROLLESTON	41	V 48 SE
MT ROSS	27	L 40 SE
MT RUAPEHU	16	M 28 SW

Mountains, Passes & Land Features - Skifields, Tracks, Parks & Forests

Location	Map No.	Ref
MT RUTLAND	29	E 39 NE
MT RYALL	33	V 45 NW
MT SEBASTOPOL (BULLER)	34	B 44 SW
MT SEBASTOPOL (MACKENZIE)	44	Q 53 NW
MT SEFTON	44	P 53 NE
MT SHEWELL	29	F 37 SW
MT SHRIMPTON	48	N 56 NW
MT SIBBALD	44	R 52 NE
MT SINCLAIR	44	T 52 SW
MT SOAKER	51	F 63 NW
MT SOLITARY	57	E 65 NE
MT ST BATHANS	49	O 58 SE
MT ST MARY	49	O 56 NE
MT STEVENS	31	Z 36 SW
MT STEVENSON	44	R 54 NW
MT STOKES	29	G 38 NW
MT STRACHAN	43	O 53 SE
MT STRAUCHON	43	O 54 SE
MT STUDHOLME	50	T 58 NW
MT SUTTON	44	R 57 NW
MT TANILBA	51	F 60 SW
MT TARAWERA	12	R 22 SW
MT TASMAN	44	Q 52 NW
MT TAYLOR	45	U 51 SE
MT TE AROHA	10	N 18 SE
MT TECHNICAL	34	Z 45 SW
MT TEKOA	39	A 47 NW
MT THOMAS	42	Z 49 SW
MT TINLINE	35	C 45 SW
MT TITIROA	58	G 64 SE
MT TONGARIRO	16	N 27 SW
MT TRAVERS	34	A 43 NE
MT TREACEY	38	V 47 NW
MT TURNBULL	52	J 61 NW
MT TUTOKO	47	I 58 NW
MT UNA	34	A 44 NW
MT UNION	36	E 43 SW
MT URIAH	33	W 43 SW
MT VICTORIA	34	Y 43 SW
MT WARD (SOUTHLAND)	57	F 64 NW
MT WARD (WESTLAND)	43	P 54 NW
MT WENDON	55	M 65 NW
MT WHITCOMBE	37	T 50 NW
MT WILLIAM	7	K 16 SE
MT WILSON	40	D 47 NW
MT ZION	7	I 15 SW
MOUTOHORA	13	V 23 NW
MURCHISON GLACIER	44	R 52 SW
MURCHISON MOUNTAINS	51	G 62 NW
NEEDLES POINT	36	G 42 SE
NEUDORF SADDLE	32	B 39 NE
NEUMANN RANGE	43	P 54 SW
NGAMOKO RANGE	19	T 25 SE
NGAPUKETURUA (TARARUA)	25	M 36 NW
NGAPUKETURUA (TAUPO)	17	O 27 NE
NGARAHU	2	F 5 NW
NGATOKA	4	H 9 SE
NGATUTURU	4	G 7 NE
NGAUTUKU	10	O 23 SE
NORTH ROUGH RIDGE	49	P 61 NW
OBELISK	54	N 62 NW
OHIWAI	8	O 16 NW
OKAPA	4	G 7 SE
OKIA FLAT	80	D 8 NW
OKIWA	22	J 31 NE
OKUKU PASS	42	Z 49 SE
OKUKU SADDLE	41	Y 49 NE
OLD MAN PEAK	49	O 58 NE
OLD MAN RANGE	54	M 62 SE
OLIVINE RANGE	47	J 56 SE
OMOEROA SADDLE	44	Q 51 SW
OPANGO	1	D 6 NW
ORANGE PEEL CORNER	7	I 15 SE
OROWHANO	1	C 5 SE
OTAINGA	2	E 5 SW
OTAUNOA RANGE	18	S 26 NE
OTEPO	1	D 5 SW
OTUPAE	17	P 29 SW
OTURIA	2	E 6 NW
PAEROA RANGE	10	P 23 SE
PAIHIKOKURI	1	D 5 SE
PAIKAURI	2	E 4 NE
PAKIHIKURA	23	N 32 NW
PAKIRARAHI	8	N 16 SE
PANTHAMS PEAK	15	G 28 SW
PAPAKURA	2	E 4 NE
PAPAROA RANGE	33	V 44 SW
PARAPARA PEAK	31	A 36 SW
PAREOKAWA	1	D 6 NW
PARIPOKAI	16	K 28 SE
PATUHA	21	F 27 SE
PATUTU	17	O 28 SW
PAUANUI (FAR NORTH)	1	C 6 NE
PAUANUI (THAMES COROMANDEL)	5	O 16 NE
PIHANGA	16	N 27 NE
PIKIAWATEA	70	F 4 SE
PILBROW HILL	4	H 10 SE
PINELHEUGH	54	O 63 NW
PINNACLE	35	C 42 NE
PIRONGIA	8	L 21 NW
PISA RANGE	54	M 60 NE
POHUKURA	18	R 26 SE
POKAKA	2	F 6 NE
POLLUX	48	L 56 NW
PORTERS PASS	41	W 50 SE
POSEIDON PEAK	47	I 58 NE
POTTS PEAK	14	X 20 SE
POUAKAI	15	G 28 NW
POUATU	15	J 27 NE
POUERUA	2	F 6 SE
PRINCESS MOUNTAINS	57	F 65 SW
PUAKATO	14	Y 23 NW
PUDDING HILL	36	D 42 NE
PUKEAKURA	14	X 24 SE
PUKEAMARU	14	Y 19 SE
PUKEHINAU	2	E 5 NE
PUKEKOHE	4	H 10 NW
PUKEMAIRE	59	L 66 SW
PUKEMATEKEO	5	I 15 NE
PUKEMIRO	3	F 7 SE
PUKEMOREMORE	25	M 36 NW
PUKENUI	18	T 26 NW
PUKETAHA	27	K 39 NW
PUKETERAKI	41	Y 49 NW
PUKETERAKI RANGE	41	Y 49 NW
PUKETOETOE	13	W 21 NW
PUKETOI RANGE	26	O 35 SE
PUKETOTARA	5	I 14 SW
PUKETUTU (BAY OF ISLANDS)	2	E 4 NW
PUKETUTU (FAR NORTH)	1	D 5 NW
PUKEWHAKATARATARA	6	M 15 NE
PUKEWHARARIKI	3	F 9 NW
PUREORA	11	N 25 SW
PUROA	6	N 13 NW
PUTAUAKI	12	S 22 NW
RADIANT RANGE	34	Y 40 SW
RAETEA	1	D 5 SE
RAGGED RANGE	38	T 50 NE
RAGGEDY RANGE	49	O 61 NE
RAGLAN RANGE	35	B 43 NE
RAHU SADDLE	33	V 45 NW
RAKAUMAHI	22	J 29 SE
RAMSAY GLACIER	37	T 50 NW
RANGANUI	9	M 23 NE
RANGIPO	8	O 16 SE
RANGIPOUA (MT HARDY)	14	W 20 SE
RANGITOTO	9	N 15 NE
RANGITOTO RANGES	9	M 23 NE
RATORURUTU	2	E 5 NE
RAUKAWA RANGE	24	R 31 SW
RAUKUMARA	14	Y 20 SW
RAUKUMARA RANGE	14	W 22 NE
RAUNGAEHE RANGE	12	S 22 NE
RAUTOUTO	2	E 5 SW
RED HILL	35	C 41 NW
REEFTON SADDLE	33	W 44 NE
REWA	28	O 38 NW
RICHARDSON MOUNTAINS	52	K 60 NW
RICHMOND RANGE	29	D 40 SW
RIMUTAKA RANGE	27	K 39 SW
ROB ROY PEAK	48	K 57 NE
ROCK AND PILLAR RANGE	56	Q 62 SW
ROCK PEAK	9	K 22 NW
ROCKY MOUNT	53	M 62 SW
ROCKY TOR	34	Y 41 SW
ROLLESTON RANGE	38	U 49 SE
ROUGH RIDGE	54	O 62 SE
ROUND PEAKS	52	J 60 SE
ROYS PEAK	48	M 58 SW
RUAHINE RANGE	23	O 33 NW
RUAOTUWHENUA	5	I 15 NE
RUATEREI	8	N 15 NE
RUGGEDY MOUNTAINS	61	H 70 SE
SADDLE HILL	29	D 39 NW
ST ARNAUD RANGE	34	A 43 SE
ST BATHANS RANGE	49	O 58 NE
ST BERNARD	36	D 44 NE
ST MARYS RANGE	49	Q 58 SE
SCOTTS KNOB	35	C 42 SW
SEAWARD KAIKOURA RANGE	36	D 44 NE
SEVERN	35	C 43 SW
SHENANDOAH SADDLE	34	Y 43 SE
SHINGLE PEAK	35	D 43 NW
SIBBALD RANGE	44	R 52 NE
SILVER PEAK	56	R 64 NE
SIMLA	5	I 15 NW
SKIPPERS RANGE	47	I 57 SE
SMYTH RANGE	37	S 49 SW
SMYTHE CORNER	5	I 15 NW
SNOWDEN RANGE	31	Z 38 NE
SNOWDON	52	I 62 NE
SOMNUS	47	I 58 SE
SOUTHERN ALPS	37	S 51 NW
SOUTRA HILL	57	P 63 NE
SPENCE PEAK	58	H 64 SE
SPENSER MOUNTAINS	34	Z 44 SE
STONEHENGE	54	Q 62 SW
STRACHAN RANGE	43	O 53 NW
STUART MOUNTAINS	51	G 61 NE
STYX SADDLE	38	U 48 NE
SUMMIT	26	P 35 NW
TAIERI RANGE	56	Q 62 SE
TAIERI RIDGE	56	R 62 SW
TAKITIMU MOUNTAINS	58	H 64 SE
TAMAHUNGA	5	J 11 SW
TANGIHUA	4	G 9 NE
TANGIHUA RANGE	4	G 9 NE
TANGOWAHINE	3	F 9 NE
TAPUAENUKU	36	E 43 NE
TAPUKETURU	3	F 8 NW
TARAKAHU	3	F 7 SW
TARAMOUKU	15	H 27 NE
TARAPONUI	18	S 27 SW
TARARU	5	N 16 NW
TARARUA RANGE	25	M 36 NW
TARATARA (FAR NORTH)	2	E 5 NE
TARATARA (WHANGAREI)	2	G 6 NW
TAREREPO	15	I 28 NW
TARINGATURA HILL	58	J 65 NW
TARINGATURA HILLS	58	J 64 SW
TASMAN GLACIER	44	Q 52 NE
TASMAN MOUNTAINS	31	Z 38 NW
TATERE	21	I 30 NW
TATU	16	K 26 NW
TAUHARA	12	P 25 NE
TAUMATAWHAKATANGI-HANGAKOAUAUOTAMATEA-POKAIWHENUAKITANATAHU	24	Q 34 SE
TAUROA	1	C 5 SW
TAUWHARE	1	C 5 SW
TAWHIUAU	12	S 24 NW
TE ARAI	2	E 5 NW
TE AROHAKERE	16	K 26 NW
TE ATUAHAUTAPU	13	V 22 NE
TE IRINGA	18	P 26 SE
TE KAKA	8	N 15 SW
TE KAPU	20	W 28 NE
TE KEHO	8	O 17 SE
TE MAPOU	15	J 28 SE
TE MATA PEAK	71	F 3 NE
TE PAKI	1	A 1 SE
TE RANGA	2	E 5 NE
TE ROTOMANOAO	4	G 9 SE
TE URA	4	G 9 SE
TE WAITI HILL	13	V 22 SW
TE WAKA	18	R 28 NE
TE WHAKAUMU	12	S 23 NE
TE WHARANGI	1	D 6 NW
TEHEOIRI	2	F 4 SE
TERAWHITI HILL	27	I 39 NE
THE CHASM	80	E 7 NE
THE DOME	5	J 12 NW
THE HAYSTACK	34	Z 41 NW
THE HUMP	57	F 66 SE
THE HUNTER HILLS	50	T 57 NW
THE PAPS	61	I 70 SE
THE PIKES	36	F 43 NE
THE PINNACLES	36	D 42 SE
THE REMARKABLES	53	L 61 SW
THE STOPPER	57	D 65 SW
THE THUMBS	44	S 52 NE
THE TWINS	31	A 39 NW
THOMPSON	25	L 36 SW
THOMSON MOUNTAINS	52	J 61 SW
THOMSON RIDGE	61	I 71 NE
THREE KINGS RANGE	17	O 29 NW
TIN RANGE	61	I 72 NW
TIRAUMEA SADDLE	34	A 42 SW
TIRIKAWA	1	A 1 SE
TITAHA	1	D 5 SW
TITIHUATAHU	2	F 6 SE
TOETOEHATIKO	3	E 8 NW
TOITOI FLAT	61	I 72 NE
TOOTH PEAK	52	J 60 SE
TOREADOR PEAK	47	J 57 NE
TORLESSE RANGE	41	W 50 NE
TOTARA	15	H 28 NE
TOTARA SADDLE	37	T 49 NW
TOWER PEAK	57	E 66 SE
TOWNLEY MOUNTAINS	57	F 64 NW
TRAVERS SADDLE	34	A 43 SE
TREBLE CONE	48	L 58 NE
TREBLE MOUNTAIN	57	D 66 SE
TRIG HILL	5	J 11 SW
TRIPS PEAK	45	U 54 NW
TUBMAN HILL	31	Y 37 NE
TUBMAN RANGE	31	Y 37 NE
TUHINGAMATA	11	N 25 NW
TUMAI	15	I 27 NE
TUNNEL RIDGE	65	J 2 NW
TUNUPO	23	O 32 NE
TUPARI	17	P 30 SW
TURIWIRI	3	F 9 SE
TUTAMOE (FAR NORTH)	3	F 8 SW
TUTAMOE (GISBORNE)	14	X 23 NE
TUTUTAWA	15	I 28 SE
TWO THUMB RANGE	44	S 54 NW
UMBRELLA MOUNTAINS	54	M 64 NE
UNUWHAO	1	B 1 NW
VICTORIA RANGE	34	Y 44 NW
VIEW HILL SADDLE	34	X 40 SE
WAEWAEPA RANGE	26	O 35 NE
WAHATUARA	27	P 34 SW
WAIKARUKU	1	D 6 NE
WAIKIEKIE	4	H 9 SW
WAIKUKU	26	O 35 NW
WAIMEA PLAINS	59	K 65 NW
WAINUI RIVER	68	D 1 SE
WAIOPEHU	25	L 36 SE
WAITAHUNA HILL	55	P 65 NE
WAITAWA	1	D 5 SE
WAITEWAEWAE	25	L 36 SE
WAKAMARAMA RANGE	31	Z 37 NW
WANGAPEKA SADDLE	31	Z 40 NE
WARDS PASS	35	C 43 SE
WEDNESDAY PEAK	57	E 67 NW
WEKA PASS	42	A 48 SE
WEST DOME	53	J 63 SW
WETA	2	E 4 NW
WHAKAANGI	1	D 6 NW
WHAKAMARU	10	O 23 SW
WHAKAPUNAKE	20	V 26 NE
WHAKARARA	2	E 4 NW
WHAKATAKA	12	T 25 SW
WHALES BACK SADDLE	40	C 45 SE
WHANGAAHEI	6	N 13 SW
WHIRINAKI	16	K 28 NE
WHITCOMBE PASS	38	T 50 NE
WHITE PEAK	57	F 65 SW
WHITECOOMB	25	M 63 SW
WILBERG RANGE	37	S 50 SW
WISP HILL	55	O 67 SW
YOUNG RANGE	43	N 55 SE

Skifields, Tracks, Parks & Forests

	Map No.	Ref
ABEL TASMAN NATIONAL PARK	32	B 37 NE
ABEL TASMAN TRACK	32	B 37 NE
ADAMS GIFT BLOCK	7	L 15 SE
AHU AHU TRACK	65	H 2 SW
AHURIRI BUSH	78	F 6 SE
AHURIRI WALKWAY	88	B 1 NW
AKATERE HISTORIC RESERVE	2	E 4 SE
ALBERT DENNIS SCENIC RESERVE	5	J 13 NW
ALFORD FOREST	41	V 52 NE
AMURI SKIFIELD	34	A 45 SE
ANAKIWA TRACK	29	F 39 NE
ANATOKI TRACK	31	A 37 SW
ANAURA BAY WALKWAY	14	Z 23 NW
ANAWHATA BEACH TRACK	65	G 2 SW
ANDERSON TRACK	65	G 3 NW
ANDREWS KAURI RESERVE	5	I 12 SW
AONGATETE FOREST	68	D 1 NE
AORANGI SCENIC RESERVE	38	U 46 NW
ARAWHATA FOREST	47	K 56 NW
ARMSTRONG KAURI RESERVE	5	I 12 SW
ARTHUR'S PASS NATIONAL PARK	41	W 48 SE
ASHBURTON WALKWAY	41	W 54 SE
ASHLEY FOREST	42	A 50 NW
ATENE SKYLINE WALKWAY	22	L 30 SW
ATHENREE FOREST	68	B 1 NE
ATIU ATIU CONSERVATION AREA	22	K 30 SE
ATUATUI FOREST	5	I 12 SW
AUCKLAND CITY WALK	65	G 2 NW
AUPORI FOREST	1	B 2 SW
AWA AWA RATA RESERVE	41	V 52 NE
AWAHONUI FOREST	18	O 27 SE
AWAKINO SKIFIELD	49	R 59 NW
BALMORAL FOREST	39	A 48 NE
BAY OF ISLANDS MARITIME & HISTORIC PARK	2	H 5 NW
BEAUMONT FOREST	55	O 65 NW
BEEHIVE CREEK TRACK	23	N 33 NE
BEN LOMOND TRACK	52	K 60 SW
BERWICK FOREST	56	Q 65 SW
BIG BUSH CONSERVATION AREA	34	A 41 S
BILLY GOAT TRACK	8	N 16 N
BOB GORDON TRACK	65	J 2 N
BOUNDARY STREAM WALKWAY	18	S 27 S
BREAM HEAD SCENIC RESERVE	4	I 9 NE
BRITANNIA WALKWAY	33	W 41 S
BROKEN RIVER SKIFIELD	41	W 49 SW
BROWNE TRACK	65	H 2 N
BRYNDERWYN HILLS WALKWAY	4	I 10 SW
BUCK TAYLOR TRACK	65	J 2 NE
BYERS WALK	65	H 2 NE
CABLE BAY WALKWAY	29	D 38 SW
CANNON POINT WALKWAY	27	K 38 SW
CAPE FOULWIND WALKWAY	33	V 42 NW
CAPE REINGA WALKWAY	1	A 1 NW
CAPE RODNEY - OKAKARI POINT MARINE RESERVE	6	K 11 S
CAPLES TRACK	52	J 60 SW
CARDRONA SKIFIELD	53	L 59 S
CASCADE FOREST	47	J 55 SW
CATLINS FOREST PARK	60	N 68 SW
CENTENNIAL TRACK	65	J 2 N
CHARMING CREEK WALKWAY	33	X 41 NW
CHASM CREEK WALKWAY	33	X 41 NW
CHATEAU MOSQUITO TRACK	65	G 2 S
COLONIAL KNOB TRACK	27	J 38 SW
COMANS TRACK	65	J 2 N
COOKS COVE WALKWAY	14	Z 24 NW
COPLAND TRACK	43	P 52 SW
CORNWALLIS PARK	65	J 3 N
COROMANDEL FOREST PARK	6	M 13 NW
COROMANDEL TRACK	6	M 13 NW
CORONET PEAK SKIFIELD	53	K 60 NE
CRAIGIEBURN FOREST PARK	41	V 49 S
CRAIGIEBURN SKIFIELD	41	W 49 SW
CROWS PARK	65	J 3 N
CROYDON BUSH	59	L 66 N
CUTTY GRASS TRACK	65	J 2 N
DENNISTON WALKWAY	33	W 41 S
DIAMOND TRAIL	65	G 3 N
DOME FOREST	5	J 12 N
DOME FOREST WALKWAY	5	J 12 N
DON MCLEAN TRACK	65	J 2 N
DUN MOUNTAIN WALKWAY	29	D 39 SV
DUSKY SOUND TRACK	57	F 64 SV
EAST BEACH RESERVE	1	C 3 S
EASTERN & WESTERN OKATAINA WALKWAY	10	Q 22 N
EGMONT NATIONAL PARK	15	G 28 NV
ERUA CONSERVATION AREA	16	L 28 N
ESK FOREST	18	R 28 S
EYREWELL FOREST	41	V 51 N
FAIRY FALLS TRACK	65	G 3 SV
FENCELINE TRACK	65	G 3 SV
FERNDOWN TRACK	65	G 3 SV
FILTER TRACK	65	G 3 SV
FIORDLAND NATIONAL PARK	52	H 59 SE
FLAGSTAFF HILL HISTORIC RESERVE	81	A 3 SE
FLAGSTAFF WALKWAY	56	R 64 SE
FLETCHER TRACK	65	J 3 NE
FLEXMAN SCENIC RESERVE	5	I 11 SV
FOX PEAK SKIFIELD	44	T 54 NE
GIBBONS TRACK	65	J 3 NE
GLENBERVIE FOREST	4	I 9 NE
GLENDHU FOREST	55	O 64 SE
GOLDEN DOWNS FOREST	32	B 40 NE
GOLDEN STAIRS WALKWAY	65	G 2 N
GOLDIE BUSH SCENIC RESERVE	5	J 14 NW
GRANVILLE FOREST	33	W 45 SE
GREENSTONE TRACK	52	I 60 NE
GWAVAS FOREST	22	Q 31 NV
HAKARIMATA WALKWAY	9	L 19 NV
HANMER FOREST	8	B 46 NV
HANMER FOREST PARK	39	A 46 NE
HAPUAKOHE TRACK	8	M 17 SV
HARPER PASS TRACK	39	X 47 NE
HARRY KAURI PARK	3	J 12 NV
HAURANGI FOREST PARK	27	L 41 NV
HAUTURU TRACK	65	K 22 NE
HAWKE BAY COASTAL WALKWAY	18	T 28 NV
HEAPHY TRACK	31	Y 37 NE
HERBERT FOREST	56	S 61 SE
HEREKINO FOREST	1	C 5 SE
HIHITANI SANCTUARY	17	N 30 NE
HIKURANGI SCENIC RESERVE	3	F 7 SE
HIRA FOREST	29	D 39 NV
HOCHSTETTER FOREST	33	W 45 SV
HOKIANGA TRACK	3	D 7 SE
HOKONUI FOREST	59	L 66 SV
HOLLYFORD TRACK	47	I 58 NE
HOME TRACK	65	H 2 NE
HOROHORO FOREST	10	O 22 SE
HOROMANGA RIVER TRACK	12	S 24 NV
HOROTIU SCENIC RESERVE	81	D 1 NV
HOUTO FOREST	4	G 8 SV
HOWARD CONSERVATION AREA	34	A 42 NV
HUATOKI WALK	89	C 2 NV
HUIA RIDGE TRACK	65	J 2 NE
HUKATERE SCENIC RESERVE	4	H 11 NV
HUNTER FOREST	43	O 55 NV
HUNUA RANGES REGIONAL PARKLANDS	7	L 16 NW
HUTIWAI CONSERVATION AREA	15	J 25 SW
IANTHE FOREST	37	S 49 NW
KAHURANGI NATIONAL PARK	34	Z 40 SE
KAIHU FOREST	3	F 8 SW
KAIIWI LAKES WALKWAY	3	E 9 NE
KAIKOURA PENINSULA WALKWAY	36	E 45 SE
KAIMAI MAMAKU FOREST PARK	10	O 21 NE
KAIMANAWA FOREST PARK	17	O 27 SW
KAINGAROA FOREST	12	Q 25 NE
KAITAIA WALKWAY	1	C 5 SE
KAITUNA TRACK	31	Z 36 NE
KAKAMATURA RIDGE TRACK	65	J 3 NE
KAKEPUKU HISTORIC RESERVE	67	E 2 NW
KANIERE WATER RACE TRACK	38	U 47 NW
KAPARA CONSERVATION AREA	22	I 29 SE
KARA FOREST	16	K 25 SW
KARAKA FOREST	5	L 24 SW
KARAMATURA TRACK	65	J 2 NE
KARAMU RESERVE	67	D 1 SW
KARANGAHAKE WALKWAY	8	O 18 NW
KARIOI FOREST	17	N 29 NW
KAURI GROVE TRACK	65	H 2 SE
KAURI PARK	65	G 2 NE

Location	Map No.	Ref
AWEKA CONSERVATION AREA	18	Q 29 NW
AWERUA RESERVE		D 8 NE
AWHAKA FOREST	38	U 47 SE
ENNEDYS BUSH	78	F 6 NE
ENNEDYS BUSH TRACK	78	E 6 SW
EPLER TRACK	51	G 63 NE
ERIKERI WALKWAY	2	F 5 SE
INLEITH FOREST	10	O 23 NE
IRIPAKA WILDLIFE SCENIC RESERVE	7	L 15 SE
OHI POINT WALKWAY	13	T 21 NE
OHITERE FOREST	25	L 35 SE
OROREREKA POINT SCENIC RESERVE	81	A 3 SW
UATAIKA TRACK	65	G 2 NW
A TROBE TRACK	65	H 2 SW
AKE KANIERE WALKWAY	38	T 48 NE
AKE OHIA RESERVE	1	D 4 NW
AKE SUMNER FOREST PARK	39	Y 46 SW
AKE TAUPO FOREST	17	P 26 SW
AKE WAIKAREITI WALKWAY	19	T 25 SE
AKE WAIKAREMOANA TRACK	19	T 25 SW
AKE WAINAMU RESERVE	65	G 2 NW
AKE WAINAMU TRACK	65	G 2 NW
AKESIDE ROTOROA TRACK	34	A 42 SW
ESLIE - KARAMEA TRACK	31	Z 39 NE
ISMORE FOREST	22	L 31 SW
ONG BAY REGIONAL PARK	6	J 13 SE
ONG ROAD TRACK	65	G 2 NE
ONGWOOD FOREST	58	H 67 SE
OWER KAURI TRACK	65	G 2 NE
UCY CRANWELL TRACK	65	H 2 SE
YELL WALKWAY	34	Y 42 NW
IAHINAPUA WALKWAY	37	T 48 NW
IAHOE FOREST	9	K 22 SW
IAHOENUI FOREST	15	J 24 SE
IAHURANGI REGIONAL PARK	6	J 12 SE
IAIMAI FOREST	33	W 43 SW
IAKARA WALKWAY	27	I 39 NE
IAKINO CONSERVATION AREA	15	J 26 SW
IAMAKU FOREST	10	O 22 SW
IANGAKAHIA FOREST	6	G 8 NW
IANGAMUKA GORGE SCENIC RESERVE	2	E 5 SW
IANGAMUKA GORGE TRACK	1	D 5 SE
IANGANUI FOREST	15	J 24 NW
IANGANUI SKIFIELD	15	G 28 NE
IANGAONE WALKWAY	25	K 37 NE
IANGATAHAE CONSERVATION AREA	19	U 25 NE
IANGATAWHIRI FOREST PARK	7	L 16 SW
IANGATU FOREST	14	X 23 NW
IANGAWHAI CLIFFS WALKWAY	4	J 10 SW
IANGAWHAI FOREST	4	J 11 NW
IAPARA FOREST	11	L 24 SE
IARERETU FOREST	4	H 10 NE
IARLBOROUGH FOREST	3	F 8 NW
IARLBOROUGH SOUNDS MARITIME PARK	30	H 37 SW
IARUIA FOREST	34	Y 43 SE
IATAHURU SCENIC RESERVE	8	M 17 SE
IATARAUA FOREST	3	F 8 NW
IATAUWHI BAY RESERVE	81	B 3 SE
IATEMATEAONGA TRACK	15	J 28 SE
IATIRANGI CONSERVATION AREA	15	I 27 SE
IAUNGAHAWA SCENIC RESERVE	10	N 20 SW
IAUNGANUI BLUFF SCENIC RESERVE	3	E 8 SW
IAUNGANUI BLUFF TRACK	3	E 8 SW
IAUNGAPOHATU TRACK	19	T 25 NE
IAUNGAROA TRACK	65	H 2 NW
IAUNGATAPERE WALKWAY	4	H 9 NW
IAUNGATAUTARI MOUNTAIN SCENIC RESERVE	67	F 4 NE
IAWHERA FOREST	38	V 46 NE
IICKENZIE TRACK	65	H 2 SE
IETHVEN WALKWAY	41	W52 SW
IIKONUI FOREST	37	S 49 NE
IILFORD TRACK	52	H 59 NE
IOHAKA FOREST	18	S 27 NE
IOHAKATINO CONSERVATION AREA	15	J 25 NE
IOIR HILL WALKWAY	5	I 12 SE
IOKAIKAI SCENIC RESERVE	1	B 1 SE
IOKI CONSERVATION AREA	15	J 26 SW
IOKIHINUI FOREST	34	Y 41 NW
IOLE TRACK	34	Z 43 NE
IONCKTON WALKWAY	24	P 32 SE
IONTGOMERY SCENIC RESERVE	4	G 10 NW
IOTUTAPU FARM WALKWAY	6	K 14 NW
IOTUTARA CONSERVATION AREA	16	L 26 NW
IOUNT ASPIRING NATIONAL PARK	43	L 55 NE
IMT AUCKLAND WALKWAY	5	I 12 SW
IMT BRUCE TRACK	25	N 36 SW
IMT CHEESEMAN SKIFIELD	41	W 49 SW
IMT COOK NATIONAL PARK	44	R 52 NE
IMT DOBSON SKIFIELD	54	S 54 SW
IMT HERBERT WALKWAY	46	A 52 SE
IMT HUTT FOREST	41	V 51 SE
IMT HUTT SKIFIELD	41	V 51 SE
IMT LYFORD SKIFIELD	40	C 46 NW
IMT MESSENGER CONSERVATION AREA	15	I 26 NE
IMT NIMROD SCENIC RESERVE	50	T 57 NW
IMT OLYMPUS SKIFIELD	41	V 50 NE
IMT RICHMOND FOREST PARK	29	F 39 SW
IMT ROBERTS SKIFIELD	34	B 42 SW
IMT SOMERS WALKWAY	45	V 52 SW
IMT THOMAS FOREST	41	Y 49 SE
IMT TUTAMOE TRACK	3	F 8 SE
IMT VERNON PARK	78	E 7 NW
IMT WILLIAM WALKWAY	7	K 16 SE
IMUIR TRACK	65	J 2 NW
IMURUMURU CONSERVATION AREA	16	K 28 SE
INELSON LAKES NATIONAL PARK	34	A 43 NW
INGAIOTONGA RUSSELL FOREST WALKWAY	2	H 6 SW
INGAIOTONGA SCENIC RESERVE	2	H 6 NW
INGAUMU FOREST	28	O 38 NW
INIHOIHO CONSERVATION AREA	16	K 25 SE
INIHONUI SCENIC RESERVE	81	C 1 SE
INIHOTUPU RIDGE TRACK	65	H 3 SE
INORTH KARAMEA FOREST	31	Z 38 NE
NORTHLAND CONSERVATION PARK	3	E 7 SE
NORTHWEST NELSON FOREST PARK	31	Y 36 SE
NYDIA WALKWAY	29	F 38 SW
ODLIN TIMBER TRACK	65	J 2 NE
OHAU SKIFIELD	49	O 56 NE
OHAUITI WALKWAY	22	O 20 NW
OKARITO FOREST	37	Q 50 NE
OKURA BUSH WALKWAY	8	J 13 SE
OKURA ESTUARY SCENIC RESERVE	5	J 13 SW
OMAHA FOREST	5	J 11 SW
OMAHUTA FOREST	1	E 6 NE
OMERU SCENIC RESERVE	5	I 13 NW
OMIHI FOREST	42	B 49 SW
OMOTO FOREST	38	U 46 NE
ONE MILE CREEK WALKWAY	52	K 60 SW
OPANUKU PIPELINE TRACK	65	G 3 SW
OPOUAHI WALKWAY	18	S 27 SE
OPUA FOREST	2	G 6 NE
OPUAWHANGA FOREST	4	H 7 NE
OPUNAKE WALKWAY	21	F 29 NW
ORIKAKA FOREST	33	X 42 NW
OROPI FOREST	10	P 20 SE
ORTON BRADLEY PARK	78	F 7 SE
OTAGO COAST FOREST	56	Q 66 NE
OTAIKA VALLEY WALKWAY	4	H 8 SW
OTAIO BEACH WALKWAYS	50	U 57 SE
OTANEWAINUKU FOREST	10	Q 20 SW
OTIERE PA	18	S 29 SW
OTIRA KOPARA FOREST	38	W 47 NW
OTOKO WALKWAY	13	W 24 NW
OXFORD FOREST	41	X 50 NE
PANEKIRIKIRI CONSERVATION AREA	19	T 26 NW
PANIRAU FOREST	16	K 25 NW
PANTO TRACK	65	J 3 NE
PAPA AROHA SCENIC RESERVE	6	M 14 NE
PAPAROA NATIONAL PARK	33	V 43 SW
PAPONGA RESERVE	1	D 6 NE
PARAHI SCENIC RESERVE	4	G 10 NE
PARAPARA PEAK TRACK	31	A 37 NW
PARARAHA VALLEY TRACK	65	J 3 NW
PARAU TRACK	65	J 3 NW
PARENGARENGA FOREST	1	B 2 NW
PAREOARA RIVER TRACK	50	T 56 SE
PATUNAMO FOREST	19	U 26 SW
PAXTON PT RESERVE	7	L 16 SW
PEBBLY HILLS FOREST	59	K 67 NE
PEEL FOREST WALKS	45	U 54 NE
PEGASUS BAY WALKWAY	42	A 50 SE
PIHA VALLEY TRACK	65	H 2 NW
PINEAPPLE - FLAGSTAFF TRACK	56	R 64 SE
PIRONGIA FOREST PARK	9	K 21 NE
PITANGA SCENIC RESERVE	22	L 30 SW
POARANGITUATAHI	15	J 27 SE
POERUA FOREST	37	R 50 NE
PT ELIZABETH WALKWAY	33	U 45 SW
POOR KNIGHTS MARINE RESERVE	4	J 7 NE
PORT ROBINSON TRACK	40	D 48 NW
PORTER HEIGHTS SKIFIELD	41	W50 SW
POUIATOA CONSERVATION AREA	15	I 27 NW
POUTU FOREST	5	G 11 SW
PUHIPUHI FOREST	4	H 7 NE
PUKEAMARU SCENIC RESERVE	14	I 10 SW
PUKEKARORO SCENIC RESERVE	4	H 10 NW
PUKEKOHE HILL SCENIC RESERVE	6	H 10 NW
PUKENUI FOREST	4	H 8 SE
PUKENUI FOREST WALKWAY	4	H 8 SW
PUKEPOTO FOREST	16	M 26 SE
PUKETERAKI FOREST	41	Y 49 NW
PUKETI FOREST	2	E 5 SE
PUKEWHARARIKI FOREST	2	E 6 SE
PUREORA FOREST PARK	9	M 23 SE
PURIRI RIDGE TRACK	65	J 2 NE
PUWHENUA FOREST	10	P 21 NE
PYKE - BIG BAY TRACK	47	I 57 NE
QUARRY TRACK	65	H 2 NW
RAETEA FOREST	1	D 5 SE
RAI FOREST	29	E 38 SW
RAINBOW SKIFIELD	34	B 42 SW
RAKIURA NATIONAL PARK	61	I 70 SW
RANGATAUA CONSERVATION AREA	17	M 29 NE
RANGITUKUA SCENIC RESERVE	70	D 1 NE
RANKLEBURN FOREST	55	N 65 SE
RAUKUMARA CONSERVATION AREA	14	X 21 NW
REES - DART TRACK	47	K 58 NW
REMARKABLES SKIFIELD	53	L 60 SE
REREKINO CONSERVATION AREA	15	I 26 SE
RGB TRACK	65	G 2 SE
RICKER TRACK	65	H 2 NE
RIDGE ROAD	65	G 2 SE
RIMUNI CONSERVATION AREA	22	I 30 NE
RIMUTAKA FOREST PARK	27	K 39 NE
RIVERHEAD FOREST	5	I 14 NE
ROBERT HASTIE SCENIC RESERVE	4	I 10 SE
ROBINSON RIDGE TRACK	65	G 2 SE
ROTOEHU FOREST	12	R 21 NW
ROTOKARE WALKWAY	21	H 29 NE
ROTORANGI HYDRO WALKWAY	21	I 29 SW
ROUND THE MOUNTAIN TRACK	17	M 28 SE
ROUTEBURN TRACK	52	I 59 NE
ROWALLAN FOREST	58	G 66 SE
RUA'S TRACK	19	T 24 SE
RUAHINE FOREST PARK	23	O 33 NE
RUAKAKA FOREST	4	H 9 SE
RUSSELL FOREST	2	H 6 NE
ST JAMES WALKWAY	34	Z 45 NW
SANTOFT FOREST	25	L 33 NW
SEAWARD BUSH RESERVE	59	K 68 SW
SEAWARD FOREST	41	V 48 SE
SHAKESPEAR REGIONAL PARK	6	J 13 SE
SHENSTONE FOREST	1	A 2 NE
SILVERPEAKS FOREST	56	S 64 NW
SILVERPEAKS WALKWAY	56	S 64 NW
SIMLA TRACK	65	G 2 SE
SISAM TRACK	65	G 2 SE
SIX MILE WALKWAY	34	Z 42 NW
SKYLINE TRACK	50	U 60 SW
SMYTHE RIDGE TRACK	65	H 2 SW
SOUTH HILL WALKWAY	50	U 60 SW
SOUTH KARAMEA FOREST	31	Z 38 NE
STONY BATTER WALKWAY	6	L 14 NE
STONY RIVER WALK	21	F 28 NE
SUGARLOAF RESERVE	78	E 6 SE
SUNNYBROOK SCENIC RESERVE	5	I 12 NE
SWANSON PIPELINE TRACK	65	G 3 SW
TAHA MOANA SCENIC RESERVE	3	E 8 SW
TAHEKE CONSERVATION AREA	16	K 24 SE
TAHORAKURI FOREST	12	P 24 SE
TAI RAWHITI SCENIC RESERVE	7	L 15 SW
TAINUI KAWHIA FOREST	9	J 21 SE
TAIPO FOREST	38	V 47 SW
TAIRUA FOREST	8	O 16 SW
TAKAKA FOREST	31	A 38 SE
TAKITIMU FOREST	58	H 64 SE
TANGARAKAU CONSERVATION AREA	16	K 27 NW
TANGIHUA FOREST	4	G 9 NE
TANGIHUA WALKWAY	4	G 9 NE
TANGIMOANA FOREST	25	L 34 NW
TANGOIO FOREST	18	S 29 NW
TANGOIO WALKWAY	18	S 28 SE
TAPAPAKANGA REGIONAL PARK	7	L 15 SE
TARAMOUKU CONSERVATION AREA	15	H 27 NE
TARARUA FOREST PARK	25	M 36 SW
TARAWERA FOREST	12	R 22 NW
TARERE CONSERVATION AREA	21	I 30 NE
TASMAN WILDERNESS AREA	31	Y 37 SE
TAUHARA FOREST	12	Q 25 NW
TAUMATA TRACK	65	G 3 SW
TAUMATATOTARA FOREST	9	J 22 SE
TAUPO WALKWAY	87	A 3 NE
TAUROA PT RESERVE	1	C 5 SW
TAWARAU FOREST	9	K 23 NW
TAWHARANUI REGIONAL PARK	6	K 12 NW
TE ANGIANGI MARINE RESERVE	24	S 33 SW
TE ARAI RESERVE	1	B 2 SE
TE HENGA - GOLDIE BUSH WALKWAY	5	H 14 SE
TE HENUI WALKWAY	15	G 27 NE
TE KAO FOREST	1	B 2 SW
TE MATA PEAK WALKWAY	24	S 31 NE
TE MATAI FOREST	10	P 21 NE
TE MATEAI FOREST	69	A 1 SE
TE MIRO SCENIC RESERVE	67	D 4 NW
TE PAKI RECREATION RESERVE	1	A 1 SE
TE POUAHI RESERVE	3	D 7 NW
TE RAUAMOA FOREST	9	K 22 NW
TE TUHI TRACK	68	I 54 NE
TE UREWERA NATIONAL PARK	12	S 23 NE
TE WERA FOREST	15	I 27 SE
TEMPLE BASIN SKIFIELD	41	W48 SW
THIRTEEN MILE BUSH FOREST	41	W51 NE
THOMPSON PARK	78	E 6 SE
THOMPSONS TRACK	68	C 1 SW
THOMSON KAURI GROVE	5	I 12 SW
TI POINT SCENIC RESERVE	6	J 11 SE
TIRAUMEA TRACK	34	Z 42 SE
TOATOA RESERVE	1	D 5 NE
TOKERAU BEACH WALKWAY	1	D 4 NW
TOKOMARU FOREST	14	Y 22 SW
TONGARIRO FOREST CONSERVATION AREA	16	M 27 NE
TONGARIRO NATIONAL PARK	16	N 28 NW
TONGARIRO RIVER WALKWAY	17	O 27 NE
TOPUNI SCENIC RESERVE	4	I 11 NW
TOTARA FOREST	37	T 48 SW
TRAVERS - SABINE TRACK	34	A 43 NE
TREBLE CONE SKIFIELD	48	L 58 SE
TROUNSON KAURI PARK SCENIC RESERVE	3	E 8 SE
TUKINO SKIFIELD	16	N 28 NW
TURAHU TRACK	68	C 1 SW
TUROA SKIFIELD	16	M 28 SE
TUTAKI CONSERVATION AREA	34	Z 42 SE
TUTIRA WALKWAY	18	S 28 NE
TWIN PEAKS TRACK	65	H 3 SW
UPPER KAURI TRACK	65	G 2 NE
URUTAWA CONSERVATION AREA	13	U 22 SE
VICTORIA FOREST PARK	34	X 44 NE
VICTORIA PARK	78	E 6 SE
VINING SCENIC RESERVE	7	L 16 SE
VINING TRACK	7	L 16 SE
WAIKARAKA WALKWAY	4	I 8 SW
WAIKAREITI CONSERVATION AREA	13	U 24 SW
WAIMA FOREST	3	E 7 NW
WAIMATE WALKWAYS	50	T 58 SE
WAIMEA FOREST	32	C 40 NE
WAINAMU BUSH TRACK	65	G 2 NW
WAIOEKA CONSERVATION AREA	13	U 23 NW
WAIORAU SNOW FARM	53	M 59 SW
WAIPIPI SCENIC RESERVE	7	I 17 NE
WAIPORI FOREST	56	Q 65 NW
WAIPOUA COAST TRACK	3	D 8 NE
WAIPOUA FOREST	3	D 7 SE
WAIPU GORGE FOREST	4	H 10 NE
WAIROA GORGE SCENIC RESERVE	7	K 16 NE
WAIRORO PARK	81	D 3 SE
WAITAANGA CONSERVATION AREA	15	J 26 NE
WAITAHA FOREST	37	S 49 SW
WAITAKERE RANGES REGIONAL PARK	1	I 15 NE
WAITAKERE TRAMLINE	65	G 2 NE
WAITANGI FOREST	2	G 5 SW
WAITANGI NATIONAL RESERVE	81	B 1 NW
WAITARA WEST WALKWAY	15	H 26 SW
WAITARERE FOREST	25	L 35 SE
WAITEWHENA FOREST	16	K 25 NE
WAITOTARA CONSERVATION AREA	22	J 29 NE
WAIUKU FOREST	7	J 17 SW
WAKAMARINA - OAMATUTU TRK	29	E 40 NE
WALKER RIDGE TRACK	65	J 2 NE
WANGANUI FOREST	37	R 49 SE
WANGAPEKA FOREST	31	A 40 NW
WANGAPEKA TRACK	31	Y 39 SE
WAOKU COACH RD TRACK	3	E 7 SE
WARAWARA FOREST	1	D 6 SW
WENDERHOLM REGIONAL PARK	6	J 13 NE
WESTLAND NATIONAL PARK	44	P 52 NE
WHAKAPAPA SKIFIELD	16	M 28 NW
WHAKAREWAREWA FOREST	10	Q 22 SW
WHAKATANE RIVER TRACK	12	T 23 SW
WHAKATIWAI REGIONAL PARK	7	L 16 NE
WHANGAMARINO WALKWAY	7	L 17 NW
WHANGAMARINO WETLAND MANAGEMENT RESERVE	7	L 17 SW
WHANGAMOMONA CONSERVATION AREA	15	J 28 NW
WHANGANUI NATIONAL PARK	16	K 28 NW
WHARAU REGIONAL PARK	7	L 16 NE
WHAREATA WALKWAY	20	W 27 NE
WHAREORINO FOREST	9	J 23 SE
WHARERATA FOREST	20	W 26 NE
WHIRINAKI CONSERVATION AREA	18	R 25 SE
WHIRINAKI TRACK	18	R 26 NE
WHITE TRACK	15	H 2 NW
WHITECLIFFS FOREST	15	I 26 NE
WHITECLIFFS WALKWAY	15	I 25 SW
WHITFORD FOREST	6	K 15 NE
WINSTONE TRACK	65	H 2 NW
WITHER HILLS WALKWAY	29	F 41 NE
WOODHILL FOREST	5	H 14 NE
WOODLAW FOREST	58	I 66 NW
ZION HILL TRACK	65	J 2 NW
ZION RIDGE TRACK	65	J 2 NW

Ashburton Central

Street	Map No.	Ref
ADAMS ST	98	C 4 SW
AITKEN ST	98	B 3 SW
ALBERT ST	98	C 4 NW
ALFORD FOREST RD	98	A 1 NW
ASCOT PL	98	B 3 NE
BAKER ST	98	B 1 NE
BARING SQ EAST	98	B 2 SE
BARING SQ WEST	98	C 3 SW
BEATTY CRES	98	A 2 NE
BELT RD	98	C 2 SW
BIRD ST	98	C 3 SE
BREMNERS RD	98	A 4 NW
BRIDGE ST	98	B 4 SW
BRUCEFIELD AVE	98	A 1 NW
BUCHANAN PL	98	A 1 NW
BULLOCK ST	98	C 2 NE
BURNETT ST	98	B 2 SW
CAMBRIDGE ST	98	B 2 SW
CAMERON ST	98	B 1 NE
CASS ST	98	C 2 NW
CATHERWOOD AVE	98	A 3 NW
CHALMERS AVE	98	C 2 SE
COLLINS ST	98	B 3 NE
CONNOR PL	98	A 1 NE
COX ST	98	C 2 NE
CREEK RD	98	A 2 NE
CROSS ST	98	C 3 SE
DAVIS CRES	98	B 4 SW
DIGBY PL	98	C 1 SW
DOBSON ST	98	C 1 NE
DOBSON ST WEST	98	C 1 NW
EAST ST	98	B 2 NE
ELIZABETH PL	98	D 5 NE
ELIZABETH ST	98	B 2 NE
ETON ST	98	A 1 NW
FERRIMAN ST	98	C 2 SW
GALBRAITH ST	98	A 3 NW
GREY ST	98	B 2 SW
GRIGG ST	98	C 2 NE
HAVELOCK ST	98	C 2 NE
HILLIER PL	98	A 3 NE
HUGH ST	98	C 2 SW
JOHN ST	98	B 1 NE
KERMODE ST	98	C 2 SW
KERR ST	98	B 3 NE
KILN CL (PVT)	98	A 2 NE
KING ST	98	A 3 SE
KITCHENER ST	98	B 4 NW
MALCOLM MCDOWELL AVE	98	A 4 NE
MAYNARD ST	98	A 3 NE
MCDONALD ST	98	C 4 NW
MCLEAN ST	98	B 3 NW
MCNALLY ST	98	B 1 NW
MIDDLE RD	98	A 2 NE
MILLER AVE	98	A 1 SE
MILLSTREAM LN (PVT)	98	A 3 NW
MITCHELL PL	98	A 3 SE
MONA SQ	98	C 2 SW
MOORE ST	98	C 2 SW
NELSON ST	98	B 3 NE
OAK GR	98	A 1 SE
ORR ST	98	B 3 NE
OXFORD ST	98	B 2 NE
PAGES RD	98	A 1 NW
PARK LN	98	B 2 SW
PARK ST	98	B 1 SE
PATCHING ST	98	C 4 NW
PETER ST	98	B 2 SE
PHILIP ST	98	B 4 SW
PORTER ST	98	B 4 SW
PRATLEY CRES	98	C 3 SE
PRINCES ST	98	B 3 NE
QUEENS DR	98	A 3 SE
RAPLEY ST	98	C 3 NE
REDDECLIFFE CRES	98	C 3 SE
REID CRES	98	A 1 NE
RIVER TCE	98	B 1 NE
ROBINSON ST	98	A 1 NW
RUSSELL AVE	98	A 3 NE
SAUNDERS RD	98	A 4 NW
SEAFIELD RD	98	B 1 NE
SEALY ST	98	B 1 SE
SHORT ST	98	B 1 NW
SMALLBONE DR	98	A 1 NW
SOMERSET LN (PVT)	98	C 2 NW
SOUTH ST	98	C 1 SE
TANCRED ST	98	B 2 SE
THE TERRACE	98	C 1 SE
TRELLECH PL	98	A 3 SW
TREVORS RD	98	B 4 NE
TUARANGI RD	98	B 3 NW
VICTORIA ST	98	C 3 NE
WAKANUI RD	98	C 3 NE
WALKER ST	98	A 1 SE
WALNUT AVE	98	C 3 NE
WALSHS RD	98	B 1 NW
WATSON ST	98	B 1 NW
WELLINGTON ST	98	C 3 SW
WEST ST	98	B 2 SE
WESTCOTT PL	98	A 2 NE
WILLIAM ST	98	C 2 SW

Skifields, Tracks, Parks & Forests - Ashburton Central

Ashburton Central - Auckland District Roads

Location	Map No.	Ref
WILLS ST	98	B 2 SE
WINTER ST	98	B 1 SE
WOODS ST	98	A 3 NW

Auckland

Auckland Central

Location	Map No.	Ref
ABBEY ST	83	D 1 NE
ACE PL	83	E 1 NW
ADA ST	83	E 4 NW
ADELAIDE ST	83	B 1 SE
AIREDALE ST	83	C 2 NE
AKAROA ST	83	C 4 NW
AKEPIRO ST	83	E 1 NW
AKIRAHO ST	83	E 2 NW
ALBERT ST	83	B 2 SW
ALBURY AVE	83	F 3 NW
ALDERLEY RD	83	E 1 SE
ALEX EVANS ST	83	D 2 NW
ALEXANDER ST	83	D 1 SW
ALFRED ST	83	B 3 SW
ALMA ST	83	D 4 SW
ALMORAH PL	83	E 3 NE
ALMORAH RD	83	E 3 NE
ALPERS AVE	83	F 3 NE
ALTEN RD	83	B 3 SE
ANZAC AVE	83	B 3 NE
AORERE ST	83	C 4 SW
ARAWA ST	83	D 2 SE
ASHTON RD	83	F 1 NE
AUBURN ST	83	D 2 SE
AUGUSTUS TCE	83	B 4 SW
AVENHAM WALK	83	F 1 NW
AYR ST	83	D 4 SE
BACONS LN (PVT)	83	B 3 NW
BALFOUR RD	83	B 4 SE
BALM ST	83	C 4 SW
BANKSIDE ST	83	B 3 NW
BARNETT CRES (PVT)	83	C 2 SE
BASQUE RD	83	D 2 SW
BASSETT RD	83	F 4 NE
BATGER RD	83	F 2 SW
BATH ST	83	C 4 NW
BEACH RD	83	B 3 NE
BEATRICE RD	83	E 4 SE
BEAUMONT ST	83	B 1 NW
BECKHAM PL	83	D 2 NE
BEDFORD ST	83	C 4 NW
BELLEVUE RD	83	E 1 SW
BELMONT TCE	83	E 4 SE
BERESFORD ST	83	C 1 NW
BIRCH PARK LN (PVT)	66	H 8 NW
BIRDWOOD CRES	83	C 4 SE
BOARDMAN LN	83	C 4 NW
BOSTON RD	83	D 2 SE
BOURKE ST	83	E 4 SW
BOURNE ST	83	F 2 SW
BOUZAID WAY	83	B 2 NW
BOWEN AVE	83	B 3 SW
BOWEN LN	83	B 3 SW
BOX LN	83	B 3 NW
BOYLE CRES	83	D 3 NW
BRADFORD ST	83	C 4 NW
BRADNOR LN	83	B 2 NE
BRENTWOOD AVE	83	E 1 NE
BRIDGE ST	83	D 2 NE
BRIGHAM ST	83	A 1 NE
BRIGHT ST	83	D 1 SW
BRIGHTSIDE RD	83	F 3 SW
BRITOMART PL	83	B 3 NE
BROADWAY	83	E 4 NW
BUCHANAN ST	83	D 1 NW
BURGOYNE ST	83	D 1 NW
BURLEIGH ST	83	D 2 SW
BURNS ST	83	D 1 NW
BURTON ST	83	D 2 SE
CANADA ST	83	C 3 SE
CARGILL ST	83	D 1 NE
CARLAW PARK AVE	83	C 3 NE
CARLTON GORE RD	83	D 3 SW
CARRICK PL	83	F 1 NW
CASCADE ST	83	B 1 NW
CASTLE DR	83	E 3 SW
CATHEDRAL PL	83	C 2 SE
CECIL RD	83	F 2 SE
CENOTAPH RD	83	D 4 NW
CENTRE ST	83	B 1 SE
CHANCERY ST	83	B 3 NW
CHAPMAN ST	83	D 1 NW
CHARLES ST	83	C 1 SE
CHARLOTTE ST	83	D 1 SE
CHARLTON AVE	83	F 1 NE
CHESHIRE ST	83	C 4 NW
CHURCHILL ST	83	B 3 SE
CINTRA PL	83	C 2 SE
CITY RD	83	C 2 SE
CLAREMONT ST	83	D 3 SW
CLAYBROOK RD	83	D 4 NE
CLAYTON ST	83	C 4 SW
CLEVELAND RD	83	C 4 NE
CLIVE RD	83	E 2 SE
CLOVERNOOK RD	83	E 3 SW
CLYDE ST	83	F 4 SW
COBDEN ST	83	C 1 SE
COLES AVE	83	F 2 SW
COLLEGE HILL	83	B 1 NW
COMMERCE ST	83	B 3 NW
CONWAY RD	83	F 1 SW
COOK ST	83	B 1 SE
COPELAND ST	83	D 1 SW
CORUNNA AVE	83	C 4 SE
COTESMORE WAY	83	E 4 NW
COULDRY LN	83	D 1 SE
COURTHOUSE LN	83	B 2 SE
COVENTRY LN	83	E 3 SE
COWIE ST	83	D 4 SW
CRACROFT ST	83	C 4 NW
CROMWELL ST	83	F 1 NW
CROSS ST	83	C 2 SW
CROWHURST ST	83	E 3 NE
CRUISE LN	83	B 3 NW
CUSTOMS ST EAST	83	A 2 SE
CUSTOMS ST WEST	83	B 2 NW
D'URVILLE HGTS	83	E 4 NW
DACRE ST	83	D 1 NE
DALDY ST	83	A 1 SE
DARBY ST	83	B 2 SE
DAVIS CRES	83	D 4 SW
DAY ST	83	C 1 SE
DENBY ST	83	C 4 NW
DEVON ST	83	D 1 SE
DIAMOND ST	83	D 1 SE
DILWORTH AVE	83	F 4 NE
DILWORTH TCE	83	B 4 SE
DOCK ST	83	B 1 NE
DOMAIN DR	83	D 3 NE
DOMETT AVE	83	E 4 NW
DOMINION RD	83	E 1 SW
DOVEDALE PL	83	B 4 SW
DRAKE ST	83	B 1 SE
DUNDONALD ST	83	D 2 SW
DURHAM LN	83	B 2 NE
DURHAM ST EAST	83	B 2 NE
DURHAM ST WEST	83	B 2 NE
EARLE ST	83	B 4 SW
EAST ST	83	C 1 SE
EDEN CRES	83	B 3 NE
EDEN ST	83	E 2 NW
EDENVALE CRES	83	E 1 SE
EDENVALE PARK RD	83	E 1 SE
EDGERLEY AVE	83	E 3 SE
EDINBURGH ST	83	C 1 SE
EDWIN ST	83	E 1 NW
EGLON ST	83	B 4 SW
ELLIOTT ST	83	B 2 SE
ELY AVE	83	E 4 SE
EMILY PL	83	B 3 NW
ENFIELD ST	83	E 2 NW
ERIN ST	83	E 2 NW
ESPLANADE RD	83	F 2 NW
ESSEX RD	83	F 2 SE
EVELYN ST	83	D 1 SW
EWINGTON AVE	83	F 1 SW
EXCHANGE LN	83	B 2 SW
EXMOUTH ST	83	D 2 SW
FALCON ST	83	C 4 NW
FANSHAWE ST	83	B 1 NE
FARADAY ST	83	B 4 SE
FARNHAM ST	83	B 4 SW
FEDERAL ST	83	B 2 SW
FENTON ST	83	E 1 NE
FERNCROFT ST	83	C 3 SW
FIELDS LN	83	B 3 NW
FLEET ST	83	D 1 SE
FLOWER ST	83	D 2 SW
FOOTBALL RD	83	D 3 SE
FORT ST	83	B 3 NW
FOX ST	83	B 4 SW
FRANCE ST SOUTH	83	D 1 NE
FRANKLIN RD	83	B 1 SW
FREYBERG PL	83	B 2 NE
FURNEAUX WAY	83	E 4 NW
GALATOS ST	83	C 1 SE
GALWAY ST	83	B 3 NW
GARDEN RD	83	C 3 SE
GARFIELD ST	83	C 4 NW
GAUNT ST	83	A 1 SE
GEORGE ST (KINGSLAND)	83	E 1 NW
GEORGE ST (NEWMARKET)	83	D 3 SE
GIBRALTAR CRES	83	E 1 SE
GILGIT RD	83	E 3 SW
GILLIES AVE	83	E 3 SE
GLASGOW TCE	83	D 3 NW
GLENFELL PL	83	E 2 SW
GLENSIDE CRES	83	E 2 SW
GORE ST	83	B 3 NW
GORE ST STH	83	B 3 NE
GRAFTON BRIDGE	83	C 2 SE
GRAFTON MEWS	83	C 3 SW
GRAFTON RD	83	D 2 NE
GRAHAM ST	83	B 2 NW
GRANDSTAND RD NTH	83	D 3 NE
GRANDSTAND RD STH	83	D 3 NE
GRANGE RD	83	F 1 SW
GRATTAN ST	83	E 2 SW
GRAYSON AVE	83	E 2 SW
GREAT NORTH RD	83	D 1 NW
GREAT SOUTH RD	83	F 4 NW
GREYS AVE	83	C 2 NW
GUDGEON ST	83	B 1 NW
GUNDRY ST	83	D 1 NE
GWILLIAM PL	83	B 1 SW
HALSEY ST	83	A 1 NE
HAMER ST	83	A 1 NE
HARBOUR ST	83	B 1 NE
HARDINGE ST	83	B 1 NE
HAROLD ST	83	D 2 SW
HASLETT ST	83	D 1 SW
HAULTAIN ST	83	E 2 NE
HAYDEN ST	83	C 1 NE
HEATHER ST	83	C 4 NW
HEPBURN ST	83	C 1 SW
HEREFORD ST	83	C 1 SW
HIGH ST	83	B 2 NE
HILLSIDE CRES NORTH	83	F 2 NW
HILLSIDE CRES SOUTH	83	F 2 NW
HOBSON ST	83	B 2 SW
HOPETOUN ST	83	C 1 SE
HOROEKA AVE	83	E 1 SE
HOROPITO ST	83	E 1 NW
HOWE ST	83	C 1 SE
HUNTLY AVE	83	D 3 SW
IAN McKINNON DR	83	D 1 NW
IRELAND ST	83	B 1 SW
JAMES COOK CRES	83	E 4 NW
JEAN BATTEN PL	83	B 2 NE
JELLICOE ST	83	A 1 NE
JOHN STOKES TCE	83	E 4 NW
JOSEPH BANKS TCE	83	E 4 NW
KAMAHI ST	83	F 1 NW
KARAKA ST	83	C 1 SE
KARANGAHAPE RD	83	C 1 SE
KARI ST	83	C 3 SW
KAWAKA ST	83	E 1 SE
KELLY ST	83	E 1 NW
KENT ST	83	E 3 NE
KENWYN ST	83	B 4 SE
KENYON AVE	83	F 1 NW
KEPPELL ST	83	D 1 SW
KHARTOUM PL	83	B 2 SE
KHYBER PASS RD	83	D 2 SW
KINGDON ST	83	D 4 SW
KINGSTON ST	83	B 2 NE
KIOSK RD	83	D 3 NE
KIPLING AVE	83	F 3 SE
KIRK ST	83	D 1 SW
KITCHENER ST	83	B 3 SW
KOHEKOHE ST	83	E 2 NW
KOHUTU ST	83	E 2 NW
KORARI ST	83	D 2 SW
LAUDER RD	83	E 2 NE
LAURIE AVE	83	D 4 NE
LAURISTON AVE	83	E 4 SW
LAXON TCE	83	D 4 SW
LEAMINGTON RD	83	F 1 NW
LEEK ST	83	D 4 SW
LION PL	83	E 3 NW
LISNOE AVE	83	E 1 SW
LITTLE GEORGE ST	83	D 3 SE
LIVERPOOL ST	83	C 2 SE
LORNE ST	83	C 2 NE
LOVELOCK AVE	83	F 2 NW
LOVERS LN	83	C 3 SE
LOWER ALBERT ST	83	A 2 SE
LOWER DOMAIN DR	83	C 3 NE
LUCY LN	83	B 2 NW
LYNDOCK ST	83	C 2 NE
MACAULAY ST	83	D 1 SE
MACMURRAY RD	83	F 4 NE
MADDEN ST	83	A 1 SE
MADEIRA LN	83	D 2 SE
MADEIRA PL	83	D 2 SE
MAHON WAY	83	C 1 SE
MAHUHU CRES	83	B 3 NE
MAHURU ST	83	E 4 NW
MAIDSTONE ST	83	C 1 SW
MAMIE ST	83	E 4 NW
MARAMA AVE	83	F 2 SE
MARGOT ST	83	F 4 SW
MARKET LN	83	A 2 SW
MARKET PL	83	A 2 SW
MARMION ST	83	C 2 NE
MARSTON ST	83	B 4 SW
MARY ST	83	E 2 NW
MAUI GR	83	E 4 NW
MAUNGAWHAU RD	83	E 3 NW
MAUNSELL RD	83	D 4 NE
MAUNSELL RD EXTENSION	83	D 4 NW
MAURANUI AVE	83	F 4 NW
MAYORAL DR	83	C 2 NE
McCOLL ST	83	E 3 NE
MELROSE ST	83	E 3 NE
MERCURY LN	83	C 2 SW
MIDDLE ST	83	B 1 SW
MIDDLETON RD	83	E 4 NW
MILLS LN	83	B 2 NE
MINNIE ST	83	D 1 SE
MOEHAU ST	83	C 3 SW
MONMOUTH ST	83	D 1 SW
MORGAN ST	83	E 3 SE
MORROW ST	83	E 3 SE
MORTIMER PASS	83	E 4 NW
MORTON ST	83	B 1 SW
MOSTYN ST	83	F 2 SW
MOUNT EDEN RD	83	F 4 SE
MOUNT HOBSON RD	83	F 4 SE
MOUNT ST	83	C 2 NE
MOUNTAIN RD	83	E 3 SW
MUSEUM CIRCUIT	83	D 4 NW
MUTU ST	83	C 4 NW
NAPIER LN	83	B 1 SW
NAPIER ST	83	B 1 SW
NELSON ST	83	C 1 NE
NEW NORTH RD	83	D 1 SE
NEWTON RD	83	D 1 NE
NGAHERE TCE	83	C 4 NW
NGAHURA ST	83	D 1 SE
NGAIRE AVE	83	F 4 SW
NGAOHO PL	83	B 4 SW
NICHOLAS ST	83	B 2 SW
NICHOLLS LN	83	C 3 NE
NIKAU ST	83	D 2 SW
NIXON ST	83	D 1 NW
NORMANBY RD	83	E 2 SE
NUFFIELD LN	83	E 4 SW
NUFFIELD ST	83	E 4 SW
NUGENT ST	83	D 2 SE
O'CONNELL ST	83	B 3 NW
OAKLANDS RD	83	F 2 SW
OMANA AVE	83	F 3 NW
ONSLOW RD	83	E 1 SW
OPHIR ST	83	D 1 NE
OSBORNE ST	83	D 4 SW
OUTHWAITE LN	83	D 3 SW
OWENS RD	83	F 2 SW
PAKENHAM ST EAST	83	A 2 SW
PAKENHAM ST WEST	83	A 2 SW
PARK AVE	83	D 3 NW
PARK RD	83	D 3 NW
PARKFIELD TCE	83	D 3 SE
PARLIAMENT ST	83	B 3 SE
PARNELL RD	83	D 4 SW
PARNELL RISE	83	C 4 NW
PARTRIDGE ST	83	D 1 SW
PENTLAND AVE	83	F 1 SE
PERCY PL	83	C 2 NW
PERCY ST	83	F 2 NW
PITT ST	83	C 2 NW
PLUMER ST	83	B 3 NE
POLLEN ST	83	D 1 NW
PORT LN	83	C 4 NW
PORTERS AVE	83	E 1 NE
POYNTON TCE	83	C 2 NW
PRATT ST	83	C 1 NW
PRINCES ST	83	B 3 SW
PROSPECT TCE	83	F 1 SW
PUKA ST	83	E 1 SE
PUNGA ST	83	E 1 SE
PUTIKI ST	83	D 1 NW
QUAY ST	83	A 2 SE
QUEEN ST	83	B 2 SE
RAILWAY ST	83	D 4 SW
RANDOLPH ST	83	D 1 NE
RAUTANGI RD	83	E 1 SE
REMUERA RD	83	E 4 SW
RENDALL PL	83	D 1 SE
ROBERT HALL AVE	83	F 4 NW
ROCKWOOD PL	83	E 3 SW
RONAYNE ST	83	B 3 SE
ROXBURGH ST	83	E 3 NW
RURU ST	83	D 1 SE
RUSKIN ST	83	C 4 NW
RUTLAND ST	83	C 2 NE
ST BENEDICTS ST	83	D 2 NW
ST GEORGES BAY RD	83	C 4 SW
ST JAMES ST	83	C 1 SW
ST KEVINS ARCADE	83	C 1 SW
ST MARKS RD	83	F 4 NW
ST MARTINS LN	83	C 2 SW
ST PATRICKS SQ	83	B 2 SW
ST PAUL ST	83	C 2 NE
ST STEPHENS AVE	83	C 4 SW
SALE ST	83	B 1 SE
SAM WRIGLEY ST	83	B 4 SW
SARAWIA ST	83	D 4 SW
SAVANNAH ST	83	F 2 NW
SCARBOROUGH LN	83	C 4 SW
SCARBOROUGH TCE	83	C 4 SW
SCOTIA PL	83	C 2 SW
SCOTLAND ST	83	B 1 NW
SEAFIELD VIEW RD	83	D 2 NW
SEAVIEW RD	83	E 3 NW
SECCOMBES RD	83	E 4 SW
SEVERN RD	83	D 2 SE
SHADDOCK ST	83	D 2 SW
SHARPE RD	83	F 3 NW
SHERBOURNE RD	83	F 1 NW
SHERIDAN LN	83	D 1 NW
SHIPHERDS AVE	83	F 3 SW
SHIPHERDS CL	83	F 3 SW
SHORT ST (CITY)	83	B 3 NW
SHORT ST (NEWMARKET)	83	E 4 NW
SHORTLAND ST	83	B 3 NW
SILVER RD	83	F 3 NW
SMITH ST	83	C 1 NW
SOUTH ST	83	C 1 SE
SOUTHERN MOTORWAY	83	D 2 SE
STABLE LN	83	D 2 NE
STANLEY ST	83	C 3 NW
STURDEE ST	83	B 2 NE
SUDBURY TCE	83	B 4 SE
SUFFOLK ST	83	D 1 SW
SUITER ST	83	D 3 SE
SWANSON ST	83	B 2 NE
SWINTON CL	83	E 1 SE
SYDENHAM RD	83	E 1 SE
SYLVAN AVE	83	E 1 NE
SYMONDS ST	83	D 2 NE
TAHUNA ST	83	C 1 NW
TAKAU ST	83	D 1 SW
TANGIHUA ST	83	B 3 NW
TAPORA ST	83	B 3 NW
TARATA ST	83	F 1 SS
TAWARI ST	83	E 1 SW
TE TAOU CRES	83	B 3 NW
TEED ST	83	E 3 NE
THE CRESCENT	83	D 3 NE
THE GLEN	83	E 4 NW
THE STRAND	83	C 4 SW
TIKA ST	83	C 4 NW
TILDEN ST	83	C 4 NW
TINLEY ST	83	B 3 NE
TITOKI ST	83	D 4 NW
TOOLEY ST	83	A 3 S
TURNER ST	83	C 2 N
TYLER ST	83	A 3 SW
UNION ST	83	C 1 N
UPPER QUEEN ST	83	C 2 SW
VAILIMA WAY	83	D 1 SW
VALENTINES LN	83	B 2 N
VALLEY RD	83	F 1 N
VERNON ST	83	B 1 S
VIADUCT HARBOUR AVE	83	B 1 N
VICTORIA ST EAST	83	B 2 S
VICTORIA ST WEST	83	B 2 S
VIEW RD	83	E 1 S
VINCENT ST	83	C 2 N
VIRGINIA AVE EAST	83	D 1 S
VIRGINIA AVE WEST	83	D 1 S
VULCAN LN	83	B 2 N
WAIATARAU PL (PVT)	83	C 1 N
WAITEMATA ST	83	A 1 S
WAKEFIELD ST	83	C 2 N
WARIMU PL	83	C 1 N
WATER ST	83	E 2 N
WATERLOO QUADRANT	83	B 3 S
WAVERLEY ST	83	D 2 S
WELD ST	83	B 1 S
WELLESLEY ST EAST	83	B 2 S
WELLESLEY ST WEST	83	B 2 S
WELLINGTON ST	83	C 1 N
WEST ST	83	C 1 S
WEST TCE	83	D 2 N
WESTHAVEN DR	83	A 1 S
WHITAKER PL	83	C 2 S
WHITE ST	83	C 2 N
WILKINS ST	83	D 1 N
WINCHESTER ST	83	D 1 N
WINDSOR ST	83	C 4 N
WINTERGARDEN RD	83	D 3 N
WITHIEL DR	83	F 3 N
WOLFE ST	83	B 2 S
WOODFORD RD	83	F 1 S
WOOTTON RD	83	E 4 S
WRIGHTS SPUR	83	E 2 N
WYNDHAM ST	83	B 2 N
WYNYARD RD	83	E 3 S
WYNYARD ST	83	C 2 N
YORK ST (NEWMARKET)	83	E 3 NE
YORK ST (PARNELL)	83	D 4 SW
YOUNGS LN	83	D 4 SW

District Roads

Location	Map No.	Ref
ABBOTTS WAY	66	G 6 NB
AHUROA RD	64	A 4 NW
AIO WIRA RD	65	G 2 NE
AIRFIELD RD	66	J 8 SV
ALBANY HIGHWAY	64	E 5 NV
ALF ACCESS RD	66	J 8 SV
ALFRISTON - ARDMORE RD	66	J 8 SV
ALFRISTON RD	66	J 8 SV
ALLENS RD	66	H 7 NV
AMREINS RD	65	H 2 NE
ANAWHATA RD	65	H 2 NV

Location	Map No.	Ref

ANNANDALE RD .... 65 F 2 NE
ANNETT RD .... 65 E 2 SE
ANZAC RD .... 64 D 3 SE
ANZAC VALLEY RD .... 65 G 3 NW
ARA KOTINGA .... 65 H 8 SE
ARARIMU VALLEY RD .... 65 D 3 SW
ARCHERS RD .... 64 E 5 SE
ARGENT LN .... 64 C 4 NE
ARMOUR RD .... 65 H 4 SW
ARROWSMITH RD .... 65 F 2 SE
ASH RD .... 65 J 7 NW
ASHWOOD AVE .... 64 D 4 NE
ATKINSON RD .... 65 H 4 NW
AUBREY RD .... 64 C 4 SE
AUSTIN RD .... 64 C 3 SE
AVIEMORE DR .... 66 G 7 SE
AWA RD .... 65 E 2 SE
AWANOHI RD .... 64 D 5 NW
AWHIORANGI PROMENADE .... 65 G 3 NW
BADER DR .... 66 H 6 SW
BAIRDS RD .... 66 H 7 SW
BAKERS LN (PVT) .... 65 F 3 NE
BALMORAL RD .... 66 G 5 NE
BARLOW RD .... 64 A 5 NW
BARR RD .... 64 E 3 NE
BARRETT RD .... 65 F 2 SE
BAVERSTOCK RD .... 66 H 7 SE
BAWDEN RD .... 64 C 4 SE
BAYER RD .... 64 B 4 NW
BEACH HAVEN RD .... 64 E 5 SW
BEACH RD .... 64 D 5 SE
BEACHLANDS RD .... 64 G 8 SE
BERENICE LN .... 64 D 4 SW
BETHELLS RD .... 65 G 1 NE
BILLING RD .... 64 A 4 SE
BIRDWOOD RD .... 64 F 3 SE
BIRKDALE RD .... 64 E 5 SW
BIRKENHEAD AVE .... 64 F 5 NW
BLACKBRIDGE RD .... 64 D 3 NE
BODHISATTVA RD .... 64 C 3 NE
BOORD CRES .... 65 E 3 SW
BOTANY RD .... 66 H 7 NW
BOUNDARY RD
(CLOVER PARK) .... 66 J 7 NE
(RIVERHEAD) .... 64 D 5 SE
(WOODHILL) .... 65 D 1 SE
BRADLY RD .... 65 D 1 SE
BRIAR LN .... 66 H 8 NE
BRIGHAM CREEK RD .... 64 E 4 SW
BRIGHAM LN (PVT) .... 64 E 3 SE
BROADY RD .... 64 B 3 NE
BROOKBY RD .... 66 J 8 NE
BROOKDALE RD .... 64 E 4 NW
BROOKVALE LN (PVT) .... 65 F 3 NW
BROOMFIELDS RD .... 66 H 8 NW
BROWNHILL RD .... 66 H 8 NW
BROWNS BAY RD .... 64 D 5 SE
BROWNS LN .... 66 H 7 NE
BROWNS RD
(RIVERHEAD) .... 65 E 3 NW
(WIRI) .... 66 J 7 NE
BUCKLANDS BEACH RD .... 66 G 7 NE
BURNS LN (PVT) .... 65 E 3 NW
BURNSIDE RD .... 66 J 8 SE
BURUNDI AVE .... 66 J 7 SW
BUSH RD
(ALBANY) .... 64 E 5 NW
(WAIATARUA) .... 65 H 3 NE
CABLE RD .... 65 F 2 NW
CAMPBELL RD
(ONE TREE HILL) .... 66 G 6 SW
(RIVERHEAD FOREST) .... 65 D 3 NW
CANDIA RD .... 65 E 2 SW
CANE RD .... 65 E 2 NE
CARBINE RD .... 66 G 7 SW
CARLISLE RD .... 64 D 5 SE
CARTER RD .... 65 G 4 SW
CASCADE AVE .... 65 H 3 NE
CASCADES RD .... 66 G 7 SE
CATON RD .... 65 F 2 SE
CAVENDISH DR .... 66 J 7 NW
CEMETERY RD .... 64 C 4 NW
CENTRAL PARK DR .... 65 G 4 NW
CENTREWAY RD .... 64 B 5 SW
CHAPEL RD .... 66 H 7 SE
CHATHAM RD .... 65 D 3 NW
CHERRY BLOSSOM LN .... 65 D 1 NW
CHRISTIAN RD .... 65 G 3 NW
CHURCH ST
(ONEHUNGA) .... 65 H 6 NE
(SWANSON) .... 65 G 3 NE
CLEVEDON RD .... 66 J 8 SE
CLEVEDON - TAKANINI RD .... 66 J 8 SE
CLIFTON RD .... 66 G 8 SE
CLYDE RD .... 64 D 5 SE
COAST RD .... 65 E 1 NW
COATESVILLE HEIGHTS .... 64 E 4 NW
COATESVILLE RIVERHEAD HWY .... 64 E 4 NW
COCHRAN RD .... 65 H 3 NE
COLLEGE RD .... 66 G 6 NE
COLLINGS DR .... 66 G 6 NE
CONSTABLE RD .... 65 F 1 SE
COOK ST .... 66 G 8 SW
CORNWALLIS RD .... 65 J 3 NE
COSTER RD .... 65 F 1 NE
COTTLE RD .... 65 F 3 NW
COULTER RD .... 65 G 3 NE
CROFT LN .... 65 D 4 SW
CROSSBRIDGE RD (PVT) .... 64 D 4 NE
CROWS RD .... 64 F 3 SE
CURRAN ST .... 64 F 5 SE
CUTHBERT RD .... 65 F 2 NE
DAIRY STREAM RD .... 64 C 4 SE
DALGETY DR .... 66 J 7 NW
DAVIDSON RD .... 65 E 1 NE
DODD RD .... 65 J 3 SE
DON BUCK RD .... 64 F 3 SE
DONALDSON DR .... 66 J 7 NW
DRUCES RD .... 66 J 7 NW
DRURY LN .... 66 D 3 NE
DUCK CREEK RD .... 64 C 5 NW
DUFFY RD .... 65 F 2 NE
DUNLOP RD .... 64 F 3 NE
DUREY RD .... 64 D 4 NE

DYSART LN .... 65 E 3 SW
EAST COAST RD
(CAMPBELLS BAY) .... 64 C 5 NE
(DAIRY FLAT) .... 64 D 5 NW
EAST TAMAKI RD .... 66 H 7 SW
ELLERSLIE PANMURE HIGHWAY .... 66 G 6 SE
ELMORE RD .... 64 C 4 NE
ESCOTT RD .... 64 D 4 NW
ESCOTT RD .... 64 D 4 NW
EVERGLADE DR .... 66 J 7 NE
EWING RD .... 65 H 4 SW
EXHIBITION DR .... 65 H 4 NW
FALLS RD .... 65 G 2 NE
FARRAND RD .... 65 E 3 SW
FIDDLERS HILL RD .... 64 A 4 SE
FITZPATRICK RD .... 66 J 8 NE
FLAT BUSH SCHOOL RD .... 66 H 7 SE
FLETCHER RD .... 65 E 2 SW
FOLEY QUARRY RD .... 64 D 4 SE
FOREST HILL RD .... 65 D 3 NE
FOREST VIEW LN .... 64 D 3 SW
FORK RD .... 65 F 2 NE
FORREST HILL RD .... 64 E 5 NW
FOSTER AVE .... 65 J 3 NW
FOSTER RD .... 64 C 4 NE
FOUNDRY RD .... 64 C 4 NE
FOWLER ACCESS RD .... 64 A 4 SE
FROST RD .... 64 C 3 SE
GEORGE BOLT MEMORIAL DR .... 66 J 6 NW
GERVIN RD .... 64 B 4 SW
GILBRANSEN RD .... 65 E 2 NE
GLADSTONE RD .... 66 F 6 SW
GLENDALE RD .... 65 G 4 SW
GLENESK RD .... 65 H 2 NW
GLENFIELD RD .... 64 E 5 SW
GLENMORE RD .... 65 H 4 NE
GODLEY RD .... 65 H 4 NE
GOLDFLATS LN .... 64 E 4 NW
GOUDIE RD .... 65 D 1 NW
GRACECHURCH DR .... 66 H 7 SE
GRANDE VUE RD .... 65 J 7 NE
GRANT RIDGE RD .... 64 A 3 SW
GRASSLANDS DR .... 67 D 3 SE
GRASSMERE RD .... 65 G 3 NW
GRAYSON RD .... 65 C 4 NW
GREAT NORTH RD .... 65 G 4 NW
GREAT SOUTH RD .... 66 H 6 NE
GREEN HOLLOWS RD .... 64 A 4 SE
GREEN RD .... 64 D 4 NE
GREENLANE WEST .... 66 G 6 NE
GREGORY RD .... 65 F 2 SE
GRIGGS RD .... 66 H 8 NE
GULF HARBOUR DR .... 64 C 6 NW
HAIGH ACCESS RD .... 64 D 5 NW
HAILES RD .... 65 F 3 NE
HAMILTON RD .... 65 E 3 SE
HAMLIN RD .... 66 J 8 SW
HANHAM RD .... 65 F 2 NE
HARRIS RD .... 66 H 7 NE
HARURU RD .... 64 B 3 SE
HASZARD RD .... 65 F 3 SE
HAWKES ACCESS RD .... 64 C 4 NW
HAYES RD .... 65 G 3 SW
HAYR RD .... 66 G 5 SE
HENDERSON VALLEY RD .... 65 G 3 SE
HENSON RD .... 66 H 8 NE
HENWOOD RD .... 65 F 3 NE
HIBISCUS COAST HIGHWAY .... 64 B 5 SW
HIGHBROOK DR .... 66 H 7 NW
HILL RD .... 66 J 7 SE
HILLCREST RD .... 64 B 4 NE
HILLSBOROUGH RD .... 66 H 5 NW
HILLTOP RD .... 65 J 7 NE
HINAU RD .... 65 E 2 SW
HOBSONVILLE RD .... 64 F 4 NW
HOLDENS RD .... 65 G 4 SW
HORSESHOE BUSH RD .... 64 C 3 SE
HORSMAN RD .... 65 F 2 SW
HOUSTON RD .... 64 D 3 NE
HUGH WATT DR .... 66 H 6 NW
HUIA DAM RD .... 65 J 3 NE
HUIA RD .... 65 J 3 NE
HULL RD .... 64 C 3 SE
HUNGRY CREEK RD .... 64 A 5 SW
HUNTER RD .... 66 J 7 NE
HURSTMERE RD .... 64 E 6 SW
HUTCHINSON RD .... 66 D 1 SE
INLAND RD
(HELENSVILLE) .... 65 D 2 NW
(WOODHILL FOREST) .... 65 D 1 SW
J. TOLHOPF RD .... 64 A 3 NE
J. TURNWALD RD .... 64 A 4 SW
JACK BARRY RD .... 64 C 3 SE
JACK LACHLAN DR .... 66 G 8 SE
JACKSON WAY .... 64 A 4 NW
JAMES FLETCHER RD .... 66 H 6 NE
JAMES MACKIE RD .... 65 D 1 SE
JAMIESON RD .... 64 A 5 NW
JEFFS RD
(DAIRY FLAT) .... 64 D 5 NW
(EAST TAMAKI) .... 66 H 8 SW
JERVIS RD .... 64 B 5 NW
JOBLIN RD .... 65 C 4 NW
JONKERS RD .... 65 F 2 NW
JOYCE ADAMS PL .... 65 E 2 NE
KAHIKATEA FLAT RD .... 64 C 3 NE
KAIPARA VIEW RD .... 65 E 2 NE
KAREKARE RD .... 65 E 2 SW
KAURI CRES .... 65 E 2 SW
KAURI LOOP RD .... 65 H 3 SE
KELLYS RD
(WAIATARUA) .... 66 G 3 SE
(WHITFORD) .... 66 H 8 NW
KENNEDY RD .... 64 D 4 NE
KENNEDYS RD .... 64 E 3 SE
KERRS RD .... 66 J 7 NW
KILLARNEY ST .... 64 E 6 SW
KINROSS ST .... 65 H 4 SW
KIRKBRIDE RD .... 66 H 6 SW
KITCHENER RD .... 64 E 6 NW
KITEWAHO RD .... 65 G 3 NW
KIWITAHI RD .... 65 D 2 SW
KNOX RD .... 65 G 3 NE
KORAHA RD .... 65 G 3 NE
KOWHAI RD .... 64 B 4 SW
KRIPPNER RD .... 64 A 4 SW
LADIES MILE .... 66 G 6 NW
LAGOON DR .... 66 G 7 SW
LAKE RD .... 64 F 5 NE

LASCELLES DR .... 64 C 4 SE
LATHROPE RD .... 64 E 3 SE
LAUDERDALE RD .... 64 E 5 SW
LEIGH RD .... 64 A 4 NE
LENNON ACCESS RD .... 64 C 5 NW
LENZEN RD .... 64 A 4 SW
LIME ACCESS RD .... 64 C 4 SW
LINCOLN RD .... 65 G 4 NW
LINE RD .... 66 G 7 NW
LINK RD .... 64 E 3 NE
LLOYD RD .... 64 E 4 NW
LOG RACE RD .... 65 H 2 SW
LONE KAURI RD .... 65 J 2 NW
LONELY TRACK RD .... 64 D 5 SW
LONG BUSH RD .... 64 D 3 NE
LONG RD .... 65 G 2 NE
LOOKOUT RD .... 65 D 1 SW
LOOP RD .... 64 A 4 NE
LUNN AVE .... 66 G 6 SE
LYNTON MASTERS LN .... 64 E 4 NW
LYON RD .... 65 E 1 NE
MAHANA RD .... 65 E 1 NW
MAHOENUI VALLEY RD .... 64 D 4 SE
MAHUNGA DR .... 66 H 6 NW
MAHURANGI WEST RD .... 64 A 5 NW
MAIORO ST .... 66 G 5 SW
MANGERE RD .... 66 H 6 SE
MANUEL RD .... 64 C 4 NW
MANUKAU RD .... 66 G 6 SW
MASSEY RD .... 66 H 6 SW
MATUA RD .... 65 E 2 NE
MAYS RD .... 66 H 6 NE
MCCATHIE RD .... 64 B 4 NE
MCENTEE RD .... 65 F 3 SW
MCGIVEN PL .... 64 E 4 NW
MCKENZIE RD .... 66 H 6 SW
MCPIKE RD .... 65 E 1 SE
MCQUOIDS RD .... 66 J 8 NW
MEOLA RD .... 66 G 5 NW
MERTON AVE .... 66 G 6 NE
MERYL AVE .... 65 E 2 NE
MESSENGER RD .... 64 C 5 NW
MILDON RD .... 65 F 2 SW
MILL FLAT RD .... 64 D 3 SE
MILL RD .... 66 J 8 NW
MISSION RD .... 65 D 1 SW
MOKOIA RD .... 64 F 5 NW
MONOWAI RD .... 64 B 3 NE
MOONTIDE RD .... 64 E 3 SE
MOTT LN .... 66 H 8 NW
MOTU RD .... 65 E 2 SE
MOTUTARA RD .... 65 F 1 NE
MOUNT ALBERT RD .... 66 G 5 SE
MOUNT SMART RD .... 66 G 6 SW
MOUNT WELLINGTON HIGHWAY .... 66 G 6 SW
MOUNTAIN RD .... 65 G 3 SW
MUDGWAYS RD .... 64 F 3 SE
MULLINS RD .... 66 J 8 SE
MURIWAI RD .... 65 F 1 NE
MURIWAI VALLEY RD .... 65 F 2 NW
MURPHYS RD .... 66 J 7 NE
MUSHROOM RD .... 65 E 1 SE
NEILSON ST .... 66 H 6 NW
NELSON RD .... 65 F 3 NW
NEW NORTH RD .... 66 G 5 NW
NEWMAN RD .... 64 C 4 NE
NGAREWA DR .... 64 A 5 NW
NIXON RD .... 64 F 3 NE
NOBILO RD .... 65 E 3 SW
NOBILO RD .... 66 J 6 NE
NORTH PIHA RD .... 65 H 2 NW
NORTH WESTERN MOTORWAY
(AVONDALE) .... 66 G 5 NE
(LINCOLN) .... 64 F 4 SW
NORTHERN MOTORWAY .... 64 E 5 SE
O'BRIEN RD .... 64 D 4 SE
O'NEILLS RD .... 65 G 3 NE
OAIA RD .... 65 F 1 SE
OCEAN VIEW RD .... 64 F 5 NE
OKURA RIVER RD .... 64 D 5 NW
OLD NORTH RD .... 65 E 2 NE
OLD RAILWAY RD .... 64 E 3 SE
OLD TELEPHONE RD .... 65 E 1 NW
ONEHUNGA MALL .... 66 G 6 SW
ONEWA RD .... 64 F 5 NE
OPAHI BAY RD .... 64 A 5 NW
OPANUKU RD .... 65 G 3 SE
ORAHA RD .... 65 E 3 SW
ORAMS RD .... 66 J 7 NE
OREGON PARK .... 64 C 4 SE
ORMISTON RD .... 66 H 7 SE
ORPHEUS RD .... 66 G 5 SW
ORRS RD .... 66 J 6 NE
OWAIRAKA AVE .... 66 G 5 NW
PAH RD .... 66 G 6 SW
PAKURANGA RD .... 66 G 7 SW
PALMERS RD .... 66 J 7 SW
PANAMA RD .... 66 H 6 NW
PAREMOREMO RD .... 64 E 4 NE
PARISH LINE RD .... 66 J 8 SE
PARKER RD .... 65 H 3 NE
PARKLANDS AVE .... 65 G 3 NW
PATIKI RD .... 65 G 4 NW
PEAK RD .... 65 D 2 NE
PEBBLE BROOK RD .... 64 C 3 NE
PENROSE RD .... 66 G 6 SE
PERRIS RD .... 65 G 3 NW
PETERS LN .... 65 G 2 SW
PHILLIP RD .... 66 J 8 SW
PICTON RD .... 66 G 8 SW
PIHA RD .... 65 H 2 NE
PILKINGTON RD .... 66 G 7 SW
PINE AVE .... 65 J 3 NE
PINE VALLEY RD .... 64 C 4 NW
PINETONE RD .... 65 D 1 NW
PIONEER LN .... 66 F 2 NE
PLEASANT RD .... 65 G 4 SE
PLUNKET AVE .... 66 J 7 NW
POINT VIEW DR .... 66 H 8 NW
POLO LN .... 66 H 8 SE
POMONA RD .... 65 E 2 SE
POPES RD .... 66 J 8 SW
PORCHESTER RD .... 66 J 7 SE
PORTAGE RD .... 66 H 4 NE
PORTERFIELD RD .... 66 H 8 NE
POSTMAN RD .... 64 C 4 NW
POTTS RD .... 66 H 8 NE
PRESTON RD .... 66 J 7 SW
PRICE RD .... 66 J 6 NE

PRINCES ST .... 66 H 6 NE
PUHINUI RD .... 66 J 7 NW
PUHOI AHUROA RD .... 64 A 4 NE
PUHOI RD .... 64 A 4 SE
PUKAKI RD .... 66 J 6 NE
PUKAPUKA RD .... 64 A 4 NE
PUKE RD .... 65 E 1 SE
PUKETAPU RD .... 65 E 1 NW
PULPIT RD .... 65 E 1 SE
PUMP RD .... 64 A 4 NW
RAHANUI RD .... 65 D 3 NW
RAILSIDE AVE .... 65 G 4 NW
RALEIGH RD .... 66 F 5 NE
RANFURLY RD .... 66 J 7 SE
RANGATIRA RD .... 64 E 5 SW
RANGE RD .... 65 G 3 NW
RANGIMARIE RD .... 64 A 4 NE
RANGITOPUNI RD .... 64 D 4 SW
RATA ST .... 65 G 4 NW
RAUHUIA CRES .... 65 H 3 SE
RAUTAWHIRI RD .... 65 D 2 NW
RAYNER RD .... 65 H 2 SW
RED HILLS RD .... 64 E 4 SE
REDOUBT RD .... 66 J 7 NE
REMIGER RD .... 64 A 6 NW
REMUERA RD .... 66 G 6 NE
RESTAL RD .... 65 E 1 NW
RICHARD RD .... 64 C 4 SW
RICHARDSON RD .... 66 G 5 SW
RIDGE RD
(HOWICK) .... 66 G 7 SE
(RIVERHEAD) .... 64 E 4 NE
RIMMER RD .... 65 D 1 NW
RIMU RD .... 65 H 3 NE
RIVERHEAD RD .... 64 E 3 NE
RIVERLAND RD .... 64 E 3 SE
ROBINSON RD .... 64 E 3 SE
ROGAN AVE .... 65 D 1 NE
RONGOMAI RD .... 66 J 7 NW
ROSCOMMON RD .... 66 J 7 NW
ROSEBANK RD .... 65 G 4 NE
ROSEDALE RD .... 64 E 5 NW
ROSELLA GR .... 65 E 2 SE
ROSS LN (PVT) .... 65 E 2 SE
ROYAL RD .... 64 E 3 SE
RUSSELL RD .... 64 B 4 SW
ST HELIERS BAY RD .... 66 G 7 NW
ST JOHNS RD .... 66 G 6 NE
SALEYARDS RD
(OTAHUHU) .... 66 H 6 NE
(PUHOI) .... 64 A 4 SE
SANDRINGHAM RD .... 66 G 5 NE
SANDSTONE RD .... 65 H 8 SW
SCENIC DR .... 65 G 3 NW
SCENIC DR NORTH .... 65 G 3 NW
SCHISCHKA RD .... 64 A 5 NW
SCHOOL RD .... 65 E 2 SW
SCREEN RD (PVT) .... 64 D 4 SW
SEAVIEW RD .... 65 H 2 NW
SEIBEL RD .... 65 G 3 NE
SELMAN RD .... 64 C 4 SW
SELWYN RD .... 65 D 1 SW
SELWYN ST .... 66 G 6 NE
SEYMOUR RD .... 65 G 4 SW
SHAW RD .... 65 H 3 SW
SHIRLEY RD .... 65 G 5 NE
SHORE RD .... 66 G 6 NW
SHORT RD .... 64 E 3 NE
SIMON BAYER RD .... 64 E 3 SE
SLOWATER LN (PVT) .... 64 A 4 NE
SMALES RD .... 66 H 7 NE
SMALL RD .... 64 C 4 NE
SMITH RD (PVT) .... 65 E 1 SW
SOUTH BLOCK RD .... 65 E 1 SW
SOUTH WESTERN MOTORWAY .... 66 H 6 SE
SPINLAY RD .... 64 D 3 NE
SPRINGS RD .... 66 H 7 NE
SPUR RD .... 64 C 4 NE
STALEY RD .... 65 H 4 SW
STANCOMBE RD .... 66 H 7 SE
STATION RD .... 65 E 3 SW
STEAM HAULER TRACK .... 65 G 2 NE
STEED RD .... 65 G 2 NE
STONEY CREEK DR .... 65 F 2 SE
STRATHFIELD LN .... 66 G 8 SW
STRIP RD .... 65 D 3 SW
SUNNYBRAE RD .... 64 E 5 SE
SUNNYNOOK RD .... 64 E 5 NE
SUNNYSIDE RD .... 64 D 4 SW
SUNNYVALE RD .... 65 F 3 SW
SUTTON RD .... 66 J 8 NE
SWANSON RD .... 65 G 3 NE
SYCAMORE DR .... 64 E 5 NE
SYLVIA PARK RD .... 66 H 6 NE
TAHA RD .... 66 E 2 SW
TAIAPA RD .... 65 F 1 SE
TAKANINI SCHOOL RD .... 66 J 7 SE
TAMAKI DR .... 66 F 6 SE
TAPU RD .... 65 E 3 NW
TARGET RD .... 64 E 5 SE
TARRANT RD .... 65 G 3 NE
TASMAN AVE .... 65 G 1 NE
TASMAN VIEW RD .... 64 E 3 SE
TAUPAKI RD .... 64 E 5 NW
TAWA DR .... 65 E 2 SE
TAWA RD .... 65 E 2 SE
TAYLOR RD .... 65 H 2 SW
TE AHUAHU RD .... 65 F 4 SE
TE ATATU RD .... 65 G 2 NW
TE AUTE RIDGE RD .... 65 G 2 NE
TE HENGA RD .... 64 C 4 SW
TE TENDER RD .... 64 D 4 SE
THE AVENUE .... 64 A 5 NW
THE BULLOCK TRK .... 64 A 5 NW
THOMAS RD .... 65 J 7 NE
TI RAKAU DR .... 66 H 7 NE
TITIRANGI RD .... 65 H 4 NW
TIVERTON RD .... 66 G 5 NW
TOP RD .... 64 C 4 SE
TOWNSHIP RD .... 65 F 3 SW
TRIANGLE RD .... 65 F 3 SW
TRIG RD
(RIVERHEAD FOREST) .... 64 D 3 SE
(WHENUAPAI) .... 64 F 4 NW
(WHITFORD) .... 66 H 8 NE
TRIGG RD .... 65 E 2 SE
TRISTRAM AVE .... 64 E 5 SE
TUDOR PARK DR .... 66 H 8 NW

Auckland District Roads - Christchurch Central

Location	Map No.	Ref
TUNNEL RD	64	A 4 NW
TURANGA RD	65	G 3 SW
TURLEY RD	64	C 4 SW
TWIN SPRINGS DR	65	D 1 SE
UNION RD	66	G 7 SE
UNITY RD	65	G 2 NE
UNIVERSAL DR	65	G 4 NW
UPLAND RD	65	J 3 NW
UPPER HARBOUR DR	64	E 4 SE
UPPER OREWA RD	64	B 4 SW
UPPER WAIWERA RD	64	B 3 NE
VALLEY RD	65	F 2 NW
VAUGHANS RD	64	D 5 NW
VICTORY RD	65	H 4 SW
VIEW RD	65	G 4 NW
WADES RD	66	H 8 NW
WAIKAREKARE LN	65	J 2 NW
WAIKOPUA RD	66	H 8 NE
WAIKOUKOU VALLEY RD	65	C 2 NE
WAINUI RD	64	B 4 SW
WAIPUNA RD	66	G 6 SE
WAIRAU RD	64	E 5 SE
WAIRERE RD	65	F 2 SE
WAITAKERE RD	65	F 3 SW
WAITEA RD	65	F 1 SE
WAITOKI RD	64	C 3 NE
WAKE RD	64	E 4 NW
WALMSLEY RD	66	H 6 SW
WATER ST	66	H 7 NW
WATERLOO RD	64	C 4 NE
WATSON RD	64	A 4 NW
WEIGHBRIDGE RD	65	E 3 NE
WEITI RD	64	C 4 SE
WELSH HILLS RD	65	G 3 NW
WENDY RD	65	G 3 NW
WENZ - BAYER RD	64	A 4 SW
WENZLICK RD	64	A 4 NW
WERANUI RD	64	B 4 SW
WEST COAST RD	65	H 3 NE
WEST END RD	64	F 5 SW
WEST HOE RD	64	B 4 SE
WEYMOUTH RD	66	J 7 SW
WHAKATAHI RD	64	D 3 SE
WHANGAPARAOA RD	64	C 5 NW
WHAREPAPA RD	65	D 1 SE
WHATIPU RD	65	J 2 SE
WHITE SWAN RD	66	G 5 SW
WHITEHILLS RD	64	C 3 NE
WHITES RD	66	H 8 NW
WHITFORD MARAETAI RD	66	H 8 NE
WHITFORD PARK RD	66	H 8 NW
WHITFORD RD	66	H 8 NW
WHITFORD WHARF RD	66	H 8 NW
WILKS RD	64	C 4 SE
WILKS RD WEST	64	C 4 NE
WILLET RD	65	D 1 SW
WILSON RD	64	D 4 NE
WINDMILL DR	64	C 4 NW
WINTOUR RD	65	E 2 SE
WIRI STATION RD	66	J 7 NW
WISHART RD	65	D 2 NW
WOOD ACCESS RD	64	B 4 NW
WOODHILL PARK RD	65	E 2 NE
WORRALL RD	65	F 2 NE
WRIGHT RD	64	D 5 NW
YELASH RD	64	F 3 SE
YOUNG ACCESS	64	C 4 NE
ZANDERS RD	65	D 3 SW

Bay Of Islands

Bay Of Islands Towns

Location	Map No.	Ref
ARABELLA RD	81	E 2 SE
ASHBY ST	81	B 4 NW
AUCKS RD	81	E 4 NW
AUSTIN ST	81	F 3 NW
BACK ST	81	F 3 NW
BAFFIN ST	81	F 3 NW
BAKER ST	81	F 3 NW
BARRACKS PL	81	C 3 SW
BAYVIEW RD	81	C 1 SE
BEDGGOOD CL	81	D 2 NW
BEECHY ST	81	F 3 NE
BERESFORD ST	81	A 4 SW
BINNIE ST	81	B 4 NW
BROADVIEW RD	81	B 4 NW
BRODIE PASSAGE	81	B 3 NE
CASS ST	81	B 3 NE
CHAPEL ST	81	B 3 NE
CHURCH ST	81	B 3 NE
DAVIS CRES	81	C 1 SE
DE HAVEN ST	81	E 3 SE
DEEMING RD	81	E 3 SE
ENGLISH BAY RD	81	E 3 SE
FLAGSTAFF RD	81	A 3 SE
FLORANCE ST	81	B 4 NW
FRANKLIN ST	81	F 3 NW
GILBERT MAIR RISE	81	C 3 SE
GOULD ST	81	B 4 NW
GRANTS AVE	81	A 4 SW
GREYS LN	81	D 2 NW
HAZARD ST	81	B 4 NW
HITITAHI RISE	81	B 4 SW
HOPE AVE	81	A 4 SW
JAMES CLENDON PL	81	E 3 NE
JAMES ST	81	A 4 SW
JOYCES RD	81	C 1 SE
KAHA PL	81	E 3 SE
KAKAPU ST	81	E 3 SE
KANE ST	81	F 3 NE
KELLET ST	81	F 3 NE
KENNEDY ST	81	F 3 NE
KENT ST	81	A 3 SE
KINGS RD	81	D 1 NE
KOWHAI CRES	81	D 2 SW
LONG BEACH RD	81	F 3 NW
LYON ST	81	F 3 NW
MACMURRAY RD	81	D 2 NW
MAJOR BRIDGE DR	81	C 4 SW
MAKO LN	81	D 2 NW
MARINA RISE	81	D 2 SW
MARSDEN RD	81	C 1 NE
MATAUWHI RD	81	B 4 NW
MOANA AVE	81	C 1 SE
OKIATO RD	81	E 3 NE
ONEROA RD	81	A 4 SW
OROMAHOE RD	81	F 2 NE
OSBORNE ST	81	F 3 NW
PAIHIA RD	81	C 3 SE
PAINE BROWN WAY	81	C 3 SE
PANORAMA AVE	81	D 2 NW
PENNEY ST	81	F 3 NW
PINE TREE LN	81	C 3 SW
PIPIROA RD	81	E 3 NE
PITT ST	81	B 3 NE
POINT VERONICA DR	81	E 2 SE
POMARE AVE	81	B 4 NW
POMARE RD	81	C 3 SE
PROSPECT ST	81	A 3 SE
QUEEN ST	81	A 3 SE
QUEENS VIEW RD	81	A 4 SW
RICHARDSON ST	81	F 3 NW
RICHARDSON ST WEST	81	F 3 SW
ROBERTSON ST	81	B 3 NE
ROSELLA RD	81	D 1 NE
ROSS ST	81	F 3 SW
RUSSELL HEIGHTS	81	A 4 SW
RUSSELL RD	81	B 3 NE
SCHOOL RD	81	D 1 NE
SCORESBY ST	81	F 3 NW
SEAVIEW RD	81	D 2 NW
SELWYN RD	81	C 1 SE
SULLIVANS RD	81	A 3 NE
TAPEKA RD	81	B 1 NW
TAU HENARE DR	81	B 1 SW
TAUMATA CL	81	E 2 NW
TE HAUMI DR	81	E 2 NW
TE KARUWHA PDE	81	C 1 NW
TE KEMARA AVE	81	C 1 NW
TE WAHAPU RD	81	E 3 SE
THE STRAND	81	B 3 NE
TIRAIRAKA TCE	81	A 3 NE
TITORE WAY	81	A 3 NE
TOHITAPU RD	81	D 2 SW
TUI GR	81	D 2 SW
VERONICA ST	81	D 2 NW
WALKER PASSAGE	81	B 3 NE
WARD DR	81	E 2 SE
WELLINGTON ST	81	A 3 SE
WILLIAMS RD	81	E 2 NE
YORK ST	81	A 3 SE

District Roads

Location	Map No.	Ref
ACCESS RD	63	C 2 SE
AERODROME RD (PVT)	63	F 1 NE
AKERAMA RD	63	F 4 NE
AUCKS RD	63	D 4 SE
BANNISTER RD	63	E 2 SW
BARNES RD	63	E 2 SW
BAYLY RD	63	D 4 NW
BLUE GUM LN	63	C 2 SE
BOLERO RD	63	F 4 SW
BROWN RD	63	E 2 SW
BROWNS RD	63	F 1 NE
BULLMAN RD	63	D 1 SE
CALLAGHAN RD	63	F 4 SW
CAMPBELL RD	63	A 1 SW
CHERRINGTON RD	63	E 3 SW
COOKSON RD	63	E 4 SW
COPPER MINE RD	63	B 1 SW
COTTLE HILL DR	63	D 3 NW
CROWS NEST RD	63	E 3 SW
CUMBER RD	63	E 1 SE
DAVIS RD	63	B 3 SW
DIP RD	63	B 1 NE
DONALDSON RD	63	D 1 SW
DOONSIDE RD	63	C 3 NW
DOVES BAY RD	63	C 3 SE
EDMONDS RD	63	C 3 SE
EDWARD RD	63	F 1 NE
FORD RD	63	F 4 NE
FRASER RD	63	E 4 SW
GOING RD	63	F 4 NW
HAILE RD	63	C 3 NW
HANSEN RD	63	C 3 NE
HARIRU RD	63	D 2 SW
HARRISON RD	63	D 1 SW
HARURU FALLS RD	63	B 3 SW
HAURIRI RD	63	B 2 NW
HAUTAPU RD	63	E 4 SW
HAY RD	63	E 4 SW
HAYTERS RD	63	F 4 NE
HENARE RD	63	F 3 NE
HIKURUA RD	63	B 2 NE
HORAHORA RD	63	F 3 SE
HOREKE RD	63	B 1 NE
HUIA RD	63	B 1 NE
HUPARA RD	63	E 3 NW
IMMS RD	63	D 1 SW
INKSTER RD	63	F 4 NE
JAMES RD	63	F 3 SW
JENNINGS RD	63	C 2 NE
JORDAN RD	63	E 1 SW
KAKA RD	63	C 2 NE
KAPIRO RD	63	C 2 NE
KARAKA RD	63	D 1 NW
KARETU RD	63	E 4 NE
KEOGH RD	63	C 2 SE
KERIKERI INLET RD	63	C 3 SE
KERIKERI RD	63	C 2 SE
KNUDSEN RD	63	F 1 SE
KORANAE RD	63	C 2 NW
KOROPEWA RD	63	C 2 NW
KUPA RD	63	C 3 NW
KURAPARI RD	63	C 3 NW
LAKE RD	63	D 1 NE
LAMBERG RD	63	D 1 NW
LANES RD	63	D 4 SE
LEACOCK RD	63	B 1 NE
LODORE RD	63	D 1 NE
LUDBROOKS RD	63	E 2 NE
MAHINEPUA RD	63	A 2 NW
MAKO ST	63	A 1 NW
MANGAKAHIA RD	63	F 2 NW
MANGAKARETU RD	63	C 2 SW
MANGATOA RD	63	A 1 SW
MARLIN DR	63	A 1 NW
MARLOW RD	63	F 4 SW
MAROMAKU RD	63	F 4 NW
MAROMAKU SCHOOL RD	63	F 4 NW
MARSHALL RD	63	E 3 NW
MARTIN RD (KAEO)	63	B 1 SE
MARTIN RD (POKERE)	63	F 3 NW
MASON RD	63	E 2 SE
MATANGIRAU SCHOOL RD	63	A 1 SE
MATARAUA RD	63	F 1 SW
MATAURI BAY RD	63	B 2 NW
MATAWAIA RD	63	F 3 NW
MATAWHEROHIA RD	63	B 1 SW
MATENE RD	63	F 2 NW
MAWSON AVE	63	C 2 SE
MCCAUGHAN RD	63	C 2 NE
MCDONALDS RD	63	D 3 SE
MCINTYRE RD	63	D 3 SE
MIHI RD	63	D 1 SW
MIHIRATA RD	63	F 3 SE
MILL RD	63	E 3 NE
MONUMENT RD	63	F 4 NE
MOTATAU RD	63	F 3 SE
NESS RD	63	C 2 NE
NGAPIPITO RD	63	F 2 NW
NGAWHA SCHOOL RD	63	E 2 NW
NGAWHA SPRINGS RD	63	E 2 NW
NGAWHITU RD	63	F 2 NW
NINIHI RD	63	F 1 NW
NOY RD	63	E 3 SE
OETZMAN RD	63	F 4 SW
OKOKAKO RD	63	D 2 NE
OKURA BAY RD	63	A 1 SW
OLD BAY RD	63	D 2 SE
OLD VALLEY RD	63	D 1 SE
OMAPERE RD	63	E 1 SE
OMAUNU RD	63	B 1 SW
ONEKURA RD	63	C 2 NW
OPAHI RD	63	F 3 NW
OPITO BAY RD	63	C 3 NE
ORAKAU RD	63	F 2 NE
ORANGEWOOD RD	63	C 3 NW
OROMAHOE RD	63	D 3 SW
OTA POINT RD	63	A 1 SE
OTAERE RD	63	D 1 SE
OTAHA RD	63	B 2 SE
OTIRIA RD	63	E 3 SE
OWAE RD	63	E 4 NE
PACKERS RD	63	F 4 SE
PAIAKA RD	63	F 4 SE
PAKARU RD	63	E 4 NW
PARAHA RD	63	F 4 SE
PAROA RD	63	D 4 NE
PARROT RD	63	F 1 SW
PERI RD	63	F 3 NW
PICADILLY RD	63	F 1 NE
PIPIWAI RD	63	F 3 SW
POKAPU RD	63	F 3 NW
POPLAR LN	63	C 2 SE
PUHITIA RD	63	F 3 SE
PUKEPOTO RD	63	D 1 NW
PUKETI RD	63	D 1 NW
PUKETONA RD	63	D 3 NE
PUKETOTARA RD	63	C 2 SW
PUNGAERE RD	63	C 1 NE
PUPUKE MANGAPA RD	63	B 1 NW
PURERUA RD	63	C 3 NW
RAINBOW FALLS RD	63	C 2 SE
RAKAUWAHIA RD	63	E 1 SW
RANGE RD	63	E 3 SE
RANGIHAMAMA RD	63	E 1 SE
RANGIHOUA RD	63	B 4 SW
RANGITANE RD	63	C 3 NW
RANUI RD	63	E 1 SW
RATA TIPENE RD	63	F 3 SW
RATAROA RD	63	B 1 NW
REDCLIFFS RD	63	C 3 NW
REMUERA SETTLEMENT RD	63	E 1 NE
RESERVOIR RD (KAIKOHE)	63	E 1 NE
RESERVOIR RD (KAWAKAWA)	63	E 4 NW
RIGDEN RD	63	F 1 NW
ROGER RD	63	E 2 SE
ROGERS RD	63	E 2 SE
RUAPEKAPEKA RD	63	E 4 SW
RUSK RD	63	F 4 SE
RUSSEK RD	63	F 4 NE
RUSSELL RD	63	C 2 NW
SANDYS RD	63	D 1 NE
SCOTT RD	63	D 1 NE
SETTLEMENT RD	63	E 3 SE
SHOWGROUND RD	63	D 2 SW
SIGNAL RD	63	D 1 NE
SKUDDERS BEACH RD	63	C 3 NW
SMEATH RD	63	E 3 NW
SMITH RD	63	E 3 NW
SOMERVILLE RD	63	C 2 NE
SQUIRES LN	63	E 1 NE
STANNERS RD	63	C 2 NE
STEWARD RD	63	F 1 SW
TAKOU BAY RD	63	B 2 SE
TANA RD	63	E 2 SW
TANEKAHA LN	63	C 2 NE
TAPUI RD	63	A 2 SE
TAURANGA BAY RD	63	A 1 SE
TE AHU AHU RD	63	D 2 SE
TE AUTE RD	63	D 3 SW
TE IRENGA RD	63	D 1 NW
TE IRENGA WEST RD	63	F 1 NW
TE PUA RD	63	E 1 NE
TE TII RD	63	B 3 SW
TE WAHAPU RD	63	D 4 NE
TEPENE TABLELANDS RD	63	B 2 NE
TIMPERLEY RD	63	E 2 NE
TIPENE RD	63	F 3 SE
TIROHANGA RD	63	E 4 NW
TOIA RD	63	E 1 NW
TOTARA NORTH RD	63	A 1 SW
TOUWAI BEACH RD	63	A 1 SE
TOUWAI - OTOROA RD	63	B 2 NW
TOWAI RD	63	F 4 NW
TREVOR RD	63	F 4 NW
TUNA PL	63	A 1 NW
UPOKORAU RD	63	D 2 SE
UTAKURA VALLEY RD	63	D 1 SW
VALENCIA LN	63	C 2 SE
WAIARE RD	63	C 1 SE
WAIKARAMU RD	63	D 2 SE
WAIKARE RD	63	E 4 NW
WAIKINO RD	63	E 4 NW
WAIKOURA RD	63	B 1 NE
WAIKUKU RD	63	D 2 N
WAIMATE RD	63	D 2 N
WAINUI RD	63	A 2 S
WAINUI VALLEY RD	63	A 2 S
WAIOHANGA RD	63	E 1 S
WAIOMIO RD	63	E 4 S
WAIPAPA RD	63	C 2 S
WAIPAPA WEST RD	63	C 2 N
WAKELIN RD	63	D 2 N
WALLIS RD	63	E 1 N
WEBER RD	63	B 1 N
WEHIRUA RD	63	D 1 S
WHAKAIRE - TARAIRE RD	63	B 2 N
WHAKATAHA RD	63	D 2 N
WHANGAE RD	63	E 4 N
WHANGAROA RD	63	B 1 N
WHARAU RD	63	C 3 S
WHARENGAERE RD	63	F 1 S
WHAREPUNGA RD	63	F 1 S
WIROA RD	63	D 2 N
YORKE RD	63	D 4 N

Christchurch

Christchurch Central

Location	Map No.	Ref
ABBERFIELD LN	97	A 3 S
ABBERLEY CRES	97	C 4 N
ABERDEEN ST	97	E 3 N
ACTON ST	97	A 1 S
AIKMANS RD	97	C 3 N
AIREDALE PL	97	A 2 S
AKELA ST	97	A 2 S
ALBANY ST	97	E 3 N
ALBEMARLE ST	97	F 4 N
ALCESTER ST	97	E 3 N
ALLARD ST	97	E 4 N
ALLEN ST	97	C 2 S
ALLISTER AVE	97	A 1 S
ALPHA AVE	97	A 1 N
AMURI PARK LN	97	B 4 S
ANDERSON ST	97	E 1 N
ANDOVER ST	97	B 2 S
ANDREWS CRES	97	F 1 S
ANTIGUA ST	97	F 3 N
ARGYLE ST	97	F 4 N
ARMAGH CT	97	C 3 S
ARMAGH ST	97	D 4 S
ASH ST	97	D 4 S
ATLAS LN	97	E 4 N
AYR ST	97	C 1 S
BALFOUR TCE	97	E 2 N
BARBADOES ST	97	E 4 S
BARNETT AVE	97	F 3 S
BARRIE ST	97	F 1 N
BARRINGTON ST	97	F 1 N
BARTLETT ST	97	D 1 N
BATH ST	97	E 3 N
BATTERSEA ST	97	E 3 N
BEALEY AVE	97	B 4 S
BEDFORD ROW	97	D 3 S
BELLS ARCADE	97	D 3 S
BERNARD ST	97	E 1 S
BERRY ST	97	B 3 N
BERWICK ST	97	A 4 N
BEVERIDGE ST	97	C 3 N
BEVERLEY ST	97	A 2 S
BISHOP ST	97	B 4 S
BLETSOE AVE	97	F 2 S
BOLTON AVE	97	E 2 S
BRADDON ST	97	F 2 S
BRISBANE ST	97	F 4 N
BRISTOL ST	97	D 1 N
BROCKWORTH PL	97	F 2 S
BROUGHAM ST	97	A 2 N
BROWNING ST	97	A 2 N
BROWNS RD	97	F 4 N
BUCHAN ST	97	F 4 N
BURKE ST	97	F 2 N
BURLINGTON ST	97	F 3 S
BURNS ST	97	E 4 S
BYRON ST	97	E 4 S
CADOGAN ST	97	F 4 S
CALEDONIAN RD	97	B 3 S
CAMBRIDGE TCE	97	D 3 S
CANON ST	97	B 4 N
CARLTON MILL RD	97	B 2 S
CARLYLE ST	97	F 4 N
CASHEL PLAZA	97	D 3 S
CASHEL ST	97	E 3 S
CASS ST	97	E 3 S
CATHEDRAL SQ	97	D 3 S
CATON ST	97	F 3 N
CHANCERY LN	97	D 3 N
CHATHAM ST	97	E 1 S
CHAUCER ST	97	F 4 S
CHELTENHAM ST	97	B 2 S
CHESTER ST EAST	97	C 4 S
CHESTER ST WEST	97	C 3 S
CHURCH LN	97	B 2 N
CHURCH SQ	97	F 1 S
CIRCUIT ST	97	A 2 N
CITY MALL	97	D 3 S
CLARE RD	97	B 3 S
CLARENCE ST SOUTH	97	E 1 S
CLISSOLD ST	97	A 1 S
CLUB LN	97	D 3 N
COLERIDGE ST	97	D 3 N
COLES PL	97	A 3 S
COLLINS ST	97	F 1 N
COLOMBO ST	97	D 3 S
COLONIAL LN	97	D 3 N
CONFERENCE ST	97	A 4 S
CORNWALL ST	97	A 4 S
CORONATION ST	97	F 2 S
COTTERILL ST	97	F 2 N
COURTENAY ST	97	A 3 N
COVENTRY ST	97	E 4 S
COX ST	97	A 1 S
CRANFORD ST	97	A 4 S
CRANMER SQ	97	C 3 S
CROHANE PL	97	D 3 S
CRYSTAL PLAZA	97	D 3 S
DARVEL ST	97	C 1 S
DEANS AVE	97	D 1 S
DERBY ST	97	B 3 S
DESMOND ST	97	A 2 S
DEVONPORT LN	97	A 2 S

Location	Map No.	Ref
EWSBURY LN	97	F 3 NE
EYELL CRES	97	F 3 SW
CKENS	97	E 1 SE
SRAELI ST	97	E 1 NE
OLLANS ST	97	B 4 SW
ONALD PL	97	A 2 SE
ORSET ST	97	C 3 NW
OVER ST	97	A 3 SE
OYLE LN	97	F 1 NW
UBLIN ST	97	B 3 SW
UNDAS ST	97	A 1 NW
URHAM ST NTH	97	C 3 SE
URHAM ST STH	97	E 4 NW
ATON PL	97	E 4 NW
DGEWARE RD	97	A 4 SE
DWARD AVE	97	A 4 SE
LGIN ST	97	C 4 NE
LMWOOD RD	97	A 1 SW
LY ST	97	C 4 NE
MERSON ST	97	F 1 NE
VERSLEIGH ST	97	B 3 NE
XETER ST	97	B 2 SE
AIRFIELD AVE	97	F 2 NE
ARADAY ST	97	F 3 SE
EAST PL	97	F 1 NE
IELDING ST	97	F 1 NW
ENDALTON RD	97	E 4 NE
ERRY RD	97	E 4 NE
RANKISH LN	97	E 1 SE
REYBERG AVE	97	D 1 NW
ULTON AVE	97	B 1 NW
ARDEN RD	97	B 1 NW
ASSON ST	97	B 1 NW
LANDOVEY RD	97	A 1 SW
LOUCESTER ARCADE	97	D 3 NE
LOUCESTER ST	97	D 4 NW
ORDON AVE	97	B 1 SW
RACEFIELD AVE	97	C 3 NE
RESSONS LN	97	D 4 NW
ROVE RD	97	E 2 SW
UTHRIES ARCADE	97	D 3 SE
ALKETT ST	97	E 3 NW
ALKETT ST	97	E 1 SE
ARGEST CRES	97	F 4 SE
ARMAN ST	97	F 1 NE
AROLD DENTON PL	97	A 3 SW
AROLD ST	97	A 3 SE
ARPER AVE	97	C 2 NW
ASTINGS ST EAST	97	F 4 SE
ASTINGS ST WEST	97	F 3 SE
AWDON ST	97	A 4 SE
AZELDEAN RD	97	E 1 SE
EATON ST	97	A 1 SE
ELMORES LN	97	B 1 SE
EREFORD ST	97	D 4 NE
EWITTS RD	97	B 2 SW
IGH ST	97	D 4 SW
IGHGATE AVE	97	B 1 NE
OLLY RD	97	B 2 NE
OLMWOOD RD	97	B 1 SW
ORATIO ST	97	E 2 NE
UMBOLDT ST	97	F 4 SE
UTCHESON ST	97	F 3 SE
UXLEY ST	97	F 4 SW
NNES RD	97	A 2 NW
AMES K BAXTER PL	97	F 1 SW
ERROLD ST NORTH	97	F 1 NW
ERROLD ST SOUTH	97	F 1 SW
OHNSON ST	97	F 3 SE
ORDAN ST	97	E 1 SW
ENILWORTH ST	97	E 3 SW
ENT ST	97	A 3 SE
EOGHS LN	97	C 1 SW
ILMARNOCK ST	97	C 3 SW
ILMORE ST	97	F 4 NW
INGSLEY ST	97	A 3 SW
INLEYS LN	97	A 3 SW
INLOCH ST	97	F 2 SW
IPLING ST	97	D 4 SW
IVERS LN	97	A 2 NE
NOWLES LN	97	B 3 SW
NOX LN	97	D 1 NW
YLE ST	97	D 4 NE
ATIMER SQ	97	F 3 NE
AWSON ST	97	A 1 SW
E CASCINA LN	97	A 1 SE
EINSTER RD	97	D 1 SW
ESLIE HILLS DR	97	E 1 NW
ESTER LN	97	E 1 SE
ICHFIELD ST	97	D 3 SE
INCOLN ST	97	E 1 SE
INCOLN RD	97	F 1 NW
INDSAY ST	97	A 4 SW
ITTLE HILLIER PL	97	F 1 SE
IVERPOOL ST	97	D 4 NW
OWE ST	97	F 1 NE
MACAULAY ST	97	F 2 NE
MACGIBBON PL	97	A 2 NW
MADRAS ST	97	E 4 NE
MALDON ST	97	E 4 NW
MANCHESTER ST	97	E 4 NW
MANHIRE ST	97	F 3 SE
MANSFIELD AVE	97	A 2 SE
MASSEY CRES	97	C 1 NW
MATAI ST EAST	97	C 1 SE
MAYFAIR ST	97	D 1 SE
MCDOUGALL AVE	97	C 4 NE
MELROSE ST	97	F 1 NW
MEREDITH ST	97	F 1 NW
MERIVALE LN	97	A 2 NW
MILFORD ST	97	A 2 NW
MILLBANK LN	97	F 3 SE
MILTON ST	97	C 4 NE
MOA PL	97	D 3 SE
MOLLETT ST	97	C 1 SW
MONA VALE AVE	97	F 3 NW
MONTREAL ST	97	E 4 NW
MOORHOUSE AVE	97	E 4 NW
MORTIMER PL	97	A 2 NW
MURRAY PL	97	B 1 NE
NASEBY ST	97	B 1 NW
NEW REGENT ST	97	D 1 SE
NORMANS RD	97	A 2 SW
NOVA PL	97	C 4 SE
OAKFORD CL	97	D 1 NW
OFFICE RD	97	A 2 SW
OGB LN	97	D 4 NW
ONSLOW ST	97	B 2 NE
ORBELL ST	97	F 3 NW
OTLEY ST	97	B 4 SE
OXFORD TCE	97	D 3 SW
OXLEY AVE	97	A 4 NW
PACKE ST	97	B 4 SE
PALAZZO LN	97	D 1 SW
PAPANUI RD	97	A 2 SE
PARK TCE	97	C 2 NE
PARLANE ST	97	F 1 NE
PEACOCK ST	97	B 3 SE
PEEL ST	97	A 1 NW
PENBURY ST	97	E 3 SE
PETERBOROUGH LN	97	C 3 NE
PETERBOROUGH ST	97	C 3 SW
PILGRIM PL	97	E 4 SW
PITT PL	97	A 3 SW
PLYMOUTH LN	97	D 3 SE
POPE ST	97	E 1 NW
POPLAR ST	97	D 4 SW
POULSON ST	97	F 1 NE
POYNDER AVE	97	B 1 NW
PRESS LN	97	D 4 NW
PURCHAS ST	97	B 4 SW
QUEENS AVE	97	B 1 SW
QUILL LN	97	E 4 NE
RADNOR ST	97	A 3 SE
RANFURLY ST	97	B 3 NW
RASTRICK ST	97	F 2 SE
REDRUTH AVE	97	F 2 SE
REHUA LN	97	B 3 NW
REPTON ST	97	B 1 SE
RHODES ST	97	B 1 SE
RICCARTON AVE	97	D 1 NE
RICCARTON RD	97	C 1 SW
ROLLESTON AVE	97	D 3 NW
ROPE ST	97	E 4 NW
ROSEWARNE ST	97	F 2 SW
ROSSALL ST	97	B 1 NE
RUGBY ST	97	F 2 NE
RUSKIN ST	97	A 2 SE
ST ALBANS ST	97	A 1 NW
ST ANDREWS SQ	97	D 4 SW
ST ASAPH ST	97	E 3 NW
ST DAVID ST	97	E 3 NW
SALISBURY ST	97	C 3 NW
SANDYFORD ST	97	E 3 SW
SCOTT ST	97	F 3 SW
SEARELLS RD	97	A 1 NW
SELWYN ST	97	F 4 SE
SHADES ARCADE	97	D 3 NE
SHEPPARD ST	97	A 3 NE
SHERBORNE ST	97	B 4 NW
SHREWSBURY ST	97	B 2 SE
SIMEON ST	97	F 1 SE
SOMERSET CRES	97	F 2 SW
SOMME ST	97	A 3 NW
SOUTHWARK ST	97	E 4 NW
SPENCER ST	97	F 1 NE
SPRINGFIELD RD	97	B 3 SE
STANLEY ST	97	F 3 NE
STEWART ST	97	E 2 NE
STIRLING ST	97	A 1 SE
STONEYHURST ST	97	B 3 SW
STRAND LN	97	D 3 NE
STROWAN RD	97	A 1 SW
STRUTHERS LN	97	D 4 SW
STUART MILL ST	97	E 2 NE
SYDNEY ST	97	F 2 SW
TARAMEA PL	97	F 1 NW
TATTERSALLS LN	97	D 4 NW
TONBRIDGE ST	97	B 2 SE
TRAFALGAR ST	97	A 3 NE
TRAMWAY LN	97	D 4 NW
TUAM ST	97	D 4 SE
TYNE ST	97	E 1 NW
ULSTER PL	97	C 4 NW
VICTORIA ST	97	C 3 NW
WAIRARAPA TCE	97	B 1 SW
WALKER ST	97	E 3 NW
WALLER TCE	97	E 2 NW
WALSALL ST	97	E 1 SW
WALTHAM RD	97	F 4 NE
WALTON ST	97	F 3 SE
WARD ST	97	F 2 NW
WARRINGTON ST	97	A 4 NE
WASHINGTON WAY	97	E 4 SE
WAVERLEY ST	97	F 3 NE
WEBB ST	97	B 2 NE
WELLES ST	97	E 4 NE
WESTMINSTER ST	97	A 3 NW
WESTPAC LN	97	D 4 NW
WESTWOOD TCE	97	C 3 NW
WILLARD ST	97	F 2 SW
WILLIAMS ST	97	E 4 NW
WILMER ST	97	E 3 NE
WINCHCOMBE ST	97	E 3 NE
WINCHESTER ST	97	B 2 NW
WINTON ST	97	A 4 NW
WISE ST	97	E 1 NE
WOOD LN	97	C 1 NE
WOOLSACK LN	97	D 4 NW
WORCESTER BOULEVARD	97	D 3 NW
WORCESTER ST	97	E 4 NW
WORDSWORTH ST	97	F 4 NW
WROXTON TCE	97	B 1 NW
YORK TONG PL	97	E 2 SE

District Roads

Location	Map No.	Ref
ADAMS RD	77	D 3 NE
ADDINGTONS RD	77	C 1 SW
ALAMEDA PL	77	E 4 SE
ALBERT JAMES PL	77	F 1 SE
ALPINE VIEW RD	77	D 3 SW
ALSTON RD	77	E 4 NW
ANDERSONS RD	78	F 7 SE
ANSONS RD	77	D 1 SW
ARMACK DR	77	E 3 SE
ASCHENS RD	78	A 5 SE
ASHLEY DENE RD	77	F 3 SW
ASHWORTHS RD	78	A 5 SE
AUCHENFLOWER RD	77	C 1 NW
AYLESBURY RD	77	D 2 SE
BAILEYS RD	78	B 5 SE
BAMFORDS RD	78	F 6 SE
BARKERS RD		
(OHOKA)	78	A 5 SE
(WOODEND)	78	A 7 SW
BARNES RD	77	D 1 SE
BARRYS RD	77	D 4 SE
BARTERS RD	78	C 6 NW
BAYNONS RD	78	C 6 NW
BAYVIEW RD	78	F 7 NE
BEACH RD	78	B 7 NW
BEALEY RD	78	D 1 SE
BELFAST RD	78	C 6 SE
BELLAM RD	78	E 4 SW
BELLS RD	77	D 3 NW
BERKETTS RD	77	F 3 SW
BETHELS RD	77	F 3 SW
BIELA PL	78	B 5 NE
BIRCHS RD	78	F 5 NW
BLAKES RD		
(BELFAST)	78	C 6 SE
(PREBBLETON)	77	E 4 NE
BLOCK RD	77	E 4 NE
BOULTONS RD	77	C 1 NW
BOUNDARY CREEK RD	77	F 2 SW
BOUNDARY RD		
(LINCOLN)	77	A 4 NE
(SWANNANOA)	77	A 4 NE
BOWERS RD	78	A 4 SW
BOYS RD	78	A 6 NW
BRADLEY RD	77	D 3 SW
BRADLEYS RD	78	B 5 NE
BRAMLEYS RD	78	A 6 SE
BRANTHWAITE DR	77	E 4 SW
BRIDGE RD	78	A 5 NE
BROOKSIDE RD	77	F 3 NW
BROWNS RD		
(DUNSANDEL)	77	F 1 SE
(OXFORD)	77	A 1 NW
(SWANNANOA)	77	B 4 SW
BUCHANANS RD	77	D 4 NE
BURDONS RD	77	F 2 NE
BURGESS RD	77	F 1 SW
BURGESSES RD	78	B 6 SW
BURNHAM RD	77	F 2 SE
BURNHAM SCHOOL RD	77	F 2 NE
BURNT HILL RD	77	B 1 NW
BUSCH LN (PVT)	78	E 5 NE
BUTCHERS RD	78	B 6 NE
CALDERS RD	77	D 3 NW
CAMEO DR	78	A 5 SE
CAMP BAY RD	78	F 8 NW
CANDYS RD	78	E 5 SE
CARLETON RD	77	A 2 NW
CASHMERE RD	78	E 6 SW
CHAMBERLAINS RD	77	F 3 SE
CHAPMANS BOUNDARY RD	77	B 4 NW
CHARTERIS BAY RD	78	F 7 SW
CHATTERTONS RD	77	D 4 NW
CHILTONS RD	78	B 5 SE
CHINNERYS RD	78	A 7 NW
CHRISTCHURCH NORTHERN		
MOTORWAY	78	B 6 NE
CHRISTMAS RD	78	B 6 NE
CHURCH BUSH RD	78	A 6 SE
CLINTONS RD	77	E 1 NW
CLOTHIERS RD	78	C 5 NE
COALTRACK RD	77	C 1 NW
COLLINS RD	77	F 4 SE
COLLINS RD EAST	78	F 5 SW
CONSERVATORS RD	78	C 5 SW
COOKS RD	77	C 1 SE
CORBETTS RD	77	F 3 SW
COSSARS RD	78	F 5 SE
COURT RD	78	F 5 SE
COURTENAY RD	77	F 3 SW
COUTTS ISLAND RD	78	C 6 NW
COX RD	77	D 1 NW
CREYKE RD	77	D 1 NW
CROSS RD	77	F 1 NW
CUNNINGHAMS RD	77	F 1 NW
CURRAGHS RD	77	A 3 NE
CUST RD	77	A 3 NE
DALZIELS RD	78	A 5 NE
DAVIS RD	78	F 5 SW
DAWN PL	77	D 2 NW
DAWSONS RD		
(MANDEVILLE NORTH)	78	B 5 NE
(TEMPLETON)	77	F 4 SW
DAYS RD	77	A 1 NW
DEPOT RD	78	C 6 NE
DICKEYS RD	77	B 1 NW
DIXON RD	77	B 1 NW
DOG TRIAL RD	77	A 1 NE
DOMAIN RD	78	E 5 SE
DOWNIES RD	77	B 3 NE
DOWNS RD	77	B 3 NE
DUNNS CROSSING RD	77	E 3 SW
DUNSANDEL & BROOKSIDE RD	77	F 1 SE
DYERS PASS RD	78	E 6 SE
DYNES RD	77	F 3 NE
EARLY VALLEY RD	78	F 6 NW
EARLYS RD	77	A 3 NE
EAST MADDISONS RD	77	F 3 SE
EASTERBROOK RD	78	A 6 SW
EDMUNDS RD	78	B 6 SW
EDWARDS RD	78	A 5 SE
EGANS RD	78	A 5 SE
ELDERS RD	78	B 6 SW
ELLESMERE JUNCTION RD	77	F 1 SW
ELLESMERE RD	78	F 5 SW
ESSENDON RD	78	D 1 SW
FAITH PL	78	D 1 SW
FERNLEA PT RD	78	F 8 SE
FERNSIDE RD	78	B 7 NW
FERRY RD	78	F 8 SE
FIELDS RD	77	D 3 SE
FINLAYS RD	78	A 6 SW
FLAXTON RD	78	B 6 SW
FOLEYS RD	77	F 1 NW
FRASERS RD	78	A 7 SW
FULLERS RD	78	A 7 SW
GARDINERS RD	78	A 6 NW
GARTERYS RD	77	A 4 NW
GENESIS DR	78	A 6 SE
GERALD ST	77	F 4 NE
GILES RD	78	F 5 SW
GILMOURS RD	78	F 5 SW
GLADSTONE RD	78	A 6 SW
GLADSTONE ST	77	F 4 NE
GODLEY HEAD RD	78	E 8 SW
GODLEY RD	77	F 2 NE
GOLF LINKS RD		
(RANGIORA)	78	A 6 NW
(TAITAPU)	78	F 5 SE
GOULDS RD	77	F 4 SW
GOVERNORS BAY RD	78	F 6 SE
GOVERNORS BAY -		
TEDDINGTON RD	78	F 6 SE
GRANGE RD	77	E 2 SW
GRAYS RD	78	D 5 NE
GREENS RD	78	A 6 SE
GREIGS RD	78	B 6 SE
GRESSONS RD	78	A 6 NE
GUTHRIES RD	78	C 6 NE
GUYS RD	78	D 5 NW
HALKETT RD	78	D 2 NE
HALSWELL JUNCTION RD	78	E 4 NE
HAMPTONS RD	77	E 4 NE
HAREWOOD RD	77	A 1 NW
HARPERS RD	78	C 5 NE
HARRIS RD		
(EYRETON)	78	B 5 SW
(RANGIORA)	78	A 6 NW
HARRS RD	78	C 5 NE
HASKETTS RD	77	D 3 SE
HAYES RD		
(AYLESBURY)	77	D 2 SE
(LADBROOKS)	78	F 5 NE
HENDERSON RD	77	C 2 SE
HENDERSONS RD	78	C 6 NW
HETHERTON RD	78	A 5 SW
HEYDERS RD	78	C 7 NE
HEYWARDS RD	78	A 6 SW
HICKLANDS RD	78	A 6 SW
HIGH ST	77	A 1 NE
HIGHFIELD AVE	77	F 1 NW
HIGHFIELD RD	77	E 1 SE
HODGENS RD	78	E 5 SW
HOLMES RD	78	F 5 NE
HOMEBUSH RD	77	C 1 SW
HOON HAY VALLEY RD	78	E 6 NW
HORORATA DUNSANDEL RD	77	E 1 NW
HORRELLS RD	77	A 3 SW
HOSKYNS RD	77	A 3 NE
HOWSONS RD	78	A 4 SW
HUDSONS RD	78	F 5 SW
INTAKE RD	77	C 2 SE
IRVINES RD	77	F 1 SE
ISAAC RD	78	B 6 NE
ISLAND RD	78	D 6 NW
IVEY RD	78	B 6 NW
JACKSONS RD	78	A 7 NW
JEFFS DRAIN RD	78	A 7 SE
JELFS RD	78	A 7 SE
JENNINGS RD	78	B 6 SE
JOHNS RD		
(BELFAST)	78	C 6 SW
(RANGIORA)	78	A 5 NE
JOHNSON RD	77	D 3 SE
JONES RD	77	E 4 NW
JOWERS RD	77	A 3 NE
JUDSONS RD	78	A 7 NW
KAIAPOHIA RD	78	B 7 SW
KAINGA RD	78	B 7 SW
KANES RD	77	F 1 SE
KEANDS RD	78	B 1 SW
KEETLY PL	78	B 6 NW
KENNEDYS BUSH RD	78	E 6 SW
KENNEDYS HILL RD	77	A 4 SE
KENNEDYS RD	77	E 3 SW
KERRS RD	78	A 6 SW
KETTLEWELL DR	78	D 4 NW
KINGCRAFT DR	78	E 5 SW
KIRK RD	77	D 4 SE
KIVERS RD	77	E 2 SW
KNIGHTS RD	77	E 3 NE
LAIRD PL	77	D 3 SE
LANGDALES RD	77	D 4 NW
LARCOMBS RD	77	D 4 NW
LAWFORD RD	77	E 2 SW
LEADLEYS RD	78	E 5 SW
LEAVINGTON CL	78	F 5 SW
LEES RD	78	A 7 SW
LEESTON DUNSANDEL RD	77	F 1 SE
LEESTON RD	77	D 4 SE
LEGGETT RD	78	A 5 NE
LEHMANS RD	78	A 5 NE
LEIGHS RD	77	F 3 NE
LILLY RD	78	A 5 NE
LINCOLN ROLLESTON RD	77	E 3 SE
LINCOLN TAITAPU RD	78	F 5 SW
LINESIDE RD	78	A 6 SE
LITTLES RD	78	A 2 NW
LOGANS RD	78	B 5 SE
LONGSTAFFS RD	78	C 6 NW
LORIMAS RD	78	C 7 SW
LOWER STYX RD	77	E 3 SE
LOWES RD	78	B 6 SE
MABERS RD	77	E 3 SE
MADDISONS RD	78	C 6 NW
MADELEYS RD	78	A 5 SE
MAIN DRAIN RD	78	C 6 SE
MAIN NORTH RD	77	B 2 SE
MAIN RACE RD	78	A 5 NE
MAIN RD	78	F 6 NE
MAINDONALDS RD	77	A 3 SW
MAIRAKI RD	77	A 4 NE
MANDALEA RD	78	A 5 SW
MANDEVILLE RD	78	B 5 NE
MANNA PL	77	D 3 SE
MARINE DR	78	F 7 SE
MARSH RD	78	A 6 NW
MARSHALLS RD	78	A 5 SE
MARSHLAND RD	78	C 7 SW
MARSHS RD	78	C 5 NW
MCCLELLAND RD	77	E 4 NW
MCDONALD RD	77	A 3 SE
MCDRURYS RD	78	F 5 NE
MCHUGHS RD	78	B 5 NE
MCINTOSHS RD	78	A 5 NE
MCKAYS LN	77	D 3 NE
MCKAYS RD	78	A 5 SE
MCLEANS ISLAND RD	78	C 6 SW
MCROBERTS RD	78	A 5 SE
MEADOWLANDS RD	78	E 5 NW
MELTON GRANGE RD	77	D 3 NE
MEMORYS LN	77	F 4 SW
MERTON RD	78	A 5 NE

Side margin (vertical): Christchurch District Roads - Dunedin Central

Location	Map No.	Ref
MEYER RD	78	F 5 SE
MIDHURST RD	77	E 1 NE
MILES RD	77	D 1 NW
MILL RD		
(CUST)	77	A 3 SE
(MANDEVILLE NORTH)	78	A 5 NE
MILTON RD	77	E 1 SW
MINERS RD	77	D 4 NE
MODENA PL	78	B 5 NE
MODERATES RD	77	E 2 NE
MOFFATTS RD	78	B 5 SE
MOIRS LN	78	F 5 SW
MONOLUA AVE	78	F 8 NW
MOODYS RD	78	B 6 NE
MOUNCES RD	77	A 4 SW
MT THOMAS RD	78	A 5 NE
MULCOCKS RD	78	A 6 SE
MURRAY RD	77	B 3 SE
NEAVE RD	77	D 4 SW
NEEVES RD	78	B 6 SE
NEWTONS RD	77	E 3 NW
NO. 10 RD	78	B 5 SW
NORTH EYRE RD		
(BENNETTS)	77	A 2 NE
(MANDEVILLE NORTH)	78	B 5 NW
NORTHBROOK RD	78	B 6 NW
NORTHWOOD RD	77	A 4 SW
NORWOOD RD	77	F 2 SE
O'FARRELLS RD	77	A 5 NE
O'ROARKES RD	78	A 5 NE
OHOKA MEADOWS DR	78	B 6 NE
OKAIHAU RD	78	A 6 NE
OLD SOUTH RD	77	F 1 SW
OLD TAITAPU RD	78	F 5 SE
OLD WEST COAST RD	77	D 3 NE
OSBORN RD	78	F 5 SE
OSTERHOLTS RD	78	F 5 SE
OTAHUNA RD	78	F 5 SE
OXFORD RD	77	A 2 NE
PA RD		
(PORT LEVY)	78	F 8 SE
(WOODEND)	78	A 7 SW
PAINTERS RD	77	D 2 NE
PARISH RD	77	A 1 SW
PARK LN	77	E 3 SE
PATERSONS RD	77	A 1 NW
PATTERSONS RD	78	A 5 SW
PEACOCK PL	78	B 5 NW
PEARCES RD	77	E 3 NW
PERYMANS RD	78	F 5 SW
PESARO LN	78	B 5 NE
PESTERS RD	77	B 3 NW
PINEWOOD CL	78	C 1 NW
PITTS RD	77	B 3 NW
PLASKETT RD	78	A 5 NE
POTTERS LN	77	F 6 NW
POUND RD	78	D 5 SW
POWELLS RD	77	F 4 SW
POWER RD	78	A 6 SE
POYNTZS RD	77	C 2 NW
PREECES RD	78	A 7 NW
PURAU AVE	78	F 7 NE
PURAU PORT LEVY RD	78	F 8 SW
QUAIFES RD	78	E 5 SE
QUIGLEYS RD	77	A 2 NW
RADCLIFFE RD	78	C 6 SE
RADDENS RD	78	B 6 NW
RAILWAY RD	77	E 3 NW
RAINEYS RD	78	F 5 NW
RANGE RD	77	C 3 NE
RANGIORA WOODEND RD	78	A 6 NE
RATTLETRACK RD	77	F 4 SW
RAVEN DR	77	F 3 SE
REED RD	77	A 2 NE
REVELLS RD	78	B 6 NE
RHODES RD	78	F 5 SE
RIDGENS RD	77	E 1 NW
RIVER RD	78	F 5 SW
ROBERTSONS RD	77	C 2 SW
ROBINSONS RD	77	E 4 NE
ROLLER RD	78	B 1 NW
ROSCREA PL	78	B 5 NW
ROSSENDALE RD	77	E 3 NW
RUNNERS RD	77	F 4 SW
RUSSLEY RD	78	D 5 NE
RYANS RD	78	D 5 NW
RYDERS RD	77	A 3 SW
SANDHILL RD	78	A 7 SW
SANDY KNOLLS RD	77	E 3 SW
SARAHS LN	78	F 5 NW
SAVILLS RD	78	D 5 NW
SCARLET OAK DR	77	D 4 NW
SCHOFIELD RD	77	A 1 SW
SCHOOL RD		
(HORRELLVILLE)	77	A 3 SE
(YALDHURST)	78	D 5 NW
SELWYN LAKE RD	77	F 1 NE
SELWYN RD	77	F 2 SE
SERGEANTS RD	77	F 4 SE
SETTLEMENT RD	78	F 5 NE
SHANDS RD	77	F 4 NE
SHARPS RD	77	D 2 NE
SHEATS RD		
(BANKSIDE)	77	F 1 NW
(HORRELLVILLE)	77	A 3 SW
SHIPLEYS RD	77	E 1 SW
SIENA PL	78	B 5 NE
SILLANO PL	78	B 5 NE
SKEWBRIDGE RD	78	B 6 NE
SMARTS RD	78	A 6 NE
SOUTH EYRE RD		
(CLARKVILLE)	78	B 6 SW
(EYRETON)	77	E 3 NW
SPENCERVILLE RD	78	C 7 NW
SPRINGBANK RD	77	A 1 NW
SPRINGS RD	77	F 2 SE
SPRINGSTON ROLLESTON RD	77	F 4 NW
STACKHOUSE RD	77	D 3 NW
STALKERS RD	78	A 7 SE
STATION RD	77	D 2 SE
STEFFENS RD	77	A 2 SW
STONE EYRE PL	78	B 5 NW
STRANGES RD	77	E 1 SW
STYX MILL RD	78	C 6 NE
STYX RIVER PL	78	C 7 NE
SUMMIT RD	78	F 6 SE
SUMNER RD	78	E 7 SE
SWAMP RD		
(CUST)	77	A 3 NE
(ELLESMERE)	77	F 3 SW
SWANNANOA RD	78	A 5 NE
TAITAPU RD	78	F 5 SE
TALLOTTS RD	77	A 4 SW
TANCREDS RD	77	E 4 SE
TASMAN LN (PVT)	77	C 2 SW
TAYLORS RD	78	B 6 SE
TE POUAPATUKI RD	78	A 6 NE
TELEGRAPH RD	77	E 1 SE
THOMPSONS LN (PVT)	77	A 3 NE
THOMPSONS RD	77	C 3 SW
THOMSONS RD	77	F 2 NE
THONGCASTER RD	77	C 3 NE
THRELKELDS RD	78	B 6 NW
TIPPINGS RD	77	A 3 NW
TOPITO RD	77	D 3 SW
TORLESSE RD	77	D 3 SW
TOSSWILL RD	78	E 5 SW
TOWNSEND RD	78	A 6 NW
TRAM RD	77	A 3 SE
TRENTS RD	77	E 4 NE
TRESILLIAN DR	77	E 3 NW
TRICES RD	78	E 5 SW
TRICKETTS RD	77	D 3 SE
TUAHIWI RD	78	B 6 NW
TURIWHAIA RD	78	A 6 NE
TURNERS RD	78	C 7 NW
TWO CHAIN RD		
(BURNHAM)	77	F 2 NW
(SWANNANOA)	78	B 5 NE
VELINO PL	78	B 5 NE
VERONA PL	78	B 5 NE
VICENZA DR	78	B 5 NE
VOSS RD	78	F 5 NE
WAIKORURU RD	78	A 6 NE
WAIORA LN (PVT)	78	B 5 NE
WAIPUNA RD	77	E 4 NE
WAITUTURI LN	77	F 8 SW
WALKERS RD	77	E 3 SW
WARDS RD		
(CHARING CROSS)	77	E 2 NE
(MANDEVILLE NORTH)	78	B 5 NW
(WAIKUKU)	78	A 7 NW
WARDSTAY RD	78	F 5 SE
WARREN RD	77	A 1 NE
WASHINGTON PL (PVT)	77	A 3 SE
WATERHOLES RD	77	F 4 NW
WATERLOO RD	77	D 4 SE
WATLINGS PL	78	E 6 SW
WEEDONS RD	77	D 3 NE
WEEDONS ROSS RD	77	D 3 NE
WEST COAST RD	77	D 4 NE
WEST MELTON RD	77	D 4 NE
WESTVIEW CRES	77	D 3 NE
WHARF RD	78	F 8 SE
WHITES RD	78	B 5 NE
WHITEWOOD CRES	77	D 3 SE
WILD RD	78	E 4 NW
WILSON DR	78	B 6 NW
WINNIE VINE PL	77	F 1 SE
WINTER RD	78	B 5 NW
WOLFFS RD	78	B 2 SW
WOODEND BEACH RD	78	A 7 SW
WOODFIELDS RD	78	A 5 SW
WOODS RD	78	B 6 SW
WOODSTOCK RD	77	A 1 NE
WOOLSHED RD	77	C 2 SW
WORLINGHAM RD	78	F 8 SW
WRIGHTS RD	78	E 5 SE
WROOTS RD	78	E 5 SE
WYLIES RD	77	D 3 SE
YALDHURST RD	78	D 5 NW
YANKEE CROSSING RD	77	F 1 NE
YOUNGS RD	78	A 6 SE

Dunedin

Dunedin Central

Location	Map No.	Ref
ADAM ST	100	D 1 SE
AGNEW ST	100	B 4 SE
AILSA ST	100	B 3 NE
AIREDALE ST	100	D 2 SW
AITKEN PL	100	E 1 SW
AKAROA ST	100	C 4 NW
ALBANY ST	100	C 4 NW
ALBION PL	100	C 3 SW
ALISON CRES	100	D 1 NW
ALVA ST	100	E 1 NE
ANDERSONS BAY RD	100	F 3 SW
ANN ST	100	C 1 NW
ANZAC AVE	100	D 3 NE
APPIAN WAY	100	C 2 NW
APPOLD ST	100	F 1 NW
ARDMORE DR	100	F 2 NW
ARTHUR ST	100	D 2 NW
AVOCA ST	100	F 1 NW
AVON ST	100	C 2 NW
BALMACEWEN RD	100	A 1 NE
BANK ST	100	A 4 NW
BATH ST	100	D 3 NW
BAUCHOP ST	100	D 4 NW
BAXTER ST	100	B 2 NE
BELLEKNOWES TCE	100	B 1 SW
BERESFORD ST	100	B 1 NW
BIRCH ST	100	E 3 NW
BISHOPS PL	100	C 2 NE
BISHOPS RD	100	D 2 NW
BLACKET LN (PVT)	100	C 3 SW
BLANTYRE RD	100	A 1 NW
BOMBAY ST	100	D 3 NE
BOND ST	100	D 2 NE
BOW LN	100	E 2 NE
BRACKEN ST	100	F 3 SW
BRAEMAR ST	100	F 2 SE
BRAEVIEW CRES	100	A 3 NW
BRAID RD	100	D 1 NE
BRANDON ST	100	F 3 SW
BRENT ST	100	B 2 NE
BRIDGE ST	100	F 1 NE
BRIDGMAN ST	100	E 2 NE
BROADWAY	100	D 2 SW
BROOK ST	100	A 4 SW
BROUGHTON ST	100	F 2 NW
BROWN ST	100	D 2 NW
BROWNVILLE CRES	100	A 3 SW
BRUCE ST	100	C 1 SW
BULLER ST	100	E 3 NE
BURLINGTON ST	100	D 3 NW
BURNS ST	100	F 1 SE
BURT ST	100	A 1 SE
BURWOOD AVE	100	B 2 NE
BUTE ST	100	B 2 NE
BUTLER ST	100	B 2 NW
CAIRNHILL ST	100	C 1 SW
CAMBRIA PL (PVT)	100	C 3 NW
CAMERON ST	100	F 2 SE
CANNINGTON RD	100	A 3 SW
CANONGATE	100	D 2 SW
CARGILL ST	100	C 2 SE
CARLYLE ST	100	A 4 NE
CARROLL ST	100	E 2 NE
CASTLE ST	100	D 3 NE
CASTLE ST NORTH	100	B 4 SW
CHACOMBE AVE (PVT)	100	A 4 NE
CHAMBERLAIN ST	100	A 3 SW
CHAPEL ST	100	B 1 SW
CHAPMAN ST	100	B 1 NE
CHARLOTTE ST	100	C 1 NE
CHETHAM AVE	100	A 4 NW
CITY RD	100	C 1 SE
CLAREMONT ST	100	B 2 NW
CLARENDON ST	100	C 3 NE
CLARK ST	100	D 2 SE
CLIFFORD ST	100	A 3 NE
CLYDE ST	100	C 4 NW
COBDEN ST	100	C 3 NW
COCHRANE ST	100	E 1 SE
COHEN PL	100	A 1 SE
COLERIDGE ST	100	C 2 SE
COMO ST	100	B 3 NW
CONSTITUTION ST	100	C 3 NW
CORNHILL ST	100	A 4 NE
CORRIE ST	100	B 3 SW
COSY DELL RD	100	C 2 NE
COUNTY RD	100	A 1 SE
CRAIGHALL CRES	100	A 1 SE
CRAWFORD ST	100	E 2 NE
CRESSWELL ST	100	D 3 SE
CRICHTON ST	100	A 1 SW
CROSS ST	100	F 1 NW
CUMBERLAND ST	100	C 4 NW
CUMBERLAND ST NTH	100	B 4 SW
DACRE CT	100	F 1 NW
DALE ST	100	B 1 NE
DALMORE CRES	100	A 3 SE
DALRY ST	100	E 1 SW
DERWENT ST	100	D 4 NW
DEVON ST	100	D 4 NW
DOLPHIN ST	100	B 2 NE
DOWLING ST	100	D 3 NW
DRIVERS RD	100	B 2 NE
DRUMMOND ST	100	A 3 SW
DUCHESS AVE	100	B 1 SW
DUDLEY PL	100	A 3 NE
DUKE ST	100	A 4 SE
DUNBAR ST	100	D 3 NE
DUNBLANE ST	100	B 2 NW
DUNCAN ST	100	C 2 NE
DUNDAS ST	100	B 4 NW
EGLINTON RD	100	E 1 SE
ELBE ST (PVT)	100	E 1 SE
ELDER ST	100	C 3 NW
ELLIS ST	100	A 3 NE
ELM ROW	100	D 2 NW
EMILY SIEDEBERG PL	100	C 3 NE
ERIN ST	100	C 1 NE
ETHEL BENJAMIN PL	100	C 3 NE
ETHEL MCMILLAN PL	100	C 3 NE
ETON ST (PVT)	100	B 1 SE
FAIRFAX ST	100	B 2 NW
FAIRLEY ST	100	D 3 SE
FALCON ST	100	C 1 SW
FALKLAND ST	100	B 1 SE
FARLEY ST	100	B 1 NE
FERNHILL ST	100	E 2 SW
FIFIELD ST	100	C 2 NW
FILLEUL ST	100	C 3 NW
FISH ST	100	D 3 SE
FONT ST	100	F 1 NW
FORFAR ST	100	F 1 NW
FORTH ST	100	B 4 SE
FREDERICK ST	100	C 3 NE
FRENCH ST	100	E 3 NE
FRYATT ST	100	D 4 NW
GARFIELD AVE	100	B 2 SW
GEORGE ST	100	C 3 SW
GILMORE ST	100	B 1 NW
GLEN RD	100	F 1 NE
GLENCAIRN ST	100	A 4 NE
GORDON ST	100	E 2 SE
GORE PL	100	B 4 NW
GOWLAND ST	100	C 3 NE
GOWRY PL	100	C 1 NW
GRAHAM ST	100	D 2 SW
GRANGE ST	100	C 3 SE
GRANT ST	100	D 2 SW
GRANVILLE TCE	100	D 1 NW
GRATER ST	100	A 2 SE
GREAT KING ST	100	C 3 SW
GREAT KING ST NTH	100	B 3 SE
GREENHILL AVE	100	A 1 SW
GRENDON ST	100	B 2 NE
GROSVENOR ST	100	F 2 NE
HADDON PL	100	C 2 SE
HAIG ST	100	E 1 NW
HALSEY ST	100	C 4 SW
HAMEL ST	100	B 2 NE
HANOVER ST	100	C 3 SE
HARBOUR TCE	100	B 4 SE
HARCOURT ST	100	D 1 NW
HARROP ST	100	C 4 NW
HARROW ST	100	C 4 NW
HART ST	100	E 1 NE
HASTINGS ST	100	B 1 NW
HAWK LN (PVT)	100	C 4 NW
HAWTHORN AVE	100	D 1 NW
HAYWOOD ST	100	F 1 NE
HELENSBURGH RD	100	A 1 NW
HENRY ST	100	A 3 SW
HEREFORD ST	100	C 1 NW
HERIOT ROW	100	C 3 NW
HIGH ST	100	E 2 NW
HIGHGATE	100	C 1 SW
HILLSIDE RD	100	E 2 SE
HOLYROOD AVE	100	A 1 SW
HOPE ST	100	E 2 NE
HOWE ST	100	A 4 SE
HOWELLS LN	100	C 3 SW
HUNTLEY AVE (PVT)	100	C 4 NW
HYDE ST	100	C 4 NW
INVERLEITH ST	100	A 3 SW
IONA ST	100	E 1 NE
JASON ST	100	E 1 SW
JELLICOE CRES	100	B 1 SW
JERVOIS ST	100	E 2 SE
JETTY ST	100	D 2 SE
JONES ST	100	D 2 SE
JUTLAND ST	100	D 4 SW
KAIKORAI VALLEY RD	100	C 1 NW
KENSINGTON AVE	100	F 2 NE
KEVIN ST	100	C 1 SW
KILGOUR ST	100	C 1 SW
KING EDWARD ST	100	F 2 NE
KINSMAN ST	100	B 1 NW
KIRRIEMUIR ST	100	E 3 NE
KITCHENER ST	100	E 3 SW
KNOX ST	100	A 4 NE
KYBER PASS	100	B 3 SE
KYLE ST	100	B 3 NE
LACHLAN AVE	100	A 3 SW
LANE END	100	E 1 SE
LAWSON ST	100	D 1 NW
LECKHAMPTON CT	100	E 2 SW
LEES ST	100	E 1 NE
LEITH ST	100	B 4 SE
LEITH ST NORTH	100	B 4 SE
LEITHBANK	100	C 4 SW
LEVEN ST	100	C 1 SW
LISMORE LN (PVT)	100	C 2 NE
LITTLEBOURNE RD	100	C 2 NW
LIVERPOOL ST	100	C 2 SE
LOGAN ST	100	C 2 SE
LONDON ST	100	C 2 SE
LOOM ST (PVT)	100	C 1 NE
LORNE ST	100	C 3 SE
LOTHIAN ST	100	A 2 SE
LOVELOCK AVE	100	B 3 SE
LUNDIE ST	100	C 1 SW
LYNN ST	100	A 1 SE
LYNWOOD AVE	100	A 3 SE
MACKENZIE ST	100	D 2 SE
MACLAGGAN ST	100	D 2 SE
MACNEE ST	100	E 1 NW
MAHENO ST	100	E 1 NW
MAILER ST	100	F 2 NW
MAITLAND ST	100	E 2 NW
MALCOLM ST	100	C 1 NW
MALTA ST	100	C 3 SW
MALVERN ST	100	E 1 SE
MANOR PL	100	E 2 NW
MANSE ST	100	D 2 SE
MAORI RD	100	B 1 SE
MARDALE ST	100	B 1 SE
MARNE ST	100	F 4 SW
MARYHILL TCE	100	A 1 SE
MASON ST	100	F 1 NW
MAYFIELD AVE	100	A 1 SW
MCBRIDE ST	100	F 2 SE
MCCREA ST	100	E 1 NW
MCGEORGE AVE	100	A 4 NW
MCMILLAN ST	100	B 2 NE
MEADOW ST	100	A 3 SE
MELLOR ST	100	B 1 SW
MELROSE ST	100	A 1 SW
MELVILLE ST	100	E 2 NW
MERLIN ST	100	D 1 NW
MICHIE ST	100	D 1 NW
MIDLAND ST	100	C 4 SW
MINERVA ST	100	A 3 SE
MOAT ST	100	C 4 SW
MONRO ST	100	A 2 SW
MONTGOMERY AVE	100	A 3 SW
MONTPELLIER ST	100	E 1 NW
MORAY PL	100	C 3 SE
MOUNT ST	100	B 1 NW
MUNICIPAL LN (PVT)	100	C 3 NE
MURRAYFIELD ST	100	F 1 SW
NAIRN ST	100	B 1 SE
NEIDPATH RD	100	E 1 SW
NEVILLE ST	100	F 1 SE
NEWINGTON AVE	100	B 1 SW
NORTH RD	100	B 3 SE
OATES ST	100	C 1 NW
OBAN ST	100	B 2 SE
OPOHO LOOP RD	100	C 2 NE
OPOHO RD LOWER	100	C 2 NE
ORARI ST	100	F 3 NW
ORBELL ST	100	F 2 SE
OSBORNE TCE	100	E 1 SE
OTAKI ST	100	F 3 NW
PACIFIC ST	100	B 3 SW
PARK ST	100	C 1 SE
PARKHILL AVE	100	E 1 NE
PARKSIDE AVE	100	A 1 SW
PARRY ST	100	C 4 SW
PASSMORE CRES	100	A 3 SE
PATRICK ST	100	E 1 NW
PEEL ST	100	C 3 SE
PENNANT ST	100	B 1 NW
PERCY ST	100	F 2 SE
PHILLIPS ST	100	F 2 SE
PILKINGTON ST	100	A 4 NW
PINE HILL RD	100	A 4 NE
PIONEER CRES	100	A 1 NE
PITT ST	100	B 3 SE
POLICE ST	100	D 2 SE
POLLOCK ST	100	B 2 SE
PORTEOUS ST	100	E 1 NW
PORTOBELLO RD	100	F 4 SW
PORTSMOUTH DR	100	D 4 SW
PRESTON CRES	100	D 1 SE
PRESTWICK ST	100	A 2 SE
PRINCES ST	100	E 2 SE
PROSPECT BANK	100	B 3 NE
QUEEN ST	100	C 3 SE
QUEENS DR	100	D 1 SW
QUEENS GARDENS	100	D 3 SE
QUENTIN AVE	100	A 4 NE
RAMSAY ST	100	A 4 NE
RANKEILOR ST	100	F 2 SE

Location	Map No.	Ref
ATTRAY ST	100	D 3 SW
EGENT RD	100	B 3 NE
EYNOLDS ST	100	F 1 NW
IEGO ST	100	C 4 NE
OBERTS ST	100	E 3 NW
OSEBANK AVE	100	A 1 SW
OSS ST	100	C 1 SW
OYAL TCE	100	C 2 NE
USSELL ST	100	D 2 SW
T ANDREW ST	100	D 3 NE
T DAVID ST	100	B 4 SE
T HELIERS CT	100	F 1 SW
AMUEL ST	100	F 2 SW
ARGOOD ST	100	B 2 SW
CARBA ST	100	C 1 SE
CHOOL ST	100	C 3 NW
COTLAND ST	100	C 1 SE
ELKIRK ST	100	C 1 NE
ERPENTINE AVE	100	E 1 SE
HEEN ST	100	B 1 NW
HETLAND ST	100	F 4 SE
HORE ST	100	F 2 NE
IM ST	100	A 2 SE
LIGO TCE	100	C 1 SE
MALL ST	100	B 3 NE
MITH ST	100	D 2 NE
OUTH RD	100	F 1 SE
PYLAW ST	100	E 2 NW
TAFFORD ST	100	A 1 SE
TEEP ST	100	A 3 SW
TONELAW TCE	100	C 2 NE
TOUTGATE	100	C 3 NW
TRATHALLAN ST	100	F 3 NW
TRATHEARN AVE	100	A 1 SW
TRATHMORE CRES	100	A 1 SE
TUART ST	100	D 3 NW
TURDEE ST	100	D 4 NW
UTHERLAND ST	100	D 2 SW
AIERI RD	100	B 1 SW
ENNYSON ST	100	C 1 SE
EVIOT ST	100	F 4 SW
EWSLEY ST	100	D 3 SE
HE OCTAGON	100	D 3 NW
HOMAS BURNS ST	100	D 3 SE
IMARU ST	100	F 1 SW
ITAN ST	100	B 3 NE
OLCARNE AVE	100	C 4 NW
RENT AVE	100	F 3 SW
URAKINA RD	100	F 3 SE
WEED ST	100	C 2 NW
YNE ST	100	B 1 SE
NION PL (PVT)	100	B 4 SW
NION ST EAST	100	B 3 SE
NION ST WEST	100	B 3 SE
PLAND ST	100	A 1 NW
VICKERY PL	100	F 1 NW
VIEW PARK LN	100	B 3 SE
VIEW ST	100	C 4 SW
VIRE ST	100	C 4 SW
VOGEL ST	100	E 2 NE
WAIN ST	100	C 2 SW
WALBERTON TCE (PVT)	100	A 4 SE
WALES ST	100	C 2 NW
WALLACE ST	100	C 2 SW
WALSH LN (PVT)	100	A 2 NE
WALSH ST	100	C 3 NE
WALTER ST	100	F 1 NW
WALTON ST	100	B 1 SE
WARD ST	100	D 3 NE
WARRENDER ST	100	B 3 NE
WATER ST	100	D 3 SW
WAVERLEY ST	100	E 4 SE
WHARF ST	100	E 3 NE
WHITE ST	100	C 4 SE
WICKLIFFE ST	100	C 4 SE
WILKIE RD	100	F 2 SW
WILLIAM ST	100	E 1 NE
WILLIS ST	100	D 1 SE
WILLOWBANK	100	A 4 SW
WOLSELEY ST	100	A 3 NW
WOODHAUGH ST	100	A 3 NW
WRIGHT ST	100	B 1 SE
YORK PL	100	D 2 NW

District Roads

	Map No.	Ref
ALFS RD	80	C 7 NW
ALLANS BEACH RD	80	D 7 SE
ALLANTON RD	79	E 3 NW
APES RD	80	A 7 NW
BACK RD	79	E 2 NW
BEACH ST	80	C 7 NW
BEEHIVE RD	79	E 2 NE
BERWICK RD	79	E 2 SW
BIG STONE RD	79	F 3 NW
BLUCHER RD	80	A 5 NE
BLUESKIN RD	80	C 7 NW
BRAIDWOOD RD	80	E 7 NW
BREMNERS RD	79	E 2 SE
BRIGHTON RD	79	F 4 NW
BRIGHTON - SCROGGS HILL RD	79	E 3 SE
BRUCE RD	79	E 2 SE
BULL CREEK RD	79	F 1 SE
BUSH RD	79	E 3 NE
CAMP ST	80	D 7 NW
CAPE SAUNDERS RD	80	D 8 SW
CENTRE RD		
(HENLEY)	79	F 2 NE
(HIGHCLIFF)	80	D 7 SE
CHALMERSTON RD	80	D 5 SW
CHRISTIES GULLY RD	79	F 2 SE
CHURCH RD	80	A 6 SE
CHURCH RD EAST	79	E 2 SE
CHURCH RD WEST	79	D 2 SE
CLARENDON - BERWICK RD	79	F 1 SW
CLARK RD	80	C 6 NW
COAST RD	80	A 7 SW
CRAIGLEA RD	79	D 3 NW
CROSSFELL ST	79	D 2 SW
CURRIE RD	79	E 2 NW
DAWSON RD	80	D 6 NW
DEANS VALLEY RD	80	C 6 NE
DICK RD	80	D 8 NW
DOCTORS POINT RD	80	C 6 NW
DONALDS HILL RD	80	C 6 NW
DOUBLE HILL RD	80	B 6 SW
DOW RD	79	E 2 NE
DRIVER ST	80	C 7 NW
DUKES RD NORTH	79	D 4 NW
DUKES RD SOUTH	79	E 3 NE
EAST BOUNDARY RD	79	F 1 NE
EVANSDALE GLEN RD	80	B 6 NE
FARM RD EAST	79	F 2 NW
FARM RD WEST	79	F 2 NW
FLAGSTAFF - WHARE FLAT RD	80	D 5 NE
FORMBY ST	80	D 7 SE
FRIENDS HILL RD	79	E 2 NE
GEORGE KING MEMORIAL DR	79	D 3 NW
GLADFIELD RD	79	E 3 NE
GORDON RD	79	D 4 SW
GRAINGER RD	79	E 2 NE
GRANTON RD	79	E 2 NE
GREEN RD	80	C 6 SE
HALFWAY BUSH RD	80	D 5 SW
HAMILTON BAY RD	80	C 7 SE
HARINGTON PT RD	80	D 7 NE
HARWOOD ST	80	D 7 NE
HAZLETT RD	79	D 4 SW
HEENAN RD	79	E 1 SE
HELVELLYN ST	79	D 2 SW
HENLEY BERWICK RD	79	F 1 NE
HENLEY RD	79	F 2 SW
HEYWARD POINT RD	80	C 7 SE
HICKEYS RD	79	E 2 SE
HIGHCLIFF RD	80	E 6 NE
HIGHLAND RD	79	F 3 NE
HOLLAND RD (PVT)	79	D 1 NE
HOOPERS INLET RD	80	E 7 SE
HUNTLY RD	79	D 2 NE
ILFORD RD	79	D 2 NE
JAFFRAY RD	79	E 4 NW
JEFFCOATES RD	79	E 4 SE
JONES RD	80	A 7 SW
KAIMATA RD	80	D 8 SW
KARETAI RD	80	E 6 NW
KEMPSHALL RD	80	E 2 NW
KILGOUR ST	80	A 7 SW
KILMOG CREEK RD	80	B 6 NW
KILPATRICK RD	80	C 6 NE
KING ST	80	B 6 SE
KIRKS DRAIN RD	79	F 2 NW
KOEFORDS RD	79	E 1 SW
LAMB HILL RD	80	A 5 NW
LAW RD	79	E 3 SE
LAWSON RD	80	A 6 SW
LEE CANAL RD	79	E 2 SW
LEE CREEK RD	79	E 2 NE
LEITH VALLEY RD	80	C 6 SW
LEWIS ST	80	C 7 NW
LOAN METAL RD	79	E 2 NE
LONGRIDGE RD	80	D 5 NW
MANN RD	79	D 2 NE
MANSE RD	80	B 6 SE
MAORI KAIK RD	79	F 2 NE
MAORI RESERVE RD	79	F 2 SE
MARKS RD	80	A 7 NW
MARSHALL RD EAST	79	F 2 NW
MARSHALL RD WEST	79	F 2 NW
MAUNGATUA RD	79	E 2 SW
MCDONALD RD	79	D 2 SW
MCINTOSH RD	79	E 3 SE
MCKAY RD	80	D 8 SW
MCKENDRY RD	79	D 2 SW
MCLACHLAN RD	80	A 7 NE
MCLAREN GULLY RD	79	F 2 NE
MCLAREN RD	79	E 1 SE
MCLEOD RD	79	E 2 SE
MCMEEKING RD	80	E 6 SE
MIHIWAKA STATION RD	80	C 7 NW
MILL RD	79	D 2 SW
MILLER RD		
(MOMONA)	79	E 2 SE
(WAITATI)	80	C 6 NW
MILNERS ST	79	D 4 SE
MOORE RD	80	A 7 NW
MOPANUI RD	80	C 7 NW
MOPANUI ST	80	C 7 NW
MT CARGILL RD	80	C 6 SE
MOUNTAIN RD	80	B 6 SW
MUNRO RD	79	E 1 SE
MURDERING BEACH RD	80	C 7 NE
NICHOLS RD	79	E 3 NW
O'CONNELL ST	80	C 6 SE
O'CONNOR RD	79	F 1 NE
OLD BRIGHTON RD	79	E 4 SW
OTAKOU GOLF COURSE RD	80	C 8 SW
OTOKIA - KURI BUSH RD	79	F 2 SE
OTOKIA - KURI BUSH RD WEST	79	F 2 SE
OTOKIA RD EAST	79	E 2 SE
OTOKIA RD WEST	79	E 2 SW
OTOKIA STATION RD	79	F 2 NE
PALMER RD	80	A 7 SW
PAPANUI INLET RD	80	D 7 SE
PIGEON FLAT RD	80	C 6 SW
PIPIKARETU RD (PVT)	80	C 8 SW
POPLAR RD EAST	79	F 2 NW
POPLAR RD WEST	79	F 2 NW
PORTEOUS RD	80	B 6 NE
PRENTICE RD	79	F 1 NW
PRYDE RD	80	A 6 SE
PUDDLE ALLEY	79	D 4 SE
PULLAR RD	80	A 6 SE
PURAKANUI RD	80	C 7 NW
QUEEN ST	80	B 6 SE
RAVENSBURN ST	79	D 2 SW
REID RD	79	D 2 SE
RESERVOIR RD	80	B 7 NE
RIDGE RD	80	E 7 NE
RIVERBANK RD NORTH	79	F 2 SW
RIVERBANK RD SOUTH	79	F 2 SW
RIVERSIDE RD	79	E 3 NE
ROLLINSONS RD	80	D 5 NW
ROUND HILL RD	80	A 7 NW
RUSSELL RD NTH	80	A 6 NE
RUSSELL RD STH	80	A 7 NW
SADDLE HILL RD	79	E 4 SW
SANDYMOUNT RD	80	D 7 SE
SAUNDERS RD	79	D 4 SW
SCHOOL RD NTH	79	D 4 NW
SCHOOL RD SOUTH	79	D 3 SE
SCROGGS HILL RD	79	E 3 SE
SCURR RD	79	E 4 SW
SEAL POINT RD	80	E 7 NE
SEMPLE RD	79	E 4 SW
SHAW RD	79	F 1 NW
SHEPPARD RD	80	D 7 SE
SHORTCUT RD	80	C 6 NE
SILVERSTREAM VALLEY RD	79	D 4 NE
SINCLAIR RD	79	D 4 NW
SOUTHDALE RD	80	E 6 NE
SPROULL DR	79	E 3 SE
STEEP HILL RD	80	A 6 SW
TAIERI VIEW RD	79	D 3 NE
TAIOMA RD	79	D 3 NE
TAKITAKITOA RD	79	F 2 SE
TAREWAI RD	80	C 8 SW
TAURIMA RD	79	E 2 SE
THORNICROFT RD	80	B 6 SE
THREE MILE HILL RD	79	D 4 SE
TIDEWATER DR	80	D 7 NE
TIROHANGA RD	79	D 3 SE
TREE RD	79	E 2 NW
TWELVETREES RD	79	E 1 SE
WAIPORI FALLS RD	79	F 1 NW
WAIRONGOA RD	79	D 4 SW
WAITATI VALLEY RD	80	C 6 SW
WEATHERSTONE RD	80	C 6 NE
WEIR RD	80	D 7 NE
WHITE RD	80	B 7 SW
WHITES RD	80	A 6 SE
WILSON RD	80	B 6 NE
WOODSIDE RD	79	D 2 SW
WOOLSHED RD	79	D 2 NE
WRIGHT RD	80	B 6 NW

Gisborne Central

	Map No.	Ref
ABERDEEN RD	87	D 3 NE
ANZAC CT	87	E 2 NE
ANZAC ST	87	E 2 NW
ATTLEE PL	87	D 3 SE
AWAPUNI RD	87	E 2 SW
BANKS ST	87	E 1 NW
BAYLY ST	87	D 2 NW
BEACON ST	87	E 2 SW
BERRY ST	87	D 3 SE
BLACKPOOL ST	87	D 1 SW
BRIGHT ST	87	E 3 SE
CARNARVON ST	87	E 3 SW
CENTENNIAL CRES	87	D 1 SE
CENTENNIAL MARINE DR	87	F 1 NW
CENTRAL ST	87	D 4 NE
CHEESEMAN RD	87	D 2 NW
CHILDERS RD	87	E 3 SE
CLIFFORD ST	87	E 3 NW
COBDEN ST	87	E 3 NW
COLEMAN RD	87	D 1 NE
COLLINS ST	87	D 1 NE
CRAWFORD RD	87	F 4 NE
CUSTOMHOUSE ST	87	F 3 NE
DERBY ST	87	E 3 NW
DESMOND RD	87	D 2 NW
DISRAELI ST	87	D 4 SE
DOMETT ST	87	D 2 SE
DOMINION RD	87	E 3 NW
EDEN LN	87	D 3 SW
ENDEAVOUR ST	87	F 4 NW
ESPLANADE	87	F 4 NW
FITZHERBERT ST	87	E 4 NW
FOSTER ST	87	D 1 NE
FOX ST	87	F 3 NE
GLADSTONE RD	87	D 3 SW
GREY ST	87	E 3 SW
HALL ST	87	D 4 NW
HARDY LN	87	E 4 NE
HARRIS ST	87	F 4 NE
HICKS ST	87	E 1 NW
HIRINI ST	87	F 4 NE
HUNTER ST	87	D 2 NW
INNES ST	87	D 1 SW
KAHUTIA ST	87	E 3 NW
LEITH ST	87	D 3 NW
LOWE ST	87	E 3 SE
LYNDHURST ST	87	D 1 SE
MACLEAN ST	87	D 4 SW
MATAI ST	87	E 2 NW
NGAIO ST	87	E 1 NE
NORMAN RD	87	D 3 NW
NORTHCOTE RD	87	D 3 NW
ORMOND RD	87	D 4 NW
PALMERSTON RD	87	D 4 NW
PARAU ST	87	F 4 SE
PEEL ST	87	E 3 SE
PITT ST	87	E 4 SW
QUEENS DR	87	F 4 SW
RAILWAY RESERVE RD	87	D 2 NW
RANFURLY ST	87	F 4 SE
RAWIRI ST	87	E 4 SE
READS QUAY	87	E 4 SW
RICHARDSON AVE	87	D 4 NE
ROBERTS ST	87	E 2 SE
ROEBUCK RD	87	D 2 NW
ROOT ST	87	D 3 NW
RUSSELL ST	87	E 4 NW
RUTENE RD	87	E 3 NW
SALISBURY RD	87	E 2 SW
SCHOOL RD	87	D 1 NW
SHEEHAN ST	87	D 3 NE
SOLANDER ST	87	E 1 NW
STAFFORD ST	87	E 1 NE
STANLEY RD	87	E 1 NE
STEVENSON LN	87	E 4 NE
STOUT ST	87	D 2 NW
TEMPLE ST	87	D 3 NE
THOMSON ST	87	D 3 NE
TOTARA ST	87	D 1 NE
TOWNLEY ST	87	D 1 NE
VOGEL ST	87	F 4 NE
WAINUI RD	87	F 4 NE
WAITANGI RD	87	E 2 NW
WHITAKER ST	87	E 3 SW
WHITMORE ST	87	E 4 NW
WILLIAMS ST	87	D 3 NW

Greymouth Central

	Map No.	Ref
ACHILLES ST	96	B 1 SE
AERODROME RD	96	C 1 SE
ALBERT ST	96	B 3 NE
ALEXANDER ST	96	B 3 NE
ALEXANDER TCE	96	B 4 NW
ARNEY ST	96	A 3 SW
ASHTON LN	96	A 3 SW
BADGER LN	96	A 3 SE
BLACKMORE ST	96	A 2 SW
BLAKE ST	96	A 2 SW
BOUNDARY ST	96	B 3 SW
BRUNNER ST	96	B 3 SW
BUCCLEUGH ST	96	C 2 SE
CHAPEL ST	96	B 3 NE
COAKLEY ST	96	A 2 NW
COLLINS ST	96	A 2 NW
CONVENT LN	96	B 3 NE
COOK TCE	96	C 3 NE
COWPER ST	96	A 4 SW
CUSTOM ST	96	C 3 NW
DEVON ST	96	B 1 NE
DOYLE ST	96	B 1 SE
ELMER LN	96	B 3 NE
FLOWER ST	96	B 1 SE
FRANKLIN ST	96	C 3 NW
FREDERICK ST	96	B 3 NW
FREYBERG TCE	96	C 3 NW
FRICKLETON ST	96	A 2 SE
GILBERT ST	96	A 2 SE
GRESSON ST	96	B 3 NE
GROGAN LN	96	A 3 SE
GUINNESS ST	96	B 3 NE
HEAPHY ST	96	B 3 NW
HERBERT ST	96	B 3 NW
HIGH ST	96	C 2 SW
HINCHY LN	96	C 3 NE
JOHNSTON ST	96	B 3 NE
KILGOUR RD	96	C 3 SW
LEONARD ST	96	B 3 NE
LOMBARD ST	96	B 3 NE
LORD ST	96	C 3 SW
LYDIA ST	96	A 3 SE
MACKAY ST	96	B 3 NE
MARLBOROUGH ST	96	C 2 SW
MAWHERA QUAY	96	A 3 SE
MERRICK ST	96	C 1 NE
MORICE ST	96	B 3 NW
MOUNT ST	96	B 4 NW
MURRAY ST	96	B 3 SE
NELSON QUAY	96	A 3 NE
NGARIMU ST	96	A 3 SE
NIKAU VALLEY RD (PVT)	96	B 3 SE
O'DONNELL ST	96	A 2 SW
O'GRADY ST	96	A 4 SW
OMOTO RD	96	A 4 SW
PACKERS QUAY	96	C 2 SE
PALMERSTON ST	96	C 2 SE
PEROTTI ST	96	C 3 NW
PRESTON RD	96	B 3 NE
PUKETAHI ST	96	B 3 NE
RALEIGH ST	96	C 2 NW
REID ST	96	C 1 NE
RICHMOND QUAY	96	A 2 SW
RIGG ST	96	B 1 NE
ROBINSON ST	96	B 3 SE
ROCHFORT ST	96	C 3 NE
RUSSELL TCE	96	B 2 NW
RYAN ST	96	B 3 SE
SCHOOL LN	96	C 2 SW
SHAKESPEARE ST	96	A 2 SE
SHORT ST	96	A 4 SW
SMITH ST	96	B 3 SE
SPRING ST	96	A 3 SE
STAFFORD ST	96	B 2 NW
STEER AVE	96	A 2 SE
SWAINSON ST	96	B 1 SE
SWIFT ST	96	B 3 SE
TAINUI ST	96	A 3 SE
TARAPUHI ST	96	A 3 NE
TAYLOR ST	96	B 3 SW
THOMPSON ST	96	B 3 SE
THREADNEEDLE ST	96	C 3 NW
TINDALE ST	96	B 3 SW
TURUMAHA ST	96	A 3 SE
WAITE ST	96	C 1 SE
WATER WALK RD	96	A 4 NW
WELD ST	96	A 3 SE
WERITA ST	96	A 3 SE
WHALL ST	96	B 3 NW
WILLIAM ST	96	B 3 NE
WILLIS ST	96	B 3 NE
WILSON LN	96	B 3 NE
WINNIE ST	96	C 3 SW

Hamilton

Hamilton Central

	Map No.	Ref
ABBOTSFORD ST	84	B 2 NE
AIRDRIE LN (PVT)	84	A 2 NW
ALEXANDRA ST	84	C 3 SE
ALFRED ST	84	A 4 NW
ALISON ST	84	E 2 SE
ALLEN ST	84	D 1 NW
ALLENBY ST	84	E 4 SE
ALMA ST	84	C 3 NE
AMBER LN (PVT)	84	C 3 SE
ANGLESEA ST	84	F 4 SE
ANSFORD PL	84	F 4 SE
ANSON AVE	84	F 4 SE
ANTHONY CRES	84	B 2 SW
AVON ST	84	A 2 NW
AWATERE AVE	84	E 1 SE
AZTEC PL	84	F 4 NE
BADER ST	84	A 3 NW
BALLOCH ST	84	A 3 NE
BANBURY CRES	84	A 2 NE
BANDON ST	84	D 1 NW
BARTON ST	84	C 4 SE
BEALE ST	84	F 3 NE
BEATTY ST	84	D 2 SW
BELFAST PL	84	A 3 SE
BETTINA RD	84	D 1 SW
BLACKBURN ST	84	E 4 NE
BLEDISLOE TCE	84	A 1 SW
BOLLARD ST	84	B 1 NE
BOLMUIR ST	84	A 1 NE
BOUNDARY RD	84	D 4 NW
BRIDGE ST	84	B 4 SE
BROOKLYN RD	84	B 2 SW
BRYCE LN (PVT)	84	C 4 NE
BRYCE ST	84	E 2 SE
CAMELLIA PL	84	A 2 SW
CARDRONA RD	84	A 2 SW

Hamilton Central - Hamilton District Roads

Location	Map No.	Ref	
CAREY ST	84	A 1	SW
CARO ST	84	C 3	SE
CASEY AVE	84	A 3	SW
CHARLEMONT ST	84	A 2	SW
CHRISTIE ST	84	A 1	NW
CHURCHILL AVE	84	B 1	NE
CLARENCE ST	84	D 3	NE
CLAUDE ST	84	A 4	SW
CLAUDELANDS RD	84	C 3	NE
CLEVELAND ST	84	F 4	SE
CLIFTON ST	84	B 3	NW
CLOW PL	84	F 2	NW
COBHAM DR	84	E 4	SE
COLLINGWOOD LN	84	C 3	SE
COLLINGWOOD ST	84	C 3	SE
COLOMBO ST	84	C 1	SE
COMMERCE ST	84	C 2	SE
CORRIN ST	84	F 3	SW
CRESCENT CT	84	F 3	NE
DARLEY ST	84	A 1	SE
DAVEY PL	84	A 4	NW
DAWSON ST	84	C 4	NE
DENZ ST	84	B 1	NE
DERMONT ST	84	F 4	SE
DEVON RD	84	C 2	NE
DILLICAR ST	84	A 2	SE
DILLON PL (PVT)	84	A 4	SE
DOMAIN DR	84	D 2	NE
DOMAIN VIEW LN (PVT)	84	D 2	NE
DOWDING ST	84	F 4	NW
DRYDEN RD	84	A 4	SE
DUDLEY TCE	84	B 1	SE
DUKE ST	84	E 1	NW
DUNSFORD MEWS (PVT)	84	D 4	NW
DYER ST	84	A 2	SE
EAST ST	84	B 4	NE
EDGAR ST	84	C 1	SW
EDGECUMBE ST	84	B 2	NW
ELLIS ST	84	C 1	NE
EMPIRE ST	84	C 1	SE
FAIRFIELD RD	84	A 2	NE
FERGUSSON ST	84	A 4	NE
FILMER PL	84	F 2	SE
FOREST LAKE RD	84	A 1	SW
FOW ST	84	D 3	SE
FOWLERS AVE	84	A 3	NW
FRASER ST	84	D 2	NW
FRENCH ST	84	D 2	NW
GALLAGHER DR	84	F 2	NW
GALWAY AVE	84	D 4	SE
GEORGE ST	84	B 4	NW
GILBASS AVE	84	E 2	SE
GILLIES AVE	84	B 4	NE
GOLDSMITH ST	84	B 1	SE
GRANTHAM ST	84	C 4	SW
GRASSLANDS PL	84	E 1	SW
GREEN ST	84	E 1	SW
GREENWOOD ST	84	C 1	NE
GREY ST	84	C 4	NE
GWYNNE PL	84	B 3	NW
HAIG ST	84	C 1	NE
HALL LN	84	C 2	NW
HALL ST	84	C 1	SE
HAMILTON PARADE	84	B 3	SE
HAMMOND ST	84	D 4	SW
HARDLEY ST	84	B 3	NW
HARWOOD ST	84	B 3	SW
HASTINGS PL	84	E 2	SW
HAWK ST	84	C 1	SW
HEAPHY TCE	84	A 3	NE
HEATHER PL	84	F 3	SE
HIBISCUS AVE	84	E 2	SE
HIGGINS RD	84	E 1	NW
HIGH ST	84	C 1	SE
HILL ST	84	C 3	SW
HILLSBOROUGH TCE	84	D 4	SE
HINAU ST	84	B 1	NW
HINTON AVE	84	A 1	NW
HOBSON ST	84	A 1	NE
HOLDEN AVE	84	A 4	NE
HOLLAND RD	84	A 3	NE
HOOD ST	84	C 1	SW
HORNE ST	84	E 3	SE
HOWDEN RD	84	A 3	NE
HUNTER ST	84	D 3	NE
INGLETON TCE	84	D 1	SW
IRVINE ST	84	C 2	SW
ISLINGTON ST	84	C 2	SW
JELLICOE DR	84	E 4	NE
JOFFRE ST	84	D 2	NW
JOLLY ST	84	C 1	NE
JONES CRES	84	F 4	NW
KAHIKATEA DR	84	E 1	SE
KEDDELL ST	84	C 2	SW
KELLS PL	84	E 1	SE
KENT ST	84	C 1	NE
KERERU ST	84	D 1	SW
KILLARNEY RD	84	C 2	SW
KING ST	84	C 1	NE
KITCHENER ST	84	B 4	NW
KNOX ST	84	C 4	SW
KOTAHI AVE (PVT)	84	A 1	SW
KOTUKU ST	84	C 1	SW
KOWHAI ST	84	E 2	SE
LAFFERTY ST	84	B 1	NW
LAKE CRES	84	E 2	NE
LAKE RD	84	C 2	NE
LANCEWOOD AVE	84	F 2	SE
LANGDON LN (PVT)	84	F 2	NE
LATHAM CT	84	F 1	NE
LEE PL	84	F 4	NE
LEMON ST	84	C 1	NE
LINCOLN ST	84	C 1	NW
LITTLE LONDON LN (PVT)	84	B 3	SE
LIVERPOOL ST	84	B 4	SE
LONDON ST	84	C 3	NW
LORNE ST	84	F 3	SE
MACDIARMID RD	84	A 1	NE
MACFARLANE ST	84	D 4	SE
MAEROA RD	84	B 1	NE
MAHOE ST	84	F 3	SW
MAKOMAKO ST	84	D 1	SW
MANNING ST	84	D 4	SW
MARAMA ST	84	C 1	SE
MARIRE AVE	84	B 2	SE
MARLBOROUGH PL	84	C 4	SW

Location	Map No.	Ref	
MARNE ST	84	A 3	SE
MARSHALL ST	84	A 3	NE
MARY ST	84	D 2	SW
MASONS AVE	84	B 4	SE
MASSEY ST	84	C 1	SW
MATAI ST	84	B 1	NW
MEMORIAL DR	84	C 4	NW
MENZIES ST	84	A 1	NW
MILL LN	84	B 2	NE
MILL ST	84	B 1	NW
MIRO ST	84	C 1	NW
MOANA ST	84	C 1	NW
MONCRIEFF AVE	84	A 3	SE
MONTGOMERY CRES	84	F 4	SW
MOULE PL	84	A 3	NW
MOUNT VIEW RD	84	F 3	SE
MURRAY ST	84	A 1	SE
MYRTLE ST	84	B 4	SW
NEW ST	84	E 1	SW
NEWTON PL	84	C 3	SW
NISBET ST	84	C 3	SW
NORMANDY AVE	84	A 3	SE
NORTON RD	84	C 2	NW
O'NEILL ST	84	B 4	NW
OAKLEY AVE	84	B 3	NE
ODETTE ST	84	F 4	SE
OHAUPO RD	84	C 1	SW
OPOIA RD	84	C 4	NW
OXFORD ST	84	A 3	NE
PALMER ST	84	B 4	SE
PALMERSTON ST	84	D 3	SE
PARK TCE	84	E 4	NW
PARR ST	84	A 3	SE
PEACHGROVE RD	84	A 4	SW
PEARSONS AVE	84	E 3	SW
PEMBROKE ST	84	E 3	SE
PERRY PL	84	F 4	NE
PIAKO RD	84	B 4	NW
PINE AVE	84	E 4	NW
PLUNKET TCE	84	E 4	NW
PRIMROSE ST	84	D 1	NW
PRINCES ST	84	B 3	SW
QUEENS AVE	84	D 2	NW
QUENTIN DR	84	F 2	NW
RADNOR ST	84	D 4	NW
RAMSAY ST	84	D 1	SW
RANFURLY AVE	84	A 3	NW
RAWHITI ST	84	C 2	SW
RAWLINGS ST	84	F 4	SE
RICHARDSON RD	84	F 3	SW
RICHMOND ST	84	B 2	NW
RIDOUT ST	84	A 1	SW
RIMMINGTON RD	84	E 2	NW
RIMU ST	84	B 1	NW
RIRO ST	84	C 4	NW
RIVER RD	84	A 2	NE
RIVERVIEW TCE	84	A 2	SW
ROACH ST	84	B 1	SE
ROSE ST	84	A 1	SE
ROSTREVOR ST	84	C 2	NE
ROTHBROOK ST	84	C 4	NW
RUA ST	84	B 1	SW
RUAKIWI RD	84	D 3	NW
ST CLAIR CT (PVT)	84	A 4	SE
ST LUKES PL	84	F 4	SW
SALE ST	84	A 3	SE
SANDLEIGH RD	84	E 3	SW
SAYER ST	84	D 1	SW
SEDDON ST	84	D 1	SW
SELWYN ST	84	B 2	SW
SILKWOOD LN (PVT)	84	F 2	NE
SLIM ST	84	F 2	SE
SLOPER AVE	84	C 2	NW
SMITH ST	84	D 1	NW
SOMERSET ST	84	C 2	SE
SOUTHEY WAY	84	A 4	NE
STANLEY ST	84	B 3	NE
STEELE RD	84	B 1	NE
STEWART PL	84	F 4	SW
STOKES CRES	84	B 1	NE
STOREY AVE	84	A 1	SW
TAHI ST	84	C 3	SW
TAINUI ST	84	C 3	SW
TAKAHE ST	84	C 1	SW
TAMIHANA AVE	84	A 3	SW
TAWA ST	84	F 2	SW
TE AROHA ST	84	A 4	SW
TEDDY ST	84	A 2	SE
THACKERAY ST	84	D 3	NE
THAMES ST	84	C 3	NE
THORBURN CT (PVT)	84	F 4	NW
TIDD ST	84	B 1	NE
TISDALL ST	84	D 4	NW
TISDALL TCE	84	D 4	NW
TORRINGTON AVE	84	C 2	NW
TORU ST	84	B 1	SW
TRELOAR ST	84	A 3	SE
TRIGG PL	84	F 4	NE
TRISTRAM ST	84	C 3	NW
ULSTER ST	84	B 2	NW
UNION ST	84	B 3	NE
UPPER KENT ST	84	C 1	NE
VALLEY TCE	84	E 4	NW
VEREL ST	84	A 3	NE
VIALOU ST	84	B 2	SE
VICTORIA ST	84	B 2	SE
VIVIAN ST	84	F 3	SW
VON TEMPSKY ST	84	C 4	SE
WALTER ST	84	A 4	NW
WARD LN	84	C 3	NE
WARD ST	84	C 3	NE
WATERLOO ST	84	A 1	SE
WEKA ST	84	C 1	SW
WEST ST	84	A 1	SW
WESTNEY PL	84	A 1	SW
WHA ST	84	B 1	SW
WHYTE ST	84	B 4	SE
WICKHAM ST	84	F 4	NE
WILLIS ST	84	F 4	NE
WILLOUGHBY ST	84	F 4	NE
WINDLEBORNE LN (PVT)	84	F 3	NW
WINDSOR RD	84	A 3	NE
WINTER ST	84	A 3	NE
WOODSTOCK RD	84	A 2	NE
WOODWARD ST	84	E 1	SW
WORLEY PL	84	C 3	NE

Location	Map No.	Ref	
WYE ST	84	B 2	SW
YEATS CRES	84	A 4	NW
YOUNG ST	84	B 4	NE

District Roads

Location	Map No.	Ref	
ACACIA GR	67	D 3	NW
AIRPORT RD	67	D 2	SE
AKATARERE RD	67	F 4	SE
ALCOCK RD	67	E 1	NE
ALEXANDER RD	67	F 1	NE
ALLEN RD			
(KIHIKIHI)	67	F 3	SW
(MORRINSVILLE)	67	B 4	NE
AMBER LN			
(KARAPIRO)	67	E 4	SW
(PUKETAHA)	67	C 3	NW
ANDERSON RD	67	D 3	SW
ANGUS RD	67	D 3	SW
ANZAC ST	67	B 1	SE
APPLEBY RD	67	D 4	SW
ARAPUNI RD	67	F 3	SW
ARTHUR RD	67	E 1	NW
ASPIN RD	67	D 4	NW
AWA RD	67	A 4	NE
BADGER CL	67	C 3	SW
BAKER RD	67	D 4	SE
BALLARD RD	67	B 2	SE
BANK RD	67	E 2	SE
BANKIER RD	67	B 2	SW
BANKS RD	67	D 3	SE
BARRETT RD	67	D 1	NE
BAVERSTOCK RD	67	C 2	SW
BEDFORD RD	67	C 1	NW
BEER RD	67	D 3	SE
BELL RD			
(KIWITAHI)	67	C 4	NE
(TE RORE)	67	E 4	SW
(WHATAWHATA)	67	D 1	NW
BELLEVUE RD	67	D 3	NE
BENN RD	67	E 4	NW
BERKERS RD	67	C 1	NE
BERN RD	67	C 1	NE
BERQUIST RD	67	D 3	SW
BERRYMANS ACCESS RD (PVT)	67	A 1	NW
BIRD RD	67	C 1	SW
BLACKETT RD	67	C 1	SW
BLUE HERON PL	67	D 3	SW
BOLLARD RD (PVT)	67	D 3	NW
BOLTON RD	67	B 4	SE
BOND RD	67	F 2	NE
BORMAN RD	67	C 2	NE
BOWE RD	67	E 1	NW
BOWMAN RD			
(MANGAPIKO)	67	E 2	SW
(WHATAWHATA)	67	D 1	NE
BOYD RD			
(HORSHAM DOWNS)	67	B 2	SE
(RUKUHIA)	67	D 2	NE
BRILL RD	67	F 2	SW
BRINKWORTH RD	67	D 3	NW
BROTHERHOOD RD	67	F 3	SW
BROWN RD	67	C 1	SW
BRUCE RD	67	F 2	NE
BRUNSKILL RD	67	D 4	NE
BRUNTWOOD RD	67	D 3	NW
BRYMER RD	67	C 2	SW
BUDDEN RD	67	F 2	NW
BUNYARD RD	67	C 1	SE
BURBUSH RD	67	C 1	NE
BURNS RD	67	F 2	NW
BUTCHER RD	67	C 3	SW
BUTLER RD	67	F 1	NE
CAMBRIDGE RD	67	E 3	SE
CAMERON RD	67	A 4	SW
CANDY RD	67	F 1	NE
CANNON RD	67	C 1	SW
CASEY RD	67	C 1	SW
CATE RD	67	C 2	NW
CATLEY RD	67	A 2	SW
CEMETERY RD	67	C 1	SE
CHAMBERLAIN RD	67	F 3	NW
CHEPMELL RD	67	C 4	SE
CHITTY RD	67	C 3	SE
CHRISTIE RD	67	C 1	SW
CHURCH RD	67	D 3	NE
CLARK RD	67	D 1	NW
CLOTHIER RD	67	E 1	NE
CLOVERFIELD LN	67	B 2	SW
COCHRANE RD	67	E 1	NE
COLLEGE DR	67	C 1	SW
COLLIE RD	67	C 1	SW
COLLINS RD	67	D 2	SW
COMINS RD	67	A 1	NW
CORCORAN RD	67	E 1	NW
COUCH RD	67	C 1	SW
COULTER RD	67	F 3	NW
COWAN RD	67	F 3	NE
COX RD	67	E 3	SE
CRAIG RD	67	C 3	SW
CRAWFORD RD	67	C 1	NE
CROSS RD	67	B 4	NW
CRUICKSHANK RD	67	E 3	NW
DAVENPORT RD	67	E 3	NW
DAVIES RD	67	A 3	NW
DAVIS RD	67	A 3	NW
DAVISON RD	67	C 2	SE
DAWSON RD	67	B 2	NW
DAY RD			
(KAIPAKI)	67	D 3	SW
(MANGAPIKO)	67	D 3	NW
DEVINE RD	67	D 3	NW
DILLON RD	67	F 4	NW
DINGLE RD	67	E 2	NE
DISCOMBE RD	67	D 3	SE
DIVERS RD	67	C 1	NE
DODD RD	67	C 4	NW
DOUCH RD	67	E 2	NE
DRIVER RD	67	B 1	SE
DRIVER RD WEST	67	B 1	SE
DUCK RD	67	B 4	SE
DUNCAN RD	67	D 3	SW
DUNNING RD	67	E 4	NE
DUVAL WAY	67	F 3	NE
ELGOOD RD	67	B 1	SW
ELLICOTT RD	67	F 3	SE
ELMWOOD LN (PVT)	67	D 2	NE
ERIC LN	67	D 1	SE

Location	Map No.	Ref	
EUREKA RD	67	C 3	
EVANS RD	67	A 1	N
EXELBY RD	67	D 1	N
EYRE RD	67	D 1	N
FENCOURT RD	67	D 4	N
FERGUSON RD	67	D 1	N
FERGUSSON GULLY RD	67	E 4	S
FINLAYSON RD	67	D 1	S
FISHER RD	67	A 1	N
FLAXMILL RD	67	A 3	N
FLETCHER RD	67	D 1	N
FLUME RD	67	D 4	N
FORKERT RD	67	E 2	N
FORREST RD	67	D 3	S
FOX RD	67	B 1	N
FRENCH PASS RD	67	D 4	S
FRIEDLANDER RD	67	C 3	N
FRONTIER RD	67	F 2	N
FROST RD	67	A 1	N
FUCHSIA LN	67	D 3	N
FULLERTON RD	67	C 1	S
GARFIELD ST	67	B 2	S
GENEVIEVE WAY	67	D 1	N
GIBBON RD	67	B 4	S
GILLARD RD	67	D 1	S
GILMORE RD	67	D 1	S
GLASSON RD	67	F 3	N
GODFREY RD	67	E 1	N
GOILE RD	67	D 1	N
GOLF RD	67	F 2	N
GOOD ST	67	D 3	N
GOODWIN RD	67	E 3	N
GORDONTON RD	67	C 2	N
GORTON RD	67	E 4	N
GOWER RD	67	B 2	N
GRAHAM RD	67	C 2	N
GRANTHAM LN (PVT)	67	C 2	N
GRAY RD	67	D 4	N
GRAYDEN RD	67	B 4	N
GREENHILL RD	67	C 2	N
GREY RD	67	E 1	S
GRICE RD	67	E 3	S
GRIGGS RD	67	F 4	N
GROVE ACCESS RD	67	D 1	S
GROVE RD	67	E 1	N
GUDEX RD	67	D 4	S
HAIRINI RD	67	F 3	N
HAKARIMATA RD	67	B 1	N
HALL RD	67	D 2	N
HAMS RD	67	B 4	N
HANGAWERA RD	67	B 4	N
HANLIN RD	67	D 3	S
HANNING RD	67	F 1	N
HANNON RD	67	D 3	S
HAPUAKOHE TRK	67	A 3	N
HARBOTTLE RD	67	C 4	N
HARBUTT RD	67	D 4	N
HARRIS RD	67	F 2	N
HARTSTONE RD	67	C 1	N
HAUMIA RD	67	A 4	S
HAUTAPU RD	67	D 3	S
HAWKSGRIP RD	67	C 1	N
HAWTHORNE RD	67	C 4	N
HAYNES RD	67	C 4	N
HEAD RD	67	E 4	S
HEDDON RD	67	D 1	N
HENDERSON RD	67	B 2	S
HENRY RD	67	D 1	N
HERBERT RD	67	A 4	S
HEREFORD DR	67	C 2	N
HERMAN RD	67	D 2	S
HETHERINGTON RD	67	E 4	S
HEWSON RD	67	E 4	S
HICKEY RD	67	E 4	S
HICKS RD	67	E 1	N
HIGGINSON RD	67	D 1	N
HIGHAM RD	67	F 3	S
HIGHBROOK WAY	67	D 1	N
HILLSIDE HEIGHTS RD	67	A 1	S
HINTON RD	67	C 3	S
HIWI RD	67	C 3	S
HODGSON RD	67	E 1	S
HOEKA RD	67	C 3	S
HOGAN RD	67	D 4	S
HOLLAND RD	67	C 3	S
HOLLINSHEAD RD	67	E 1	N
HOLMWOOD DR	67	D 1	S
HOOKER RD	67	D 3	S
HOOPER RD	67	C 3	S
HOROTIU BRIDGE RD	67	C 1	N
HOROTIU RD	67	C 1	N
HORRELL RD	67	B 4	N
HORSHAM DOWNS RD	67	C 2	N
HORWOOD RD	67	B 2	N
HOUCHENS RD	67	D 2	N
HOUGHTON RD	67	D 1	N
HOWARD RD	67	B 2	S
HOWDEN RD	67	C 1	S
HUHU RD	67	A 1	S
HUNTER RD	67	C 3	N
HURRELL RD	67	C 2	N
HUTCHINSON RD	67	C 2	N
HYDRO RD	67	E 4	N
INGRAM RD	67	D 2	S
JACOBS LN	67	B 1	S
JAMES RD	67	A 1	S
JANE CAVE LN NORTH	67	D 1	N
JANE CAVE LN SOUTH	67	D 1	N
JARY RD	67	E 2	S
JEW RD	67	B 1	N
JOHNSON RD	67	E 2	S
JUDD LN	67	E 4	N
JUDGE RD	67	F 3	N
JURY RD	67	D 1	N
KAHUI AVE	67	C 3	S
KAHUWERA RD	67	F 4	S
KAINUI RD	67	B 3	N
KAIPAKI RD	67	D 3	S
KAIRANGI RD	67	F 4	N
KAKARAMEA RD	67	E 1	S
KAKEPUKU RD	67	F 2	S
KANUKA RD	67	B 1	S
KARAKARIKI RD	67	C 1	S
KARAKARIKI VALLEY RD	67	C 1	S
KARAPIRO RD	67	E 4	N
KARL RD	67	E 2	N

Hamilton Central - Hamilton District Roads

Location	Map No.	Ref		
AURI LN	67	B	1	NE
AURI RD	67	A	4	NW
AY RD				
(HORSHAM DOWNS)	67	C	2	NW
(PUAHUE)	67	F	3	NW
ELM RD	67	B	1	SE
ERIE RD	67	C	2	NW
ERNOTT RD	67	F	3	NW
MBERLEY RD	67	A	1	NE
MIHIA RD	67	D	3	NW
PPEN LN (PVT)	67	C	3	NW
ROA RD	67	C	3	NW
TE ACCESS RD	67	E	3	NW
TE RD	67	E	3	NW
WI RD				
(HOE O TAINUI)	67	A	3	NE
(PUKETOTARA)	67	F	1	SE
WITAHI RAILWAY RD	67	C	4	NE
WEEBONE RD	67	A	2	NW
OPPENS RD	67	D	3	NW
OROKO RD	67	F	4	SW
OROMATUA RD	67	D	1	NE
OTARE RD	67	B	2	NW
URANUI RD	67	B	4	SW
AKE RD				
(HOROTIU)	67	B	2	SW
(OHAUPO)	67	E	2	NE
ANG RD	67	C	4	SW
AURENT RD	67	D	3	SE
AW CRES	67	C	1	NE
AW RD	67	B	3	NW
AXON RD	67	C	1	SE
EE MARTIN RD	67	D	3	NE
EGER GR	67	F	2	NE
IMEWORKS LOOP RD	67	E	1	NW
IMMER RD	67	C	1	SE
INDSAY RD	67	C	1	SE
ISSETTE RD	67	C	3	SW
IVINGSTONE RD	67	D	1	SE
OCHIEL RD	67	D	3	SW
OCKERBIE LN	67	D	1	NW
ONG RD	67	F	3	NW
OVELLS RD	67	E	4	NW
OWE RD	67	D	2	NE
UCIEN PL	67	A	3	SW
UCK AT LAST RD	67	E	4	SE
YND RD	67	E	3	NW
MACKY ACCESS RD	67	E	1	SE
MACKY RD	67	A	1	SW
MAHUTA STATION RD	67	D	1	NE
MAISEY RD	67	D	3	NE
MANGAPIKO SCHOOL RD	67	E	2	SW
MANGATEPARU LOOP RD	67	B	4	NW
MANGATI RD	67	F	1	SW
MANGAUIKA RD	67	F	1	NE
MANHIRE RD	67	A	4	SE
MANUEL RD	67	A	3	SE
MAORI POINT RD	67	C	1	SW
MARKEVIN LN (PVT)	67	D	3	SW
MARSHMEADOW RD	67	E	1	NW
MARTELLETTI RD	67	F	4	SE
MARU RD	67	C	1	SW
MARWOOD RD	67	D	3	NE
MARYCHURCH RD	67	D	3	NE
MASSEY RD	67	E	3	NE
MASTERS RD	67	C	3	NE
MATANGI RD	67	D	3	NW
MATUKU RD	67	B	3	NE
MAUNGA RD	67	F	4	SE
MAUNGAKAWA RD	67	D	4	NE
MAUNGATAUTARI RD	67	E	4	NE
MCCANDLISH RD	67	D	1	NE
MCCLURE ST	67	F	1	NE
MCCONNELL RD	67	A	2	SW
MCCRACKEN LN (PVT)	67	D	1	NW
MCELDOWNIE RD	67	D	3	SW
MCFALL RD	67	E	2	NE
MCGLYNN RD	67	A	1	NE
MCGREGOR RD	67	D	2	SW
MCLARNON RD	67	A	1	NE
MCVIE RD	67	A	1	NE
MEADWAY RD	67	E	2	NW
MELLOW RD	67	D	3	SW
MELLSOP RD	67	F	3	SE
METCALFE RD	67	D	1	SE
MIDDLE RD				
(GORDONTON)	67	B	3	SW
(RUKUHIA)	67	D	2	SE
MILL RD	67	E	2	NE
MILLS RD	67	D	3	NE
MOHRING RD	67	A	3	NE
MONCKTON RD	67	F	3	SE
MORGAN RD	67	F	1	SE
MORGAN RISE (PVT)	67	D	1	NW
MORRINSVILLE - TAHUNA RD	67	B	4	NW
MORRINSVILLE WALTON RD	67	B	4	SW
MOSS RD	67	A	2	SW
MOTUMAOHO STATION RD	67	B	3	SE
MOXHAM RD	67	E	2	SE
MUIR RD	67	E	3	SW
MYSTERY CREEK RD	67	D	3	SW
NAGAR LN	67	D	3	SE
NARROWS LN	67	D	3	NW
NARROWS RD	67	D	2	NE
NEILSON AVE (PVT)	67	C	2	NW
NEWELL RD	67	D	2	NE
NEWMAN RD	67	A	4	SW
NGAHINAPOURI RD	67	D	2	SE
NGAHUIA PL	67	F	2	SE
NGAROTO RD	67	E	2	SE
NGARUAWAHIA RD	67	C	1	NE
NGUTUNUI RD	67	F	1	SW
NICHOLLS RD	67	C	4	NW
NICKLE RD	67	E	4	SW
NO. 1 RD	67	A	4	NE
NO. 4 RD	67	A	4	SW
NO. 7 RD	67	A	4	NE
NO. 8 RD	67	A	4	NE
NO. 8 RD EXTN	67	A	4	NE
NO. 9 RD	67	A	4	NE
NORFOLK RD	67	E	2	NW
NORRISH RD	67	E	2	NE
NORWEGIAN RD	67	C	3	NW
NUZUM RD	67	B	1	SE
O'DEA RD	67	D	1	NE
O'REGAN RD	67	D	2	SW
O'SHEA RD	67	E	1	SE
OAK VIEW PL	67	C	3	SE
OAKLEA LN	67	D	3	NW
OAKSHOTT RD	67	E	1	NE
OKOWHAO RD	67	A	1	NW
OLD MOUNTAIN RD	67	D	1	NW
OLD RD	67	A	2	SW
OLD SCHOOL RD	67	E	1	NE
ONION RD	67	C	1	NE
ORINI RD	67	A	3	SW
ORMSBY RD				
(HOROTIU)	67	B	1	SE
(TIHIROA)	67	F	1	SE
OSBORNE RD	67	C	2	NW
OWEN RD	67	E	1	SE
PAEROA - TAHUNA RD	67	A	4	NE
PAPESCH RD	67	F	2	NW
PARALLEL RD	67	E	3	NE
PARAWERA RD	67	F	3	SE
PARIHORO RD	67	F	1	SE
PARK RD	67	B	1	SE
PARKER RD	67	F	3	NE
PARKLANDS RD	67	E	1	SE
PATERANGI RD	67	C	2	NW
PATERSON RD	67	C	1	SW
PATTERSON RD	67	E	1	SE
PAYNE RD	67	F	3	SE
PEACH RD	67	F	3	SE
PEACOCKE RD	67	A	2	NW
PEACOCKES RD	67	D	2	NE
PEAKE RD	67	D	3	SE
PENCARROW RD	67	D	3	SW
PENNIKET RD	67	D	2	SE
PENNY CRES	67	B	1	NE
PENNY RD	67	E	1	SE
PERCIVAL RD	67	C	2	SE
PERKINS RD	67	C	1	SE
PERRIN RD	67	E	2	NW
PHEASANT CL	67	C	1	SE
PIAKO RD	67	B	3	SW
PICKERING RD	67	D	3	NE
PIRI RD	67	A	2	SE
PIRONGIA RD	67	E	2	SW
PIZZINI RD	67	A	2	NW
PLATT RD	67	C	3	SE
POKURU FACTORY RD	67	F	2	NW
POKURU RD	67	F	2	NE
POLLOCK LN (PVT)	67	D	3	NW
POWELLS RD	67	C	2	SE
PROCTOR RD	67	A	3	NW
PUAHUE QUARRY RD	67	F	3	SE
PUAHUE RD	67	F	3	NW
PUKE RD	67	B	2	SE
PUKEKAPIA RD	67	A	1	NW
PUKEMOREMORE RD	67	D	4	NW
PUKERIMU LN	67	E	3	NE
PUKETAHA RD	67	C	2	NE
QUINE RD	67	A	4	NW
RACECOURSE RD	67	D	3	SE
RAHIRI RD	67	F	4	NW
RALPH RD	67	A	1	NE
RANBY RD	67	E	2	NE
RANGIAOWHIA RD	67	F	3	NW
RANSTEAD RD	67	D	4	NW
RAY RD	67	F	2	NW
RAY RD (PVT)	67	B	1	NE
RAYNER RD	67	A	1	SE
RAYNES RD	67	D	2	NE
REAY & WATSON RD	67	B	3	NE
REDBROOK DR	67	B	1	NW
REDOUBT RD	67	E	4	SE
REDWOOD GR (PVT)	67	D	2	NE
REID RD				
(NGAHINAPOURI)	67	E	1	NE
(PUKETAHA)	67	B	3	SE
REWA RD	67	A	4	SW
REYNOLDS RD				
(CAMBRIDGE)	67	E	3	SE
(HORSHAM DOWNS)	67	C	2	NW
RICE RD	67	E	1	NE
RICHARDS RD	67	C	1	NW
RIDGE PARK DR	67	C	1	NW
RIMU ST	67	A	4	NW
RINGER RD	67	D	3	NE
RIVER RD	67	C	2	NW
RIVERVIEW RD	67	A	1	SE
ROACHE RD	67	B	4	SE
ROBERTSON PL (PVT)	67	D	2	SE
ROBERTSON RD				
(NGUTUNUI)	67	F	1	SW
(WHATAWHATA)	67	C	1	SE
ROBINSON RD	67	F	4	NW
ROBSON RD	67	D	1	NE
ROGERS RD	67	B	1	SE
ROSBOROUGH RD	67	E	1	NE
ROSEBANKS DR	67	D	3	NW
ROTO - O - RANGI RD	67	E	3	SE
ROTOKAURI RD	67	C	1	SE
ROWE RD	67	D	1	NE
RUAKURA RD	67	C	2	SE
RUKUHIA RD	67	D	2	NE
RUKUMOANA RD	67	C	4	NE
RUTHERFURD RD	67	D	1	NE
RYAN RD	67	E	2	SW
RYBURN RD	67	E	2	NW
RYE RD	67	A	2	SE
SAEGER RD	67	C	1	SE
SAINSBURY RD				
(PIRONGIA)	67	F	1	NE
(PUKETAHA)	67	C	2	SE
ST KILDA RD	67	D	4	SW
ST LEGER RD	67	E	2	SE
SANCTUARY LN	67	D	3	NW
SAULBREY RD	67	B	1	SE
SCHOLLUM RD	67	C	4	SW
SCOTSMAN VALLEY RD	67	C	4	SW
SCOTSVALE DR	67	C	1	SE
SCOTT RD	67	B	4	SE
SEDDON RD	67	C	1	SW
SEIFERT RD	67	B	3	NW
SETTLEMENT RD	67	C	3	SE
SHAW RD	67	C	3	SE
SHERWOOD DOWNS RD	67	C	3	NW
SHEWAN RD	67	C	3	NW
SIMMOND RD	67	D	1	SW
SING RD	67	D	1	SW
SITTAUER RD	67	E	2	NW
SKEET RD	67	E	1	SE
SMART RD	67	D	4	SW
SMITH RD				
(HOROTIU)	67	B	1	SE
(KARAMU)	67	D	1	SW
SOWERBY RD	67	E	2	NE
SPEAKE RD	67	E	3	NW
SPEEDY RD	67	B	1	SE
STARKY RD	67	C	4	NE
STATE HIGHWAY 39	67	C	1	SE
STATION RD	63	E	1	SE
STEELE RD	67	D	2	SE
STOKES RD	67	B	2	NW
STOREY RD				
(RANGIAOWHIA)	67	E	3	SW
(WAITERIMU)	67	A	2	NE
STRONG RD	67	E	1	NW
STUART JAMES LN (PVT)	67	D	3	NW
SULLIVAN RD	67	B	1	SE
SUMMERFIELD LN	67	D	3	SW
SUTTON RD	67	E	2	SE
SWALLOW LN (PVT)	67	D	2	NW
SWAYNE RD	67	D	4	SW
TAANE RD	67	E	4	SE
TAHUNA RD	67	A	2	NE
TAHUROA RD	67	C	4	SW
TAI PATENA PL	67	C	3	SE
TAINUI RD	67	A	3	SE
TAITUA RD	67	D	1	NE
TAMAHERE LN	67	D	3	NW
TAPLIN RD	67	D	3	NW
TARI RD	67	F	4	SE
TARR RD	67	E	4	SW
TAUHEI QUARRY RD	67	A	3	SW
TAUHEI RD	67	B	4	NW
TAUKORO RD	67	B	4	NW
TAUWHARE RD	67	D	3	NW
TAWA RD	67	A	1	NE
TAYLOR RD	67	A	2	SE
TE AWA RD	67	D	3	SW
TE HOE RD	67	C	1	NE
TE KOWHAI RD	67	B	1	SE
TE MAWHAI RD	67	D	3	NW
TE MIMI RD	67	B	4	NW
TE MIRO RD	67	D	4	NW
TE OHAKI RD	67	A	1	NE
TE PAHU RD	67	E	1	NW
TE PUROA RD	67	C	1	NW
TE RAHU RD	67	F	2	NE
TE RETI RD	67	F	4	SW
TE TAHI RD	67	F	1	NW
TELEPHONE RD	67	C	3	NW
TENFOOT RD	67	A	2	SE
THIRLWALL LN	67	E	3	NE
THOMAS RD	67	C	2	NE
THOMPSON RD	67	E	2	SW
THORNTON RD	67	D	4	SW
TIKI RD	67	E	4	SW
TIROHANGA RD	67	E	4	SW
TOM RAWSON LN (PVT)	67	C	1	SW
TOPVIEW RD	67	C	3	SW
TRENTHAM RD	67	D	1	NE
TUHIKARAMEA RD	67	D	1	NE
TUI RD	67	E	4	NE
TUNAKAWA RD	67	A	3	NE
TURKINGTON RD	67	C	1	SW
UAPOTO RD	67	A	2	SW
UMUTAWA RD	67	F	4	SE
VAILE RD	67	C	3	SW
VALINTINE RD	67	B	3	NE
VICTORIA RD				
(CAMBRIDGE)	67	D	3	SE
(PUKEMOREMORE)	67	E	2	SW
WAIARI RD	67	D	3	NW
WAIKERIA RD	67	F	3	SW
WAIKOHA RD	67	D	1	SW
WAIKUKU RD	67	C	4	NE
WAIMANA RD	67	C	1	SE
WAIMANU RD	67	A	1	NE
WAINGARO RD	67	B	1	SW
WAIPA HEIGHTS RD	67	C	1	NW
WAIPUNA MINE RD	67	B	1	NW
WAIRAMA RD	67	C	4	SE
WAITE RD	67	E	1	SW
WALKER RD	67	B	2	NW
WALLACE RD	67	C	1	SW
WALLBANK RD	67	D	1	NE
WALSH RD	67	B	2	NW
WARING RD	67	C	4	SW
WASHBOURNE RD	67	B	1	SE
WASHER RD	67	D	4	SW
WATKINS RD	67	C	3	NE
WAVERLEY RD	67	C	3	NE
WEBSTER RD	67	A	2	NW
WELCH RD	67	A	2	NW
WEST MINE RD	67	A	1	NW
WEST RD	67	E	2	NE
WEST ST	67	E	2	NE
WHAKAHORO RD	67	A	4	NE
WHITEHALL RD	67	E	4	NE
WHITIKAHU RD	67	B	2	NW
WHITTAKER RD	67	E	1	NW
WILLIAMS RD	67	B	3	NE
WILLIAMSON RD	67	D	1	NE
WILLIS RD	67	C	1	NE
WILLOW BROOK LN	67	D	1	NW
WILLOW CREEK LN	67	D	3	NW
WILLOWWOOD LN (PVT)	67	A	2	SW
WILSON RD	67	B	4	NE
WILTON RD	67	D	2	SE
WINDLEBORN RD	67	D	1	NE
WINDMILL RD	67	D	3	NW
WISEMAN RD	67	D	1	NE
WOOD RD	67	D	3	NW
WOODCOCK RD	67	B	2	SE
WOODLANDS RD	67	C	3	SW
WOODSIDE RD	67	E	3	SW
WOODSTOCK RD	67	A	3	SW
WOODWARD RD	67	C	1	SW
WOOLRICH RD	67	D	1	NW
WRIGHT RD	67	F	1	NE
WYATT RD	67	D	1	NE
ZIG ZAG RD	67	D	3	SE

Hokitika Central

AIRPORT DR	96	E	3	NE
ALPINE VIEW	96	E	1	NW
BEACH ST	96	E	1	NE
BEALEY ST	96	E	2	NE
BONAR DR	96	D	3	SW
BRITTAN ST	96	E	1	SE
CAMP ST	96	F	3	NW
DALTON ST	96	F	3	NW
DAVIE ST	96	F	3	NW
ELCOCK LN	96	E	2	NW
FITZHERBERT ST	96	F	2	NE
GIBSON QUAY	96	F	2	NE
HALL ST	96	F	2	NE
HAMILTON ST	96	E	2	SW
HAMPDEN ST	96	E	2	NE
HAU HAU RD	96	F	4	NW
HEENAN PL	96	E	3	NE
HOFFMAN ST	96	F	3	NE
HOWITT PL	96	E	3	SE
INDUSTRIAL RD (PVT)	96	F	3	NW
JOLLIE ST	96	F	4	NW
KANIERE RD	96	F	4	NW
LIVINGSTONE ST	96	E	3	SE
PARK ST	96	E	2	SW
PERRY LN	96	E	2	SW
RAILWAY TCE	96	E	2	NW
REVELL ST	96	E	2	NW
RICHARDS DR	96	F	3	NW
ROLLESTON ST	96	F	2	NW
SALE ST	96	F	2	NE
SEAVIEW HILL RD	96	D	3	NW
SEWELL ST	96	D	2	NE
SPENCER ST	96	D	2	NE
STAFFORD ST	96	E	2	SE
TANCRED ST	96	E	2	SE
TOWN BELT EAST	96	F	4	NW
TUDOR ST	96	F	3	NE
WALKER PL	96	E	1	NE
WELD LN	96	E	1	NE
WELD ST	96	E	2	NE
WHARF ST	96	E	1	SE
WHITCOMBE TCE	96	D	3	SE

Invercargill

Invercargill Central

55 ARCADE	101	D	1	SE
ABBOT ST	101	A	4	SE
ADAMSON CRES	101	C	4	SE
ADAMSON PL	101	C	4	SE
ALBERT CRES	101	A	2	SE
ALBERT ST	101	A	2	SW
ALICE ST	101	B	1	NE
ANNAN ST	101	A	4	NE
ANNE ST	101	A	1	NE
ANTRIM ST	101	B	3	SE
ARTHUR ST	101	B	1	SE
ARUNDEL CRES	101	F	4	SE
AVENAL ST	101	B	1	SE
BAIRD ST	101	D	3	NE
BALMORAL DR	101	F	2	NE
BAMBOROUGH ST	101	C	4	NW
BANKS ST	101	C	3	SE
BASSTIAN ST	101	A	2	SW
BAY RD	101	A	1	NW
BEATRICE ST	101	B	1	SE
BEATTY ST	101	F	4	NW
BIGGAR ST	101	F	3	NE
BLUFF HIGHWAY	101	D	1	NW
BOND PL	101	D	1	NW
BOND ROW NORTH	101	D	1	NW
BOND ROW SOUTH	101	D	1	NW
BOND ST	101	B	3	SE
BOURKE ST	101	E	2	SE
BOWMONT ST	101	E	1	NW
BUTE ST	101	C	1	SE
CAMBRIDGE PL (PVT)	101	D	2	SW
CAMDEN ST	101	D	3	SE
CATHERINE ST	101	B	3	NE
CENTRE ST	101	E	4	SW
CHAPMAN ST	101	C	3	SE
CHARLOTTE ST	101	D	4	NE
CHELMSFORD ST	101	A	3	NE
CHEYNE ST	101	B	3	SE
CLIFTON ST	101	F	4	SE
CLYDE ST	101	E	1	NE
COLLINGWOOD ST	101	F	1	NW
COMPTON ST	101	E	3	SE
CONON ST	101	E	4	SE
CONYERS ST	101	D	1	NW
COURTVILLE PL (PVT)	101	D	1	NE
CRAWFORD ST	101	C	4	NE
CRINAN ST	101	F	2	SE
CRUICKSHANK CRES	101	A	4	NW
DALRYMPLE ST	101	F	2	SE
DAVID ST	101	D	4	NE
DEE ST	101	D	1	NE
DEVERON ST	101	D	2	NW
DOME ST	101	D	2	NW
DON ST	101	D	2	NW
DOON ST	101	D	3	NW
DOUGLAS ST	101	A	1	NW
DRURY LN	101	A	1	NW
DUBLIN ST	101	B	3	SE
DUDLEY ST	101	A	1	NW
DUKE ST	101	F	4	SE
DUNDEE PL	101	F	4	SE
DUNDEE ST	101	F	3	SE
EARN ST	101	C	1	SE
EARNSLAW ST	101	D	3	SW
ELLES RD	101	D	3	SW
ELM CRES	101	A	2	NE
ELSTON LN EAST	101	F	4	SW
ELSTON LN WEST	101	F	4	SW
ENWOOD LN	101	E	3	SE
ESK ST	101	D	2	SW
ESK ST WEST	101	D	1	SE
ETTRICK ST	101	E	1	SW
EXMOUTH ST	101	A	4	SW
EYE ST	101	E	2	NE
FERN ST	101	A	1	NE
FILLEUL ST	101	A	1	NE
FORTH ST	101	D	2	SW
FOX ST	101	C	1	NE
FULTON ST	101	B	1	NE
GALA ST	101	C	2	SW
GEORGE ST	101	B	3	NE
GLADSTONE TCE	101	A	4	NW
GORDON ST	101	F	3	SE
GRACE ST	101	F	2	SE

Location	Map No.	Ref
GREY ST	101 A 2	SE
GUTHRIE LN	101 B 1	SE
HAMILTON ST	101 F 4	NE
HARDY ST	101 F 3	NE
HENSLEY ST	101 B 1	NE
HERBERT ST	101 B 3	NE
HERRIOT CT	101 D 3	NE
HERRIOT ST	101 D 3	NE
HIGH ST	101 A 3	SE
HOLYWOOD LN	101 A 1	SE
HOLYWOOD TCE	101 A 1	SE
HOPE ST	101 E 4	NW
HOWORTH ST	101 A 2	NE
ISABELLA ST	101 C 4	NW
ISLINGTON ST	101 D 3	SE
JACKSON ST	101 D 3	NE
JAMES ST	101 C 4	NW
JANET ST	101 F 2	SE
JED ST	101 D 2	NE
JOHN ST	101 F 2	SW
JOSEPH ST	101 A 4	NE
KAURI TCE	101 A 4	NE
KELVIN ST	101 B 2	SW
KING ST	101 B 3	SE
KIRKWOOD LN	101 C 2	SE
KOWHAI AVE	101 A 4	NW
LAMOND ST EAST	101 A 4	NE
LAMOND ST WEST	101 A 3	NE
LAYARD ST	101 A 2	SE
LEES ST	101 A 2	SE
LEET ST	101 C 3	SW
LEITH ST	101 B 4	SW
LEVEN ST	101 D 1	NE
LEWIS ST	101 B 2	NW
LIDDEL ST	101 E 1	SE
LIFFEY ST	101 C 1	NE
LINDISFARNE ST	101 C 3	SW
LOCKERBIE ST	101 D 4	NE
LORN ST	101 C 1	NW
LOUISA ST	101 B 1	NE
LOWE ST	101 C 1	SE
MACMASTER ST	101 C 3	SW
MAITLAND ST	101 F 3	SE
MARGARET ST	101 C 4	NW
MARTIN ST	101 F 3	SE
MARY ST	101 C 3	SW
MATAI PL	101 A 4	NE
MATAI ST	101 A 4	NE
MCGILVRAY RD	79 A 1	NE
MCLEOD COURT	101 A 3	NW
MELBOURNE ST	101 B 3	SW
MERSEY ST	101 E 1	SW
METZGER ST	101 E 4	SW
MILLER ST	101 E 4	NW
MITCHELL ST	101 C 3	SE
MOANA ST	101 A 3	NW
MONOWAI ST	101 F 4	SW
MONTROSE ST	101 A 2	NE
MORAY CRES	101 F 3	SW
MORELL ST	101 F 3	NE
MORTON ST	101 F 4	SW
MURPHY ST	101 F 4	SW
NELSON ST	101 C 3	SE
NESS ST	101 E 3	SW
NEWBIE ST	101 F 4	SE
NEWCASTLE ST	101 B 3	SW
NICHOL ST	101 F 4	NE
NITH ST	101 D 2	SW
NORTH RD	101 A 1	NE
OTEPUNI AVE	101 D 4	SE
PALL MALL ARCADE	101 D 1	NE
PARK ST	101 A 2	SE
PERTH ST	101 B 4	SW
PHILIP ST	101 B 1	SW
PINE CRES	101 A 4	NE
POMONA ST	101 E 4	SW
PRESTON ST	101 A 1	NE
PRINCES ST	101 C 3	SE
QUEENS DR	101 B 3	SW
RAMRIG ST	101 A 2	SE
RAYMOND ST	101 E 3	NE
RIMU ST	101 F 4	NE
RITCHIE ST	101 C 3	SE
RIVER ST	101 A 2	NW
ROBERTSON ST	101 D 3	NE
RODNEY ST	101 E 3	SE
ROSEWOOD DR	101 A 3	NW
ROSS ST	101 A 4	NW
ROWAN ST	101 A 4	NE
ROY ST	101 F 3	NE
RUGBY ST	101 E 3	SE
RUSSEL ST	101 A 4	SE
ST ANDREW ST	101 C 3	NE
SALFORD ST	101 A 4	NW
SATURN ST	101 F 4	SW
SELWYN ST	101 F 2	SE
SHORT ST	101 C 3	NE
SPEY ST	101 D 2	NW
STEAD ST	101 E 1	SW
STIRLING ST	101 B 4	SW
STOBO ST	101 A 1	NW
SURREY PARK ST	101 C 4	SE
SWINTON ST	101 A 2	SE
SYCAMORE PL	101 A 4	NE
SYDNEY ST	101 B 3	SW
TALBOT ST	101 A 4	NE
TAY ST	101 D 2	NW
TERRACE PL	101 A 3	NW
TERRACE ST	101 A 3	NW
TEVIOT ST	101 E 2	SW
THAMES ST	101 C 1	NE
THE CRESCENT	101 D 1	SE
THOMSON ST	101 C 2	NW
TOTARA ST	101 E 4	SE
TRUSTBANK ARCADE	101 D 2	NW
TURNBULL ST	101 A 3	NW
TWEED ST	101 E 2	NW
TYNE ST	101 E 2	SW
URE ST	101 B 4	SW
VENUS ST	101 F 4	SW
VICTORIA AVE	101 C 1	SW
VIEW ST	101 F 1	NE
WACHNER PL	101 D 1	SE
WAIHOPAI ST	101 A 1	NW
WARD ST	101 A 4	NE
WAVERLEY ST	101 B 4	SE
WELLESLEY AVE	101 B 1	SE
WELLINGTON ST	101 E 3	SE
WILFRID ST	101 E 4	SE
WILLIS ST	101 A 1	NW
WILTON ST	101 A 3	NE
WINDSOR ST	101 A 3	SE
WOOD ST	101 D 1	SE
YARROW ST	101 D 2	NW
YTHAN ST	101 E 2	SE

District Roads

Location	Map No.	Ref
ACKERS RD	79 B 1	SE
ACTAEON RD	79 A 2	NE
AERODROME RD	79 A 3	NE
AICKEN RD	79 C 2	NW
ALLISON RD	79 B 1	NW
ANGLE RD	79 A 1	NE
AVON RD	79 C 3	SW
AWARUA SCHOOL RD	79 C 3	SW
BAINFIELD RD	79 B 4	SW
BATH RD	79 C 3	SE
BAY VIEW RD	79 A 4	SE
BENZIE RD	79 A 4	SE
BLACK RD	79 A 2	SE
BLONDELL RD	79 B 4	SW
BLYTH ST	79 C 3	NE
BOLGER RD EAST	79 C 3	NE
BOLGER RD WEST	79 C 3	NE
BOYLE RD	79 A 2	NW
BRAND RD	79 B 3	SE
BRIDGE INN RD	79 A 4	NE
BRIDGE RD	79 A 2	SE
BROWN RD	79 B 3	NE
BUTSON RD	79 B 4	NW
CALYPSO RD	79 C 2	NW
CAMERON RD	79 A 4	NE
CAMP RD	79 B 1	NE
CAULFIELD RD	79 A 4	NE
CHRISTES RD	79 C 1	SE
CLEARWATER RD	79 C 4	NE
CLYDE ST	79 A 2	NW
COGGINS RD	79 B 1	SE
COLYER RD	79 C 3	SW
CROWE RD	79 A 2	SW
CURRAN RD	79 B 2	SW
CURRY RD	79 B 4	NW
DAFFODIL BAY RD	79 C 2	NW
DAVIDSON RD	79 A 4	NE
DAWSON RD	79 B 4	NW
DERBY ST	79 C 3	SW
DIANA RD	79 A 2	NE
DOWLING RD	79 A 3	SE
DRYSDALE RD	79 A 3	SE
DUNLOP RD	79 A 1	SE
DUNNS RD	79 B 2	SW
EDENDALE WOODLANDS HWY	79 A 4	SE
ENDOWMENT RD	79 B 3	SE
ERSKINE RD	79 C 2	NW
EVANS RD		
(INVERCARGILL)	79 C 3	NW
(TISBURY)	79 A 4	SE
FAIRWEATHER RD	79 B 3	NE
FERGUSON ST	79 B 2	NW
FERRY RD	79 B 2	NW
FINDLAY RD	79 B 3	NW
FLEMING RD	79 A 4	SE
FLORA RD EAST	79 A 3	NW
FLORA RD WEST	79 A 4	NE
FORBES RD	79 A 4	NE
FORDE RD	79 B 2	NW
FOSBENDER RD	79 B 1	NE
FOWLER RD	79 A 2	SW
FRASER RD	79 A 1	NW
FROGGAT RD	79 A 4	SW
GARDINER RD	79 B 3	NE
GORGE ROAD -		
INVERCARGILL HWY	79 C 4	NW
GRAY RD	79 B 2	SW
GREIG RD	79 B 2	SW
GROVE BUSH WOODLANDS RD	79 A 4	NE
HARDWICK RD	79 B 1	SE
HEADS RD	79 A 4	SE
HELENA RD	79 A 3	NE
HOWELL RD	79 B 1	NE
HUGHES RD	79 B 1	NE
IRVING RD	79 A 4	NW
KENNEDY RD	79 A 2	NE
KENNINGTON ROSLYN BUSH RD	79 A 3	SE
KENNINGTON - WAIMATUA RD	79 B 3	NE
KENT ST	79 C 3	SW
KING RD	79 C 3	NE
LAKE RD	79 B 4	NE
LEE RD	79 C 3	NW
LEONARD RD	79 A 2	SW
LONGBUSH SOUTH RD	79 B 4	NW
LONGFORD RD	79 B 2	SW
LORNE DACRE RD	79 A 3	SW
MACKAY RD	79 C 3	SE
MARAMA AVE STH	79 C 3	SE
MASON RD	79 B 3	SE
MASSEYS TRAMWAY RD	79 C 4	NE
MATHESON RD	79 B 3	NE
MATUA RD	79 C 2	NW
MCDOWALL RD	79 A 1	NW
MCIVOR RD	79 A 4	NE
MCKERCHAR RD	79 A 4	NE
MCLEOD RD	79 A 1	NW
MCSTAY RD	79 A 4	NE
MILL RD NORTH	79 B 4	NW
MILL RD SOUTH	79 B 3	NE
MINERVA RD	79 A 2	NE
MOFFETT RD	79 A 2	SW
MONA BUSH RD	79 A 4	SW
MOORE RD	79 C 3	NE
MOTU RIMU RD	79 C 3	NE
MURPHY RD	79 C 3	NE
MYROSS RD	79 A 3	SE
NALLY RD	79 B 4	SW
NEAS RD	79 B 4	NW
NICHOL RD	79 B 4	NW
O'NEIL RD	79 C 3	NW
O'ROURKE RD	79 A 3	NW
OKI ST	79 A 1	SE
OPORO FLAT RD	79 A 1	NE
ORETI RD	79 C 1	NE
ORION RD	79 A 2	NE
ORR RD	79 B 3	NE
OTATARA RD	79 B 2	SW
OTERAMIKA RD	79 B 3	NE
PACIFIC AVE	79 C 1	NE
PIERCY RD	79 A 4	SE
PIT RD	79 C 1	NE
POMONA RD EAST	79 A 2	NE
POMONA RD WEST	79 A 2	NE
PRICE RD	79 A 1	NE
RAKAHOUKA CHURCH RD	79 A 4	NW
RAKAHOUKA GROVE BUSH RD	79 A 4	NW
RIMU RD	79 B 4	NW
RIMU SEAWARD DOWNS RD	79 B 4	NE
RIMU SOUTH RD	79 B 4	SE
ROSE RD	79 A 3	NE
ROSLYN RD	79 A 3	SE
RYAL BUSH WALLACETOWN RD	79 A 1	NE
SANDY POINT RD	79 C 1	NE
SHAND RD	79 B 4	SE
SHORT RD	79 A 2	SW
SIM RD	79 B 4	SE
SIMON RD	79 A 3	SE
SOMERVILLE ST	79 C 3	NW
SPRIGGS RD	79 C 3	NE
STAUNTON RD	79 B 1	NE
STEAD ST	79 B 4	SE
STEEL RD	79 A 2	SW
STEWART RD	79 B 4	NE
TAPPER RD	79 B 4	SE
TARAMOA RD	79 A 1	NE
TARAMOA WEST PLAINS RD	79 A 1	SE
TAYLOR RD	79 A 3	NW
TAYLOR RD EAST	79 A 3	NW
TIWAI RD	79 C 3	SW
TROTTER RD	79 A 4	NW
TUFFERY RD	79 B 4	SE
UNDERWOOD LINDS BRIDGE RD	79 A 2	NW
WAIHOPAI DOWNS RD	79 B 4	NE
WAIMATUKU BUSH RD	79 A 1	SW
WALLACETOWN		
LORNEVILLE HIGHWAY	79 A 2	NW
WATT RD		
(INVERCARGILL)	79 C 2	NW
(RIMU)	79 B 4	NW
WELSH RD	79 C 4	NW
WEST PLAINS RD	79 A 1	SE
WEST PLAINS SCHOOL RD	79 A 2	NE
WILCOX RD	79 B 3	NE
WILSON RD		
(MOTU RIMU)	79 C 3	SE
(WALLACETOWN)	79 A 1	NE
WIXON RD	79 C 3	NW
WOODLANDS CEMETERY RD	79 A 4	SE
WOODLANDS SOUTH RD	79 A 4	SE

Masterton Central

Location	Map No.	Ref
ALAMEIN CT	90 E 4	NW
ALBERT ST	90 E 2	NW
ALLENBY ST	90 D 4	SE
ARCHER ST	90 F 2	NE
BANNISTER CT	90 F 2	NE
BANNISTER ST	90 D 1	SE
BENTLEY ST	90 D 1	SE
BLAIR ST	90 F 2	NE
BRUCE ST	90 F 2	NW
BUNNY ST	90 F 2	NW
CAMBRIDGE TCE	90 E 1	SE
CAMERON CRES	90 F 3	SE
CASEL ST	90 F 2	NW
CHAPEL ST	90 F 1	NE
CHURCH ST	90 F 1	NE
CHURCHILL AVE	90 E 4	NW
CODDINGTON CRES	90 E 1	NE
COLE ST	90 E 1	NE
COLOMBO RD	90 E 2	SW
COOPER ST	90 E 3	NE
CORADINE ST	90 F 1	NW
CORNWALL ST	90 F 1	NW
CRAYNE ST	90 F 2	SE
CRICKET ST	90 E 2	SE
DEE PL	90 F 3	SE
DIXON ST	90 E 1	SW
ELIZABETH ST	90 F 3	NW
ESSEX ST	90 E 1	NE
FIRST ST	90 D 3	NE
FOURTH ST	90 D 3	NE
FRENCH ST	90 D 4	NE
GORDON ST	90 E 4	NE
GORT PL	90 F 1	SW
GRANT CRES	90 F 3	SE
GREY ST	90 D 2	SW
HACKER ST	90 F 3	NW
HARLEQUIN ST	90 F 1	NE
HERBERT ST	90 F 1	NE
HEREWINI ST	90 D 1	NE
HESSEY CT	90 F 2	NW
HESSEY ST	90 F 2	NW
HINAU PL	90 D 4	SW
HOGG CRES	90 E 2	NE
HOPE ST	90 E 2	NE
JACKSON ST	90 E 2	SE
JEANS ST	90 F 3	NW
JORDAN TCE	90 D 3	NW
KAKA ST	90 D 4	SW
KEATON ST	90 F 2	NE
KEIR CRES	90 D 4	NE
KERERU PL	90 D 4	SW
KING EDWARD ST	90 D 3	NW
KING ST	90 E 2	NE
KIPPENBERGER ST	90 E 4	NW
KIRTON ST	90 D 3	SE
KITCHENER ST	90 D 4	NW
KOWHAI PL	90 D 4	SW
KUMMER CRES	90 D 1	SW
KURIPUNI ST	90 F 1	SW
LANSDOWNE CRES	90 F 3	SE
LETT ST	90 F 2	SE
LINCOLN RD	90 D 2	SW
MABSON TCE	90 D 3	NW
MACARA ST	90 F 2	SE
MARCHBANK PL	90 F 2	NE
MASONIC ST	90 F 1	NE
MATAI ST	90 D 3	NE
MATIPO ST	90 D 4	SW
MCKENNA ST	90 F 1	NE
MEMORIAL DR	90 E 3	NW
MICHAEL ST	90 F 1	NW
MILLER PL	90 E 2	NW
MIRIAM ST	90 F 2	NW
MIRO ST	90 D 3	NW
MONTGOMERY CRES	90 E 3	NW
MONTGOMERY PL	90 E 4	NW
NEWLAND PL	90 E 1	NW
NGAIO PL	90 D 4	NW
NGAUMUTAWA RD	90 D 1	NW
OLIVE ST	90 D 2	NW
OXFORD ST	90 D 2	SW
PARK AVE	90 E 2	SE
PARK ST	90 E 2	SE
PERRY ST	90 E 1	NW
POWNALL ST	90 E 1	NW
PURIRI CRES	90 D 4	NW
QUEEN ALEXANDRA ST	90 D 3	NW
QUEEN ST	90 F 1	SW
RAGLAN ST	90 D 4	SW
RAHIWI PL	90 D 3	NW
RAILWAY CRES	90 D 2	SW
RATA PL	90 D 4	NW
RENALL ST	90 E 1	SW
REWA PL	90 D 4	NW
RIMU ST	90 D 3	NW
ROBERTS RD	90 D 4	SW
ROGERS LN	90 F 2	NW
RUSSELL ST	90 F 1	NW
SECOND ST	90 D 3	SW
SMITH ST	90 F 2	NW
STAMFORD PL	90 D 3	NW
STUART CRES	90 F 3	SW
SUSSEX ST	90 F 2	SW
TAKAHE ST	90 D 4	SW
TAWA ST	90 D 4	NW
TAY PL	90 F 3	SW
TE ORE ORE RD	90 E 3	NW
TERRACE END	90 D 3	NW
THE CROSSING	90 E 1	NW
THIRD ST	90 D 3	NW
TOTARA ST	90 D 3	SW
TRUSTEE ST	90 E 2	NW
VICTORIA ST	90 E 2	NW
VILLA ST	90 D 1	SW
WAVELL CRES	90 E 4	NW
WORKSOP RD	90 E 4	NW
WRIGLEY ST	90 E 2	NW

Napier - Hastings

Hastings Central

Location	Map No.	Ref
ADA ST	88 F 4	NW
AKINA ST	88 F 1	NW
ALBERT ST	88 E 3	NW
ALEXANDRA CRES	88 D 3	SW
ALEXANDRA ST	88 E 3	NW
AMANDA PL	88 D 3	NW
ANSON ST	88 E 4	NW
AVENUE RD EAST	88 E 2	NW
AVENUE RD WEST	88 D 1	NW
AWATEA ST	88 F 1	NW
BEATSON RD	88 F 4	NW
BEATTY PL	88 E 4	NW
BEATTY ST	88 E 4	NW
BEECH RD	88 D 1	NW
BERESFORD ST	88 D 1	NW
BULLER ST	88 F 2	NE
CAMBRIDGE ST	88 E 3	NW
CAROLINE RD	88 D 2	SW
CHARLES ST	88 D 1	SW
CHARLOTTE CRES	88 D 3	NW
CHURCHILL ST	88 F 2	SW
CLIVE ST	88 F 2	SW
COLLINGE PL	88 D 4	NW
COLLINGE RD	88 D 4	NW
COPELAND RD	88 F 2	SW
CUNNINGHAM CRES	88 D 4	SW
DALCROSS ST	88 D 4	NW
DUCHESS CRES	88 D 3	NW
DUFFERIN ST	88 F 2	NE
EASTBOURNE ST EAST	88 E 2	NW
EASTBOURNE ST WEST	88 D 1	SE
ELLISON RD	88 D 3	NW
ELM RD	88 F 2	SW
FENWICK ST	88 D 4	NW
FERGUSON ST	88 D 2	NW
FITZROY AVE	88 F 2	NW
FRANCES ST	88 F 1	SW
FREDERICK ST	88 D 3	NE
FRENCH ST	88 F 2	NW
GASCOIGNE ST	88 F 1	NW
GROVE RD	88 D 3	SE
HAIG ST	88 F 4	NW
HASTINGS ST NORTH	88 E 2	NE
HASTINGS ST SOUTH	88 F 1	NE
HEATHCOTE AVE	88 D 3	NW
HENRY ST	88 E 1	NW
HERETAUNGA ST EAST	88 E 2	SE
HERETAUNGA ST WEST	88 D 2	SE
HOLT PL	88 D 2	SE
HOOD ST	88 F 2	SW
HOWARD ST	88 F 4	SW
JELLICOE ST	88 E 4	NW
JERVOIS PL	88 E 4	NW
JERVOIS ST	88 D 3	SW
JUBILEE ST	88 D 4	SE
KARAMU RD NORTH	88 E 1	SW
KARAMU RD SOUTH	88 F 1	NW
KATHLEEN ST	88 F 4	SE
KING ST NORTH	88 D 2	SW
KING ST SOUTH	88 E 1	NE
KNIGHT ST	88 E 1	NE
LASCELLES ST	88 D 1	SW
LAWRENCE ST	88 F 2	SE
LEO ST	88 F 1	SW
LOUIE ST	88 F 1	SW
LOVEDALE RD	88 D 1	NW
LUMSDEN RD	88 F 3	SW
LUMSDEN RD	88 F 3	SW
LYELL ST	88 F 2	NE
LYNDON RD EAST	88 E 2	SW
LYNDON RD WEST	88 D 2	SE
MADDISON ST	88 F 2	NE
MAITLAND CRES	88 D 2	SW
MARKET ST NORTH	88 D 2	SW

Location	Map No.	Ref
ARKET ST SOUTH	88	E 1 NE
ARTIN DALE	88	F 1 NE
ASSEY ST	88	F 4 NE
AXVILLE DR	88	D 3 NE
AYFAIR AVE	88	D 3 NE
CLEAN ST	88	D 1 NE
ETHUEN ST	88	E 2 SE
ILLER ST	88	F 1 SW
ONA ST	88	F 1 SW
URDOCH RD EAST	88	D 2 SW
ELSON ST NORTH	88	D 2 SW
ELSON ST SOUTH	88	E 1 NE
ORFOLK CRES	88	E 4 NE
ORTON RD	88	F 3 SW
AK RD	88	F 2 NW
MEGA PL	88	F 4 SE
UTRAM RD	88	F 2 SE
ALMER PL	88	F 4 SE
ARK RD NORTH	88	F 3 NE
ARK RD SOUTH	88	F 4 SE
ATTISON RD	88	E 1 SW
OPLAR PL	88	F 1 SE
RINCES ST	88	E 2 SE
ROSPECT RD	88	E 1 NW
UEEN ST EAST	88	E 1 NE
UEEN ST WEST	88	D 1 NE
AILWAY RD	88	F 1 NW
AINBOW AVE	88	F 4 NE
EKA ST	88	F 1 SW
IVERSLEA RD NORTH	88	F 3 NW
IVERSLEA RD SOUTH	88	F 2 SW
OBERTS ST	88	D 2 NE
ODNEY ST	88	D 1 NW
USSELL ST NORTH	88	E 2 NE
USSELL ST SOUTH	88	E 2 NW
T AUBYN ST EAST	88	E 2 NE
T AUBYN ST WEST	88	D 1 NE
T LEONARDS AVE	88	D 1 NW
OUTHAMPTON ST EAST	88	E 2 SW
OUTHAMPTON ST WEST	88	D 1 SW
OUTHLAND RD	88	E 1 NW
USSEX ST	88	E 4 SE
YLVAN RD	88	F 3 NW
YMONS ST	88	F 4 SW
ERRACE RD	88	F 3 NE
OMOANA RD	88	D 1 NE
OWNSHEND ST	88	D 1 NW
UDOR AVE	88	D 3 NE
VICTORIA ST	88	E 3 NW
WARREN ST NORTH	88	E 2 NE
WARREN ST SOUTH	88	E 2 NW
WHITEHEAD RD	88	D 2 NW
WILLOW PL	88	F 1 SE
WILLOWPARK RD NORTH	88	F 2 NW
WILLOWPARK RD SOUTH	88	F 2 NW
WINDSOR AVE	88	F 3 SE
WOLSELEY ST	88	D 3 SE

Napier Central

Location	Map No.	Ref
ALBION ST	88	C 4 NW
ALPERS TCE	88	C 1 SE
AMNER PL	88	A 3 SW
ANDREW ST	88	C 2 SW
BALQUHIDDER RD	88	B 2 SE
BARRY ST	88	A 2 NW
BATTERY RD	88	B 2 NW
BAY VIEW RD	88	C 4 SW
BOWER ST	88	B 2 NE
BRACKEN ST	88	A 4 NW
BREAKWATER RD	88	A 4 NW
BREWSTER ST	88	B 4 NW
BRIDGE ST	88	A 1 SE
BROWNING ST	88	B 4 SW
BULL ST	88	A 3 NW
BURKE ST	88	B 1 NE
BURLINGTON RD	88	B 3 NW
BURNS RD	88	B 2 NE
BYRON ST	88	B 4 NW
CAMERON RD	88	B 3 SE
CAMERON TCE	88	B 3 SE
CAMPBELL ST	88	A 2 SW
CARLYLE PL	88	C 2 NE
CARLYLE ST	88	C 2 SE
CARNELL ST	88	C 2 SE
CATHEDRAL LN	88	B 4 SW
CHARLES ST	88	A 1 NW
CHATHAM ST	88	A 3 NW
CHAUCER RD NORTH	88	B 2 NE
CHAUCER RD SOUTH	88	B 2 SE
CHAUCER STEPS	88	B 3 NE
CHILDERS RD	88	B 4 NW
CHILTON RD	88	A 3 SW
CLIVE SQUARE EAST	88	C 3 NE
CLIVE SQUARE WEST	88	B 3 NE
CLYDE RD	88	B 4 NW
COBDEN CRES	88	A 3 SE
COBDEN LN	88	A 3 SE
COBDEN RD	88	A 3 SW
COLEMAN TCE	88	A 3 SW
COLENSO AVE	88	B 3 SE
CONVENT RD	88	B 4 NW
COOTE RD	88	B 4 NW
CORONATION ST	88	A 2 SW
CORRY AVE	88	B 1 NE
CORUNNA BAY	88	C 3 NE
CRAVEN ST	88	A 2 SW
CUSTOMS QUAY	88	C 4 NW
DALTON ST	88	C 2 NW
DELHI RD	88	C 4 NW
DENHOLM RD	88	B 2 NW
DICKENS ST	88	C 4 NW
DOMETT ST	88	B 4 NW
EDWARDES ST	88	C 2 NE
ELIZABETH RD	88	A 4 SE
EMERSON ST	88	C 4 NW
ENFIELD RD	88	C 2 NE
FARADAY ST	88	C 4 NW
FAULKNOR LN	88	C 4 NW
FAULKNOR ST	88	C 3 NW
FINNIS LN	88	B 3 SW
FITZROY RD	88	B 3 NE
FITZROY STEPS	88	A 3 SW
FRANCE RD	88	A 3 SE
GEORGE ST	88	B 2 NE
GEORGES DR	88	C 2 SE
GLADSTONE RD	88	B 2 NW
GOLDSMITH RD	88	B 2 NW
GOLDSMITH TCE	88	C 2 SW
GRIFFIN ST	88	C 2 SW
GUYS HILL RD	88	B 2 SE
HADFIELD TCE	88	B 4 NW
HALL ST	88	C 3 SE
HARDINGE RD	88	A 2 NE
HARVEY RD	88	B 3 NE
HASTINGS ST	88	C 4 NW
HAVELOCK RD	88	C 2 NE
HAVELOCK TCE	88	C 2 NW
HENRY HILL ST	88	C 1 SE
HERRICK ST	88	C 2 SW
HERSCHELL ST	88	B 4 NW
HOLTS LN	88	B 3 NE
HOOKER AVE	88	B 3 SE
HORNSEY RD	88	A 4 NW
HOSPITAL LN	88	B 1 SE
HOSPITAL TCE	88	B 2 SW
HUKARERE RD	88	B 4 NW
HUMBER ST	88	C 1 NW
HYDERABAD RD	88	C 1 NE
JAMES ST	88	A 1 NE
JULL ST	88	C 3 SW
KARAKA RD	88	A 4 NW
KAVANAGH RD	88	C 2 NW
KELSALL ST	88	C 2 NE
KENNEDY RD	88	C 3 SW
KENNY AVE	88	C 2 NE
KIPLING AVE	88	B 3 NW
KOWHAI RD	88	B 3 NE
LAMBTON RD	88	B 2 NE
LAWRENCE RD	88	B 2 NE
LEVER ST	88	A 2 SW
LIGHTHOUSE RD	88	A 4 SW
LINCOLN RD	88	B 3 NE
LITTLE BURKE ST	88	B 1 SW
LOGAN AVE	88	C 2 SW
LUCKNOW TCE	88	C 2 NE
LUCY RD	88	A 4 SW
MACAULAY ST	88	A 2 NW
MADEIRA RD	88	B 4 SW
MADEIRA STEPS	88	B 4 SW
MAHIA ST	88	A 2 SW
MAIN ST	88	C 1 NE
MARINE PDE	88	B 4 NW
MARKET ST	88	C 2 SE
MAY AVE	88	C 3 NW
MCDONALD ST	88	C 2 SE
MEEANEE QUAY	88	A 1 SW
MERSEY ST	88	C 3 NE
MILLAR ST	88	C 3 NE
MILTON RD	88	B 3 NE
MILTON TCE	88	B 3 NE
MORGAN AVE	88	C 1 SE
MORSE ST	88	C 3 NW
MUGGERIDGE ST	88	C 3 NW
MUNROE ST	88	C 3 SE
NAPIER TCE	88	B 2 SE
NELSON CRES	88	C 3 SE
NELSON QUAY	88	A 2 NW
NORMANS LN	88	C 1 NE
NORTHE ST	88	C 2 NE
OLIVER RD	88	B 4 NW
ONSLOW RD	88	B 2 SE
ORMOND RD	88	B 2 NW
OSSIAN ST	88	A 3 NW
OUTRAM RD	88	A 3 NW
OWEN ST	88	A 1 SW
PANDORA RD	88	A 1 SW
PARADE ST	88	C 2 NE
PARADISE RD	88	A 3 SW
PRIESTLEY RD	88	A 4 SW
PRIESTLEY TCE	88	A 4 SW
RAFFLES ST	88	C 3 NW
RAGLAN ST	88	A 3 NW
RANDALL PL	88	B 1 NE
RICHARDSON PL	88	B 1 NE
RIDDELL ST	88	B 1 NE
ROACH ST	88	C 3 SE
ROSLYN RD	88	A 3 SW
ROUTLEDGE ST	88	C 2 SW
SANDERS AVE	88	B 3 NE
SEALY RD	88	B 3 SE
SEAPOINT RD	88	B 4 NW
SEAVIEW TCE	88	B 4 NW
SELWYN RD	88	C 3 SE
SHAKESPEARE RD	88	B 3 NE
SHAKESPEARE TCE	88	B 3 NE
SHELLEY ST	88	B 3 NE
SIMLA TCE	88	C 1 SE
SIXTY FIFTH ST	88	C 3 NW
SMALE TCE	88	C 3 NW
SPENCER RD	88	A 2 NW
STAFFORD ST	88	C 4 NW
STATION ST	88	C 2 NW
STOPFORD ST	88	C 2 NW
STUART ST	88	A 2 SW
SWAN ST	88	C 4 SW
TAMATEA DR	88	C 1 SW
TANGAROA ST	88	A 2 SE
TARADALE RD	88	C 2 NW
TAREHA ST	88	B 3 NE
TENNYSON ST	88	B 3 NE
TERRACE LN	88	B 3 NW
THACKERAY ST	88	C 2 NE
THAMES ST	88	B 1 NW
THOMPSON RD	88	A 4 NW
TU ATU ST	88	B 1 SW
TYNE ST	88	C 4 SE
VAUTIER ST	88	C 4 NW
VIGOR BROWN ST	88	C 4 NW
WAGHORNE ST	88	A 2 NW
WELLESLEY RD	88	C 3 SE
WEST QUAY	88	A 1 SE
WHAKARIRE AVE	88	A 1 NE
WINIFRED ST	88	C 2 SE
WINSTON LN	88	A 2 NE
WRIGHT ST	88	A 2 NW

District Roads

Location	Map No.	Ref
ALLEN RD	71	C 3 SW
ANDERSON RD	71	B 1 NE
APLEY RD	71	B 1 NE
ARATAKI RD	71	A 3 NW
AVERY RD	71	C 1 SW
AWAHURI RD	71	B 3 NW
BALLANTYNE RD	71	E 3 SE
BLACKBARN RD	71	F 2 SE
BLIND RD	71	B 3 SW
BOYD RD	71	B 3 SW
BROOKFIELDS RD	71	C 3 SW
BURMA RD	71	F 1 SW
CARRICK RD	71	D 2 NE
CHARLTON RD	71	E 4 NE
CHESTERHOPE RD	71	D 3 NW
CLIFTON RD	71	D 4 SE
COHRS RD	71	F 1 SE
CRAGGY RANGE RD	71	F 4 NW
CRYSTALL RD	71	E 2 SE
DARTMOOR RD	71	B 1 NE
DOUGLAS RD	71	F 1 SW
DUNCAN RD	71	A 2 SE
DUNVEGAN RD	71	D 1 NE
EAST RD	71	A 3 SW
ELWOOD RD	71	E 3 SW
ENDSLEIGH RD	71	E 3 SW
EVANS RD	71	D 2 NE
EVENDEN RD	71	D 3 SW
FARNDON RD		
(CLIVE)	71	D 3 NE
(PAKIPAKI)	71	E 2 SW
FRANKLIN RD	71	D 3 NW
GILBERTSON RD	71	D 3 NW
GILLIGAN RD	71	A 2 SE
GIMBLETT RD	71	D 1 NE
GLENGARRY RD	71	A 2 SW
GLENOGLE RD	71	F 1 NE
GORDON ST	71	E 1 SW
GREEN HILL RD	71	D 3 SE
GROOME PL	71	D 2 NW
HAKIWAI RD	71	C 3 SE
HALES RD	71	D 3 NW
HAVELOCK RD	71	D 3 NW
HAWKES BAY EXPRESSWAY	71	A 2 NW
HEDGELEY RD	71	E 1 NE
HIGBEE PL	71	E 1 NE
HIGBEE RD	71	E 1 NE
HILL RD		
(BAY VIEW)	71	A 3 NW
(FLAXMERE)	71	D 2 NW
HODGSON RD	71	A 2 SE
HOLT RD	71	F 1 NE
HORONUI RD	71	D 2 NW
HOTEL RD	71	A 3 NW
JARVIS RD	71	E 1 SW
JESSEP RD	71	C 3 SE
JOHNSTON WAY	71	D 3 SE
KAHURANAKI RD	71	F 3 SW
KAIMATA RD	71	C 1 NW
KAWERA RD	71	C 3 SE
KING RD	71	D 3 NE
KOHUPATIKI RD	71	D 3 NE
LAWN RD	71	A 3 NE
LE QUESNE RD	71	A 3 NE
LINKS RD	71	B 2 SW
LONGLANDS RD EAST	71	E 2 NW
LONGLANDS RD WEST	71	E 2 NW
LONGVIEW RD	71	B 2 SE
MALCOLM RD	71	F 1 SE
MANGAROA RD	71	E 2 NW
MARAEKAKAHO RD	71	E 1 NE
MARAETOTARA RD	71	F 4 SW
MATANGI RD	71	F 3 NE
MATAPIRO RD	71	C 1 NW
MCFARLANE RD	71	E 2 NW
MCLEAN RD	71	D 2 NE
MCNAB RD	71	D 1 NE
MERE RD	71	D 1 NE
MIDDLE RD	71	F 2 SW
MILL RD	71	D 4 NW
MILLAR RD	71	E 4 NE
MITCHELL RD	71	A 2 SE
MONTANA RD	71	D 1 SE
MOORE RD	71	E 4 NW
MORLEY RD	71	C 2 NW
MOTEO PA RD	71	C 2 NW
MT ERIN RD	71	E 2 SE
MUTINY RD	71	F 2 NW
NAPIER RD	71	D 2 NW
NGAHIRIWA PL	71	D 1 SE
NGATARAWA RD	71	D 2 NE
NICHOLL RD	71	B 3 NW
NILGIRI RD	71	F 4 NE
OCEAN BEACH RD	71	C 2 NW
OHITI RD	71	D 2 NW
OMAHU RD	71	C 2 SE
OMARUNUI RD	71	C 2 NW
OMARUNUI SETTLEMENT RD	71	C 2 NW
ONEHUNGA RD	71	A 3 SW
ORMOND RD (OAK AVE)	71	D 1 SE
PAKIPAKI RD	71	E 2 SW
PAKOWHAI RD	71	D 3 NW
PALOMINO RD	71	D 4 SW
PARKHILL RD	71	D 4 SW
PENRITH RD	71	B 2 SE
PERCIVAL RD	71	B 3 SW
PINELEIGH DR	71	B 3 SW
PIRAU RD	71	B 3 SW
PORAITI RD	71	B 3 NW
POUKAWA RD	71	F 1 SW
PUKETAPU RD	71	C 2 NE
PUKETITIRI RD	71	B 2 NE
RAILWAY RD	71	F 1 NE
RANGITANE RD	71	D 3 NW
RARATU RD	71	F 3 SE
RAUKAWA RD	71	D 1 NE
RAUPARE RD	71	D 2 NE
RAYMOND RD	71	D 4 SW
RICHARD RD	71	E 3 SE
RIVER RD	71	E 4 SW
ROCHFORT RD	71	F 2 SE
ROSSER RD	71	F 1 SE
ROYS HILL RD	71	D 1 SW
RU COLLIN RD	71	E 2 NE
RUAHAPIA RD	71	D 3 SW
SANDY RD	71	C 3 SE
SCHOOL RD	71	E 3 SW
SEAFIELD RD	71	A 2 SE
SEARS RD	71	C 3 SE
SHANLEY RD	71	C 1 SW
SILVERTON RD	71	C 3 SE
SISSONS RD	71	C 3 SE
SOLDIERS SETTLEMENT RD	71	A 1 SW
SPRINGFIELD RD	71	C 2 NE
STOCK RD	71	E 2 SE
STROME RD	71	C 2 SE
SWAMP RD	71	E 2 SE
TAIHAPE RD	71	C 1 NW
TE AUTE RD	71	F 1 SW
TE MAHANGA RD	71	D 2 NE
TE MATA MANGATERETERE RD	71	D 3 SE
TE MATA RD	71	E 3 NE
TENNANT RD	71	D 1 NE
THOMPSON RD	71	D 2 NE
TUKI TUKI HILLS RD	71	E 4 NW
TUKI TUKI RD	71	D 4 SW
TURAMOE RD	71	E 2 SW
TWYFORD RD	71	D 2 NE
VALENTINE RD	71	B 2 SW
VICARAGE RD	71	A 1 SW
WAIHAU RD	71	E 4 SW
WAIMARAMA RD	71	E 2 SE
WEST RD	71	A 3 SW
WHAKATU RD	71	D 3 SW
WOODTHORPE STATION RD	71	C 1 NW

Nelson - Marlborough

Blenheim Central

Location	Map No.	Ref
ALFRED ST	94	E 2 SE
ANDREW PL	94	E 3 SW
ANDREW ST	94	E 3 SW
ARGOSY PL	94	F 2 NE
ARTHUR ST	94	E 1 NW
ASTON ST	94	E 3 SE
AUCKLAND ST	94	D 4 SE
BALLINGER DR	94	E 1 SE
BANK ST	94	E 1 SE
BARY ST	94	F 1 SW
BATTYS RD	94	F 2 NE
BEAVER RD	94	E 3 NE
BOMFORD ST	94	E 1 SE
BOYCE ST	94	F 2 NW
BROOK ST	94	D 3 SE
BUDGE ST	94	D 3 SE
CARR ST	94	F 2 SW
CHARLES ST	94	F 2 NE
CHELSEA WAY (PVT)	94	D 3 NE
CHERRYWOOD PARK	94	D 1 SW
CHURCHILL ST	94	D 3 SE
CLOUSTON GARDENS	94	E 1 NW
COLEMANS RD	94	D 1 NE
COLLETT PL	94	D 4 SW
COSTELLO AVE	94	D 3 SW
CRICKLEWOOD LN	94	E 1 NE
CURRY ST	94	E 2 NE
DASHWOOD ST	94	E 2 SE
DAWKINS PL	94	E 4 SW
DILLON ST	94	E 2 SW
DILLONS POINT RD	94	E 4 SE
DIX CRES	94	D 3 NE
DODSON ST	94	E 2 NE
DUNBEATH ST	94	E 4 NE
ELIZABETH ST	94	E 4 NE
ELTHAM RD	94	F 2 SE
ELZY ST	94	F 4 NE
ENDEAVOUR ST	94	D 4 SW
FARMAR ST	94	D 3 SE
FARNHAM DR	94	D 1 SW
FELL ST	94	D 3 NW
FIFTH LN	94	E 1 SE
FIRST LN	94	F 3 NE
FOURTEENTH LN	94	F 3 NE
FOURTH LN	94	F 3 NE
FRANCIS ST	94	F 3 SE
FRESWICK ST	94	F 4 NE
FULTON ST	94	D 1 SE
GASCOIGNE ST	94	E 4 NE
GEORGE ST	94	F 2 NE
GIRLING AVE	94	D 3 SW
GLENROY CRES	94	D 2 NW
GRADY ST	94	E 3 NW
GROVE RD	94	E 3 NE
HENRY ST	94	F 3 NW
HERBERT ST	94	E 2 SW
HIGH ST	94	E 2 SW
HILEY ST	94	F 3 SW
HODSON ST	94	E 1 NE
HORNE PL	94	E 1 NE
HORTON ST	94	F 4 NE
HOULDSWORTH ST	94	D 3 NW
HUTCHESON ST	94	D 1 SE
JELLYMAN PL	94	D 1 SE
JOHN ST	94	E 1 NE
JONES PL	94	E 1 NE
KEISS ST	94	F 4 NE
KINGS LN (PVT)	94	F 3 NE
KINGWELL DR	94	E 1 NE
KINROSS ST	94	F 3 NE
LAKINGS RD	94	E 2 NE
LEE ST	94	F 2 NW
LEEFIELD ST	94	F 4 NE
LINTON ST	94	D 3 SW
LUCAS ST	94	F 1 NE

Blenheim Central - Nelson-Marlborough District Roads (side title)

Location	Map No. Ref
MAIN ST	94 F 4 NW
MARKET ST SOUTH	94 F 3 NE
MARSHALL PL	94 E 4 SE
MARY GRACE PL	94 F 4 SE
MAXWELL RD	94 F 3 SW
MCARTNEY ST	94 F 4 SW
MCCALLUM ST	94 D 1 SE
MCFARLANE PL	94 D 2 NW
MCLAUCHLAN ST	94 D 2 NW
MEACHEN CRES	94 F 2 NW
MEEHAN ST	94 E 4 NW
MIDDLE RENWICK RD	94 E 1 NE
MILL STREAM LN	94 E 2 SW
MOGRIDGE PL	94 D 1 SE
MOLLY CASEY PL	94 F 3 SW
MONRO ST	94 F 2 NE
MOWAT ST	94 D 1 NE
NELSON ST	94 E 2 NW
NICOLL ST	94 E 1 SW
NINTH LN	94 F 4 NE
NOSWORTHY ST	94 F 3 SE
OLD RENWICK RD	94 D 1 NW
OPAWA ST	94 F 4 NW
ORCHARD LN	94 E 1 NW
OWEN PL	94 D 1 SE
PARK TCE	94 F 4 NW
PARK VIEW LN	94 F 4 SW
PARKER ST	94 E 2 NE
PATTIE PL	94 E 1 NE
PENNY ST	94 D 3 NW
PERCY ST	94 E 1 NE
PHILIP PL	94 E 1 NW
PITCHILL ST	94 E 3 NW
POYNTER ST	94 F 2 SE
PURKISS ST	94 E 1 SE
QUEEN ST	94 F 3 NE
REDWOOD ST	94 F 3 SE
RICHMOND ST	94 F 2 NE
ROTHWELL PL	94 E 1 NE
RUSSELL TCE	94 E 3 NE
RUTHKEN CRES	94 E 1 NE
RYAN PL	94 D 1 SE
SAUL LN	94 F 3 SE
SCOTT ST	94 F 3 NE
SECOND LN	94 F 3 NE
SEQUOIA PL	94 F 1 NE
SEYMOUR ST	94 F 3 NW
SHERWOOD PL	94 E 1 SE
SHIRTLIFF ST	94 D 4 SW
SINCLAIR ST	94 E 3 SE
SMITH AVE	94 E 3 NW
SNOWDEN CRES	94 E 2 SW
SOPER LN	94 D 2 SW
SPRINGSWOOD GR	94 F 1 NE
STEPHENSON ST	94 F 1 SW
STUART ST	94 F 4 NE
SUTHERLAND TCE	94 F 4 NW
SYMONS ST	94 F 3 NE
TENTH LN	94 F 4 NE
THE WILLOWS	94 D 1 NE
THIRD LN	94 F 3 NE
TIMANDRA PL	94 F 4 SE
TREVOR CRES	94 F 4 SW
TWELFTH LN	94 E 3 SE
VEVIAN PL	94 F 2 NW
WALNUT LN	94 E 4 NW
WARD ST	94 E 1 NW
WARWICK ST	94 D 3 SE
WATERLEA GREEN	94 E 3 NW
WATSON PL	94 E 1 NE
WHITE ST	94 E 2 SE
WYNEN ST	94 F 3 NE

Nelson Central

Location	Map No. Ref
ABRAHAM HGTS	95 C 1 NW
ACHILLES AVE	95 B 2 SE
AJAX AVE	95 B 3 SW
AKERSTEN ST	95 A 2 SE
ALBANO WAY (PVT)	95 B 3 SE
ALBERT RD	95 B 1 NW
ALMA ST	95 C 3 NW
ALTON LN (PVT)	95 C 3 NE
ALTON ST	95 C 1 NE
ARROW ST	95 C 3 NE
ATAWHAI DR	95 A 4 SW
ATMORE TCE	95 C 4 SE
AVON TCE	95 C 3 NE
BARRINGTON WAY (PVT)	95 C 3 NE
BEACHVILLE CRES	95 B 1 NE
BECCLES LN	95 C 1 SE
BELLA GROVE WAY (PVT)	95 B 3 NW
BRIDGE ST	95 B 3 SW
BRITANNIA HGTS	95 B 1 SW
BRONTE ST	95 C 2 SE
BRONTE ST EAST	95 C 2 SE
BROOKSIDE (PVT)	95 C 3 SE
BROUGH TCE (PVT)	95 C 1 NW
BRUNT QUAY	95 A 1 NE
BRYDON WAY (PVT)	95 B 3 NE
BUXTON SQUARE	95 B 2 SE
CAMBRIA ST	95 B 3 NE
CARKEEK ST	95 A 1 NE
CARLTON ST	95 C 1 SE
CHRISTIANS LN (PVT)	95 B 2 SW
CHURCH LN (PVT)	95 C 2 NE
CHURCH ST	95 C 2 NE
CLEVELAND TCE	95 C 4 SW
CLOUSTON TCE	95 B 2 SW
COLLINGWOOD ST	95 C 3 NW
COLLINS ST	95 A 1 SE
CRAIGHOLM CRES (PVT)	95 B 2 NW
CRISPS LN (PVT)	95 C 2 NE
CROSS QUAY (PVT)	95 A 2 NE
DAVIES DR	95 A 4 SE
DAYMAN WAY (PVT)	95 B 3 NW
DE CESARE WAY (PVT)	95 B 3 NE
DI LEVA WAY (PVT)	95 B 3 NW
DI PIERRI WAY (PVT)	95 B 3 NW
DOMETT ST	95 C 3 NE
DUNCAN ST	95 A 2 SW
DUNDAS ST	95 A 3 SW
EASTWOOD PL	95 B 3 NE
ELLIOTT ST	95 B 3 NW
ERIN ST	95 C 3 SE
EVERETT ST (PVT)	95 A 4 NW
EXAMINER ST	95 C 2 SE
FIELD ST (PVT)	95 A 4 NW
FIFESHIRE CRES	95 B 1 NW
FOUNTAIN PL	95 B 1 NE
FOUNTAIN SQUARE	95 B 2 NW
GLOUCESTER ST	95 C 2 NW
GRAHAM ST	95 A 1 SW
GROVE ST	95 B 3 NW
HALIFAX ST	95 B 2 SE
HALIFAX ST EAST	95 B 3 SE
HALSTEAD ST	95 B 3 SW
HANBY PARK	95 C 4 NE
HARBOUR TCE	95 A 1 SW
HARDY ST	95 B 2 SW
HARDY ST EAST	95 C 4 NW
HARLEY ST	95 C 3 NW
HARPER ST	95 C 3 SE
HASTINGS ST	95 B 1 SE
HATHAWAY CT (PVT)	95 B 2 NE
HATHAWAY TCE	95 B 2 NE
HAVEN RD	95 B 2 SW
HAY ST	95 A 1 SE
HELENA WAY (PVT)	95 B 3 NW
HOPE ST	95 C 3 NW
IWA RD	95 A 4 SW
JENVILLE WAY (PVT)	95 B 3 SE
KERR ST	95 C 2 NW
KING ST	95 C 3 SW
KINGSFORD QUAY (PVT)	95 A 2 SE
KINZETT TCE (PVT)	95 A 2 SE
KONINI ST	95 C 2 NW
KOTUKU WAY (PVT)	95 B 3 SE
LANCEWOOD WAY (PVT)	95 B 3 SE
LAURIA WAY (PVT)	95 C 4 NW
LAVAL HGTS	95 C 1 NW
LEVIEN LN (PVT)	95 A 4 NW
LOCK WAY (PVT)	95 A 1 NE
LOCKING ST	95 C 2 SW
LOW ST	95 C 2 SW
LUCAS TCE	95 B 1 SW
MAITAI RD	95 C 2 NW
MAJESTIC WAY (PVT)	95 B 3 NE
MALTHOUSE LN (PVT)	95 B 3 SW
MANUKA ST	95 C 3 SW
MAORI RD	95 B 2 NW
MARY ANN LN	95 B 1 NE
MAYROYD TCE	95 C 4 SW
MCGLASHEN QUAY	95 A 1 NE
MILL ST	95 C 2 NE
MILTON ST	95 B 2 SE
MONOPOLI WAY (PVT)	95 B 3 NW
MONTCALM ST	95 C 1 NW
MONTGOMERY SQUARE	95 B 2 SW
MONTREAL RD	95 C 1 SW
MORRISON ST	95 C 3 NW
MOUNT PLEASANT AVE	95 B 1 NE
MOUNT ST	95 C 2 SW
NATALIE ST	95 C 1 NE
NEW ST	95 C 2 SE
NGAIRE LN	95 B 3 NE
NGAIRE PL	95 B 3 NE
NILE LN (PVT)	95 C 3 NW
NILE ST	95 C 3 NW
NILE ST EAST	95 C 4 NW
NILE ST WEST	95 C 2 NE
NORTH RD	95 A 3 SE
NORTHESK ST	95 C 1 SE
OLDHAM ST (PVT)	95 B 3 SE
OXFORD ST (PVT)	95 C 2 NW
PARK ST	95 C 1 SE
PARU PARU RD	95 B 2 NE
PEARCE WAY (PVT)	95 A 4 SE
PEPPER TREE WAY (PVT)	95 B 3 NE
PETTIT PL	95 B 3 SE
PIONEER CRES	95 B 1 SE
PITT ST	95 C 2 NE
POYNTERS CRES	95 B 1 NW
PROVINCIAL LN (PVT)	95 C 3 NW
QUEBEC RD	95 C 1 NW
QUEBEC RD	95 C 1 NW
QUEEN ELIZABETH 2 DR	95 A 2 SE
QUEENS RD	95 A 1 SW
RENTONE ST	95 B 1 SE
RENWICK PL	95 C 2 SW
RICHMOND AVE	95 C 1 SW
RIMU ST	95 C 3 SW
RIVERSIDE DR	95 B 3 SW
ROGERS ST	95 B 1 NE
RUSSELL ST	95 B 1 SE
RUTHERFORD ST	95 C 2 NE
ST ANN PL	95 C 1 SE
ST JOHN ST	95 C 3 NW
ST LAWRENCE ST	95 C 1 NE
ST VINCENT ST	95 C 1 SE
SCHOOL OF MUSIC LN (PVT)	95 C 3 SW
SELWYN PL	95 C 2 SE
SHAKESPEARE WALK	95 B 3 SW
SHARPS LN (PVT)	95 B 3 SW
SHELBOURNE ST	95 C 3 SW
SNODGRASS AVE (PVT)	95 A 4 NW
SORRENTO WAY (PVT)	95 B 3 NW
SOUTH ST	95 C 2 NE
SOVEREIGN ST	95 A 3 SW
STANLEY CRES	95 B 1 NE
STEPNEY LN	95 B 1 NW
SUSSEX ST	95 C 3 NW
TAHAKI ST	95 C 2 NW
TASMAN ST	95 C 3 SE
TOI TOI ST	95 C 3 SW
TORY ST	95 C 4 NW
TRAFALGAR AVE (PVT)	95 C 1 SE
TRAFALGAR SQUARE	95 C 2 NE
TRAFALGAR ST	95 B 2 SE
TRAFALGAR ST SOUTH	95 C 2 SE
VANGUARD ST	95 C 1 SE
VICKERMAN ST	95 A 2 SW
VICTORIA HGTS	95 B 1 NW
VOSPER ST	95 A 3 SW
WAINUI ST	95 A 3 SW
WAKATU LN	95 B 2 SE
WAKEFIELD QUAY	95 A 1 SW
WALTERS BLUFF	95 A 4 NE
WASHINGTON RD	95 B 1 SE
WASHINGTON TCE	95 B 1 SW
WATERS WAY (PVT)	95 A 4 NW
WATSON ST	95 B 1 SE
WEKA ST	95 B 3 NE
WELLINGTON ST	95 C 2 SW
WELLINGTON ST WALKWAY	95 C 2 NW
WELLS RD	95 B 1 NE
WESTERHAM PL	95 C 1 NW
WHITEHEAD PL	95 A 4 SE
WILDMAN AVE	95 A 1 SE
WILL WATCH WAY	95 B 1 NE
WILLOW WALK	95 C 3 SW
WIREMU WAY (PVT)	95 B 3 NW
WOLFE ST	95 B 1 SW

Picton Central

Location	Map No. Ref
AUCKLAND ST	94 B 2 SW
BROADWAY	94 C 1 NE
BRYANT PL	94 C 1 NE
BULLER ST	94 C 1 NW
CANTERBURY ST	94 C 1 SE
COLLINS PL	94 B 3 NE
CORNWALL ST	94 C 1 SW
DEVON ST	94 C 1 SW
DORSET ST	94 C 1 SW
DUBLIN ST	94 B 1 NW
DUBLIN ST WEST	94 B 1 NW
DURHAM ST	94 C 1 NE
ENDEAVOUR LN	94 B 2 SW
GEORGE ST	94 B 2 SW
GRAVESEND	94 B 1 SW
GRAVESEND PL	94 B 1 SW
HAMPDEN ST	94 A 3 SE
HEATHER PL	94 C 2 SW
HIGH ST	94 C 2 NW
KENT ST	94 C 1 NE
LAGOON RD	94 B 1 NE
LEICESTER ST	94 C 1 SE
LINCOLN ST	94 B 3 NE
LONDON QUAY	94 B 2 SW
MARKET ST	94 B 2 SW
MILTON TCE	94 C 1 SW
NELSON SQUARE	94 C 1 SE
NEWGATE ST	94 C 1 NE
OTAGO ST	94 C 2 NW
OXFORD ST	94 C 1 SW
QUEEN CHARLOTTE DR	94 B 1 NE
RUSSELL ST	94 B 2 SW
RUTLAND ST	94 B 3 SW
SCOTLAND ST	94 C 1 SE
SEAVIEW CRES	94 B 2 SW
SEYMOUR ST	94 B 2 SW
SUFFOLK ST	94 B 3 NW
SURREY ST	94 B 3 SW
SUSSEX ST	94 A 3 SE
TARANAKI ST	94 C 2 NE
VICTORIA CL	94 A 3 SE
WAIKAWA RD	94 B 2 SW
WAITOHI PL	94 C 1 NE
WELLINGTON ST	94 C 2 NW
WEST TCE	94 C 1 SW
YORK ST	94 C 1 NE

District Roads

Location	Map No. Ref
AARON CREEK RD	75 D 2 NW
ABEL TASMAN DR	75 D 2 NW
AKERBLOMS RD	76 C 4 SE
ALDOURIE RD	75 F 3 NE
ALEXANDER BLUFF RD	75 D 2 SE
AMELIA CRES	76 D 3 SW
ANAKIWA RD	76 D 3 SW
ANAKOHA RD	76 C 4 NW
ANISEED VALLEY RD	75 A 4 NW
APPLEBY HIGHWAY	75 F 4 NW
ARCHERS RD	76 C 2 NW
ARNOLD LN	75 F 3 SE
ARTHUR CRES	76 D 3 SW
AWAROA RD	75 B 3 NW
BACK RD	75 C 2 NW
BAIGENT VALLEY RD	75 F 3 SW
BARTLETT RD	75 F 4 NW
BARTLETTS RD	76 F 1 SW
BARTON LN	75 F 3 SE
BATCHELOR FORD RD	75 D 3 SW
BATON VALLEY RD	75 E 1 SE
BATTERY HILL RD (PVT)	75 F 1 SE
BATTYS RD	76 F 3 NE
BAY END	75 B 1 NE
BAY VIEW TCE	75 B 1 NE
BEACON RD	76 D 3 SW
BEATRICE PL	76 E 3 SW
BEDFORD RD	76 F 2 SW
BELL ISLAND ACCESS (PVT)	75 E 4 SW
BELL RD	75 F 2 SW
BELLS RD	76 F 3 NE
BELVIEW RD	75 D 2 SW
BEN MORVEN RD	76 F 3 NW
BENSEMANN RD	75 E 2 SE
BERRYMAN RD	75 F 2 NW
BESTS RD	76 F 2 SW
BIG POKORORO RD	75 E 2 NE
BIRD LN	75 F 3 SE
BIRD RD (CLIFTON)	75 B 2 NE
BIRD RD (WAKEFIELD)	75 F 3 SE
BISHOP RD	75 A 1 NW
BLACKBIRD VALLEY RD	75 F 3 NE
BLACKBYRE RD	76 F 1 SW
BOGEY VALLEY RD (PVT)	75 F 2 SW
BOYCES RD	76 F 2 SW
BRANCOTT RD	76 F 2 SE
BRANDY CREEK RD	75 F 2
BRISTOL ST	76 F 2
BROOKBY RD	75 F 2
BROOKLYN VALLEY RD	75 D 2
BROUGH PL	76 D 3 S
BROUGHTON BAY RD	76 C 3 N
BRYANTS RD	76 D 1 N
BULFORD RD	76 D 1 S
BULFORD RD SOUTH	76 D 1 S
BULWER RD	76 A 3 S
BYDDER TCE (PVT)	75 A 1 S
CAMERONS RD	75 C 2 S
CANAAN RD	75 C 2 S
CARLUKE RD	76 D 1 N
CARLYON RD	75 E 3 S
CEMETERY RD	75 B 2 S
CENTRAL RD	75 E 3 N
CENTRE CREEK RD	76 F 1 S
CENTRE VALLEY RD	75 F 1 S
CHALLIES RD	76 F 3 N
CHAMBERLAIN ST	75 D 3 S
CHAYTORS RD	75 F 3 N
CHING RD	75 D 3 S
CISSY BAY RD	76 B 2 S
CLARKE RD	75 F 1 N
CLOVA BAY RD	76 C 3 N
CLOVER RD EAST	75 F 4 S
CLOVER RD WEST	75 F 3 S
COBB DAM RD (PVT)	75 D 1 N
COBB VALLEY RD	75 D 2 N
COLLINGWOOD - BAINHAM MAIN RD	75 A 1 N
CONDERS BEND RD	76 F 2 S
CONNOLLYS RD	76 F 3 N
COZENS RD	75 F 2 N
CRAIGIEBURN RD	75 C 2 N
CRAIL BAY RD	76 C 3 S
CRAVENS RD	76 F 3 N
CROISILLES - FRENCH PASS RD	76 C 1 N
CROISILLES RD	76 C 1 N
CULLENSVILLE RD	76 E 2 N
DALTONS RD	76 D 1 N
DAVEY RD	75 E 3 N
DEEPDALE RD	75 F 3 N
DEHRA DOON RD	75 D 3 N
DEVIL'S BOOTS RD	75 A 1 S
DILLONS POINT RD	76 F 3 S
DOG POINT RD	76 F 2 S
DOMINION RD	76 F 2 S
DOUGLAS RD	75 D 3 S
DOUSLINS GULLY RD	76 E 2 N
DOVEDALE RD	75 F 2 N
DRUMMOND RD	76 E 3 N
DUNCAN BAY RD	76 C 2 N
EAST TAKAKA RD	75 C 2 N
ECKFORDS RD	76 F 3 S
EDEN RD	75 E 3 N
EDEN VALLEY RD	75 F 2 N
EDENS RD	75 F 4 N
EDWARDS RD	75 E 3 N
ELAINE BAY RD	76 B 2 S
ELIE BAY RD	76 C 3 S
ELLIS RIVER RD	75 F 1 N
EVES VALLEY RD	75 F 3 N
EXCELLENT ST	75 A 1 N
FABIANS VALLEY RD	76 F 1 N
FACTORY RD (KOROMIKO)	76 E 3 N
FACTORY RD (RIWAKA)	75 D 3 N
FAHEY RD (PVT)	75 F 2 N
FARADAY RISE	75 F 4 S
FAREHAM LN	76 F 2 S
FENWICK RD	75 B 1 N
FINLAY GR	76 D 3 S
FLAXMILL DR	75 F 3 N
FLAXMORE RD	76 E 3 N
FLETT RD	75 F 2 N
FOREST CREEK RD	75 F 2 N
FOX'S ISLAND RD	76 F 2 S
FRANKLIN ST	75 C 3 S
FRASER RD	75 B 1 N
FREETHS RD	76 E 2 N
FRY RD (PVT)	75 E 2 N
GARDNER VALLEY RD	75 F 2 N
GIBSONS RD	76 F 2 N
GIFFORDS RD	75 F 2 S
GLENRAE RD	75 F 2 S
GLENVIEW RD	76 B 2 S
GODFREY RD	76 F 2 S
GOLDEN HILLS RD	75 F 3 S
GOLF RD	75 F 3 S
GOODALL RD	75 D 3 N
GRAHAM VALLEY NORTH BRANCH RD	75 E 2 N
GRAHAM VALLEY RD	75 E 2 N
GRAHAM VALLEY SOUTH BRANCH RD	75 E 2 N
GRAHAMS RD	75 F 3 N
GRANT RD PURAMAHOI	75 B 1 N
GREEN TREE RD	75 D 3 N
GREENACRES RD	75 F 3 N
GREENHILL RD	75 F 3 N
GREIG LN	76 D 1 S
GREVILLE HARBOUR RD	76 A 2 N
GROVE TRACK	76 D 2 S
GUERNSEY RD	76 F 2 S
HAKAHAKA RD	75 D 4 S
HALL RD	75 C 2 S
HAMAMA RD	75 C 1 N
HAMMERICHS RD	76 F 3 N
HAMMOND RD	76 F 2 S
HANOVER RD	75 D 3 N
HARDINGS RD	76 F 3 S
HARLEY RD	75 D 3 N
HARVEY RD	75 C 3 S
HARWOOD PL	76 E 3 N
HAWKE VALLEY RD	75 F 4 S
HAWKESBURY RD	76 F 2 S
HAYCOCK RD	75 F 2 S
HEADINGLY LN	75 F 4 N
HEALYS RD	76 D 1 S
HEBBERDS RD	75 F 4 S